Demystifying School

DEMYSTIFYING SCHOOL

SCHOOL

Writings and Experiences

Assembled and Interpreted by

Miriam Wasserman

PRAEGER PUBLISHERS
New York • Washington

Published in the United States of America in 1974
by Praeger Publishers, Inc.
111 Fourth Avenue, New York, N.Y. 10003

© 1974 by Miriam Wasserman
Bibliography © 1973 by Miriam Wasserman

Library of Congress Cataloging in Publication Data
Wasserman, Miriam, comp.
  Demystifying school.

  Bibliography: p. 339.
    1. Education—United States—Addresses, essays,
lectures. I. Title.
LA217.W37   370′.973   73-16446

Printed in the United States of America

For our children's children,
two in particular

Contents

Demystifying School

Introduction

. . . the system of Copernicus in his De Revolutionibus Orbium Coelestium *and . . . the* De Humani Corporis Fabrica *of Vesalius, both published in the same year, 1543, . . . were the first pictures of how the heavenly spheres or the human body would appear to those who had eyes clear enough to see for themselves, and not through the spectacles of ancient authority. They were put forward and accepted at the outset by a new lay society also learning to see and experience for itself. It was only later, when the political consequences of the new vision began to be apparent, that authority took fright and tried, too late, to shut it out.*

—J. D. Bernal, Science in History

If the Battle of Waterloo was won on the playing fields of Eton, the jokers of Watergate were trained on the playing fields of the high schools of suburbia.

The Team—today's operative word—the Man, whose very name passes no one's lips lest the evil behind the revered institution be revealed as merely human—the fleetingly glimpsed "faithful women" (one dead)—at last the meeting in public of the parallel lines of underworld and superworld, which surprises us unnecessarily (the parallelism was all along an illusion; we were seeing double)—the entire human Package (to use Their word) was assembled and wrapped fifteen to thirty years before in the schoolrooms and high school stadiums of the nation. It remained only to tie it up with the necessary strings of power, which broke when carelessly secured, letting all the dirty tricks fall out on the living room floor.

The times were not yet ripe.

But the schools are preparing new men to go into the next package. True, many are refusing to accept the processing that intensive schooling entails. That only makes the few who do accept potentially more dangerous.

Those few will go on helping the Man cover up what goes on in the schoolroom and the Oval Room.

The coverup is a shared mythology, weirdly entangling each in the myths spun out by the other. So educators teach reverence for the sanctity of the political institutions while politicians preach reverence for the sanctity of the schools.

But the mythology that certifies the sanctity of the schools, while still commanding respect, or at least lip-service, in some quarters, induces uneasiness in others.

The most victimized of the schools' victims have been uneasy for a long time (they are "the uneasy poor"). Then, a few years ago, in the midst of civil rights struggles and peace marches and urban rebellions and youth revolts—in other words, in the midst of the wider social crisis—some of the rest of us also became uneasy. When we looked hard at the realities behind the myths, we noticed:

- Schools are not a great melting pot for Americans of every color, creed, and nationality but a sorting board, which drops the children of each generation into grooves ground out for them by their parents (with only an occasional error).

- Free public education is not a great highway to opportunity and success but a series of barriers that keep people in the enclosures society has thoughtfully provided for them.

- Schooling is not an opening of knowledge and understanding and an access-way to wisdom but a ritual and an incantation and a doctrine which blind and deafen the mind and cripple and corrupt the soul.

- Schoolchildren are not unique spirits to be nurtured to self-fulfilling adulthood but tiny soldiers to be trained to act out the strategy of the generals.

- Teachers are neither dedicated, patient angels of instruction nor devils of destruction but quite ordinary women and men earning a salary to pay the rent.

When we discovered that these and a lot of other myths were not true, we were furious, as children are when they discover that Santa Claus or God or adult virtue has been used to con them into obedience. And, like the children who blame their parents for the fraud, many people found relief in blaming the teachers.

Among those who now openly or secretly question the myths, the prevailing state of thinking appears to be about halfway between blaming the teachers and trying to understand how the system works.

This book is intended to contribute to that understanding (if only to get the teachers off the hook).

The crisis of the schools is an aspect of the wider social crisis. The school crisis at once reflects and contributes to the social crisis. The training of the Watergate men is an example of the contribution. The drug epidemic among despairing students is another. Wherever we move between the school world and our other worlds we find further examples.

If we concentrate our attention on the school world primarily, we find a series of internal contradictions whose mounting tensions are the essence of the school crisis.

School has many functions: to survive as an institution, to serve the larger society, to maintain its own credibility with itself, to meet some minimal human needs of its participants. Some of its functions interfere mildly or drastically with others. This is the meaning of the term "internal contradiction."

For example, one of the major functions of schools in any society is to disseminate and inculcate the myths which that society for one reason or another needs to tell about itself. So our textbooks and our teachers' mouths are filled with myths about our society and about the schools themselves which distort reality and interfere with our ability to deal effectively with the world that lies behind the myths. (Some are dealt with in Chapter 6, "Curriculum: Grim Competition, Alienating Language, and the Mythology of Imperialism.") In this sense the school's myth-making function interferes with its function of preparing the members of the next generation to cope with their own and society's problems, including the growing social crisis.

Moreover, the schools' myths tend to "turn students off." Recognizing how much of what passes for knowledge is "jive," students often reject the whole kit and caboodle of the school message, including those very intellectual and ethical skills that would enable them to begin to make sense of themselves and their world. But if schools were to abrogate their myth-making function, they would have ceased to serve those great powers in society whose authority guarantees their existence. This can only happen as the powers themselves begin to crumble.

This is one set of internal contradictions.

Another is the function of sex socializing. (This topic is dealt with in Chapter 4, "Preparing Girls and Boys for a Consuming-Producing Society.") School prescribes different roles for girls and boys, partly to help preserve the schoolrooms' very delicate balance of authority and autonomy, and partly to give the children practice in playing the different roles they will be expected to play as women and men. But, as it is necessary to preserve the illusion that females have equal access to prestige education and positions, many women come to be overeducated for the roles society will expect or allow them to play. Then they turn harshly on that very institution under whose auspices they achieved their superior training and aspirations. Here the fact that the little girls believed the myths rather than the reality helped them to surpass the reality. So, with great justice, the myths may sometimes be used by determined people to confront and overcome the damaging reality.

School does not have the choice of withdrawing higher education across the board for women. Any more than it has the choice of withdrawing school incarceration past grade three or grade six for all those millions of (usually poor and/or nonwhite) students whose reading and math skills usually cease to improve somewhere in elementary school. (This problem, which can be defined broadly as "tracking," is dealt with in Chapter 3, "Education's Role in the Distribution of the Social Product.") If the label "student" were removed from these millions of relatively low-status young citizens (female and poor or nonwhite), they would be left with no socially defined roles—clearly an extremely dangerous social situation.

The contradiction here is with the economy's need, not only to process future workers and consumers, but to retain them in nonworking roles for longer and longer periods of their lives, and moreover to employ *other* workers, for whom the private sector has no place, to do this. (How the economy's need for an inflationary educational sector produces other internal contradictions is dealt with in Chapter 8, "The Fiscal Crisis: Where School and Economy Intersect," and Chapter 7, "Teachers: Fulcrum of the System.")

Wherever we look, the contradictions grow out of each other. Our society needs almost all of its adults to be literate, including the lowest-status ones. But the children who are being processed to be the lowest-status adults are rejecting, along with the school's clearly apparent designation of their destiny, the school's minimal attempts to teach them to read.

Our society needs people to believe in the usefulness of schooling. But when people agree to be stultified for years in the expectation that stultification will earn them a good place in adult society and then find that the places either don't materialize or aren't good, they stop believing in the goodness and usefulness of stultification. So they are rejecting at once the myth and the reality.

As the internal contradictions mount, the school crisis mounts. Some writers and reformers have become so distraught at the crisis that they can only think to abolish schools altogether. This "solution" reaches a peak of sentimentality that very few people are prepared to go along with. If there were to be an enormous heightening of the social crisis with accompanying general collapse of major institutions, it might be that schools, too, would give way. But at this stage, proposing to abolish schools because they harm their clients, even harm them more than they help them, is like proposing to abolish generating plants because they damage the environment more than they benefit it. Most people are simply not prepared to live by candlelight—however lovely the glow. Moreover, the beneficiaries of power and profits in the world are also not prepared to abandon the sources of their power and profits which are in schools or in generating plants.

There are other sentimental or partial or shortsighted solutions. They include alternative schools, "efficiency learning" (programed learning, behavior modification, and so on), "free learning" (open classrooms, British infant school style, and so on), compensatory education, desegregation-busing, and many more. (Some of the contradictions of these are dealt with in Chapter 10, "Institutional Reform Strategies.") To the extent that these solutions address themselves to particular symptoms of the school crisis and ignore other symptoms, they are easy solutions and they tend to aggravate the internal contradictions.

Difficult solutions alone will serve. They require us to recognize that schools are part of a system of power and profits, that they are subject to the power and contribute to the profits, and that the school crisis is an aspect of the social crisis. If the children are being manipulated, oppressed, dehumanized, their manipulation, oppression, and dehumanization are on a continuum with the adults'. It is foolish to believe that we can spare the children what we allow to be inflicted on ourselves. Schools are a crucial part of the social process; to deal with them and change them, we have to deal with and change the whole social process.

But we have to begin somewhere. Those of us who are in schools can begin there. School is not "inside" and the rest of the world "outside." The schoolhouse walls, too, are an illusion. Just as the children daily pass through them their despair and their drugs, they can also pass through them their hopes and their shrewd observations of both worlds. When we adults begin to examine our illusions and the realities—to demystify school —we can help them to put their observations into an intellectual framework that will replace the mythology and serve as a basis for profound social change.

The great thinkers of the sixteenth century taught us that to control our physical world we had to tear away the myths that darken reality and our minds—to demystify the physical world. Now, four centuries later, remote and frightening men threaten us with catastrophic powers. Only by wresting those powers back into our own hands, only by assuming control of our social world, can we save it and the physical world itself from destruction. Like the giants of the sixteenth century, we must demystify in order to know how to act, and the demystifying is itself a first and continuing act.

School is a good place to begin. It is at once a source and the subject of many myths. And school, along with the family, is the major transmitter of our culture, whose most powerful internal contradiction is that it also contains within it the intellectual tools, the moral dictates, and the human energy needed to overcome its evil.

In the last three or four years, writers, teachers, and students —each from their own vantage point—have begun to build up a revisionist history and analysis of schooling in the United States. There is now a considerable body of writings and experiences analyzing and dealing with one or another segment of the institution school. This book brings together some of these writings and experiences and tries to fit the various segments into meaningful or at least recognizable patterns.

It is meant to be an essay toward understanding and action.

Some Suggestions on the Use of This Book

Each selection and each chapter represents a limited aspect of the reality we are seeking to expose. The reality is seen to deepen as we observe each aspect more closely and also as we stand back from time to time for a wider view of several aspects. The book will be most useful for the reader who does both.

The chapter introductions are intended as an aid. They propose a few connections among the pieces within each chapter and a few connections among the several chapters. They may be read as chapter introductions, as chapter summaries, or, together with the general introduction, in sequence as a kind of summary of the book. Readers may also wish to compare my short interpretations of individual selections with their own.

Many if not most of the selections can be read as independent pieces. In fact, some were specifically chosen to make available to a wider public highly valuable writings which have had a far too limited circulation. But most will gain in significance as they are considered together with related material. Where classes or discussion groups use this book, their members may wish individually to read different related pieces and then discuss them as a group.

Readers who find the book useful will find the annotated bibliography indispensable. The book can be only an introduction to the study of an area of our lives together, an area that we can very well see is beginning to go under. If we're going to rescue it—which means rescuing ourselves and our children and their children—we're going to have to go on studying and acting. The bibliography is meant to be an aid to both. Relevant works of other students, both radical and conventional, are listed. Also listed are the names of little-known publications and groups which are doing some of the most important thinking, writing, and acting in the nation in respect to the school crisis and the social crisis. Readers are urged to put themselves in touch with these publications and groups. The bibliography is deliberately offered as a whole, rather than by individual topics, so that as they introduce themselves to the complexity of the subject, readers will find new interconnections in the literature as a whole. Readers who regard the bibliography as something like a secondhand bookstore, rather than as an "assigned reading list," will be able to take pleasure in browsing along its shelves.

In fact, I hope that the book as a whole will give pleasure as well as profit. An important motive in putting it together has been my wish to share with others the pleasure and the profit that I myself have had from several years of reading in the field.

Among the people whose deeds and writings have given me the greatest pleasure and profit are many students and teachers to whom I have related in one way or another in the Bay area of California, where I live, in correspondence throughout the country and abroad, and in the several cities that I have visited. People welcomed me to their homes, their places of work, and their thoughts. I could not have put together this book without them.

In publicly giving thanks to them, I should like to point out to my readers that the serious business of understanding and changing our society requires just such widespread and mutual trust, and that I hope they will do their best to continue to spread the network of trust.

The Louis M. Rabinowitz Foundation of New York trusted me to the extent of providing a grant, which made possible the travel and a certain amount of leisure for "thinking up" the book.

Dick Lichtman started me on the way to understanding the alienation of labor, which is a key to understanding the social crisis and the school crisis.

Ann and Joe Gladstone of Pescadero provided a quiet and loving place in which I could spread out the leisure and the thinking.

The members of BARTOC, individually and as a group, provided the sense of groupness as well as some immediate ideas and experiences that have been basic to my own experiencing of the school crisis.

Miriam Wasserman

San Francisco, California
November, 1973

1 School Nightmares: The Private and the Public

There are few people over age six who know nothing of school nightmares. For some people, school is or always was a nightmare, which began in those dark corners of childhood that haunt us all our lives. For most others, school is or was sometimes a nightmare, which sometimes recurs. Now the school nightmare officially enters the public realm; in the dark corners are the haunts of a whole society.

In another part of his forty-year-old classic, from which we here reprint a description of a modest, old-fashioned teacher's nightmare, Willard Waller describes and explains schools as little despotic systems. The teacher's nightmare is of the strange dissolution of his despotism.

The teacher's nightmare could well have been identical in content with his students' most enthusiastic daydreams, in accordance with the axiom that the nightmares of the oppressor are the daydreams of the oppressed. Which doesn't mean that his students didn't have their own nightmares. Probably they were not very different from our own as students, or from our own students'. Who has not awakened in a cold sweat from the dream of having to face the final reckoning in a class whose very existence she has forgotten till the moment of the dream?

Some children are either so sensitive or so bold as to seek to escape an intolerable nightmare. "The Children's Daytime Nightmares" tells of their tragedies.

Others, more romantic or more devious, find ways of turning

the nightmare into a daydream. Then the fantasies of freedom or revenge that the reluctant pupil at the back of the room is busy dreaming away for twelve years may create for him an adulthood of incompetence and idleness that is its own night-mare in a nightmare society. Willie, a good and gifted human being who dreamed away his pleasant childhood, says of his dreams and nightmares, "All your life, been having a dream you was going to make it. And didn't make it nowhere. . . . When I face it, I want to run. When I want to run . . . I *can't* run. . . . My life, I'll change with anybody. I don't want it no more."

But our private fears and fantasies are born of and return to the soil of our life in society. The teacher's modest private night-mare of pre—World War II days has become the daily reality of the days of and after a war of extermination in Southeast Asia. Solemn school-board members, as we see in the selections from the *American School Board Journal,* now concern themselves at public meetings with matters that the teacher-dreamer dared to acknowledge only in the darkness of his dreams.

In New York City in 1968, many people's private daydreams and nightmares erupted into a public nightmare whose mean-ness surprised even the protagonists themselves. The teacher-dreamer's private nightmare of forty years earlier became the agony of a city of 8 million adults and children. After the op-pressed children had already shattered the insecure despotism of the classroom, their parents and spokesmen undertook on a mass scale to rescue them from the grimness of illiteracy and semiliteracy. And, in the cosmopolitan city in which all races, religions, and nationalities had sometimes been said to live in harmony, those who felt they had the least to gain from what harmony there was began a struggle for equality, with or without harmony. The two documents here included about the Great School Strike of 1968 (popularly known as "Ocean Hill—Browns-ville") were chosen for their moderation; they barely hint at either the ugliness or the revolutionary hopes of those struggles.

At the time of this writing, both the gross ugliness and the exhilarating hopes have subsided. But the seedbed for the pub-lic and the private nightmares is still fertile. There is a crisis of the schools that none of us and none of our schools can escape. It is part of, and it contributes to, the crisis of our society. The chapters that follow explore some manifestations and meanings of that crisis. We must understand our nightmares and the real life of which they are fragments in order to begin to cope with

them, and also in order to begin to realize our most humane
daydreams.

An Old-fashioned Nightmare

by Willard Waller

Following is the recurrent dream of a male teacher of twenty-six.
He has an excellent reputation as a disciplinarian, and has succeeded with some difficult schools.

The record of the dream follows:

Each year as the horrid conflict of the first month was going on
and the feeling against me was considerable and bitter, I would
have a dream. It ran as follows:

It is morning. The nine o'clock bell calling the school formally
to attention has not rung yet. Part of the pupils are in the school
building visiting and playing; others are outside doing likewise. All
is going nicely. I bend intently over my work at the desk for
several minutes.

Finally a noise in the room draws my attention. Annoyed, I look
up quickly. To my surprise a big boy is scuffling with a smaller
one. I loudly command them to stop. They do, but reluctantly.
About that time some girls start running noisily up and down the
aisles. This on top of the scuffling is too much. I tell them to take
their seats. They do, but I can see by their faces that they have a
notion not to. There is rebellion in the air. By this time the boys in
the corner are throwing books at each other. I am amazed. Why,
what ails them? Throwing things inside is strictly against the rules.
And these boys are usually so docile. But there is Alfred Davis
among them, and he is a very mischievous boy and antagonistic
towards me. And it was Bernice Keller, ever slow to mind, who
led the girls in their racing among the seats. I shout at the boys.
They do not heed me. I bawl them out and remark that if they
can't find anything better to do they had better wash the blackboards for me. They interpret the remark in the imperative mode,
which is correct, and scowling and muttering begin the task.

From Willard Waller, *The Sociology of Teaching* (New York: John Wiley
& Sons, 1932, 1967).

There is a commotion on the playground. From the window I see the boys fighting over a swing. I go out. They do not stop as I approach. I speak to them. I cuff them. They pay no attention. I am aghast. *Neither look, nor speech, nor action, nor presence of the teacher avails.* I note some girls running back and forth across the street in front of the passing automobiles. I call to them, but in vain. Wrathfully I start toward the street. The girls run away down the street. I am no child; I will not run after them. Baffled I ring the school bell. It is past nine o'clock anyhow.

Inside pandemonium reigns. The girls whom I left in their seats are dashing about the room upsetting the loose furniture. The boys at the blackboards are pelting each other with chalk and erasers. They pelt me as I appear. I charge upon them. They elude me. This is terrible, *terrible*!

But where are the boys and girls from outdoors? Why do they not come in? Did they not hear the bell? The boys have stopped fighting and are standing looking sullenly at the building. What shall I do? What can I do? They heed neither teacher nor bell. I attempt to expel them. They will not go home. The girls are standing tantalizingly across the street. I shall take it up with the school board. They laugh at me. They even scorn the board! Then I shall settle this thing by force. I go inside to get a club. They follow me in. The sight of the club quiets them somewhat. They all take their seats.

I preach to them. Smirkingly they listen. We start the lessons, but the conflict reasserts itself everywhere. I leave the desk and the club to help a student whose hand is raised. In the other end of the room a titter arises and increases in volume. Aha! So they're at it again. I seize the club. A few blows restore order. But it is no use. No matter where I turn the club must be used. Nor can I use it fast enough to be effective, to keep order. I shall have to call in the board. I have failed! But no, I will not fail! I redouble my efforts. The students begin breaking up desks and tearing down casements so that they too may have clubs. I seek refuge behind my desk and pound upon it for order. They ignore the act. The whole school gathers itself to rush upon me with clubs. Pale with fear, I square myself for the finish. They start . . . but never reach me because I awaken, cold with sweat. Parts of the dream and the faces appear and fade away in the darkness before my eyes. I recall a few pupils—good students, "teacher's pets," friends of mine outside of school or students with whom my associations in school have been close—who took no part. Vernon Hart, Lucille

Ollinger, Harold Childers, and Oscar Olson had nothing to do with it. They stood off in the corners and at the edges staring without expression. They were neutral. They favored neither side. God bless them! I must be better to them in the future. The dream is still real. I begin to plan what I shall do tomorrow to get even with them and to restore order. I excuse myself for letting such a thing get started. I wasn't feeling well, my head ached so, or this would never have happened. Well, if I can't control them, I'll just disappear, I'll skip the country.

Then I become fully conscious. I wonder what I really would do if such a thing should happen. I resolve not to rule with quite such an iron hand. Well, if it ever does happen, they'll never see me again. And thus for an hour or so until I fall asleep again. The dream, however, haunts me for several days.

During my first year of teaching, when this dream came, it frightened me. I thought it must be a bad sign. But nothing of the kind ever happened. Only one little red-haired chap even so much as dared to talk back to me that year. And at the end of the term I was asked to return at an increase in salary; and so in the years of teaching after that I looked upon this dream, when it came, as a good omen, as a portent that the year would be a successful one.

Nightmares of the 1970's

A Journal Special Report—Fires and Vandals: How to make them both unwelcome in your schools, by Ernest E. Juillerat, Jr.

School fires will cost boards $64.5 million this year

Most school fires are *set*. They are not accidents. They're called "touch offs"—fires that somebody deliberately starts. They are frequent and . . . they can be devastating. . . .

How to (just about) vandal-proof every school in your district

How much did your school district contribute to the more than $100 million that school boards paid last year to correct the damage inflicted by school vandals? Vandalism is a dark cloud hanging over most schools, but a board and superintendent may find one silver lining. That is, if they can diminish the problem, their district may have additional funds for its educational program next year—funds that were used this year to remove paint-splattered obscenities from the principal's office, for example. . . .

(January, 1972)

(from the tables of contents of selected issues)

Nightmares of 1984

BARTOW, FLA. (Ramparts/FPS). Just a few miles from the spires of Disney World's Tomorrowland is an Orwellian future that didn't wait until 1984. In Polk County, Florida, a flat, sleepy stretch of land, world renowned for frozen orange juice, the school board has begun installing a series of special cameras which will monitor junior and senior high school students during class, in the halls and while eating lunch.

The School Board of Polk County, plagued with the typical problems of drug dealing, student unrest and vandalism, became the first system in the nation to install Kodak Analyst Super-8 security cameras. The police, banks and retail shops have been using similar cameras for over a year.

W. W. Reed, superintendent of the Polk County School Board, said that the surveillance equipment, although in use only a short time, has had a psychological impact on the 10 senior and 16 junior high schools where they are in use. "They have had a definite effect on the total tenor at the schools," said Reed.

The cameras, "the latest Super-8 advance" according to a Kodak Company release, cost around $240 apiece and are set to snap a picture every 30 seconds. Because they are encased in a sound-absorbent box, students never know when a picture is being taken. The time-lapse camera can operate for days without changing film.

. . . Reed takes great pains to emphasize that the school board has no intention of snooping on the students. "We're neither interested, nor do we have the time to 'spy' on our students when they are conducting themselves in manners normal for their age level," he said.

"We process and look at the film only when incidents have occurred that require establishing responsibility for them," Reed continued. "It is a completely innocent way of taking remedial action."

But students at Polk County schools and the American Civil Liberties Union of Florida disagree with the superintendent as to the innocence of the Analyst Super-8's. "We are inhibited from being ourselves," said one senior student body president from a school where the cameras have been used. "It doesn't say much for our teachers when they need spy cameras to keep control," he added.

Florence Wills, spokeswoman for the American Civil Liberties Union of Florida, said that the Polk County School Board's installation of the cameras constituted "a definite invasion of privacy." . . .

"We feel the Polk County School Board has attempted to rewrite the Constitution of the United States," she continued. "We feel this type of surveillance should be stopped before it spreads to other school boards around the country. We already have information that the Palm Beach County Board is about to install a similar system by Kodak."

In the meantime Kodak is mounting a major effort to put its Analyst Super-8 cameras in every school, retail store, government office and warehouse in the country. "The present crime emergency may be more important than almost any other environmental problem," states the narrator of Kodak's sales presentation for their security cameras.

. . . Students loudly proclaim that school rules are as widely ignored as they were before the installation of the cameras. . . . "Nothing has changed but the amount of subterfuge and fear," said a student.

The Children's Daytime Nightmares

Boy Skips School to Be at Mother's Bedside—Police Jail Him

STUART, FLA. A 12-year-old boy spent 30 hours in the Martin County Jail after bolting from school to be near his ailing mother.

"I had no choice," Juvenile Court Administrator Jerry Prewitt explained. He said that he had ordered the youth to be held in jail "until we could come up with an answer of what to do with him."

The youngster, whose name was not disclosed because of his age, had been a chronic truant since his mother suffered a stroke four months ago. Prewitt said the boy skipped class in Stuart and hitchhiked to his home in Indiantown, where his mother is recuperating.

Sheriff's deputies later captured the boy at his home and returned him to Stuart where he was placed in a holding cell in the Martin County jail, Prewitt said.

(FPS, No. 19, March 20, 1972)

A Change of Mind on Way. 16-Year-Old Air Hijacker

MIAMI. A teen-ager who said he was having problems at home hijacked an airliner yesterday but then changed his mind and allowed the plane to land at Miami, where he gave himself up.

[The boy], 16, a high school sophomore at Mobile, Ala., took over National Airlines Flight 745 at gunpoint while it was on the ground in Mobile and ordered the pilot to go to Montreal. . . .

[The pilot] said the boy was a "gentleman the whole time," but very nervous. [He] said the youth told him his "main problem was at home. He was getting bad grades in school and his parents were on his back."

(*San Francisco Chronicle,* March 9, 1971)

Missing Girl Hid Under a House for 23 Days

An 11-year-old Millbrae girl, who apparently was so afraid to return to school after cutting classes that she hid for 23 days under a neighbor's house, underwent psychiatric observation yesterday. . . .

The girl, described by the family as a loner who had few friends and liked to read, told the [police] officers [who found her] she went on night prowls of the neighborhood and lived mainly on canned goods taken from her father's camper truck, parked nearby. . . .

"She was harder to find than a squirrel," an officer said. "It was as if she had escaped to another planet."

(*San Francisco Chronicle*, January 5, 1972)

Poem*

He always wanted to explain things, but no one cared.
Sometimes he would draw and it wasn't anything.
He wanted to carve it in stone or write it in the sky.
He would lie out in the grass and look up in the sky
And it would only be him and the sky and the things inside him
    that needed saying.
And it was after that that he drew the picture.
He kept it under his pillow and would let no one see it.
And he would look at it every night and think about it.
And when it was dark, and his eyes were closed, he could still see it
And it was all of him. And he loved it.
When he started school he brought it with him
Not to show to anyone, but just to have it with him like a friend
It was funny about school.
He sat at a square, brown desk
Like all other square, brown desks.
And he thought it should be red.
And his room was a square, brown room
Like all the other rooms.
And it was tight and close. And stiff.
He hated to hold the pencil and chalk.
With his arm stiff and his feet flat on the floor, stiff.

* This poem, later widely reprinted, was given to a teacher in Regina, Saskatchewan, by a twelfth-grade boy. Although it is not known if he wrote the poem, it is known that the boy committed suicide a few weeks afterward.—Ed.

With the teacher watching and watching.
The teacher came and spoke to him.
She told him to wear a tie like all the other boys.
He said he didn't like them.
And she said it didn't matter.
After that they drew.
And he drew all yellow and it was the way he felt about morning.
And it was beautiful.
The teacher came and smiled at him.
"What's this?" she said. "Why don't you draw like Ken's drawing?
Isn't that beautiful?"
After that his mother bought him a tie.
And he always drew airplanes and rocketships like everyone else.
And he threw the old picture away.
And when he lay alone looking at the sky,
It was big and blue and all of everything,
But he wasn't anymore.
He was square inside, and brown,
And his hands were stiff.
And he was like everyone else.
And the thing inside him that needed saying didn't need it anymore.
It had stopped pushing.
It was crushed. Stiff.
Like everything else.

Private Nightmares and the Public Realm

Children's Strikes in 1911

A Ruskin docker-student . . . described the children's strikes in nearly 60 port towns in 1911. These strikes were always in the poorest, roughest parts of town, and often truants and "bad elements" took a leading role. Their demands are fascinating. These varied from place to place, but usually included: abolition of the attendance officer, one day's holiday a week excluding Saturday, one hour's schooling in the morning and one in the afternoon, a shilling a week to be paid to all schoolgoers. 1911 was a year of dock strikes. It was in the town where the troops were called in and shot two strikers that the first school strike broke out. The school strikes had no visible effect on school discipline, but who knows what effect they had on the strikers?

(*Libertarian Teacher* [Leicester, England], No. 9, 1973)

Harlem Parents' Committee Recommendations on the Bundy Report*

Community control of schools is now a definite possibility. Such a victory is imperative for our times. Anything short of this single objective would perpetuate the current process of "programmed retardation" which has been very successful in maintaining the "status crow." Let the record speak for itself.

1966 Facts

?????   325,006 black and Puerto Rican student failures in the Elementary and Junior High schools. (Total Elementary and Junior black and P.R. enrollment: 382,360)

?????   82,509 black and Puerto Rican drop-outs from High School. (Black and P.R. High School enrollment: 147,337)

?????   3,798 black and Puerto Rican graduates with academic and commercial diplomas—out of approximately 19,000 High School graduates. (Black and P.R. are 54.6% of High School enrollment)

We cannot tolerate this kind of performance any longer. The only way we can reverse this picture is, first, to take responsibility

* The Harlem Parents' Committee was a small group of volunteer working people who devoted great efforts to exposing and seeking to overcome the inadequacy of teaching and learning of the mainly black children of New York City's central Harlem. The Committee was headed by a politically and educationally moderate man, Isaiah Robinson, who was later appointed a member and then President of the Board of Education of the City of New York. The terminology of guerrilla warfare in the HPC statement is mild compared to the rhetoric of many more militant groups that participated in the decentralization–community control struggle.

The Bundy Report was the work of a committee funded by the Ford Foundation and headed by McGeorge Bundy (who before that was a top foreign-affairs aide to President Kennedy) that recommended decentralization of the city's school system as a way of overcoming its administrative and educational bankruptcy.—ED.

through complete control of all schools in our communities and to hold the professionals accountable to us for quality performance and production. This means a change in power relationships. Only then can we effect change in our children's present and future condition.

This will not be an easy battle. In any war of liberation (in this case against the dual school system), the first strategy is to establish a beachhead. The time is now! We must "dig in" and fight here. This is the front line of the fight.

Our first assault should be on the basis of a few simple but direct and non-negotiable objectives around which we must unite:

(1) Complete community control and autonomy over:
     (a) Schools
     (b) Personnel
     (c) Budget
(2) The District should elect its entire School Board.
(3) Tenure rights should be protected for all personnel that are responsive and accountable to the community.
(4) The Central Education Agency [should] be comprised of three (3) appointed and salaried commissioners, responsible for research, planning, analysis and incentive programs, maintaining legal services, public information services and other functions (applicable citywide) not specifically vested in the community boards.

These four simple objectives are by no means all of our concerns, but they are direct and easily understood. Our battle lines should be drawn around these only—pinpointing specific targets that get to the heart of the struggle. Our telegrams, letters, conferences and other contacts with legislators should drive home these objectives.

From the Statement of the Special Committee on Racial and Religious Prejudice, the Honorable Bernard Botein, Chairman

In November, 1968, Mayor John V. Lindsay of New York City created a Special Committee on Racial and Religious Prejudice, under the chairmanship of Bernard Botein, formerly presiding justice of the Appellate Division, "to report back to him within five weeks on the current conditions of racial and religious prejudice, focusing primarily on the school dispute." ...

An appalling amount of racial prejudice—black and white—in

New York City surfaced in and about the school controversy. Over and over again we found evidence of vicious anti-white attitudes on the part of some black people.

The anti-white prejudice has a dangerous component of anti-Semitism.* Black leaders sincerely tend to regard this anti-Semitism as relatively unimportant in the school controversy, since in their struggle for emergence their preoccupation is with discrimination, notably in education, employment and housing, and not with defamation, oral or written. Jews, in turn, are outraged by anti-Semitic defamation itself, fearful that such apparent indifference may spark violence and other forms of anti-Semitism well beyond defamatory expressions.

The black-white hostility also has a small measure of bigotry emanating from or directed against Puerto Ricans. Puerto Ricans found themselves split in their relationships between whites and Negroes.

Further, although it has long been known that bigotry has many shapes, it has become clear to us, at least in this controversy, that the prejudice emanating from blacks generally takes a form somewhat different from that which has emerged among whites. The countless incidents, leaflets, epithets and the like in this school controversy reveal a bigotry from black extremists that is open, undisguised, nearly physical in its intensity—and far more obvious and identifiable than that emanating from whites.

On the other hand, anti-black bigotry tended to be expressed in more sophisticated and subtle fashion, often communicated privately and seldom reported, but nonetheless equally evil, corrosive, damaging and deplorable. . . .

Clearly, . . . the episodes of alleged bigotry require more investigation and further analysis to assess with finality their extent, depth of meaning, scope and impact. Further study is needed, too, before gauging their permanent effect on community attitudes, and the extent to which racial and religious hatred will persist after the decentralization issue has been resolved.

There have been a number of desecrations of synagogues in recent months. . . .

Aside from the immorality, the destructive atmosphere and

---

* Some people, including the editor of this book, believe that Judge Botein's account of the anti-white and anti-Semitic expressions during this struggle is incomplete and therefore inaccurate. For an account expressing a different view of these matters, see Miriam Wasserman, *The School Fix: NYC, USA* (New York: Outerbridge & Dienstfrey, 1970).

personal insult which arise from racial and religious defamation are disruptive and confusing to the analysis which many in the black and Puerto Rican communities are now making of the various establishments they feel have failed them. Concentrating on the religion and race of those involved does not contribute to an understanding of control of institutions or of how that control can be rearranged.

Jews, Negroes and Puerto Ricans in this city constitute a very large proportion of its inhabitants. These groups, on the whole, have endeavored for years to live in a spirit of amity, respect and mutual helpfulness. This attitude has been encouraged by other groups which have been a part of the friendly effort to achieve unity in diversity which has characterized this great community. The present state of affairs, with hostility escalating on all sides, presents an intolerable situation. Of course, these tensions did not spring full blown from the current school confrontation. In a city inhabited by so many diverse groups, so many underprivileged people, it would appear that a certain amount of resentment and hatred has been simmering below the surface for many years. It is likely that similar emotions in some other cities spread and were spent, if only temporarily, in bloody riots. But in any event, there can be no doubt that the recent school conflict touched off the spate of religious and racial bigotry which this city is now experiencing. It is ironic that this conflict should develop so speedily and massively between Jews and blacks—two groups who for many years have so successfully cooperated with each other in attempting to promote a higher level of human dignity, racial and religious understanding and equality of opportunity for men of all colors and creeds. With these groups on edge, with new antagonisms fired by the school decentralization controversy, with some people using bigotry as a weapon, racial antagonism to some extent has been encouraged as an echo of the main struggle. Thus the entire community has been riven and stirred by the spreading antagonism between these two groups of old friends.

In this controversy some persons have distorted the issues by the injection of bigotry. These shrill voices have espoused racism, anti-Semitism, and intimidation. Hate-mongers have engendered an atmosphere of fear. It is time for concerned citizens—blacks and whites—who have been too silent, to speak up for the vast majority of citizens committed to an orderly process of change in a dynamic democratic society. Their failure to do so early, clearly and sufficiently, we found, was in itself a contributing factor to the exacerbation of hostilities; the persistent allegations of "racism" by each side against the other—ill-defined and unspecified—themselves became harmful epithets.

There is room for dissent, protest and militancy, but anti-Semitism, racism and violence are out of bounds in any community discussion of complex problems. If citizens do not speak out against racism and bigotry and support an orderly process, the tension between the races will intensify and tear our city apart. They must condemn and repudiate racism and anti-Semitism and all other manifestations of bigotry. We must maintain an atmosphere in which issues will be discussed without the injection of prejudice. It would be constructive for the leadership on all sides to come together in a collective statement repudiating further intrusion of bigotry in the decentralization debate.

The Quiet Daydreamers: Growing Up Illiterate

by John Reimann and Willie Gallagher

I first met Willie in the summer of 1964, when he was seventeen years old. That was before he dropped out of school. . . . he had a warm, open smile. He used to come up to the basement on 147th Street, where we were running an art workshop, to be tutored in reading.

Willie had managed to get all the way to tenth grade on the slide. His survival in school depended on his ability to fake it. He had one way or another of getting around the fact that he was completely illiterate. It was a pattern that he developed as far back in school as he can remember.

In fourth grade, he recalls, the class used to get a weekly assignment of words to learn to spell. He'd go home, do the assignment, which consisted of looking the words up in the dictionary and copying out dictionary definitions. He knew the alphabet and could do this, sometimes with the help of a younger sister, without knowing at all what he was writing.

From Miriam Wasserman, *The School Fix: NYC, USA* (New York: Outerbridge & Dienstfrey, copyright 1970). Reprinted by permission.

The teacher knew he didn't know anything and wasn't learning anything, and conspired with him to help him avoid confronting the problem. The weekly spelling tests were arranged as a contest between one half of the class and the other. . . . Willie, however, never participated in them. According to him, the teacher and he "worked together" to keep him out of the contest. He wanted to stay out, he says, to avoid embarrassment in front of his fellow students. God knows why she wanted to keep him out; she probably told herself that she was doing him a favor.

This was typical of Willie's school career. He was always a good boy in class, he says, so the teacher never had it in for him. The way he saw it, the teachers called on—"bothered"—the more unruly students. "You so smart—tell me the answer to this," is the way he describes their attitude. About himself, he says, "I was quiet. I always find out, if you be quiet, since I couldn't read, you could get by. Just lay in the back and be quiet. 'Cause anybody that know they couldn't read would know if you stay in the back and stay quiet, you won't be embarrassed about learning to read. If you be a big mouth—start trouble—you be singled out all the time." . . .

When they gave tests, sometimes he just didn't take them, sometimes he "just scribbled stuff, and the teacher never picked it up."

"How did that make you feel?" I asked, "that you scribbled something and she didn't even bother to look at it?" I was sure that would have hurt him.

"I felt all right. Nice. Like, I knew it was wrong. Like I was getting away with something."

In the series of conversations we had, I often returned to that point, because I couldn't believe that somewhere, he didn't feel hurt, neglected. One time when we were talking about ways in which school helps "to keep black people down," I suggested that a teacher's not going out of her way to draw a student out could be one way in which she might be telling him he's not very valuable, that a teacher should make a student work, so he would feel worth something.

"But the kid won't get the idea," he said. "He just be glad that you not bothering him. He'll feel he's getting away with something. 'Cause he's afraid to be embarrassed, and know he don't know it. He just getting away. He feels great about it [not having to work]. Least I did." . . .

Twice, once in fifth and once in sixth grade, he got left back.

Otherwise, he did fine. He got A's on his report card—for good conduct.

If his teachers weren't pushing him, neither was his grandmother. . . . Now he wishes they had pushed him. "You like a baby. You come up, you know, you don't know what's good for you. This is good for you, this is going to help you, this is vitamins, you know. You don't know if it's going to help you or not." . . .

Some time after he began to try to learn to read with me, his attitude toward school changed some. He began to feel that "people jigged me up. Teachers jigged me up. They supposed to help me, they didn't help me. Parents supposed to love me, they didn't help me. Everybody loved me . . . but nobody helped me."

Specifically he began to blame his teachers. I tried to say it wasn't the teachers, it was the whole system. But he argued about that: "Right, but see, what I'm trying to say is how I came all the way up through the system, and I wasn't the only one. And look at me. Why was I all juked up? I wasn't mean. So, I look back, it must have been the teachers. Like I was there. Every day. In the class. All day. And I wasn't mean. So, like, if they dishing it out, I should have got some of it. Other words, they wasn't dishing it out." . . .

The school year of 1964–65 he was on his way out of school. He couldn't read, and, as it now appears, wasn't really working at it. He occasionally used to say something about killing himself, which it was easy not to take too seriously because it was said so casually.

"I was just tired of my surroundings. Like, you know, what we used to do on the weekends? We'd mug three, four, five people at a time. Every weekend, you know, it was nothing else to do.... ."

He was doing this very shortly after I first began to tutor him, but he never said anything to me about all this at the time. He didn't want me to think he was a bad guy. From my point of view at that time, things looked pretty hopeful for him. Anyway, I was teaching him to read. From his? "Hopeless and helpless," he says. . . .

The next year he joined the Muslims, got sent to jail for mugging, came out and went to live with his uncle in Brooklyn. "I got a whole lot out of the Muslims," he says. "They made me realize it was all out there for me to get."

When he first told me the story of his arrest, he said he had had nothing to do with the mugging. . . . When he told me again recently about how he used to mug people in Harlem, I asked him

if he actually was guilty of the mugging for which he was convicted. He talked around some.

"That robbery, did I have anything to do with that? Can't
remember, John, it was so long back. Let me see . . . let me see.
. . . Yeah. It was the night I had left my money at my man's
house. Went all the way up in the Bronx. We was going to Topps.
Saw this man. They said, 'Come on.' I said, 'Naw.' They said,
'Yeah.' I said, 'Well, why not?' So it just happened.

"Got busted. Paid the cost."

"How come you're telling me now?" I asked him.

"John. You know, who's John? You know, John is John. After
you get to know somebody, you feel that you can tell them something, it won't bother them, you know. 'Cause they know that you
ain't as bad as you . . . you know. . . . Like, if you kill somebody,
John, I know that you not a real killer, so I won't be afraid of
you or anything like that there. I'd think, 'He's all right,' you
know. If you told me why you killed him, I'd understand, you
know. . . . After a while you feel that you can trust this person
and tell them these things, and they would trust you in that way."

After Willie got out of jail, he got married to a girl he had got
pregnant. He became, half-seriously, involved in a black militant
group. He's had a series of jobs none of which pay enough to keep
him up to date with his household bills and also buy him the
clothes and partying that he loves. . . .

One evening recently I came home and put on a tape of what
was supposed to be a reading lesson that Willie was to have done.
I heard the following:

"Wow. Life is a drag. You ain't got money. More likely, you
ain't got a chance. Everything's against you—everything. Get
ahead—live good. Not knowing how to read, every time you want
to eat, that works hand in hand. Can't read, you can't eat what you
want to eat. If you can read, that dollar there. All your life is
money. You look at yourself—you could be like the man around
the corner.

"Little old man—twenty-two years old. All your life, been
having a dream you was going to make it. And didn't make it
nowhere.

"The whole world in front of you. Feel like reaching out for it;
and you just can't get it. Every time you get up on it, it moves
away. You get a job, making some money, but, you still not happy.

You want more money! Why you want more money? 'Cause the money you getting—it's going too fast. The Man allows you to make enough money—not enough to get by—enough to strain, to scrape by. He got you straining every week, every year, to get by. It's a thing. A circle. . . .

"Look where I am today: Twenty-two. Got a half-assed job. Got a family. And I got bills. Do I deserve all this? . . . Hell no. Didn't do nothing to nobody all my life. Nobody. Maybe a couple of girls when I got older, but they didn't mind. . . .

"Supposing you have a problem—find it, and then deal with it. Problem at home—I'm not ready for it. Not ready for it at all. Can't back out—can't get away from it—so I got to face it. When I face it, I want to run. When I want to run I . . . I *can't* run. So therefore I'm stuck. Stuck in a rut. And trying to get out. Been trying to get out of a rut for twenty-two years. . . .

"My life, I'll change with anybody. I don't want it no more.

"Did I say I don't want it no more? I wouldn't say that. I've had some good times in my life. Had some good times last weekend! Probably have some good times next weekend! But it's all in the middle of those good times, which you're hurting. And after those, you're hurting. And *before* those good times, you're hurting.

"I got to get away. Don't care how I get away, as long as I get away. I want to take my little girl with me. Hate to go alone. My father left me; I used to hate him. Today I know how it was. Probably had it hard just like this. Making a decision. To leave, to stay, be hurt. If he stay, he hate himself. If he left, he be regretting that. I used to say, 'Why did he leave me?' Why? He want to be happy. He should have stayed with me and Mommy. But looking at me now I can see why he did it. But then you say, 'He should have known what he was doing.' I should have known what I was doing, too. Thought I knew. Evidently, I didn't know. Boy, oh boy, oh boy. Feel like killing yourself, but then you say, there's too much fun out there, you going to miss too much if you do. . . .

"You look down at your little girl. . . . She looks up at you and smile. Then you realize that you can't leave. Can't get away. Can't get away at all. Her mother know that she got you around, 'cause she got your daughter. You look at the future for you in your present job, and like it's nowhere. But then you think, if I get down to the books, my job can be somewhere for me. Only if you get down to the books. With the city, it's test after test. Each raise is a test; each test is a raise. The key to getting past the tests is reading. The key to reading is learning to read. The key to learning to read is finding time to read. The key to finding time. . . .

"Then you say, well, I better do it 'cause I want to learn and get ahead. But then you find you got struggles in yourself. A house that's divided, it can't stand. If you divided against yourself, you can't function right.

"Too many problems. Too many inner struggles . . . to do anything. And it all revolves around money. To live, to eat, to sleep, to enjoy yourself—you must have money. To get money, you must work. To get good money, have a good job. Have a job, have a good education. Have a good education, *study* for it. You must want to study. So it all lies in you again.

"Life? Who needs it?

"I do. It's a lot of fun. Lot of enjoyment. Lot of kicks. Lot of headaches. Lot of struggles. Lot of backaches. But then, it's a whole lot of partying.

"You party, you party, you party.

"You suffer, you suffer, you suffer.

"You get older, you get older, you get older.

"You find that you through with the party, and you got nowhere to go.

"Well, that's the way it is. So why not be that way? Boss if you find it happy."

2 The Hidden Curriculum: Alienation and Reification

The modern school has succeeded in doing something which, according to the law of physics, is impossible: the annihilation of once existent matter. The desire for knowledge, the capacity for acting by oneself, the gift of observation, all qualities children bring with them to school, have, as a rule, at the close of the school period disappeared. . . . There is much common-sense in the French humourist's remark, "You say that you have never gone to school and yet you are such an idiot."
                                —Ellen Key, The Century of the Child, 1909

The folk wisdom is that what schools do is to "prepare children for real life," or train them so that when they grow up they will be able to "get along in the outside world." Leaving aside the questions of why the life of an adult is more "real" than the life of a child and what is "outside" and what is "inside," it is nevertheless possible to accept the folk wisdom. Then we may ask: What kind of world is that "outside world," and what do schools do to prepare children to function as adults in it?

We all know that the schools' ostensible major task is to inculcate some bits of information and some basic skills that are indispensable to our complex society, and that the schools perform this function more or less well with various groups of children. That this task might possibly be done more effectively and pleasantly by other means and institutions doesn't matter that much: Because, over and above its ostensible purpose of teaching children to *do* the kinds of things our society says they must do, school has the far more significant purpose of teaching them to *be* the kinds of adults our society says they must be.

Among the qualities of such adults, as is suggested by the potpourri of clippings that opens this section, are more or less unquestioning respect for authority, willingness to accept authority's definitions of work and play, dependence for approval on authority more than on peers, willingness to perform relatively meaningless work with great regularity, and high valuation of money and things (customarily represented in school by credits and grades—but some "innovators" are experimenting with real money and commodities). What István Mészáros calls the "interiorization" of these values is called by the Discipline Code of the San Francisco Unified School District "self-discipline." That self-discipline can be in some mysterious way damaging to people's humanity is suggested by the selection "Something Happens to You if You Get Too Much Education" and by the few wise words of Carl Gustav Jung.

What it is that "happens to you" when you get too much education is analyzed in "Alienation and the Crisis of Education." Mészáros locates the crisis of education in alienation. It must be understood that, for a Marxist, "alienation" means something different from what it means to most non-Marxists, something more intricately interwoven with the social system. "Alienation" is commonly more or less synonymous with "turning off" or "dropping out" (psychologically speaking), as in the frequent complaint: "My students are so alienated," meaning that they aren't relating to the school world. A Marxist might say that it is the school world that is alienated, that the "alienated" students are in fact alienated from alienation, and that school alienation corresponds with the alienation of labor in the work world.

Alienation of labor refers to the fact that the wage or salary worker sells his labor power (a significant part of his life energy) for money rather than using it directly to sustain and give meaning to his life. He gives himself up to his employer. He also gives up the product of his labor and meaningful self- or group-directed cooperative relations with his co-workers. For Marxists, this social and human alienation, which constitutes the core of capitalist relations of production, violates the very nature of man, which is to seek to control and change himself and, together with others, his natural and human environment.

Another term Mészáros uses that requires some thought is "reification," which means turning human qualities, values, and relations into things (after the Latin *res*, meaning "thing"). Examples would be the ascription of either good or evil to modern technology rather than to the relations among the people who create, control, and use the technology, and the identification of education with the educated person's grades, diploma, or degree rather than with his changed consciousness, skills, and relationships. In both these cases, lifeless things at once symbolize and mask the human reality.

Through reification, people's activities become embedded in institutions in such a way that the actors lose control of their activities and the activities come to damage the actors deeply. So in reification of learning (submitting to school), children's learning activity becomes so deeply embedded in the institution school that they can barely conceive of learning except as schooling.

If self-conscious control of our life-work energies and our group destiny are, as Marx believed, characteristically and uniquely human drives, then alienation from ourselves must be learned. The institution school, with much help from the institution family, teaches the lesson. We may call it alienation training.

In "Miss White's Second Grade" we see the teacher administering the first lessons in the long course from which some of the children will graduate as certified alienated workers. Only Beryl, almost absent-mindedly, refuses to participate, devoting her energies instead to unalienated learning to read. She illustrates a central contradiction of schooling—between alienation training, on the one hand, and substantive and skill learning, on the other. For many children, alienation training exists as a block against skill learning. Boys and low-status children seem to suffer more from this contradiction than girls and middle-class children. Chapters 3 and 4 deal with this phenomenon.

Observations on Work, Play, Money, Self-Discipline, Good Citizenship, and Maturity

Practical outcomes of interaction among task, process, and intra-personal concerns are reflected in the postulate that the classroom consists of two distinct cultures: one a work, and one a play, culture.

The work culture represents a congruence with adult expectations for problem-solving behavior, serious consideration of teacher-imposed task demands. Ideally, direction for the operation of a class springs from the problem under investigation. However, society has put into each class an agent, the teacher, who may or may not take responsibility for a task's intrinsic directions; whatever the case, the teacher is a potent force or source of demands in the classroom and structures the work culture to a significant extent.

The play culture is adverse to work and may be characterized by behaviors that impede problem solving, reject imposed leadership, and meet intrapersonal needs. The tasks in a work culture are significantly different from the tasks in the play culture. The two cultures reflect differential goals, thwarting potential, role assignment, and behavioral norms. The means by which conflict may be reduced is also significantly different for the two cultures.

(Robert H. Koff, "Classroom Dynamics and Teacher Training,"
Journal of Teacher Education, Vol. XX, No. 1 [Spring, 1969])

•

The dynamic principle of fantasy is play, which belongs . . . to the child, and as such it appears to be inconsistent with the principle of serious work. But without this playing with fantasy no creative work has ever yet come to birth. The debt we owe to the play of imagination is incalculable.

(Carl Gustav Jung, quoted in *Play: A Natural History Magazine Special Supplement,* December, 1971)

•

The extrovert in the playground, the child who loves fun and is forever in scrapes, may be allergic to school. This is the finding of a survey, to be published soon, which says that the "anti-school" child is more emotional and prefers a social to an academic life.

The National Foundation for Educational Research calls this "school allergy." . . .

The allergy . . . has been defined by comparing groups of "willing workers" in school with "pupils who were failing to participate in the life and work of the school."

"The 'allergic' child emerged as an emotional, socially extroverted, pleasure-seeking, and irresponsible dilettante, unconcerned about long-term aims and emotionally geared toward social intercourse rather than toward solitary academic pursuits." . . .

[The researcher] feels that the only possible approach is to fight the allergy in those "indifferent and culturally meager" homes prone to it by "sheer, hard, out-of-school work on the part of the teacher, fostering the talents or personal interests of the child, and encouraging him in outside activities."

(*Manchester Guardian*, September 15, 1971)

•

10-SPEED BICYCLE FREE!

YOUR CHILD CAN EARN A $90.00 BICYCLE WHILE HE
IMPROVES HIS READING AND MATH SKILLS!

Sullivan materials have earned a reputation nation-wide for motivating children to learn and for developing reading and mathematics skills. . . . But even the most exciting and innovative teaching materials cannot consistently hold a child's interest . . . especially when they are supplemental to a regular study schedule. "Learning for learning's sake" is often not enough.

At Sullivan Educational Centers we are well aware of this problem . . . and we have done something about it!

We have arranged to purchase 10-speed bicycles (which retail at up to $113.50) for our students at $90.00 each. Every student will "earn" one free "BIKE BUCK" for each hour of instruction that he takes between September 20, 1972, and March 1, 1973, at any of our twenty Sullivan Educational Centers. Each "BIKE BUCK" is worth $1.00 toward the purchase of his 10-speed bicycle. If he accumulates 90 "BIKE BUCKS," he will receive his own 10-speed, absolutely free!

Of course, any number of lessons may be taken, and any number of "BIKE BUCKS" redeemed to purchase a bicycle, the difference to be made up in cash.

BICYCLES ARE ON DISPLAY AT ALL CENTERS.

(From a regularly appearing newspaper advertisement)

(From the Discipline Code of the San Francisco Unified School District)

Freedom and Discipline
Freedom is fragile. Its survival depends on the strength and self-discipline of free men.

Our public schools today must intensify their efforts to develop in children and youth the intellectual and moral self-discipline needed for maintaining and extending our democratic way of life. This calls for the pinpointing of emphases from kindergarten through the topmost grades where the student has an ever-increasing share of responsibility for his or her own conduct.

A Message about DISCIPLINE from the P.-T. A.
We believe that the greatness of our way of life depends upon equal opportunity for each citizen, the greatest opportunity being education at public expense. However, while education is a right of American youth, it is not an absolute right, but a privilege carrying with it definite responsibilities on the part of the pupil and his parents.

DISCIPLINE in the schools is best achieved when Pupils, Parents, and Teachers get together
to assist and support one another in the development of an educated, self-disciplined, useful citizenry.
to understand that the right of pupils to public education depends upon pupils and parents meeting their responsibilities.

DISCIPLINE in the schools is best achieved when Pupils perform their legal duties
to be regular and punctual in school attendance, and upon return from absence or tardiness, to bring an excuse signed by their parents.
to accept the authority and instruction of the teacher in the classroom and on or near the school premises. . . .
to come to school clean, neat, and properly dressed, in keeping with school rules and suggestions pertaining to clothing and grooming.
to be good citizens, cooperating with other pupils and respecting their rights and property. . . .

to exercise leadership toward the worthwhile goals of the school.
to conserve and respect school property, including textbooks and
instructional materials.

*DISCIPLINE in the school is best achieved when Parents perform
their legal or parental duties*
to contribute to completion of homework assignments by providing
a quiet, appropriate place for study at regular hours.
to regulate non-school activities to prevent inroads upon study.
to train their children by word and example in the essentials of
good citizenship so they respect the rights and property of others.

●

DEAR ABBY: You once gave a definition for "maturity" before
a high school audience. What was it?—LOREN D.
DEAR LOREN: To be able to stick with a job until it's finished,
to do one's job without being supervised, to be able to carry money
without spending it, and be able to bear an injustice without
wanting to get even.*

(*San Francisco Chronicle*, February 13, 1973)

"Something Happens to You if You Get Too Much Education"†

"Now, why are our people so good at working on the high steel?
They're like mountain goats up there. I'm convinced that it's an
inherited ability of some sort. And this brings me to education. In
order to function as a good steelworker, you have to have very
good reflexes, of course, and you can't really think about what
you're doing. It has to do with getting messages to your muscles

---

* Learning to bear an injustice without wanting to get even helps one to
bear injustices against others without wanting to redress them and also to
commit injustices against others without feeling guilt.—ED.

† The person being interviewed is Kahn-Tineta Horn, identified as a
"young Mohawk Indian woman who once was successful as an actress and
model and now is prominent among . . . America's Indian activists."—ED.

From *The New Yorker*, May 27, 1972. Reprinted by permission; © 1972
The New Yorker Magazine, Inc.

from a certain part of your brain—the lower part, which controls your reflexes. Something happens to you if you get too much education. I guess the electric charges go into the other part of your brain. I don't know. But for some reason your reflexes aren't as good after you start getting more education. That's why my brother had to quit working on high steel. He fell once, and he knew he was going to kill himself—as our father did—so he quit. Virtually all of the Indian steelworkers who have fallen in the past thirty years have been men who were improving their education. This is why I'm opposing the establishment of a high school in Caughnawaga. I think most Indians shouldn't go past about the seventh grade. Right now, we have about 95-per-cent employment on our reserve. The men do a certain kind of work—it suits them, it appeals to them, they make good money, they look after their families. They bring about four hundred thousand dollars a week in wages into the reserve. If they get a better education, they can't work on high steel and there are no other jobs for them, so they end up unemployed. So if we're concerned about Indians' being employed and being self-sufficient, then education is a drawback."

We asked Miss Horn if her theories about education applied to all Indians or just to those in Caughnawaga.

"Well, I'm talking principally about Caughnawaga," Miss Horn replied. "But I think most Indians shouldn't get the same education that white people get. Some of us have to get an education. We need professional people—doctors and lawyers. But not all Indians should have this education. We had fifty Indian students at McGill this year, and it was pretty sad to see what happened to some of them. We need some way to find out which Indians can go to college and not be ruined by it and degenerate the way these kids did. They're ruined for life. They can't even go back up North without infecting the communities they came from."

"Infecting them with what?"

"The diseases they picked up down in white society. The fashionable confusions, the drugs, the venereal diseases, the white values that they're taking back up there and confusing the Indians with."

Alienation and the Crisis of Education

by István Mészáros

No society can persist without its own system of education. To point to the mechanisms of production and exchange alone in order to explain the actual functioning of capitalist society is quite inadequate. Societies exist in and through the actions of particular individuals who seek to realize their own ends. Consequently the crucial issue for any established society is the successful reproduction of such individuals whose "own ends" do not negate the potentialities of the prevailing system of production. This is the real size of the educational problem: "formal education" is but a small segment of it. As Gramsci emphasized:

> There is no human activity from which all intellectual intervention can be excluded—*homo faber* cannot be separated from *homo sapiens*. Also every man, outside his own job, develops some intellectual activity; he is, in other words, a "philosopher," an artist, a man of taste, he shares a conception of the world, he has a conscious line of moral conduct, and so *contributes towards maintaining or changing a conception of the world*, that is, towards encouraging new modes of thought.[1]

Thus in addition to reproducing, on an enlarging scale, the manifold *skills* without which productive activity could not be carried on, the complex educational system of society is also responsible for producing and reproducing the framework of *values* within which the particular individuals define their own specific aims and ends. The capitalistically reified social relations of production do not perpetuate themselves *automatically*. They succeed in this only because the particular individuals *"interiorize"* the outside pressures: they adopt the overall perspectives of commodity-society as

[1] Antonio Gramsci, "The Formation of Intellectuals," in *The Modern Prince and Other Writings*, translated by Louis Marks (London: Lawrence & Wishart, 1957), p. 121.

Excerpted by permission from István Mészáros, *Marx's Theory of Alienation* (London: Merlin Press, 1970). Footnote numbers have been changed in this adaptation.

the unquestionable limits of their own aspirations. It is by doing so that the particular individuals "contribute towards maintaining a conception of the world" and towards maintaining a specific form of social intercourse which corresponds to that conception of the world.

Thus the positive transcendence of alienation is, in the last analysis, an educational task, requiring a radical "cultural revolution" for its realization. The issue at stake is not simply the political modification of the institutions of formal education. As we have seen, Marx strongly stressed the objective ontological continuity of the development of capital, embodied in *all* forms and institutions of social interchange, and not merely in the directly economic second order mediations of capitalism. This is why the task of transcending the capitalistically alienated social relations of production must be conceived in the global framework of a socialist educational strategy. The latter, however, should not be confused with some form of educational utopianism.

1. Educational Utopias

The concept of "aesthetic education" was made famous by Schiller's *Letters upon the Aesthetical Education of Man*,[2] written in 1793–4 and published in 1795. Needless to say, Schiller's idea —formulated as a possible antidote to the harmful "rationality" of capitalistic developments—remained a mere idea: it could not find a significant place in the prevailing system of educational practices. . . .

It would have been nothing short of a miracle if this idea of an "aesthetic education of man" had a different fate, in a world dominated by capitalistic alienation.* For "the sense caught up in crude practical need has only a restricted sense. . . . The care-burdened man in need has no sense for the finest play; the dealer in mineral sees only the mercantile value but not the beauty and the unique nature of the mineral: he has no mineralogical sense."[3] And "crudity" is not a fatality of *nature*; on the contrary, under the

[2] *Über die ästhetische Erziehung des Menschen, in einer Reihe von Briefen*, English edition in *Schiller: Essays, Aesthetical and Philosophical* (G. Bell & Sons, London, 1884).

* The relevance of Mészáros's comments on Schiller's "aesthetic education" to free schools, alternative schools, and so on is clear.—ED.

[3] Karl Marx, *Economic and Philosophic Manuscripts of 1844* (Translated by Martin Milligan, Lawrence & Wishart Ltd., London, 1959), pp. 108–9.

conditions of capitalism this crudity is *artificially* produced by superimposing on all physical and mental senses "the sheer estrangement of all the senses—the sense of having."[4] Consequently the remedies cannot be found in some fictitious "inner world," divorced from, and opposed to, the actual world of men. The traditional philosophical opposites: "subjectivism and objectivism, spiritualism and materialism, activity and suffering, only lose their antithetical character, and thus their existence, as such antitheses *in the social condition*; . . . the resolution of the theoretical antitheses is only possible in a practical way, by virtue of the practical energy of men. Their resolution is therefore by no means merely a problem of knowledge, but a real problem of life, which philosophy could not solve precisely because it conceived this problem as merely a theoretical one."[5] Aesthetic education is therefore only possible in a genuine socialist society which—in the global framework of a socialist educational strategy—transcended the capitalist "alienation of all the senses," and thus produces man in the "entire richness of his being—*produces the rich man profoundly endowed with all the senses—as its enduring reality.*"[6] Thus an adequate aesthetic education of man cannot be confined to an imaginary "inner world" of the isolated individual, nor indeed to some remote utopian haven of alienated society. Its realization necessarily involves the totality of social processes in their complex dialectical reciprocity with each other. This is why the separate program of an "aesthetic education of man," as an antidote to the spread of capitalistic "rationality," is condemned to a hopeless utopianism under conditions when the uncontrollable second order mediations of the reified social relations of production determine—in a narrowly utilitarian framework—the educational processes just as much as all the other aspects of commodity society.

Indeed, considering the problems closely connected with the failure of the efforts which aimed at an "aesthetic education of man," we find that this failure cannot be understood except as an aspect of a more fundamental issue: the inherently problematic character of education under capitalism. The concept of "aesthetic education" is, in fact, a specific attempt at dealing with the dehumanization of the educational processes in capitalist society, and as such it is an aspect of an ever intensifying crisis. It is necessary,

[4] *Ibid.*, p. 106.
[5] *Ibid.*, p. 109.
[6] *Ibid.*

therefore, to inquire, very briefly, into the nature of this crisis which goes back a long way in the past.

At the dawn of the modern age Paracelsus spoke in these terms about education: *"Learning is our very life,* from youth to old age, indeed to the brink of death; no one lives for ten hours without learning."[7] By the middle of the eighteenth century, however, things have significantly changed. Adam Smith, though himself a great champion of the "commercial spirit," strongly emphasizes that the division of labor is doubly damaging for education. On the one hand, it impoverishes man to such an extent that one would need a special educational effort to put things right. But no such effort is forthcoming. On the contrary—and this is the second aspect of the negative impact of the "commercial spirit" on education—since the division of labor simplifies in an extreme form the work processes, it largely diminishes the need for a proper education, instead of intensifying it. Thus in accordance with the needs of the prevailing system of production, the general level of education is not raised but lowered instead: the extremely simplified work processes make possible the spread of child labor, and consequently the children are denied the possibility of a balanced education. The "commercial spirit"—i.e., the victoriously advancing spirit of capitalism—"confines the views of men. Where the division of labor is brought to perfection, every man has only a simple operation to perform; to this his whole attention is confined, and few ideas pass in his mind but what have an *immediate* connection with it. When the mind is employed about a variety of objects, it is somehow expanded and enlarged, and on this account a country artist is generally acknowledged to have a range of thoughts much above a city one. The former is perhaps a joiner, a house carpenter, and a cabinetmaker, all in one, and his attention must of course be employed about a number of objects of very different kinds. The latter is perhaps only a cabinetmaker; that particular kind of work employs all of his thoughts, and as he had not an opportunity of comparing a number of objects, his views of things beyond his own trade are by no means so extensive as those of the former. This must be much more the case when *a person's whole attention is bestowed on the seventeenth part of a pin or the eightieth part of a button,* so far divided are these manufactures. . . . The rule is general; in towns they are not so intelligent as in the country, nor in a rich country as in a poor one. Another inconvenience attending

[7] Paracelsus, *Selected Writings,* p. 181.

commerce is that *education is greatly neglected.*"⁸ And a few pages
later Adam Smith concludes: "These are the disadvantages of a
commercial spirit. The minds of men are *contracted,* and rendered
incapable of elevation. *Education is despised, or at least neglected,*
and heroic spirit is almost utterly extinguished. *To remedy these
defects would be an object worthy of serious attention.*"⁹ . . .

Robert Owen, at a later date, describes with graphic realism the
way in which everything becomes dominated by the power of
money: "Man so circumscribed sees all around him hurrying forward, at a mail-coach speed, to acquire *individual wealth,* regardless of him, his comforts, his wants, or even his sufferings, except
by way of a degrading parish charity, fitted only to steel the heart
of man against his fellows, or to form the tyrant and the slave.
To-day he labors for one master, to-morrow for a second, then for
a third, and a fourth, until all ties between employers and
employed are frittered down to the consideration of what *immediate gain* each can derive from the other. The employer regards
the employed as *mere instruments of gain.*"¹⁰ It would be difficult
to find a more fitting description of how all human relations
become subordinated to the impersonal authority of money and
profit-seeking. . . .

Given this background, it can be no surprise to us that the great
educational utopias of the past—which were originally intended as
a countervailing force to the alienating and dehumanizing power of
the "commercial spirit"—had to remain completely ineffective
against the diffusion of alienation and reification in all spheres of
life. Even in the field of higher education, which for a long time
could shelter behind the glorified façade of its own irrelevance to
the direct needs of a "spontaneously" expanding "laissez faire"
capitalism, the erstwhile ideal of creating a "harmonious" and
"many-sided individual" has been gradually abandoned and the
narrowest of specialization prevailed in its place, feeding with
"advisers," "experts," and "experts in expertise" the cancerously
growing bureaucratic machinery of modern capitalism. "We are
well aware of the disintegration of thought and knowledge into an

⁸ Adam Smith, *Lectures on Justice, Police, Revenue, and Arms* (1763).
In *A. Smith's Moral and Political Philosophy,* edited by Herbert W.
Schneider (Hafner Publishing Co., New York, 1948), pp. 318–19.
⁹ *Ibid.,* p. 321.
¹⁰ Robert Owen, *A New View of Society and Other Writings,* Introduction by G. D. H. Cole, Everyman Edition, p. 124.

increasing number of separate systems, each more or less self-contained, with its own language, and recognizing no responsibility for knowing or caring about what is going on across its frontiers. ... The story of the Tower of Babel might have been a prophetic vision of the modern university; and the fragmentation which is spotlighted there affects the whole of society."[11] "Commercial spirit," for its full realization, required the fragmentation, mechanization and reification of all human relations. This is why the fate of the ideal of "universality" expressed in the great educational utopias of the past had to be settled in the way we are all familiar with. What decided the fate of these utopias at the very moment of their conception was the fact that they aimed at producing the desired effects *in place* of the necessary social changes, and not *through* them.

2. The Crisis of Education

No sane person would deny that education is in crisis today.[12] Nevertheless the nature of this crisis is, quite understandably, far from being generally agreed upon. Professional cold-war ideologists are mystified. As Chomsky observes: "Having settled the issue of the political irrelevance of the protest movement, Kristol turns to the question of what motivates it—more generally, what has made students and junior faculty 'go left,' as he sees it, amid general prosperity and under liberal, Welfare State administrations. This, he notes, 'is *a riddle to which no sociologist has as yet come up with an answer.*' Since these young people are well-off, have good futures, etc., their protest must be *irrational*. It must be the result of boredom, of too much security, or something of this sort.'"[13]

Others, while willing to concede some minor points (related to "research facilities," the "size of the classes," and the like) insist that only "a handful of troublemakers" and "academic thugs" are responsible for the disturbances. The persistence and the growing intensity of the crisis of education in the leading capitalist coun-

---

[11] M. V. C. Jeffreys, *Personal Values in the Modern World* (Penguin), p. 79.

[12] The extent of this crisis is well illustrated by the fact that hundreds of volumes have been published on this subject within the last few years all over the world.

[13] Noam Chomsky, *The Responsibility of Intellectuals.* In *The Dissenting Academy.* Edited by Theodore Roszac (Penguin, 1969. First published in the USA by Random House, 1967), p. 240.

tries, without a single exception, point, however, towards a very different conclusion. To anticipate it in one sentence: today's crisis is not simply that of some educational institution but the structural crisis of the whole system of capitalist "interiorization" mentioned [earlier].

Such an "interiorization," needless to say, cannot take place without the concerted effort of the various forms of "false consciousness" which represent the alienated social relations of commodity-production as the direct, "natural" expression of the individuals' aims and desires. "Normally"—i.e. when commodity-production has its undisturbed run, backed by expanding individual demand—"consumer ideology," reflecting the material framework of society, prevails in the form of generating the necessary "consensus": the easy acceptance of the pseudo-alternatives, as genuine choices, with which the manipulated individual is confronted on both the economic and the political markets. Serious complications arise, however, at the time of economic crises. In the United States, for instance, at the time of the last economic recession a few years ago, newspaper articles and advertising slogans were full of references to one's alleged "patriotic duty" to buy even the most unwanted objects, with the implicit admission —a clear departure from the normal practice of everyday advertising based on the "non-ideological" axiom of the "naturalness" of capitalism—that such goods are indeed *unwanted* and bear no relation to the individuals' "spontaneous" appetites. What the public was asked to buy were unredeemable "patriotic bonds" of the American system of capitalism. The main function of Vietnam-type operations in the American system of incentives is that the direct military involvement provides the framework of "patriotic" advertising and the multimilliard boost to the economy magnifies the appetite of the *system*—in the self-consuming way of war production—without needing to expand the heavily saturated appetite of the stuffed consumer-individual.[14] ...

The need to readjust the mechanisms of "interiorization" is great and growing. There is, however, no acceptable ideology at hand to back it up. The traditional "authorities" of bourgeois democracy are in the middle of a crisis today which dwarfs "the crisis of

[14] There are, of course, various other methods of "absorption of surplus." See Chapters 4–7 of *Monopoly Capital* by Paul A. Baran and Paul M. Sweezy (Monthly Review Press, New York and London, 1966).

democracy" that once brought Fascism to the fore as a "solution" in keeping with the needs of commodity-production. . . . The monstrous *bureaucratization* of society, in accordance with the needs of an increasingly more complex system of commodity-production, succeeded in emptying the "democratic institutions" of all their erstwhile significance, reducing even Parliament—this "pinnacle of democratic institutions"—to the status of a second-rate debating society, thanks to the "consensus" (amounting in fact, if not necessarily in intention, to sheer "collusion") which prevails on all major issues of policy. Also, the various *hierarchical* structures of society which in the past were vitally important in determining the orientation of the younger generation, now, . . . turn out to be not only ineffective in their value-orienting and stabilizing function but also prove to be definite targets for active dissent and radical opposition.

One must consider the crisis of formal education within the framework of this broader picture. For—as a Paracelsus still knew very well—education is "our very life, from youth to old age, indeed up to the brink of death," and therefore its proper assessment cannot be confined to contemplating merely a fraction of the complex phenomena involved. Formal education is closely integrated in the totality of the social processes, and even as regards the particular individual's consciousness, its functions are judged in accordance with its identifiable *raison d'être* in society as a whole. In this sense the present-day crisis of formal education is but the "tip of the iceberg." For the *formal* educational system of the society cannot function undisturbed unless it is *in accord* with the *comprehensive* educational structure—i.e., the specific system of effective *"interiorization"*—of the given society. Thus the crisis of educational institutions is indicative of the totality of processes of which formal education is an *integral* part. The central issue of the current "contestation" of the established educational institutions is not simply the "size of the classes," the "inadequacy of research facilities," etc., but the *raison d'être* of education itself. It goes without saying: such an issue inevitably involves not only the totality of educational processes, "from youth to old age," but also the *raison d'être* of the instruments and institutions of human interchange in general. Are such institutions—including the educational ones—made for men, or should men continue to serve the alienated social relations of production—this is the real subject of the debate. Thus the "contestation" of education, in this wider sense, is the greatest challenge to capitalism in general, for it directly affects the very processes of "interiorization" through which alienation and reification could so far prevail over the consciousness of the individuals.

Education has two main functions in a capitalist society: (1) the production of the skills necessary to running the *economy*, and (2) the formation of the cadres, and the elaboration of the methods, of *political* control. As Gramsci had emphasized: "In the modern world the category of the intellectuals . . . has been inordinately enlarged. They have been produced in imposing numbers by the *democratico-bureaucratic social system,* beyond what is justified by the social needs of *production*, even if justified by the *political needs* of the fundamental ruling class."[15] Accordingly, the crisis of education also manifests itself primarily on the economic and the political plane. . . .

As regards the structural overproduction of intellectuals, the fact of the matter is that an increasing amount of the economic machinery is being tied to the educational field, producing not only a growing number of graduates and postgraduates etc., but also a whole network of companies directly interested in the expansion of "culture." The fact that in the production of intellectuals—unlike that of motor-cars—the upper limit is not the sky but the availability of meaningful employment opportunities (which depends, of course, on the structure of society as a whole), is one that cannot be inserted into the system of calculations of commodity-production. Economic expansion requires an expanding intellectual production (whatever its quality and overall effects), and this is enough to keep the wheels turning. (Of course the Quixotic "Black-paper writers" who want to solve this problem by restrictive political and economic measures have no idea what kind of a capitalist society they live in.)

The problem is rendered increasingly grave by another contradiction of the system: the multiplication of "leisure" as a result of the spectacular technological advances we witness today. It goes without saying, up to a point the system is capable not only of absorbing the newly produced "free time" and the unemployment that potentially goes with it, but also of turning them into instruments of further economic expansion and boom. (The growing "industry of culture," the expansion of parasitic services, etc.) But here, again, the limits should not be overestimated. Not only

[15] Gramsci, *op cit.*, p. 125.

because the pace of technological advance is precipitous, and not only because the capitalist power groups cannot escape in the long run from the consequences of the structural weakening of their competitive position (due to the increasing share of the parasitic factors in the economy as a whole) as regards the emerging post-capitalist systems, but also because a trouble-free expansion of "leisure" is inconceivable without a radical overcoming of its senseless present-day character.

It would be illusory to expect significant changes in this respect. The only form of accountancy known to capitalism is a narrow *monetary* accountancy, while seriously tackling the problems of "free time" (not idle "leisure") requires a radically different approach: the institution of a *social accountancy* in a society which succeeded in emancipating itself from the crippling pressures of the alienated second order mediations of commodity-production. . . . Bourgeois ideology, ever since Adam Smith, could only tackle the problem of education and leisure in a narrowly utilitarian frame-work: as "amusement of the mind," destined partly to restore the worker's energies for the next day's soulless routine, and partly to keep him away from wasteful "debauchery." The conception of "free time" as the vehicle of transcending the opposition between mental labor and physical labor, between theory and practice, between creativity and mechanical routine, and between ends and means, had to remain far beyond the bourgeois horizon. Even Goethe insisted in his *Faust,* with profound ambiguity, that "to accomplish the Great Work, One spirit is enough for a thousand hands":

> *Dass sich das grösste Werk vollende,*
> *Genügt Ein Geist für tausend Hände.*

The Marxian view, in sharp contrast to "leisure" blindly subordi-nated to the needs of commodity-production, implies not only the replacement of "piecemeal" monetary accountancy by a compre-hensive social accountancy, but at the same time also the practical realization of the culture, acquired through "free time," in the form of integrating "execution" with policy- and decision-making which alone can give it a sense of purpose—thanks to the positive transcendence of the existing social hierarchies. . . .

The present-day ideological crisis is only a specific expression of the general structural crisis of capitalistic institutions. There is no space here to enter into a detailed discussion of this complex mat-ter. We have to content ourselves with merely pointing to some of its more important aspects. The main issue is that the institutions of capitalism are inherently violent and aggressive; they are built on the premise of: "war if the 'normal' methods fail." The blind "natural law" of the market mechanism, the realization of the principle of *bellum omnium contra omnes* carries with it that the social problems are never *solved*, only *postponed*, or indeed—since postponement cannot work indefinitely—transferred to the *military* plane. Thus the "sense" of the hierarchically structured institutions of capitalism is given in this ultimate reference to the violent "fighting out" of the issues, in the international arena, for the socioeconomic units—following the inner logic of their development— grow bigger and bigger, and their problems and contradictions increasingly more intense and grave. Growth and expansion are inner necessities of the capitalist system of production and when the local limits are reached there is no way out except by violently readjusting the existing relation of forces. . . .

However "irrational" may seem to be this mechanism of postponement inevitably leading to periodical collisions, it was a model of "rationality" as compared to the present situation. For it was rational in the limited senses of (1) offering to the individuals some specific objectives to achieve, no matter how monstrous they may have been (e.g., Fascist policies); (2) structuring the various institutions of capitalism in a hierarchical functional pattern, assigning to them definite tasks in pursuing the overall objectives of growth and expansion. Today—since the system has been decapitated through the removal of its ultimate sanction—an all-out war on its real or potential adversaries—even the semblance of rationality has disappeared. Exporting internal violence is no longer possible on the required massive scale. (Attempts at doing so on a limited scale—e.g., the Vietnam war—not only are no substitutes for the old mechanism but even accelerate the inevitable internal explosions, by aggravating the inner contradictions of the system.) Nor is it possible to get away indefinitely with the ideological mystifications which represented the *internal* challenge of socialism: the only possible solution to the present crisis, as an *external* confrontation: a "subversion" directed from abroad by a "monolithic" enemy. For the first time in history capitalism is globally confronted with its own problems which cannot be "postponed" much longer, nor can they be indeed transferred to the military plane in order to be "exported" in the form of an all-out war.[16]

---

[16] Of course such a war can *happen*, but its actual planning and active preparation in the open cannot function as a vital internal stabilizer.

But both the institutions and the ideology of monopoly capital are *structurally* incapable of solving such a radically new problem. The intensity and the gravity of the educational-ideological crisis of present-day capitalism is inseparable from this great historical challenge.

Miss White's Second Grade

by Miriam Wasserman

In rereading my own notes on my [school] visits, I am most struck by the way in which the teacher (the classroom situation), in teaching the child how to be a pupil, alienates him from his fellows, from his body, from his feelings and impulses, from his immediate physical surroundings, from his opinions, from his language and thoughts, from his community and daily experiences—in other words, from all that he is as a human organism living and growing in a nourishing, sustaining environment. He is denied access to the very biologic and human wellsprings whose flow is necessary to learning and growing and converted into a little automaton who makes gestures and repeats answers to please an adult to whose signals of pleasure and displeasure he must become almost pathologically sensitized. . . .

The whole school is assembled in the great dreary inside yard. The children in straight lines by size places, the teacher at the head of each line sh-sh-shing, frowning, prodding. One alert young teacher walks up and down her line arranging her children. She pulls a boy's hands out of his pockets, grabs a hand that is scratching a head and sets it down neatly along the side of the body, mutters a scold at a girl whose finger is near a nostril. Another, looking hardly more than a college girl, with twitching mouth and haunted eyes, can't manage her line at all; as fast as she pops two in, squeezing and hissing, three more pop out. What is going to happen among these thirty people when they are alone behind the closed classroom doors? The principal never once looks in her direction. I think she must be among the already condemned. The principal is walking about like Elizabeth reviewing the troops;

From Miriam Wasserman, *The School Fix: NYC, USA* (New York: Outerbridge & Dienstfrey, copyright 1970). Reprinted by permission.

where a line is crooked or whispering, she frowns at the teacher, who jabs a word or a hand at a child. Finally she dismisses the lines to their rooms in the order of the quietest and straightest. On the way up the stairs the teachers recite sharply, "Don't run, you'll fall." "Which way are you walking? Then LOOK that way." "One step at a time, Roger, one step at a time; you'll trip." "Sh-sh-sh. Sh-sh-sh. Sh-sh-sh."

I come to Miss White's room, where the principal has arranged that I am to visit.

Miss White is fortyish, tall, thin, pale, stiff in her movements, very hardworking, very energetic. Indeed, she seems to me to expend at each turn an amount of energy quite out of proportion to the task being performed. At lunch she told me that she uses herself up trying to help those children but that their home backgrounds are so poor she feels she is hardly making a dent. I suspect that if she were able to relax and forget about their unfavorable home backgrounds, both she and the children would accomplish a hundred times more than they do. She seems to be fighting herself and the children every moment.

Her room, like her person, is aseptic. It is a small class, and the children's movable chairs and desks are spread about the room as far from one another as possible, as if some centrifugal force had flung them apart, each child to be suspended alone in his allotted space. On the side bulletin board, arranged with infinite precision under a frill of yellow and green construction paper, are arithmetic and spelling exercises, with the examples and the words identically positioned on each paper. On the back bulletin board, under a frill of red and blue construction paper, are the results of an art lesson, rexographed outlines of an Easter bunny bearing a basket of flowers colored in with crayons. The bunnies are all white and the baskets all blue, but there is some-variation in the colors of the flowers. The children must have spent hours producing these pictures in which the colors remain so obediently within the bounding outlines. Only the irregularly printed names announce them to be products of individual, real-life children.

Miss White introduces me to the children. "This is Mrs. Wasserman, children, a very distinguished writer. Say 'Good morning, Mrs. Wasserman.' " "Good morning, Mrs. Wasserman." "Good morning, children." "This is a very s-l-o-w class, h-o-l-d-o-v-e-r-s," she spells, trying to enlist my gaze in an understanding complicity. I look away, ashamed.

The well-trained children stand neatly behind their chairs. At a

signal, first the girls sit, then the boys. Miss White says, "Feet flat
on the floor, heads up, sit straight, hands clasped on desk." I think
that some kind of posture exercise is about to begin, but it turns
out to be the required position of the morning except when the
class or a child is ordered to stand, go to the board, or the like.
If occasionally a child slumps, scratches, bends down to retrieve
an object he has cleverly managed to drop, or turns his head to
look at another child, the whole lesson comes to a grinding halt
as Miss White announces, "Just one minute, Alette [or whoever
is reciting], Julio isn't listening." Or, really angered, "Franklin,
you look at ME! You listen to ME!" During the hours of tutelage,
the children must give over to her keeping their bodies as well
as their souls. One ingenious boy, held immobile, has learned to
ripple his abdominal muscles behind the desk. He does this on
and off throughout the morning, looking down surreptitiously at
his jiggling belt buckle.

   Only Beryl is excepted. Small, light brown, quiet, almost always
faintly smiling, Beryl comes in late, sits when and as she wishes,
picks up a book from the book table and reads if she wishes,
plays with her fingers if she wishes. She is quiet and alone with
herself. She is never called on in the way the other children are.
When the homework assignment is to be copied, Beryl and Alonzo
turn out to have left their notebooks home. Miss White gives
Alonzo a sheet of paper, but ignores Beryl. She later explained to
me that it would have been pointless to have had Beryl copy the
assignment; as she wouldn't have done the homework anyway,
why waste a sheet of paper—one example of a teacher's expectations reinforcing a child's deviant ways. While the children are
writing, Beryl helps herself to a book and reads. I invite her to
my back corner to read to me, which she does willingly and well.
Although the other children ignore her, and she them, every
twenty minutes or so, with no external stimulus that I can see,
Miss White turns on Beryl her own and the entire class's disapproving attention. "Beryl, don't you *want* to learn? Do you want
to be left back? If you don't pay attention, you won't go on to
the third grade. Don't you *want* to go on to third grade with
the other children?" Beryl only sustains her thin smile. But Jewell
manages to catch my eye in a gaze of disapproving complicity that
is a replica of Miss White's.

   To the extent that they respond overtly to one another at all,
the children do so entirely in accordance with the teacher's needs.
So, when Miss White has three or four times downgraded one
boy for giving a series of wrong answers, the children finally all

laugh aloud at him. Then she transmits a signal quite opposite to the one she had been transmitting, saying, "You mustn't make fun of Collins. That's unkind."

The opening lesson is to read from the blackboard a list of twenty words. It seems to me that the children already know these words (i.e., can read them), but with scoldings about hands beneath the desk and Beryl's diversions, frequent reminders that these words "might, ju-u-ust might" turn up on next week's Metropolitan Reading Tests, and somewhat meandering discussions after each word, the lesson takes thirty-five minutes. The discussions, which Miss White later explained to me are a way of lightening the lesson by letting the children tell about "their own little experiences," are actually explicit reminders of the rules of middle-class morality and the irrelevance and unworthiness of their own impulses, opinions, and experiences, for which reminders the bodily regimentation serves as unremitting practice.

A child is called on, and reads, "Sling shot." Miss White, "That's right, 'sling shot.' Does anyone know what a sling shot is?" A chorus of responses, "When you take a rubber band . . ." "You go like this with a paperclip." Etc. "Hand, hands." Silence. Hands are raised. A child is called on and explains. Miss White, "Do you think it's a good idea to use a sling shot" Chorus of disapproving "No-o-o's," and one unwary "Yes." Miss White is very angry. "Who said, 'yes'?" "Not me." "It was Josie." "Josie did." "Josie, you ought to know better than that. Don't you know somebody can get hurt? You could hit a person's eye and blind him." She enlists the whole class's dismay and disapproval of naughty (too honest) Josie.

A hand is raised, "My uncle he blind, and . . ."

"My uncle *is* blind."

"My uncle he *is* blind, and one day when I be walking with him . . ."

"One day when I *was* walking with him."

A few tales of the blind and the halt are told. Miss White sometimes but not always interrupts to correct the storyteller's speech. The child dutifully parrots the revised sentence, and then like a rubber band, his tongue snaps back into the speech he first heard from his mother's lips and hears (and uses) all his waking hours except from his alien teachers or TV. He will be corrected five or ten times a day every day he is in school, for ten or twelve years, but will remain loyal all that time to his mother tongue.

Miss White points to the next word and calls on a child. It is "plow," which the child pronounces to rhyme with "snow." A chorus of spontaneous corrections. Miss White draws herself up menacingly, scolding, *"Excuse me!"* Silence. *She* corrects the mispronunciation. As in every instance when the children move or call out, they are required to suppress their natural impulse to set aright what is wrong, to respond verbally to the written symbol, to essay an answer and see if it goes ("If you don't know, don't guess.")—in other words to learn.

If the children cannot (or do not) adopt the teacher's speech as their own, she sometimes does not even understand theirs, or the ideas they seek to convey by means of it.

"What is a plow?" she asks.

"Like a trapter," Alonzo responds confidently.

"Like a *what*?" less confused than angry.

"Like a trapter," somewhat less confidently.

"Speak up, Alonzo. What are you trying to say? Talk more carefully. Now once more. What is a plow?"

"Trapter?"

Miss White is by now very annoyed and disapproving. "Trapter? Trapter? I don't know what you're saying." She makes a kind of shrug of hopelessness. Alonzo is expressionless.

"Now, somebody else. What is a plow?"

"A snowplow?" Jewell asks hopefully.

"Well. Not exactly. Look." Miss White gets out a book, and shows a picture of a farmer in overalls and straw hat walking behind a plow being pulled by a drayhorse. "That's a plow. Now I want you to remember what a plow is. You might, you just might, meet it on the reading test." She sighs.

Now Miss White points to "flower." A child reads it. Then, "Who sees a flower in the room?" Josie, straining out of his seat and grunting as if he were on the toilet, is called on and rushes toward the Easter baskets. "JOSIE! Did I tell you to get up? Go Back To Your Seat. . . . Now, can someone tell me where there is a flower, without getting out of your seat." (Ah, Josie, Josie, you have a lot to learn.)

"Flower" is followed by a long hassle in which the children describe a "trunk" (also from the Metropolitan Reading Tests, where it is illustrated by a picture of a footlocker) as "where you put the suitcases."

"Why in the world"—trying to imagine perhaps the homes they come from—"would you want to put a suitcase in a trunk? Unless," speculating, "there isn't room in the closet."

"You know, like to go on a picnic."

Outraged, "Who would take a *trunk* on a picnic?"

All of them, teacher and children, are now utterly bewildered, caught in a kind of entanglement of confusion, and helpless to extricate themselves. I think if a visitor were not present someone would have some kind of a temper tantrum, out of the fury of impotence. I violate a cardinal rule for observers and break in to say that maybe the children are referring to the trunk of a car. I shouldn't have done it; of course Miss White is embarrassed. "Oh," explaining, "it is some years since I've had a car." Then disapprovingly, "You know *they* all have cars"—one-upping after having been one-upped.

Alonzo meanwhile has fallen out of position and is languishing. "Alonzo, sit up. What did you have for breakfast, Alonzo?"

"Crackles and peanut-butter-and-jelly sandwich."

"Who gave you your breakfast, Alonzo?"

"Me myself."

"Tell your grandmother *she* should give you breakfast." To me, "He's terribly n-e-g-l-e-c-t-e-d." To Alonzo, "You make sure your grandmother gives you supper tonight, Alonzo."

"She always do."

To me, "You can see what the trouble is." Then, "Alonzo draws very well. Show Mrs. Wasserman your picture, Alonzo." I tell Alonzo it is a beautiful picture. (It is not a coloring in, but a genuine creation.) "But that's all he wants to do," she says, negating the effects of her and my praise.

Now a relief teacher comes in and Miss White sits down with me at the back of the room to perform some clerical chores and brief me on what I have observed. "This one hasn't even seen *Mary Poppins* because his mother won't take him to the movies, and that one has had three 'fathers' already. What can you expect when they come from homes like that? They don't even know how to talk in sentences. They have to be stimulated to think; they don't have an idea in their heads. They look around them and they don't know what they see." But they know that a snow-plow is a kind of plow, that a plow is related to a tractor, and that you put the picnic things in the trunk. And one too brave soul knows that he likes to use a sling shot. But what they see is declared to be not there and what they think to be wicked. "Beryl just came to us from Ocean Hill–Brownsville. It's no wonder she's so bad and doesn't know anything." I said I thought she read very well. "Yes," sighing, "but that's all she wants to do."

The relief teacher is distributing some construction-paper buckets that the children had made on a previous day. They are different colors, and on each is written the name of the child who made it. But they are passed out at random, and the children begin to demand to receive their own with their own names. The teacher says it doesn't matter who gets which one. (That is, it doesn't matter to her.) The children have had empty hands and empty desks since the morning began, and many grasp at the little pieces of colored paper like a hungry infant at the breast. The teacher says they mustn't touch them until she tells them what to do with them; they are only paper and they can tear; if they tear, then they won't have them for what they need them for; and on and on. Miss White several times nervously interrupts her conversation with me to jump up and remove one child's hands from the paper or rearrange another's limbs. Most of the children refrain from touching and content themselves with looking. It is said that slum children are not good learners because they are incapable of delayed gratification. I find my stomach in knots until finally the signal is given that the pathetic little papers may be touched. I suspect that slum children are bad learners because they are denied the gratification of being allowed to learn.

The buckets are finally employed in a mass enactment of "Jack and Jill." Miss White explains that this way the children have an opportunity to "experience some freedom and new experiences" and the teacher can "get into the children's world." Next comes "Humpty Dumpty," which is an occasion for some cultural background. It is elicited that Humpty Dumpty is an egg. "What happens when you drop an egg?" "It breaks." "What comes out when an egg breaks?" There is some hesitation. Finally a girl who has learned to read the teacher's mind faster than I says, "The yolk." No one asks what happens to the white, but "yolk" is written on the board. Then they go on to "Little Miss Muffet." One boy, enacting the spider, so far departs from the script as to snarl at Miss Muffet with clawed hands and bared teeth. The class cracks up, in the first spontaneous interaction among themselves I have seen. Miss White drops her pen and hurries to the front of the room, saying, "No, no, you must do it on the word 'frighten,' not before. Like this. Now class, recite it again and watch how I do it."

Dutifully, they recite it again, and Miss White acts the spider, while the boy spider returns quietly to his seat.

Now they copy their homework assignment and finish just in time before the bell rings for lunch.

3 Education's Role in the Distribution of the Social Product

In almost all contemporary societies the social product is distributed unequally, in accordance with quite elaborate and often deeply hidden rules governing who gets how much. (By "social product" is meant all the goods and services produced by a given society for the use of its own members or for exchange for the goods and services of another society.)

In the United States and many other countries, in addition to preparing *all* children for the "outside world," schools also play a major role in determining *which* children will play which roles in that world and will therefore receive proportionately smaller or larger shares of the social product.

Schools do this by a process sometimes called tracking. Tracking simply means directing students to educational careers that will certify them as members of approximately the same socio-economic class that their parents occupy. By means of tracking, schools help society to reproduce in each generation the class structure of the previous generation.

While in some countries this process is clear and open, in the United States the reality is clouded by an apparent equality of educational opportunity, and also by the popular myths *about* school that are taught *in* school.

The reality is exposed in Richard Rothstein's fine study "How Tracking Works." The selection from Ivar Berg's *Education and Jobs*, from which the title of this chapter is taken, helps to explode some of the myths, especially the myth that the years spent in school help people to perform better on the job. On the contrary, the book firmly documents Edgar Friedenberg's belief in the existence of a conspiracy. The conspiracy is to use selective school credentialing as a way of perpetuating all the gross, but no longer legal, discriminatory practices against the poor and the dark that have characterized our history as a nation.

In many cases, tracking involves open, vulgar racism and discrimination, as the selections from Hollingshead, Malcolm X, and others testify. In many other cases, however, there is no apparent racism or discrimination by school personnel. Quite the contrary, school personnel often seem to be making special efforts on behalf of the low-status children, but tracking continues to function smoothly nevertheless.

What is perhaps going on here is that alienation training— the very subtle process of interiorizing certain values, certain character traits, certain styles of being and behaving—does not operate similarly among the children of the middle and upper classes and the children of the working classes and the poor. The results of the "clear thinking" test used by Alameda County to qualify citizens for grand-jury duty suggest that many people in these groups have different ways of coping with life's problems than people of the middle class (and no wonder!), or else that they are less willing to play the game of "giving the tester the answer you know he wants."

"Giving the tester what he wants" lies in the same characterological syndrome as giving the teacher, the principal, the boss, what he wants. We might call it deference. What the fire chief of San Francisco describes as an "ability to get along with other men on the job" probably means not exactly that but giving proper deference to the boss. Boney of Elmtown and Mario Martinez of Los Siete were, indeed, not fit to be credentialed as suitable for the labor market, as they demonstrated by choosing to leave school rather than tolerate certain routine humiliations appropriate to their class and status.

Lower-class students, especially males, are judged more by their behavior in respect to authority than by their academic skills. Teacher-assigned grades reflect promptness, good attendance, "effort," "citizenship." By contrast, middle- and upper-class students can be far more feisty and independent and still survive: They are thought to be showing, not inappropriate impudence, but youthful and useful "spirit."

The fact that we reward low-status people for appropriate behavior and "good character" rather than for job-related skills is not, of course, an argument against the benefits of literacy and intelligence. It is only to say that wielders of power don't really care much for excessive literacy and high intelligence among the poor.

Indeed, we can observe in *Letter to a Teacher* how literacy and intelligence might flourish if they were set to overcome humility, rather than to reinforce it. The excerpts from that brilliant and deeply moving document are included here as an evidence that the school problem, which some may regard as peculiar to the United States, is worldwide. The book is also an example of a combining of careful scholarship, deep humanity, and skillful writing by some poor Italian schoolboys from which scholars everywhere might take a good lesson. A work of ordinary school-boys who, though humble, struggled against societal humiliations, it looks forward to Chapter 11, which reports the deeds of other humble people.

•

How Tracking Works

by Richard Rothstein

From the Post Office rack, you can get this glossy pamphlet,[1] prepared and distributed in the public interest by the U.S. Army:

> WOULDN'T IT BE THE SMART THING FOR *YOU* TO STAY IN SCHOOL?
> It's a great, big world out there.
> And there's a place in it for you.
> Trouble is, a lot of other guys will be out scratching for the same spot.
> It's sort of like a basketball, football or baseball game.

[1] This pamphlet was available in Post Offices in the winter of 1971.

From *Down the Up Staircase: Tracking in Schools* by Richard Rothstein for the Teacher Organizing Project of the New University Conference. Copyright, 1971, by the New University Conference. Reprinted by permission. Table and note numbers have been changed in this adaptation.

You've got to have the moves to beat out those other guys.
To get out into the open and score. Or make the double-play
or hit it up the alley.
And you know what that takes.
Training. A stick-to-it attitude. An education. The kind
you're getting right now by staying in school.

SAY YOU DROPPED OUT OF SCHOOL TO LOOK FOR A JOB?

You ought to be able to get a job of some kind. Whether
it's what you want, or would like to keep, is another question.
As a high school drop-out, you'll have three general types of
jobs open to you.
Farm jobs. Unskilled labor. Service jobs.
Openings in these jobs seem to increase slightly year after
year. But then, so do the number of people looking for them.
So even here, you'll have to beat out the next guy.

Most Americans accept the assumption of the Army pamphlet:
that people can rise in life by getting an education; that to get a
better job, stay in school. This belief in upward mobility through
education is widely accepted not just for individuals but for groups
as well. In the late 1960s liberal Americans held that black ghetto
poverty resulted from the failure of blacks to obtain a good education which would prepare them for good paying jobs. As the
Kerner Commission said, "the schools have failed to provide the
educational experience which could overcome the effects of discrimination and deprivation."[2]

Upward Mobility Is Limited—Everyone
Can't Get Ahead of Everyone Else

However, widespread mobility through education is mythical.
And like many social myths, this myth retains its strength not by
its sophistication but by our failure to question an obvious contradiction. The emperor has no clothes. In any "basketball, football or baseball game" there are as many losers as winners. When
you make the double play, two other guys are out. And while a pep
talk can sometimes determine which side wins and which side
loses, it can never make a winner out of everyone. If the same

[2] *Report of the National Advisory Commission on Civil Disorders* (Bantam edition, 1968), pp. 25, 425.

pep talk is given to everyone, it probably won't even affect who wins.

Think about the Army pamphlet for a minute. What if every kid followed its advice and stayed in school? Would the number of farm jobs, unskilled jobs and service jobs decrease? Ultimately, the pamphlet's myth of upward mobility implies that these jobs will disappear if everyone graduated from high school. If they all went on to college, we would have a society where everyone was a doctor, lawyer, teacher or business executive. Nobody would have to car-hop, run a punch press, or harvest lettuce. Absurd.

If everyone stayed in school, what mechanism would neatly choose those most qualified for the better jobs?* Everyone can't stay in school if the system is to function. The effect of the Army pamphlet depends on the refusal of large numbers of young men and women to heed its advice; moreover, they must know that they refused to heed it. For an essential ingredient of this nation's man- and womanpower channeling system is the belief by those stuck with lousy jobs that it's their own fault—I can't do better than a farm, unskilled or service job because I was too dumb to stay in school. If only I'd listened to that pamphlet . . .

If the poor believe that their poverty and alienation are the result of their own stupidity, their own failure to achieve, and their own unwillingness to stick it out in school, they will be less likely to squawk about their condition and less likely to question the occupational structure which assigns poverty and alienation to those who do the majority of the country's necessary work.† And if those who are secure financially believe their success is the result of hard work rather than a favorably stacked deck, they are likely to be more self-righteous and rigid in defending the status quo.

The economic structure of our society requires a system of vastly differentiated educational opportunities for those destined for different jobs; combined with the myth that the top educational opportunities are open to all who try to make it.

---

* This question was once asked in an education class at the University of California, Berkeley, as: "Imagine that it would be possible to bring everybody 'up to grade level' in reading and at the same time to prevent anybody from being well over grade level, how would you decide who got into the rare top jobs and professions?" A woman student quickly answered, "The ones who are the best singers," by an absurd response demonstrating the absurdity of the question.—ED.

† Rothstein's use of "alienation" is equivalent to what was defined in Chapter 2 as alienation from alienation.—ED.

In the elementary and high schools of the nation, *tracking* is the mechanism which fills this function. Students are assigned to tracks; the track sizes are proportional to the job openings in the occupations to which those tracks lead. We will show in this pamphlet that students are effectively assigned to reading groups, special classes, and special schools on the basis of income, race and sex. Yet there is a complex mechanism which persuades those involved (teachers as well as students and parents) that the assignments are made on the basis of "ability."

Tracking is not unique. It is similar to other systems whose purpose is to manipulate people to adjust to national economic policies. In 1965, the Selective Service System issued a memorandum to local draft boards justifying the use of draft deferments to pressure men into civilian occupations which were short of voluntary manpower:

> From the individual's viewpoint, he is standing in a room which has been made uncomfortably warm. Several doors are open, but they all lead to various forms of recognized, patriotic service to the nation. Some accept the alternatives gladly —some with reluctance. The consequence is approximately the same. . . .
>
> The psychology of granting wide choice under pressure to take action is the American or indirect way of achieving what is done by direction in foreign countries where choice is not permitted. Here, choice is limited but not denied, and it is fundamental that an individual generally applies himself better to something he has decided to do rather than something he has been told to do.[3]

Tracking is the "American or indirect" way of assigning occupational roles through manipulation of the school systems of the country. This pamphlet is about how tracking works.

We Teachers Were Tracked into Teaching

The fundamental principle of the tracking system is that *educational opportunities adjust to the needs of the occupational struc-*

---

[3] Called "Channeling," this document was issued by Selective Service in 1965. Its argument to draft boards was that pressuring young men into deferred occupations is a more important function of the draft than developing military manpower. *Ramparts* magazine excerpted 2 pages from the Channeling Memo in its December 1967 issue.

ture, and not vice versa. A helpful way to understand this principle is to look at our own experience as teachers and students in the last 15 years. The number of teachers in this society is not determined by the number of students who choose teacher training in college; rather, the number of students to whom teacher training is offered is determined by the number of teacher job openings.

Three years ago, nearly every school district in the country was begging for teachers. There were radio advertisements trying to induce housewives to teach, and men could get high school jobs even if they couldn't coach basketball. But in 1970 there were 38,000 teachers who couldn't find jobs, and it will get worse: the U.S. Office of Education predicts a surplus of 55,000 teachers a year by 1975.[4]

School administrators like this situation. They can afford to be fussy, get rid of teachers who exhibit the slightest independence, and cut back on improvements in teacher working conditions that teacher unions won in the 1960s.

The present teacher glut was created by a tracking plan that was stimulated by the Ford Foundation and federal government and extended down to every high school counseling office in the country. Not every administrator and official fully understood the role he was performing; many in the lower levels of bureaucracy undoubtedly believed the myth of unlimited mobility which we described earlier. But for students in the 1960s, the tracks to the teaching profession were opened wide.

In the late 1950s, high level national decisions were made to increase the supply of teachers. This was largely due to the Pentagon needs for teachers of educated workers in industries which could feed the post-Sputnik space program; the increasing automation of American industry which reduced job growth and made it necessary to have more teachers to keep children in high school and off the job market longer; and the expansion of schools in the wake of the post-war "baby boom." New colleges to train teachers were built at a breakneck pace. College enrollments jumped from 3.2 million in 1958 to almost 7 million in 1967–68.[5] In 1957, about 9,000 Ph.D.s in all fields were granted; in 1971, more than 30,000.[6]

---

[4] *New York Times,* July 19, 1970, p. 49, "Many New Schoolteachers Unable to Find Jobs as Nationwide Demand Shrinks."

[5] Lewis B. Mayhew, *Colleges Today and Tomorrow* (San Francisco, 1969), p. 230.

[6] *Time,* May 24, 1971, p. 51, "Graduates and Jobs."

In the early 1960s Admiral Hyman Rickover, developer of the nuclear submarine, became one of the leading educational theorists of the country. He warned that the U.S. would lose the Cold War if more effort were not devoted to expanding education for the "gifted" who might become scientists and engineers.

Advanced placement and honors tracks were set up and expanded in high schools to encourage college application and rapid matriculation. Corporations made vast sums available to the kids in these tracks for college scholarships (for example, the Merit Scholarship Program). The federal government established a student loan program (N.D.E.A.) which could be paid off by teaching instead of money. The Ford Foundation (through its Woodrow Wilson Program) undertook to finance the cost of graduate school for bright students who would promise to enter the teaching profession. And the Selective Service System established a draft deferment for young men who went into teaching.

All these mechanisms created a teacher glut, so today opposite mechanisms are being set in gear. The teacher supply is now being constricted to adjust to the glut—but not constricted so fast as to eliminate administrators' freedom to choose. Public college tuition is being increased by state legislatures all over the country, discouraging and prohibiting working class kids from trying to become teachers. College expansion and construction have slowed. Counselors are now directing high school students into vocational programs at two year colleges rather than to four year teacher training institutions.

Normally, schoolteachers administer the tracking system, unwittingly channeling their students into fields which the military and corporate employers wish to fill. But today's job glut is making many teachers realize that, as students, they were at the receiving end of the tracking system; tracked while being trained to track.

The American Occupational Structure Makes Rigid School Tracking Necessary

Table 1, prepared by the U.S. Department of Labor, shows how the various occupational groups will grow between 1968 and 1980.

As the economy continues to automate, and as more and more resources are directed to sales and service from production, the relative number of blue collar workers (operatives) and craftsmen will decrease. To take their places in the occupational structure,

TABLE 1. GROWTH OF OCCUPATIONAL CATEGORIES

Jobs (millions)		Occupational Group	Percent Change
1968	1980		−30 −20 −10 0 10 20 30 40 50
75.9	95.1	All workers	25
10.3	15.5	Professional	50
7.7	11.1	Service	45
12.8	17.3	Clerical	35
4.6	6.0	Sales	30
7.8	9.5	Managers	22
10.0	12.2	Craftsmen & foremen	22
1.7	2.0	Private household	15
14.0	15.4	Operatives	10
3.6	3.5	Non-farm laborers	−2
3.5	2.6	Farm workers	−33

SOURCE: *U.S. Manpower in the 1970s: Opportunity and Challenge* (U.S. Department of Labor, 1970).

there will be vastly increased numbers of service workers, clerical workers, sales workers and professional-technical workers. When we consider that approximately 20% of the professional-technical category will be specialized workers (engineering technicians, laboratory workers, etc.) with a minimum of training—often only a few months in a "vo-tech" program of a junior college—we see that the growth in the labor force in the next decade will be overwhelmingly in boring, alienating, low skill jobs which involve no more decision making or earning power than the assembly line jobs they replace (though workers who wear white collars rather than blue may be temporarily lulled into feelings of upward mobility).

In order to service this changing economy, what can we expect school systems to do in the next few years?

First, we can expect that there will be some increased pressure to get potential school drop-outs to stay and get a high school diploma, since employers in the clerical, sales and service fields will require diplomas to a somewhat greater extent than the factory blue collar employers they are replacing. . . .

Second, we can expect increased efforts to track women high school students into bookkeeping, shorthand and typing courses. In 1969 . . . although 34.5% of employed high school graduates

were in clerical occupations, 57.1% of employed women high
school graduates were in those jobs (with another 9% in sales,
and another 14% in service).

Third, we can expect college placement tracks in many high
schools to narrow, or at least to cease growing in the way they did
in the 1960s. This will be particularly true in those working class
high schools whose college placement tracks fed mainly into local
public teacher training colleges. Instead, we can expect high
schools increasingly to prepare graduates for entrance into technical schools and technical programs in junior colleges. For example, in Chicago, 17.5% of the full time students in the seven
junior colleges are now vocational-technical. The rest of the students are prepared for transfer to four year teacher training or
engineering institutions. But the City College Master Plan proposes
to increase the vo-tech program to include 60% of the full time
students in the next few years.[7]

Fourth, we can expect corporations to take a more direct hand
in the education of students, since the technical skills of production
are more specialized than the assembly line blue collar work they
replace. . . .

Within the lower (black and white working class) tracks,
increasing numbers of students must be directed to highly specialized but routine technical fields (computer programmer aide, x-ray
technician, etc.). As a fifth adjustment, elementary schools in poor
communities can be expected to place increasing reliance on teaching machines and programmed learning systems which can communicate bare technical skills without creativity or reflective
ability. . . .

Sixth, we can expect a continued unwillingness on the part of
school principals and administrators to tolerate experiments with
non-authoritarian teaching methods, particularly in inner city and
working class schools. Schools which are training the future file
clerks, typists, supermarket checkers and waitresses must, like the
blue collar training schools before them, produce workers who
submit to authority, who don't question standards of discipline,
who don't identify with the problems of fellow workers, who take
orders rather than use their own initiative, who are competitive
and who don't expect to do creative work. On the other hand,

---

[7] Chicago City College, *Food for Thought: Discussion Draft for a Master
Plan* (1970), pp. 63, 81. For a thorough discussion of the shift from general
to vocational programs in junior colleges, see Rue Wallace and Warren
Friedman, *Welcome to the Factory,* published by the New University
Conference.

suburban high schools will continue to develop a relatively per-
missive and relaxed atmosphere which is suited to the autonomy
and self-motivation which future professionals must learn. Within
some border schools, much more autonomy and teacher experimentation will be tolerated in the upper tracks and much less
permissiveness tolerated in the middle and lower tracks.

If the Occupational Structure Is Not Challenged, A Meritocratic (Equal Opportunity) Tracking System Would Be the Best We Could Hope For

Many teachers and students are critical of tracking without understanding its broader social function. They tend to see tracks,
between schools and within schools, as a violation of egalitarian
principles by offering different levels of educational programs to
different groups of students. But the tracking system cannot be
effectively challenged on these egalitarian grounds alone. For a
tracked educational system is entirely rational if we accept three
widely shared assumptions: First, that the ability or motivation
required to attain high levels of educational achievement differs
from one individual to the next in measurable ways. Second, that
different occupational categories require different levels of educational attainment. And third, that an occupational structure like
that projected for the American economy in Table 1 is necessary
and inevitable.

Later in this pamphlet we will offer grounds for challenging
each of those assumptions.* But in the absence of such challenges,
a *meritocratic* tracking system may seem to be a rational solution to the labor channeling problems of a complex industrial
society.

With Only Limited Occupational Privileges Available, Tracking Preserves Those Privileges for the Rich, for Men, for Whites

The tracking system in American elementary and secondary education is not, however, meritocratic. In addition to the rational
occupational channeling functions of a meritocratic system, American educational tracking also serves a second function; the maintenance of rigidities in the social class, race and sex role divisions
of American society. It is an essential purpose of the tracking

* For this discussion, readers are referred to the full text of *Down the Up
Staircase.*—ED.

system to prevent significant mobility between rich and poor, white and black, male and female. Tracks do insure that schools certify students for occupational openings in the required proportions, but they do this by insuring that the "upper" tracks leading to more prestigious occupations have proportionally more whites, men, and rich students; and that the "lower" tracks leading to blue collar (and now to technical, service, sales and clerical) jobs include proportionally more blacks, women and poor or working class students. . . .

TABLE 2. PER CENT OF HIGH SCHOOL GRADUATES GOING TO COLLEGE THE FOLLOWING YEAR, BY ACADEMIC APTITUDE, SOCIO-ECONOMIC BACKGROUND AND SEX, 1960

Academic Aptitude	Low	Low-Mid	Mid	Up-Mid	High	All
Male:						
Low	10	13	15	25	40	14
L-Mid	14	23	30	35	57	27
Mid	30	35	46	54	67	46
U-Mid	44	51	59	69	83	63
Upper	69	73	81	86	91	85
All	24	40	53	65	81	49
Female:						
Low	9	9	10	16	41	11
L-Mid	9	10	16	24	54	18
Mid	12	18	25	40	63	30
U-Mid	24	35	41	58	78	49
Upper	52	61	66	80	90	76
All	15	24	32	51	75	35

SOURCE: Christopher Jencks and David Riesman, *The Academic Revolution* (New York, 1968), p. 103.

Rich men have more than three times the chance of going to college than poor men (81:24). Rich women's chances are five times greater than poor women's (75:15). Men's chances are 40% better than women's (49:35); a rich man's chances are 540% greater than a poor woman's (81:15).

White children have a 30% greater chance of getting to the last year of high school than non-white children (and within the non-white group, the figure for blacks—as opposed to Orientals—is much lower); and once seniors in high school, whites have a greater chance of graduating and of entering college. If we had statistics by which college entrance could be weighted by quality

TABLE 3.   SELECTED MEASURES OF SCHOOL RETENTION, BY COLOR AND SEX, 1959

Color and Sex	Ratio of H.S. Seniors to 100 Persons 17 Years Old	% of H.S. Seniors Who Graduated	% of H.S. Grads Who Enrolled in College
Male:			
White	82.9	84.9	46.4
Nonwhite	62.3	76.0	40.5
Female:			
White	81.0	91.9	37.4
Nonwhite	60.8	84.4	38.2

SOURCE: James S. Coleman (H.E.W.), *Equality of Educational Opportunity,* p. 451.

of institution, the advantages of white students would be even more marked.

The Differences Between Suburban and Inner City Schools Are the Most Important Aspect of Tracking

From elementary school to university, tracking is mainly a question of differences in quality between entire schools. Suburban schools are newer, better equipped, with better "reputations" and prestige among admissions and employment officers than are urban, particularly black, schools. . . .

The importance of inter-school tracking is illustrated by Table 4, which shows how, shortly after Sputnik, students were chosen for a city-wide "gifted children program" in a major Northern city. Not a single student from a school which served a neighborhood

TABLE 4.   PROGRAM FOR GIFTED CHILDREN

Income Group	Number of Gifted Children Chosen	Rate per 10,000 Students
I (below $5,000)	0	0
II ($5,000-)	4	1.1
III ($6,000-)	41	6.1
IV ($7,000-)	120	20.1
V ($8,000-)	123	36.0
VI (over $9,000)	148	78.8

By income halves, the rate per 10,000 students was:
A (under $7,000) 3.7
B (over $7,000) 34.4

SOURCE: Patricia Sexton, *Income and Education* (1961), p. 60.

where families made less than $5,000 was chosen, whereas nearly 1% of the students from schools in the richest communities were chosen.

The pressures for internal school tracks *decrease* as the rigidity of the interschool tracking system increases. Both a suburban white middle class school and an urban ghetto school can eliminate extensive I.Q. testing and ability grouping within the school and within classes, without affecting tracking. In recent years, some such schools have begun to eliminate testing and ranking, in the guise of anti-tracking reform. However, the elimination of tracking within a school which is racially and socially homogeneous can have the opposite effect—to further rigidify the class and race bias of the tracking system by certifying students solely by the community in which they were schooled. Many liberal teachers cannot understand why black ghetto parents fight hard *for* increased testing, establishment of special classes, and other programs which entrench internal tracking. But the parents can see what the liberal teachers cannot: to eliminate tracking within a ghetto school will more likely mean that *no* student will have a chance at college rather than that all will. In the absence of certified tracks, all students are likely to be considered "average." Special scholarship programs were established in the late 1960s for "bright" ghetto youth. But college admissions officers are still not interested in an "average" black kid.

Similarly, many liberal teachers in privileged suburban school systems have been pleased by the willingness of a few of those school systems to experiment with less tracked forms of learning and with less competitive atmospheres. But again, while these reforms may be important for other reasons, they are not really the anti-tracking reforms they seem to be. *Any* graduate of an "untracked" school in a wealthy suburb will have an assured place in college.

Internal school tracking (or "ability grouping") becomes more essential to the maintenance of class and race stratification in schools which are not socially and racially homogeneous. Ghetto border schools, mixed middle and working class schools, changing neighborhood schools—these are places where internal tracking is most rigid. . . .

The tracking system is today a response to the problem of scarce opportunity for economic security in this country; and in the context of scarce opportunity, everyone wants to corner the market on limited privilege. Black parents want discipline and rigid tracks in their schools so that ghetto kids will at least be qualified for middle level jobs they'll have a hard time getting anyhow. White working class parents are enraged at compensatory education for blacks, for they understand too well that it is their own children who will pay for it. White middle class parents want to make sure that their children don't get caught in the scramble for the lower-middle tracks, and move to "good" neighborhoods in the suburbs with "better" schools which can guarantee admission to an elite college. . . .

There is no short run reform program which can eliminate the tracking system with its breeding of competitiveness, false hopes for upward mobility, anti-social feelings of superiority and inferiority. So long as schooling is a scarce material reward which serves as a ticket to other, more important scarce material rewards, the tracking system in some form or other will separate those rewarded in school from those not. The frustrations of tracked schools are a reflection of the class structure of a capitalist society. So long as we have doctors earning $30,000 a year alongside dishwashers earning $3,000, we will have a school system which separates the dishwasher from the doctor at an early age. And so long as we have a political system which is dominated by corporate interests, the schools will also serve to insure that the sons of doctors have a better crack at privileges than the sons of dishwashers.

Teachers upset about the tracking system and their role in it ultimately must look to the broader structure of society for the cause of their frustrations. A school reform movement which does not also become an economic structure reform movement is bound for defeat, caught up in its own contradictions.

Though Victory Is a Long Way Off, Radical Teachers Should Expose and Challenge Tracking Wherever Possible

Remember, our often perceived "failure" to educate our students is not a result of our own personal inadequacies, of undisciplined or unmotivated students, of hostile communities or even of over-crowded or underresourced classrooms. From 8:00 to 3:00 each day, facing individual kids, this is easy to forget. We make futile attempts at individual solutions in our classrooms, locking the hostile world outside our door. We may even retreat into hope-lessness, seeing the only way out is to leave for a more non-alienating situation in a "free" school. Since our basic involve-ments lie within a classroom and a school, we tend to think of

classroom and school problems as isolated. But we can't escape
the social struggle, not us, not our students, not their communities.
We must work together to create a society in which the schools
will serve the people. We can create our weapons from our own
situations in the schools of the United States.

Caste and Class in "Elmtown"*

by August Hollingshead

The high school curriculum is organized around three courses:
college preparatory, general, and commercial. Enrollment in each
course is related very significantly to class position; that is, each
course acts either to attract or repel students in the different prestige classes. In 1941, the class I's and class II's concentrated on
the college preparatory (64 per cent) and ignored the commercial
course. Fifty-one per cent of the class III's were in the general, 27
per cent in the college preparatory, and 21 per cent in the commercial course. The class IV's entered the general (58 per cent)
and commercial courses (33 per cent) and avoided the college
preparatory; only 9 per cent were in it. The pattern for the class
V's was similar to the class IV's, except that 38 per cent were in
the commercial and 4 per cent in the college preparatory course.
  The prestige bias in the different courses is particularly clear
among the girls. For instance, 12 of the 14 class II girls (86 per
cent) enrolled in the college preparatory course; none in the secretarial division of the commercial course; and only one in the
general-commercial course, and one in the general course. Sixty-
two per cent of the girls from class IV and 38 per cent from class

---

* The description here is taken from a sociologist's field study of a small
Midwestern community at the end of the Great Depression, just before the
United States entered World War II. The sons and daughters of all families,
from the very well-to-do to the very down-and-out, attended the same
comprehensive high school (if they had not already dropped out). The
families and their offspring were assigned to classes by the author in
accordance with income, wealth, occupation, and so forth, class I being the
most prestigious and class V the least.—Ed.

From *Elmtown's Youth: The Impact of Social Classes on Adolescents* by
August B. Hollingshead. Copyright © 1949 by John Wiley & Sons, Inc. By
permission.

III were concentrated in the commercial course, particularly in the secretarial division. Since most girls trained in the secretarial division find jobs as secretaries and clerks in Elmtown's offices after graduation, the high school provides these girls with specialized terminal education. . . .

. . . If a person wants to "rate," especially among the girls, it is wise to enroll in the college preparatory course. The following interview materials indicate how the process works.

Alice White (class III) and Nellie Anderson (class IV) were clique mates in Central School during the seventh and eighth grades. During the summer following their graduation from grammar school, they informally planned their high school years. Alice's father and mother expected her to go to high school, then on to college, so she had no other idea than to enter the college preparatory course. Nellie's father had deserted the family the spring she finished the seventh grade, leaving her mother with Nellie and two smaller children. Although Mrs. Anderson did not consider it necessary for Nellie to attend high school, she did not wish to violate the law; so she started her, telling Nellie many times of sacrifices necessary to send her to school "now that Daddy has run away." Nellie's mother wanted her to take the secretarial course so she could "get a job" when she was old enough to quit school.

On the first day of the fall semester, Nellie went to Alice's house, and the two girls started to school together. On the way, they met Anne Parker (class III), a third clique mate, whose mother had told her to be sure to take home economics. Anne, however, wanted to enroll in college preparatory, because most of her girl friends intended to. The three girls discussed the situation on the way to school and decided that all three would enroll in the college preparatory course.

That evening Alice reported to her parents what she had done, and her father commented, "Fine! Now I expect you to work hard on Latin and algebra. The rest will be easy." Her mother was happy until Alice told about the girls' discussion on the way to school. Then she exclaimed:

> I don't think Anne's mother realizes the girls in the home economics course are looked down upon by the girls from the better families. Alice, you did wrong in getting Nellie to sign up for the college preparatory course. Her mother can't send her to college, and the poor girl will be snubbed by the other girls in there. Why can't you ever learn you can't manage the

lives of other people? Water will seek its level. Let Nellie take the secretarial course and go her way.

Anne's mother objected to her enrollment in the college preparatory course, but let her continue it with the comment "If you do real well in your studies, your father may help you go to college, but it will be hard for us."

Nellie's mother was explosively angry with Nellie and with the high school authorities for allowing Nellie to enroll in the college preparatory course. She immediately told Nellie that she must change to the secretarial course. Nellie cried most of the night, but her mother went to school the next morning and changed Nellie's course herself. Nellie continued in school for a year and a half, but dropped out of her old clique, and then left school to work in the "dime" store. . . .

[The principal of the school, unable to control tardiness, instituted a new regime, whereby any student arriving late for school would have to serve detention that afternoon.]

The second week of the new regime, the daughter of a prominent class II family did not go to detention. Instead, she kept an appointment with a beauty parlor to have a permanent wave. The next morning the Superintendent walked into the principal's office, diffidently fingered the mail in the teachers' boxes, sauntered over to the windows with his hands in his pockets, looked at the autumn leaves moving across the yard, and in a disinterested way asked, "How is the detention room working?" The principal answered:

All right, except we are running into the old stall of some students who think they can do as they please!

[Superintendent] Yes, I know. The idea is all right, but I do not think it will work in every case. Last evening, Mrs. Newton called Evelyn [the Superintendent's wife] about the church supper next week. She mentioned that Kathy [her daughter, the girl in question] was at the hairdresser's last night!

[Principal] That is just what I had in mind. Last evening I called Mrs. Newton and told her Kathy was not in detention and I wanted to know where she was. Mrs. Newton told me she had to have her hair fixed for the dance at the Country Club tonight. When I get Kathy in here, I am going to tell her a thing or two.

[Superintendent] Now, be careful, Alfred. I do not think there is a thing we can do in this case.

The principal sat silently at his desk and shuffled excuses. The Superintendent walked out of the office.

When Kathy came in for her lecture, she was dressed neatly in a brushed wool sweater and tweed skirt. She walked coyly to the principal's desk and asked in a naive voice, "Did you want to see me last night?"

The principal looked up and quietly asked, "Did you forget about detention?"

A pause. "No, I had an appointment at Craig's to have my hair set."

"Did you have to go last night?"

"Yes, tonight I have to go to Mrs. Nettle's to get my dress for the dance."

"All right. Go on to class, but don't let this happen again."

After Kathy left the office, the principal threw a pack of excuses on the desk and muttered, "There it goes again! The next time one of these prominent families puts pressure on me, I am going to raise hell!"

The following Wednesday morning, Frank Stone, Jr. (class I), parked his father's Cadillac in front of the high school at a quarter after eight, climbed out leisurely, picked up his notebook, and walked into the office and casually remarked, "I guess I'm late again."

The principal looked hard at him and spoke firmly, "What's the story this time?"

"I didn't wake up, I guess."

"This time you are going to detention like everyone else." He wrote young Frank an excuse, placed his name on the detention list, and, as he handed him the excuse, said, "This means one hour in detention. I want to see you there at three-fifteen tonight."

When the principal checked detention at three-thirty, he noted that young Frank was absent. He walked down the hall to the Superintendent's office, where the one telephone in the building was located, and called Frank Stone, Sr., at his office. He told Mr. Stone that young Frank had been late that morning and he had not come to detention. He ended with, "I want him down here right away."

The Superintendent heard the telephone conversation from his partially enclosed office. As the principal hung up the receiver, he walked into the outer office and asked, with a studied effort to be calm, "What did Mr. Stone say?" The principal replied, "He is going to get young Frank down here right away. I have to leave now to practice my solo for this Sunday with Mrs. Henderson, but

I will tell Mr. White to check young Frank in when he comes."
(The principal sang in the Methodist choir "for policy's sake.")
The principal returned to detention, spoke to Mr. White, then
came back to his office, locked his desk, put on his coat, and left.

About a half-hour later, Mr. Stone drove to the high school with
young Frank. The Superintendent waited in his office with an eye
on the street. As Frank came into the building, the Superintendent
slowly walked down the hall toward the principal's office. The two
met at the head of the stairs, and the Superintendent asked in a
pleasant voice, "Haven't you gone home yet?" Young Frank, burn-
ing with rage, retorted, "Mr. [Principal] made me come back for
detention. Dad is really sore."

"Frank, come into my office, and let us talk this over." The two
walked into the Superintendent's office and discussed the matter.
After ten or fifteen minutes, the Superintendent told Frank to sit
in the outer office for a while and not go to detention. Some days
after this, he said to us:

> I did not want to put young Frank in the detention room with
> the rest of the kids; so I sat him there in the outer office, and
> I deliberately worked around in my office until about five-
> thirty. Then I came out and said, "Frank, I guess you have
> been here long enough. You go on home and let's not have
> any hard feelings." I talked to his father later about the whole
> thing, and I think we have come to an understanding.

The principal was enraged when he learned what had happened, but he could do nothing. This practically ended uniform
enforcement of the new detention rule. Thereafter, class I and
class II students and many class III's flaunted it on the least
pretext. . . . However, it was enforced more rigidly for many others.

Three weeks after the Frank Stone, Jr., incident, "Boney"
Johnson, a 15-year-old class IV boy, came late one morning, and
the English teacher refused to admit him to class without an
excuse. As "Boney" walked into the office, the principal was sitting
at his desk. Before "Boney" could say a word, he barked, in a
sarcastic tone:

> So my pretty boy is late again! I suppose it took you half an
> hour to put on that clean shirt and green tie! [The principal
> arose from his desk, walked around and looked at Boney's
> trousers and shoes and went on.] Ha, you have your pants

pressed today! I suppose you took a bath last night, too. New shoes, and they're shined.

"Boney" said nothing, but his face flushed and he bit his lips. The principal walked back to his desk, sat down, and wrote out an admission slip. He put "Boney's" name on the detention list and handed over the excuse with the remark, "I want to see you in detention tonight. Now go on to class and show the girls what a pretty boy you are."

"Boney" turned, and as he walked toward the door, said in a low voice, "I'm not going to your damned detention room tonight or any time."

The principal apparently did not hear him as he went on with his work. In a few minutes, he walked across the room and said:

Now there's a hot one. He's one of our wise guys. He thinks he's a hotshot. His old man is a laborer out at the fertilizer plant, and the kid thinks he's someone, umph! He'll be on the W.P.A.* if they have one twenty years from now. There's one guy I'm going to see put in detention.

When school was out that afternoon, the Superintendent stood in the hall near the side exit, Mr. White, a teacher, watched the front door, while the principal patrolled the building. Mr. Gardner, another teacher, was in the detention room. After the building was cleared of students and most of the teachers had gone home, the Superintendent walked back to his office, but the principal stood outside the front door. Suddenly the door was thrown open from the outside, and angry voices were heard. The Superintendent rushed out of his office and stood at the head of the stairs. The principal pushed and shoved "Boney" up the stairs as he repeated, "You can't get away with that stuff." As they neared the top, "Boney" broke from his grasp and started down the hall toward the side door. The Superintendent blocked his path, and "Boney" ran upstairs. The principal leaped and grabbed him by the coat collar with his left hand. "Boney" turned and started to fight. The principal spun him around, seized the visor of his cap with his right hand and yanked it down over his eyes. While "Boney" was

---

* A work-relief (welfare) program of the New Deal. Interestingly, the principal's remark is in the nature of a self-fulfilling prophecy, or a wish disguised as a prophecy. He might more accurately have said, "He'll be on W.P.A. twenty years from now if I have anything to say about it."—ED.

fighting to get the cap off his face, the principal hit him three times with the heel of his hand on the back of the neck near the base of the skull. "Boney" cursed, struggled, and hit in all directions. Soon he broke free and ran toward the Superintendent, who shook and slapped him three or four times. Both men then grabbed him by the arms and shook him vigorously. The Superintendent angrily screeched, "You're going out of this building. You're never coming back until you bring your father and we talk this over." By this time, the three had reached the front door. "Boney" was shoved outside. He stood there, cursing and threatening both men with violence. In a few minutes he composed himself, straightened his clothes, and walked away, muttering to himself.

The principal and the Superintendent came upstairs and walked into the Superintendent's office. The Superintendent dropped into his swivel chair and said, when he had caught his breath, "I can stand a lot of things from kids, but one thing I can't stand is a sassy kid. No kid's going to sass me." He puffed a few minutes more. The principal said nothing, and the Superintendent resumed, "That boy is a trouble maker. I've had my eyes on him all year. Look at the gang he's running with."

"Yes, I know. They're trouble makers around here. I had trouble with them all last year, and they're starting out again this year. If he wasn't that type, he wouldn't be running with that bunch."

After a pause, the Superintendent composed himself and remarked, "That boy will have to bring his father back here, or he'll not get in this school." The principal agreed, "Yes, I'll stand with you on that. We have got to stop this thing some way."

After the principal had walked out of the office, the Superintendent slumped wearily in his chair and said:

> I ought to know better than that. I would have really liked to smack that boy, but that's one thing I've learned. You can't pop these kids even though they deserve it. The hardest thing I have to fight all the time is to keep from popping these smart kids. I shouldn't have lost my temper but, damn it, sometimes it gets too much for me. When a kid sasses me, I see red and that's all there is to it. I don't think anything will come of this, his background being what it is.

The Superintendent was right; nothing came of it, except— "Boney" quit school.

"You've Got to Be Realistic About Being a Nigger"

by Malcolm X

I kept close to the top of the class, though. The topmost scholastic standing, I remember, kept shifting between me, a girl named Audrey Slaugh, and a boy named Jimmy Cotton.

It went on that way, as I became increasingly restless and disturbed through the first semester. And then one day, just about when those of us who had passed were about to move up to 8-A, from which we would enter high school the next year, something happened which was to become the first major turning point of my life.

Somehow, I happened to be alone in the classroom with Mr. Ostrowski, my English teacher. He was a tall, rather reddish white man and he had a thick mustache. I had gotten some of my best marks under him, and he had always made me feel that he liked me. He was . . . a natural-born "advisor," about what you ought to read, to do, or think—about any and everything. We used to make unkind jokes about him: why was he teaching in Mason instead of somewhere else, getting for himself some of the "success in life" that he kept telling us how to get?

I know that he probably meant well in what he happened to advise me that day. I doubt that he meant any harm. It was just in his nature as an American white man. I was one of his top students, one of the school's top students—but all he could see for me was the kind of future "in your place" that almost all white people see for black people.

He told me, "Malcolm, you ought to be thinking about a career. Have you been giving it thought?"

The truth is, I hadn't. I never have figured out why I told him, "Well, yes, sir, I've been thinking I'd like to be a lawyer." Lansing certainly had no Negro lawyers—or doctors either—in those days, to hold up an image I might have aspired to. All I really knew for certain was that a lawyer didn't wash dishes, as I was doing.

Mr. Ostrowski looked surprised, I remember, and leaned back

in his chair and clasped his hands behind his head. He kind of half-smiled and said, "Malcolm, one of life's first needs is for us to be realistic. Don't misunderstand me, now. We all here like you, you know that. But you've got to be realistic about being a nigger. A lawyer—that's no realistic goal for a nigger. You need to think about something you *can* be. You're good with your hands —making things. Everybody admires your carpentry shop work. Why don't you plan on carpentry? People like you as a person— you'd get all kinds of work."

The more I thought afterwards about what he said, the more uneasy it made me. It just kept treading around in my mind.

What made it really begin to disturb me was Mr. Ostrowski's advice to others in my class—all of them white. Most of them had told him they were planning to become farmers. But those who wanted to strike out on their own, to try something new, he had encouraged. Some, mostly girls, wanted to be teachers. A few wanted other professions, such as one boy who wanted to become a county agent; another, a veterinarian; and one girl wanted to be a nurse. They all reported that Mr. Ostrowski had encouraged what they had wanted. Yet nearly none of them had earned marks equal to mine.

It was a surprising thing that I had never thought of it that way before, but I realized that whatever I wasn't, I *was* smarter than nearly all of those white kids. But apparently I was still not intelligent enough, in their eyes, to become whatever *I* wanted to be.

It was then that I began to change—inside.

Demand Release of Nine Children from a Class for the Mentally Retarded

A suit was filed (1/8/70) in Federal District Court in Monterey County to remove nine Mexican-American children from classes for the mentally retarded in the Soledad Elementary School District. Victor E. Ramírez, a bilingual school psychologist, testified

From *La Mujer—en Pie de Lucha ¡Y la hora es ya!* Dorinda Moreno, editor, published in *Chicago Journal* by Espina del Norte Publications, Mexico City, 1973. Reprinted by permission.

in a statement to the court that when tests were given to the children in Spanish, seven of the nine scored above the maximum (2 to 19 points) used by the school to determine retardation. One of the other two scored right at maximum and the second only three points below. On the average, the children tested 15 points higher in Spanish than when tested in English.

The testimony included further evidence that children from Spanish-speaking homes were adjudged "retarded" on the basis of tests designed for Anglo, middle-class children. The tests contained such questions as "Who wrote Romeo and Juliet?" "What is the color of rubies?" and "Why is it better to pay bills by check than by cash?" (a difficult question for a child whose parents have never had a bank account) and to identify such words as "chattel," "hieroglyphic," and "Genghis Khan."

Placement in the "MR" classes dooms normal children to illiteracy, since these classes in this state offer limited training in reading, mathematics and other basic subjects.

The suit asked the court to prohibit the state and local school districts from placing any Spanish-speaking children in classes for the mentally retarded solely on the basis of tests administered in English. It is estimated that there are 85,000 children currently enrolled in classes for the educable mentally retarded in California. A study two years ago indicated that 26% (or 22,000) are of Spanish surname as compared to 13% of the whole student population!

Off the Track and into the Street*

by Marjorie Heins

Many of the latin immigrants were skilled and upwardly aspiring city workers. Others were professionals or semi-professionals— Nelson's father had been to college—but unlike the European

From *Strictly Ghetto Property: The Story of Los Siete de la Raza* by Marjorie Heins, copyright 1972, Ramparts Press, San Francisco.

* In May, 1969, seven young men from San Francisco's Latin Mission district were accused of murdering a policeman. Their case, which came to

workers who populated the Mission before them, the latinos faced racial discrimination in jobs and housing, profound cultural differences, and anti-latin prejudices which had developed among the Anglo population during one hundred years of California history. . . .

. . . whatever the true unemployment rate in the Mission, it is easy to see that jobs are very scarce, especially for Spanish-speaking immigrants. Mayor Joseph Alioto's application for a Model Cities Planning Grant in 1968 asserted that the Mission had the highest unemployment rate in the city, while its underemployment rate was about double the city average.

Mission High School reflected the dismal situation. With 36 percent of its student body Spanish-speaking, and 68 percent Third World (black, latin, Asian, Filipino, Samoan and other non-whites), Mission High had the lowest average family income of any school in the city. The average daily absence rate was 25 percent. In 1966, Mission High sent only 5 percent of its graduates on to four-year college, as compared to 50 percent for the city's most affluent—and mostly white—public high school. In the Mission district as a whole, the dropout rate in 1969–70 was 29 percent for males and 20 percent for females. As for the Mission's adult population, in 1966 between 40 and 60 percent had less than nine years of education.

"When school came around every year, I didn't have any enthusiasm," Mario Martinez says of his elementary and junior high school years. "Back in my country, when school was coming we used to get prepared. You buy all your new books and you fold up the covers real nice.

"When I first got here they put me back in the fifth grade. I would just sit there. This guy who spoke Spanish and English would sometimes interpret for me, but the rest of the time I would just sit, try to listen. The only thing I could do was when it was time to draw—I always drew something about my country. I passed that grade, but I don't know why they passed me."

His older brother Tony's strongest impressions were of racism

---

be called the Case of Los Siete, attracted considerable support in their community, and, after a lengthy and highly publicized trial, six of them were acquitted (the seventh having disappeared). The Martinez brothers, who appear in this selection, belong to a family that had immigrated from San Salvador both to escape a wave of right-wing repression there and to find a better education for the family's scholarly sons.—ED.

at school. "A lot of times the teachers won't even talk to you," he says. "They looked at us and thought, 'Well, this guy probably don't even understand what I'm saying.' Plus they call you names. I remember the first time I was called a Mexican was in Marshall elementary school. I remember this teacher real well; she was a drunk. You could smell it a mile away. I remember I was coming down the steps in front of the school. You wasn't supposed to walk there or something. At that time I didn't understand English. It wasn't till later I found out she had called me a fucking greaser. I remembered by the sound.

"In junior high the Dean of Boys was pretty nasty. He was always making racist remarks. Not only to the brown kids but to the black kids, calling them motherfucking niggers and shit. All the time—it would be a continuous thing. They couldn't refer to you—you never had a name. When they call Mary in the classroom, it's Mary, and John is John; but when they call us it's 'You, the Mexican kid.' Calling us farmworkers and *braceros* and peons and all this. After a while you just don't want to hear it."

Mario adds, "In junior high this one guy, if you were late to class he would call you down and hit you with a paddle. Once I was late and so he called me down. He told me to bend over, and he hit me with a paddle. I didn't know what he was going to do. He just hit me. And I got real mad. I didn't come to school for about two weeks. All I could think was, nobody has a right to hit me, only my parents. And this stranger, even though he does belong to this big school, he don't have no right hitting me.

"Even after I learned English, I still had problems. Like with the kids. There was a lot of little *pochos*—guys whose family was born in our country, but they were born here. They don't speak Spanish. Even if they know Spanish, they won't speak it to you. Like I would ask someone in Spanish to tell me something and he would say, 'I don't speak Spanish,' and I knew he did. It got me upset, because I thought, these guys, they're ashamed of our culture, ashamed of our people. So I didn't get along with them at all. 'Cause you've got to be proud of what you are.

"Our culture has never left us," Mario says. "With my parents, when I speak to them in English, you just call somebody 'you': in Spanish you have a formal thing—you say 'Usted.' That's the way I treat my parents: 'Usted.' If I wanted to say 'you,' I'd just say 'tu.' But that's a kind of friendly thing. There's no respect there. I rebelled against a lot of things, but not my culture or my parents, 'cause I don't see much to rebel against there.

"I used to go to school in the morning," Mario says. "And my friends would ask me, 'Are you going to class?' And we would just split. It was a better experience. I learned more on the streets than in school, just being with people I could relate to."

The Martinez brothers were quickly turned off to school—with its pressure to speak English and abandon their culture and its run-ins with racist teachers or administrators. Like most young latins they began to spend their time on the streets—going to dances, frequenting pool halls, tasting wine and grass.

"I would hang around with guys a lot older than myself," Tony remembers. "Hanging around with bigger guys helped me not get hung up on drugs. I seen all these guys, first smoking a lot of grass, then using a lot of hard stuff. Chicanos and latinos don't usually go for the psychedelic drugs, you know. Don't dig the synthetic kick. So they use a lot of hard drugs. But the thing about hard drugs is—people you know, they might have a job, and then they get hooked. Then they have to steal. Pretty soon they're going to jail. You see them become all skinny and weak and they're dying and they're OD'ed and stuff. So this is why I never touch the stuff. And in our case our family is tight-knit. So we always had somebody behind us. We had time to think about these things, because we wouldn't have the many problems our friends would have. All my partners on the street, they have to hassle to find a job or a room where to stay—go steal so they can pay a week in a hotel. Hassles we wouldn't have to go through."

Educational Achievements and Worker Performance

by Ivar Berg

The search for evidence to give weight to economic arguments supporting the use of educational credentials for jobs has not been conspicuously successful. . . .

The efforts of manpower and job analysts to identify the "real" educational requirements are of similarly problematical value; the difficulties of distinguishing employer *tastes* from employers' functional *needs* are in no wise eliminated by the use of the U.S.

From Ivar Berg, *Education and Jobs: The Great Training Robbery,* Praeger Publishers, 1970. Reprinted by permission.

Employment Service's descriptions of jobs. These descriptions, while apparently based on today's practices, are themselves informed by preferences generated in the marriage of yesterday's labor-market conditions with prejudices honored too well by time. Thus margins of choice with respect to manpower utilization remain open to employers after technological determinants and the sorting process of market forces have shaped a firm's occupational structure.

And managers, upon whom there are strong pressures to be guided by evidence, usually offer little more than assertions in support of practices the benefits of which are assumed.

An alternative method is to examine the actual performance of workers in identical or similar jobs whose educational backgrounds are different to determine whether differential educational achievements might be related to differences in organizationally relevant behavior. . . .

Blue-Collar Workers

In the first of the field investigations, data were collected in 1967 on the productivity, turnover, and absenteeism of 585 former and present female workers in a multiplant Mississippi textile manufacturing company. We found that educational achievement was *inversely* related to performance thus conceived. Thus, where 57 per cent of the long-tenure employees had ten or more years of schooling, the figure for short-tenure employees was 71 per cent; the statistical probability that the observed difference would occur by chance is 5 in 100.

The data with respect to educational achievement correlated with productivity, which in this company could be measured accurately from piecework earnings, and absenteeism were somewhat less clear, but they gave no support to the contention that educational requirements are a useful screening device in blue-collar employee selection. The education of high producers did not differ from that of low producers to any statistically significant degree, although the *less* productive ones were slightly *better* educated. . . .

In the same vein, there was no statistically significant relationship between educational achievement and absenteeism, another bugaboo of managers who are anxious to maintain smooth production schedules and continuous work flows, although there were slightly more high school graduates among the "low" than the "high absentee" group. . . .

. . . in our interviews regarding the "greater potential" of better-

educated workers, . . . employers insisted that the elevation of
education requirements reflects management's desire to build for
the future by assuring a pool of labor from which promotions may
be made. If their assumption is correct, we would expect to find
that personnel who have been promoted are better educated than
those who have not, especially in companies that are proud of the
essential rationality of their manpower and personnel policies.

Although this expectation is not easily tested, we might well be
skeptical of an intrinsically appealing analysis that protects its own
flank by seeing long-term benefits in an approach to a short-run
problem. In a parallel study, data were collected on the patterns
of labor-force "attachment" among (1) installation-crew members
in two privately owned urban utility companies, (2) workers in
an auto assembly plant located on the periphery of one of America's great cities, and (3) nonmanagerial employees in two large
urban department stores.[1] These data do not square with management's convenient rationale.

The patterns were substantially the same in all four employment settings; those of the installers are illustrative. In an effort
to account for the promotion rates of these workers, educational
achievement explained so few promotions that it could be dis-
counted as a factor. The results were interesting, however, in that
they offered some clues to the real nature of "organizational
mobility," to borrow a barbarism from sociology, clues that are
entirely consistent with the skeptical bias of the present study.

When the researcher who originally exploited the data examined
the job titles in these four work settings, she discovered that,
although the titles were ordered into a pay scale, the resulting
array did not correspond to a skill hierarchy except at the extreme
ends of the wages continuum. It appears, then, that education
may well be relevant to the "promotion potential" of workers in
a shop or plant where title and pay changes reflect differences in
job tasks and obligations, but it is not likely to be specifically
relevant to promotions in settings where managers have developed
a nominal hierarchy to legitimize wage differentials created by
the numerous factors that operate in urban labor markets.

It is doubtful that the uncounted masses of Americans who are
"promoted" each year are as easily fooled by nominal hierarchies
as are some senior academics who conceive of occupational titles

---

[1] Marcia Freedman, *The Process of Work Establishment* (New York:
Columbia University Press, 1969).

as ranks representing differential skills. Such ranks are merely included among the more socially significant rungs on the largely symbolic occupational "ladders." . . .

White-Collar Workers

The facts are not more reassuring with respect to white-collar workers. An analysis of the merit pay increases awarded to over a hundred secretaries employed by one of the nation's largest magazine publishers revealed no discernible relationship between these rewards for performance and the educational achievements of the recipients who had attended various post–high school programs but had not graduated from college. Nor did any associations appear when the number rather than the amount of increases was considered. In fact, while a small number of college graduates received slightly more raises than the nongraduates, the education-evaluation data were otherwise *inversely* related.

In another white-collar study, the results were in line with those already reported: Performance in 125 branch offices of a major New York bank, measured by turnover data and by the number of lost accounts per teller, was inversely associated with the educational achievements of these 500 workers.[2] The branches with the worst performance records were those in which a disproportionately (and significantly) high number of employees were attending educational programs after working hours! There was also evidence that performance was worst in precisely those branches in which, besides the educational achievements' being higher, the managers stressed education in consultations with tellers concerning their futures with the bank.

The fact that white-collar workers' job performances are more difficult to measure than those of blue-collar workers makes useful analysis in this area almost impossible. Salaried workers, for example, are not usually "docked" for the absences they incur whether they malinger, "go to the doctor," or attend to the myriad personal details of a folded, bent, and spindled society of forms, bureaus, licenses, and application blanks. Nor are formal records kept of the millions of hours spent on haircuts, apartment-hunting trips, brokerage-office visits, or headcolds by Americans whose salary checks presumably attest to their diligence and industry. The argu-

---

[2] Martin J. Gannon, "Employee Turnover and Productivity in a Branch Banking System," unpublished doctoral dissertation, Columbia University, 1969, written under the supervision of the author.

ment that these "breaks" are a factor in keeping employee morale
high is rarely applied to the blue-collar worker who seeks to escape
from the factory for no pleasure greater than his mother-in-law's
funeral.* The facts of life with respect to record-keeping guarantee
that *any* criteria used by managers to screen employees can be
made to work in the short run. And as my colleague and an
authority on manpower problems, Professor Eli Ginzberg, has
frequently observed, "The long run is, after all, only a series of
short runs."

Professionals and Managers

Survey researchers at the Opinion Research Corporation of
Princeton, New Jersey, however, have sought to identify some of
the attitudes of engineers and scientists, including a few with
administrative responsibilities, in an investigation sponsored by
industry leaders concerned about the care and feeding of these
high-priced personnel. Because employers had ranked the personnel
("A" or "B," according to their "value") from whom demographic
and attitude data were solicited, it was possible to make at least
an empirical excursion into the nettlesome issues involved.

The personnel, nearly 620 of them, were employed by the
nation's six largest manufacturers of heavy electrical equipment
and appliances; the education-income nexus could thus be viewed
in a comparative perspective, and logical inferences could be
drawn concerning the hiring and salary policies of the six companies and the connections among company characteristics, personnel characteristics, and personnel satisfactions.

It may reasonably be assumed that the distributions of educational achievements represented in each of the companies are indi-
cators of that company's hiring policies. Engineers and scientists
are more geographically mobile than most other occupational
groups; moreover, each of the companies is large enough to recruit
in a national labor market. Assuming, therefore, that the same
types of men were available to all six companies, we can regard
the fact that (for example) F had 62 Ph.D.'s among 96 employees
whereas D had one Ph.D. in 100 to be the result of management
choice.

Table 1 . . . shows that, at least with respect to men with

---

* This is a difference that the high school experiences of Frank Stone, Jr.,
and "Boney," of "Elmtown," had prepared them to expect if not, in
"Boney's" case, accept.—ED.

TABLE 1. MEAN ANNUAL SALARIES OF SCIENTISTS AND ENGINEERS AT SIX COMPANIES, BY MANAGEMENT EVALUATION AND EDUCATION, 1958

Management Evaluation	Education						
	Less than Bachelor's Degree	B.A. or B.S.	Some Graduate Courses	M.A. or M.S.	Ph.D.	Total	Tau β
Ordinary							
Mean	$7,780	$7,500	$7,840	$8,270	$10,850	$8,460	.41*
S.D.	1,550	1,720	1,570	1,590	2,060	2,200	
Number	(27)	(128)	(25)	(66)	(71)	(317)	
Valuable							
Mean	11,100	10,020	10,620	9,840	11,710	10,750	.17
S.D.	1,370	2,710	2,770	2,090	2,370	2,520	
Number	(21)	(84)	(21)	(55)	(110)	(291)	
Total							
Mean	9,230	8,500	9,110	8,980	11,370	9,550	.32*
S.D.	2,210	2,510	2,580	1,990	2,290	2,620	
Number	(48)	(212)	(46)	(121)	(181)	(608)	

* Significant at the .05 level.

graduate degrees, management in these six companies tends to reward educational achievement rather than performance! Men with master's degrees who were designated by *management* as among 20 per cent of their scientists who were "relatively most valuable in terms of present performance and potential" were paid an average salary which was *$1,000 less* than that paid to Ph.D.'s who were reportedly less valuable. Other data show that Ph.D.'s are paid substantially more even when they are younger and less experienced. Small wonder that these Ph.D.'s were a happy lot!

The data do not support the blanket inference that employers always reward educational achievement more than performance, but they afford presumptive evidence that this is the case. It is entirely likely that the numerous discrepancies between the evaluations and incomes earned by the subjects in the Opinion Research Corporation's survey are artifacts of the initial salary differentials, which reflect different educational achievements. These differentials are easily maintained when subsequent salary increases are clustered in such a way as to reduce the likelihood that personnel will make "coercive comparisons" among themselves. In these six companies, at least, it appears that some less educated men earn through *performance* salaries that men with Ph.D.'s are given for their degrees.

A thorough search of the published literature on turnover and absenteeism in industry revealed that the matter of education is rarely considered among the factors linked to these often costly organizational problems. We reviewed hundreds of these studies and conclude, as did Gaudet, that in "seeking to learn the relation of turnover to education, level of skill, and marital status we find many general statements which are valueless, or worse, for decision-making."[3]

Conclusion

The data in this chapter do not prove that educational requirements are bad; they do, however, reinforce doubts about whether the benefits that managers apparently believe accompany educational credentials do in fact materialize.

"But employers don't look for specific performance when they hire better-educated workers," some may argue. When they do, it is because they do not have evidence about the performance of the

[3] F. J. Gaudet, "Labor Turnover: Calculation and Cost," *AMA Research Study No. 39* (New York: American Management Association, 1960), p. 79.

less educated workers who come to their personnel offices through contacts and references. Managers are concerned with generalized ability, and they believe that this can be ascertained through educational achievement.

Unfortunately, the data to test this hypothesis are not available. Some *pieces* of relevant evidence, however, suggest that the selection process is not so easily described. Professor Gary Becker (with an almost opposite purpose) sought to determine whether the individual returns on marginal investments in education are explained by the fact that higher-paid, better-educated workers are more able—that is, more intelligent, and from backgrounds that make them more valuable to employers. His findings might embarrass an educator; they show that, although there *is* a positive association between ability and educational achievement, the latter accounts for *much* more of the variance in earnings. Although each of the studies he considers is deficient in one or more of the particulars of research design, the cumulative weight of the evidence, as he correctly points out, is impressive indeed.[4] "Consequently," he writes, "it may be concluded that, even after adjustment for differential ability, the private rate of return to a typical white male college graduate would be considerable, say, certainly more than 10 per cent."[5]

It is possible that there *are* benefits, and efforts to prove this point may betray a misguided empiricism on the part of researchers. But the faith of some in the benefits of education is perhaps no more valid than others' faith in the admittedly narrow issue of economic benefit. And one may well be skeptical, if not cynical, about how much *real* education can be utilized by most industrial organizations. Meanwhile, the contention that people are changed as a function of their education and thus can change the world gains at least as much horrifying as gratifying support from history. One should note that there are as many distinguished scholars advising the Department of State on Vietnam as there are among critics of that department, and that crackpot realism is no less prevalent among Ph.D.'s than among less educated members of advisory staffs in military and other governmental units. To argue that well-educated people will automatically boost efficiency, im-

[4] See Gary Becker, *Human Capital* (New York: Columbia University Press), 1964, p. 88.
[5] *Ibid.*

TABLE 2.   PROBABILITY OF ENTERING COLLEGE,
            BY ABILITY AND SOCIO-ECONOMIC STATUS[a]

Ability Quarter	Socio-economic Quarter			
	Low 1	2	3	High 4
Females				
Low 1	.06	.12	.13	.26
2	.13	.15	.29	.36
3	.25	.34	.45	.65
High 4	.48	.70	.73	.87
Males				
Low 1	.07	.07	.05	.20
2	.08	.09	.20	.33
3	.18	.23	.36	.55
High 4	.34	.67	.67	.82

[a] The samples from which these probabilities were calculated were high
school juniors in 1960.
SOURCE: John C. Flanagan and William W. Cooley, *Project Talent: One-
Year Follow-Up Studies* (Pittsburgh: School of Education, University of
Pittsburgh, 1966), p. 95.

prove organizations, and so on may be to misunderstand in a
fundamental way the nature of American education, which functions to an important, indeed depressing, extent as a licensing
agency.

Education, Class Barriers, and the Liberal Creed

The defenders of the educational establishment point out that
things could be worse and that critics have overstated their case.
Education, they assert, produces thoughtful citizens and material
well-being; the economic benefits to the society are accordingly
stressed and linked, by assertion, to social welfare. But surely, in
a discussion of education, the definition of social welfare must go
beyond aggregated tallies of material benefits to include the matter
of education's role in the distribution of social product. And when
the issues are thus joined, the defense is less compelling.

Educational credentials have become the new property in
America. Our nation, which has attempted to make the transmis-
sion of real and personal property difficult, has contrived to replace
it with an inheritable set of values concerning degrees and
diplomas that will most certainly reinforce the formidable class
barriers that remain, even without the right within families to pass
benefices from parents to their children.

As a number of my colleagues have suggested, employers can derive benefits from the employment of better-educated workers that outweigh the pathological correlates of "excessive" education; after all, the intent was only to open up the narrower economic issues. But the use of educational credentials as a screening device effectively consigns large numbers of people, especially young people, to a social limbo defined by low-skill, no-opportunity jobs in the "peripheral labor market."[6]

Barriers against greater mobility are not made less imposing by public policies that reinforce the access to formal education of middle- and upper-income youngsters through subsidy and subsidy-like arrangements. Today, tax-supported and tax-assisted universities are full of mutant spirits from families whose incomes are well above those of the average taxpayer. The personal advantages to those who hold academic credentials are sufficiently well known that the majority of Americans do not even pause to question the TV spots or subway posters that warn of the lifetime hazards facing "dropouts."

The quality of public education available to the poor and near poor is almost uniformly low, a fact that contributes increasingly to the visibility of the barrier between the haves and the have-nots. For the have-nots, especially black Americans, there is a special pain in all this, for they are underrepresented in the policy-making councils that have decreed the frightful mess in urban education and the segregated style of American living and learning, but they are overrepresented among those who suffer the penalties in fox-holes overseas and ratholes at home.

At least as sharp a pain must afflict some thoughtful liberals in America. For them formal education has been the equilibrating mechanism in a progressing industrial democracy that has been relatively free of class conflict. It was the liberal who helped to sell America on education and who saw in education the means by which merit might ultimately conquer unearned privilege. He must now acknowledge that he is the defender of a most dubious faith. For while he struggles from the edges of hard-earned privilege to help the poor, he must live off these privileges in the education of his own children.

The results of the present study do not give much weight to the economic argument in its detail, although it would be foolish to

---

[6] See Dean Morse, *The Peripheral Worker* (New York: Columbia University Press, 1969).

deny that education is involved in the nation's capacity to produce goods and services. No benefit would accrue from reviewing the detailed findings here. Let us state, however, that they give grounds for doubting that it is useful to regard education in America within a simplified framework in which a person's *years of schooling* are taken as a significant measure; schools are too diverse and people too differentiated to permit the routine and automatic confusion of the morals, motives, and capabilities of the licensed with their licenses. . . .

Finally, it is appropriate to call attention to the role of the American academic community in the processes by which credentials have come to loom so significantly in the lives of their fellow citizens. A Columbia University colleague has put one major aspect of the matter well:

> Is it not dangerously presumptuous to insist, despite our lack of understanding about the contribution of college schooling to occupational performance, that nevertheless, all professionals must pay a toll to the schools and the teachers? University administrators and college professors have been put into a position that all too closely resembles the old robber barons on the Rhine. They exact not just coin from those who wish passage to professional employment but also the more valuable asset, time—four to eight years of students' lives. . . .
>
> For those who want to do more than pass through to a career . . . college has much to offer for its cost. The offering takes the form of perspectives, understanding, and insights rather than lucrative techniques and productive skills. [However,] not all persons find such an education to their taste or in their interests; some may wish to pursue a career as immediately as possible, postponing until later, or doing without, the contribution education might make to their lives. At present, choice is denied. Entrance to a career is through college, where schooling all too often is masked as education. Would not the colleges, teachers, students, and those who look forward to professional careers be better served if other entry ways were open, available, and used?[7]

[7] James W. Kuhn, "The Misuse of Education: The Problem of Schooling for Employment," speech presented at the inauguration of Dr. Gordon C. Bjork as President of Linfield College, McMinnville, Oregon, May 20, 1969.

School Credentialing and the "Outside World"

Exam for Firemen Tightened

The San Francisco Civil Service Commission . . . acted yesterday to tighten . . . requirements for applicants wishing to take its new firemen's examination. . . .

. . . the Commission voted to:

• Require of all applicants a high school diploma or its equivalent . . .

Battalion Chief Andrew Casper told the commission that 106 of 142 fire departments in the state require the high school diploma, and that high school graduation "indicates an ability to get along with other men on the job."

(*San Francisco Chronicle*, July 8, 1971)

Alameda County Quiz: Juror Test Is Ruled Out

A "clear thinking" test that Alameda county used for years to qualify jurors is unconstitutional because it excluded most blacks and other low-income citizens, the U.S. Supreme Court ruled yesterday.

The case arose when Richard L. Carmical, convicted Nov. 4, 1966, of possession of heroin and possession of a firearm, went to U.S. District Court in San Francisco to challenge the selection of jurors in Alameda County Court.

District Judge Gerald S. Levin dismissed his claim. But the case was appealed and the U.S. Court of Appeals for the Ninth Circuit reversed Levin.

Yesterday, the U.S. Supreme Court upheld the Court of Appeals by rejecting an appeal by California Attorney General Evelle J. Younger.

Carmical objected to the use of the 25 multiple-choice question quiz, which had to be answered in ten minutes, although the participants were not told of any time limit.

For a prospective juror to qualify, he had to answer 21 questions, such as these, correctly:

"If a person asks you for something you do not have you should: 1) tell him to mind his own business; 2) say you don't have it; 3) walk away.

"If it rains when you are starting to go to the doctor, you should: 1) stay at home; 2) take an umbrella; 3) wait until it stops raining.

"Why is a man superior to a productive machine? 1) a man has a sense of humor; 2) a man can think; 3) a machine requires repairs.

"The statement that the moon is made up of green cheese is: 1) absurd; 2) misleading; 3) wicked.

"5 p.m. is a rush hour on buses because: 1) working people are going home at that hour; 2) so many people live in the country; 3) buses are the best cheap means of transportation.

"The government of the United States is sound because it: 1) follows the will of the majority; 2) does not allow representative government; 3) permits the development of dictators.

"The most desirable quality of a juror is: 1) ambition; 2) kindly attitude; 3) logical thinking.

"You should not give money to beggars on the street because: 1) it makes it hard for the beggars to get work; 2) it encourages living off of others; 3) it takes away the work of organized charities."

Andrew Schultz, who has been Alameda County Jury Commissioner for one month, says he can't find the correct answers in his files.

In the second half of 1967, according to the Appeal Court, 81.5 per cent of the registered voters from predominantly black and low-income areas of the county who took the test failed it. Failures in predominantly white areas were only 14.5 per cent.

The state had argued that Carmical must offer evidence to show that the test was intentionally designed to produce this result. But the appeal court said, "the object of the constitutional mandate is to produce master jury panels from which identifiable community classes have not been systematically excluded."

When such exclusion does occur, it said, "the subjective intent of those who develop and enforce the system is immaterial."

(*San Francisco Chronicle*, October 17, 1972)

Letter to a Teacher

by the Schoolboys of Barbiana

Barbiana is not the name of a school or the name of a town. It is a community of about twenty farmhouses in the hills of the Mugello region, in Tuscany. The church of Barbiana, a small, lovely building of the fourteenth century, stands on a hill overlooking the valley. . . .

The landscape has a harsh beauty: woods, stony slopes and a few scattered fields and orchards.

Don Lorenzo Milani, founder of the school at Barbiana, was ordered to the Barbiana church in 1954. . . . Soon after being ordered to Barbiana, Lorenzo Milani felt the needs of the children of the farms scattered nearby to be very critical. Most of the children had either flunked out of school or were bitterly discouraged with the way they were taught. He gathered about ten boys, eleven- to thirteen-year-olds, and gave them a full schedule of eight hours' work, six or seven days a week. Later, the group grew to twenty. The older children would devote a great deal of time to teaching or drilling the younger. Many hours were given by all to the study and understanding of problems directly significant to their own lives, and, along these lines, eight students of the school wrote this *Letter* as a full-year project. . . .

(From the translators' Introduction)

•

DEAR MISS,

You won't remember me or my name. You have flunked so many of us.

On the other hand I have often had thoughts about you, and the other teachers, and about that institution which you call "school" and about the kids that you flunk.

You flunk us right out into the fields and factories and there you forget us.

Two years ago, when I was in first *magistrale,** you used to make me feel shy.

From *Letter to a Teacher,* by the Schoolboys of Barbiana, translated by Nora Rossi and Tom Cole (New York: Random House, 1970). Footnote numbers have been changed in this adaptation.

* A four-year high school leading to a diploma for elementary school teachers.—Translators' note.

As a matter of fact, shyness has been with me all my life. As a little boy I used to keep my eyes on the ground. I would creep along the walls in order not to be seen.

At first I thought it was some kind of sickness of mine or maybe of my family. My mother is the kind that gets timid in front of a telegram form. My father listens and notices, but is not a talker.

Later on I thought shyness was a disease of mountain people. The farmers on the flat lands seemed surer of themselves. To say nothing of the workers in town.

Now I have observed that the workers let "daddy's boys" grab all the jobs with responsibility in the political machines, and all the seats in Parliament.

So they too are like us. And the shyness of the poor is an older mystery. I myself, in the midst of it, can't explain it. Perhaps it is neither a form of cowardice nor of heroism. It may just be lack of arrogance.

* * *

During the five elementary grades the State offered me a second-rate schooling. Five classes in one room. A fifth of the schooling that was due me.

It is the same system used in America to create the differences between blacks and whites. Right from the start a poorer school for the poor.

* * *

None of the girls from town ever came to Barbiana. Perhaps because the road was so dangerous. Perhaps because of their parents' mentality. They believed that a woman can live her life with the brains of a hen. Males don't ask a woman to be intelligent.

This, too, is racism. But on this matter we cannot blame you, the teachers. You put a higher value on your girl students than their parents do.[1]

Sandro was fifteen; five feet eight in height: a humiliated adult. His teachers had declared him an imbecile. They expected him to repeat the first intermediate for the third time.

Gianni was fourteen. Inattentive, allergic to reading. His teach-

[1] For instance, in the year 1962–63, 65.2 per cent of the boys and 70.9 per cent of the girls graduated from the first intermediate; 72.9 per cent of the boys and 80.5 per cent of the girls graduated from the second intermediate class. (*Annuario Statistico dell'Istruzione Italiana 1965* [*Yearbook of Statistics on Italian Education 1965*], page 81.)

ers had declared him a delinquent. They were not totally wrong, but that was no excuse for sweeping him out of their way.

Neither of them had any intention of repeating. They had reached the point of dropping out and getting jobs. They came over to us because we ignore your failing marks and put each person in the right grade for his age.

Sandro was put in the third intermediate and Gianni in the second. This was the first satisfaction they ever had in their unhappy school careers. Sandro will remember this forever. Gianni remembers once in a while.

* * *

We should settle what correct language is. Languages are created by the poor, who then go on renewing them forever. The rich crystallize them in order to put on the spot anybody who speaks in a different way. Or in order to fail him at exams.

You say that little Pierino, daddy's boy, can write well. But of course; he speaks as you do. He is part of the firm.

* * *

After three years of schooling at Barbiana I took, in June, my exams for the intermediate diploma as a private-school candidate. The composition topic was: "The Railroad Cars Speak."

At Barbiana I had learned that the rules of good writing are: Have something important to say, something useful to everyone or at least to many. Know for whom you are writing. Gather all useful materials. Find a logical pattern with which to develop the theme. Eliminate every useless word. Eliminate every word not used in the spoken language. Never set time limits.

That is the way my schoolmates and I are writing this letter. That is the way my pupils will write, I hope, when I am a teacher.

But, facing that composition topic, what use could I make of the humble and sound rules of the art of writing in all ages? If I wanted to be honest I should have left the page blank. Or else criticized the theme and whoever had thought it up.

But I was fourteen years old and I came from the mountains. To go to a teachers' school I needed the diploma. This piece of paper lay in the hands of five or six persons alien to my life and to everything I loved and knew. Careless people who held the handle of the knife completely in their own grasp.

I tried to write the way you want us to. I can easily believe I was not a success. No doubt there was a better flow to the papers of your own young men, already masters in the production of hot air and warmed-over platitudes.

*   *   *

The history of this half-century was the one I knew best. Russian Revolution, fascism, war resistance, liberation of Africa and Asia. It is the history lived by my father and my grandfather.

I also knew well the history of my own time. That means the daily newspaper which we always read at Barbiana, aloud, from top to bottom.

While cramming for the exams we would steal a couple of hours every day to read the paper, overcoming our stinginess. Because nothing is found in the newspaper that could help us pass your exams. This proves again how little there is in your school useful for life.

That is why we must read the news. It is like shouting in your face that your filthy certificates have not turned us into beasts. We want the diploma for our parents. But politics and the news of each day—they are the sufferings of others and are worth more than your interests or our own.

*   *   *

At the gymnastics exam the teacher threw us a ball and said. "Play basketball." We didn't know how. The teacher looked us over with contempt: "My poor children."

He too is one of you. The ability to handle a conventional ritual seemed so vital to him. He told the principal that we had not been given any "physical education" and we should repeat the exams in the fall.

Any one of us could climb an oak tree. Once up there we could let go with our hands and chop off a two-hundred pound branch with a hatchet. Then we could drag it through the snow to our mother's doorstep.

I heard of a gentleman in Florence who rides upstairs in his house in an elevator. But then he has bought himself an expensive gadget and pretends to row in it. You would give him an A in Physical Education.

*   *   *

Some people hate equality.

A school principal in Florence told a mother: "Don't you worry, madam, send your son to us. Our school is one of the least egalitarian in all of Italy."

It is quite easy to cheat the "sovereign people." One can do it

just by starting a special class for the "nice" boys. It is not necessary to know them personally. It's enough to look at their report
cards, their age, their address (farm or city), place of birth (North
or South), father's profession, and influential references or pull.

In this way, two, three and even four intermediates will coexist
in the same school. Class A is the "intermediate old-style." The
class that runs smoothly. The best teachers will fight to have it.

A certain kind of parent will go to a lot of trouble to have a
child placed in it. Class B will not be quite as good, and so on
down the line.

But these are all honorable people. The principal and the
teachers are not doing it for their own good, they are doing it for
the good of Culture.

Not even the parents act for their own good. They are acting
for the child's future. To push one's own way through is not
proper, but to do it for the child's good is a Sacred Duty. They
would feel ashamed not to.

The poorest among the parents don't do a thing. They don't
even suspect what is going on. Instead, they feel quite moved. In
their time, up in the country, they could only finish the third grade.

If things are not going so well, it must be that their child is not
cut out for studying. "Even the teacher said so. A real gentleman.
He asked me to sit down. He showed me the record book. And a
test all covered with red marks. I guess we just weren't blessed
with an intelligent boy. He will go to work in the fields, like us."

* * *

Let us start all over, this time with numbers. Giancarlo took on
himself the job of compiling statistics. He is fifteen years old. He
is another of those country boys pronounced by you to be unfit
for studying.

With us he runs smoothly. He has been engulfed in these figures
for four months now. Even math has stopped being dry for him.

The educational miracle we have performed on him comes out
of a very clear prescription.

We offered him the chance to study for a noble aim: to feel
himself a brother to 1,031,000 who were flunked,[2] as he was,
and to taste the joys of revenge for himself and for all of them.

* * *

[2] Flunked from the compulsory school during the school year 1963–64.
*This footnote and those that follow were provided by the young authors
of the book so that their peasant parents and others would be certain to
understand.*—Ed.

Schools have a single problem. The children they lose. The Giannis.

Your "compulsory school" loses 462,000 children per year. This being the case, the only incompetents in the matter of school are you who lose so many and don't go back to find them. Not we: we find them in the fields and factories and we know them at close range.

Gianni's mother, who doesn't know how to read, can see what the problems of the school are. And so will anybody who knows the pain endured by a child when he fails, and who has enough patience to look through the statistics.

Then these figures will begin to scream in your face. They say that the Giannis run into millions and that you are either stupid or evil.*

*   *   *

Let us drop in on a first grade on the first day of school, in October. Thirty-two students are there. At a glance they all seem alike. In reality there are five repeaters among them.

Seven years old, aprons and ribbons, yet already stamped "retarded," which will cost them dearly later on in the intermediate.

In the following October the teacher† of the second grade again finds thirty-two children in her classroom. She sees twenty-six familiar faces and feels at home again among *her own*, whom she has come to love.

A bit later she spots the six new students. Five are repeating the grade. One of these has already repeated twice; he is almost nine years old.

The sixth new face is Pierino,[3] the doctor's son.

* Here follows a statistical analysis of the flunking and dropout patterns in the Italian schools, demonstrating a powerful discrimination against the children of the working or farming classes. These are specifically Italian problems. However, the American reader may still be interested in these analyses and calculations as a sample of the way the students at Barbiana were taught always to make their point and base their findings on solid statistical foundations. Because of this serious effort on the part of these children, the Italian Physical Society gave a prize (generally given to promising physicists) to the school of Barbiana after the publication of this book. —Translators' note.

† As a rule, a teacher stays with the same class for a certain number of years in the elementary grades. Throughout the discussion that follows, the elementary school teacher referred to is one that has stayed with her class for all five years.—Translators' note.

[3] In our text Pierino is the symbol of 30,000 children who skip the first grade each year.

The doctor's chromosomes are powerful. Pierino could write when he was only five. He has no need for a first grade. He enters the second at age six. And he can speak like a printed book.

He, too, is already branded, but with the mark of the chosen race.

* * *

By failing the oldest of the children the teachers manage at the same time to hit the poorest.

We have made a survey of the professions of the fathers of those kids who grow old in the elementary schools. The results can be seen in Figures 1 and 2.[4]

Gianni has already reached age fourteen and will have to repeat the first intermediate. At this point, to continue becomes an absurdity. Even if he is passed each time from now on he will finish the intermediate at seventeen.

Boredom in school is at its peak. Work is easy to find.[5] In a few months it will even be legal.

Gianni is well aware that going to work is not all that great, but he does feel like bringing home a pay envelope. He is fed up with being scolded for every penny he spends.

And his parents themselves make their protests with less and less force. To do otherwise, both they and the boy would have to have a very rare ability to persevere—a self-created passion for learning, strong enough to overcome every failure.

A helping hand from you could make the difference. You did stretch out a hand—but to topple him once and for all.

Perhaps that wasn't your intention. The teacher who stuck you with a student too old for your class is certainly guilty as well. The world may also be guilty and, for that matter, so may Gianni himself be guilty.

[4] The data refer to the third, fourth and fifth elementary grades in thirty-five schools of the provinces of Florence, Milan and Mantua for a total of 2,252 students (school years 1965–66, 1966–67).

[5] With the new provision regulating apprenticeship (law of January 1955) the engaging of apprentices has become convenient. In the more technically developed regions, children are sought out even in their homes, while their unskilled fathers may have trouble finding jobs. For instance, in the province of Florence, the city of Prato has a double preeminence: high industrial development and high truancy among school children. See "L'Adempimento dell' Obligo Scholastico." Ufficio Studi della Provincia di Firenze ["The Fulfilling of the Compulsory School System." Center for Studies of the County of Florence] 1966.

Figure 1

SLAUGHTER OF THE POOR

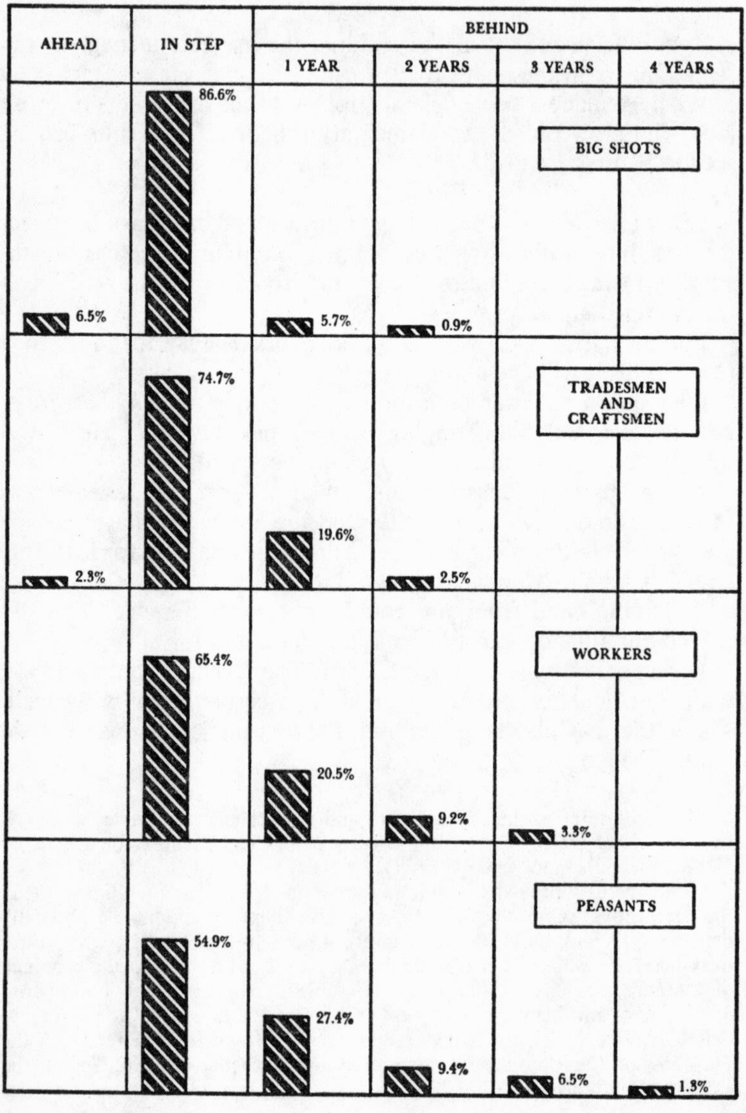

AHEAD	IN STEP	BEHIND			
		1 YEAR	2 YEARS	3 YEARS	4 YEARS
6.5%	86.6%	5.7%	0.9%	BIG SHOTS	
2.3%	74.7%	19.6%	2.5%	TRADESMEN AND CRAFTSMEN	
	65.4%	20.5%	9.2%	3.3%	WORKERS
	54.9%	27.4%	9.4%	6.5%	PEASANTS · 1.3%

Figure 2

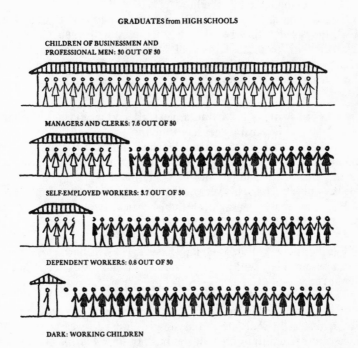

FATHER'S PROFESSION

GRADUATES from HIGH SCHOOLS

CHILDREN OF BUSINESSMEN AND
PROFESSIONAL MEN: 30 OUT OF 30

MANAGERS AND CLERKS: 7.6 OUT OF 30

SELF-EMPLOYED WORKERS: 3.7 OUT OF 30

DEPENDENT WORKERS: 0.8 OUT OF 30

DARK: WORKING CHILDREN

But when you see a little boy behind the counter of a vegetable stand, I would hate to be in your shoes knowing that I was the one who had flunked him.

If only you were able to say, "Why don't you come back to school? I've passed you, just so that you can come back. Without you, school somehow has lost its flavor."

We may seem to be implying the existence of some master who manipulates you. Someone who has cut the schools to measure.

Does he really exist? Is there a handful of men gathered around a table, holding all the strings in their hands: banks, business, political machines, the press, fashions?

We don't know. If we claim this, we feel our book takes on a certain mystery-story tone. If we don't, we seem to play the simpleton. It is like arguing that so many little gears have fallen into place by chance. Out sprang an armored car able to make war all by itself, with no driver.

Perhaps the life story of "Pierino" can give us a key. So, let us try to take a loving look at his family.

The doctor and his wife are up there on top of things. They read, they travel, they see friends, they play with their child, they take time to keep close track of him and they even do it well. Their house is full of books and culture. At five I had mastered the shovel; Pierino, the pencil.

*   *   *

As it began, so it continues, year after year. Pierino is always promoted and he hardly does any studying.

I fight my way through with clenched teeth, and I fail. He also manages to have time for sports, meetings of the Azione Cattolica,[6] or the Giovane Italia[7] or the F. G. Comunista,[8] as well as time for his puberty crisis, his year of the blues and his year of rebellion.

He is less mature at eighteen than I was at twelve. But he keeps going ahead. He will graduate with full honors. . . .

Pierino, then, will become a professor. He will find a wife much like himself. They will produce another Pierino. More of a Pierino than ever.

Thirty thousand such stories every year.

If we consider Pierino's mother in herself, she is no wild beast. She is just a bit selfish. She has simply shut her eyes to the existence of other children, though she has not kept Pierino from meeting other Pierinos. She and her husband are surrounded by other intellectuals. Clearly, they don't want to change.

As to the thirty-one mothers of Pierino's schoolmates, either they don't have time or they don't know any better. They hold jobs which pay so little that to make ends meet they have to work from childhood to old age and from dawn to night.

But *she* was able to go to school until she was twenty-four. Besides, she was helped at home by one of those thirty-one other mothers—the mother of some Gianni who neglected her own son while doing the housework for Pierino's mother.

All the free time she gets to pursue her interests—is it a gift from the poor or is it a theft by the rich? Why doesn't she share it?

---

[6] Catholic Action, the name of a Catholic political movement.
[7] Young Italy; today it is a young Fascists' organization.
[8] Federation of Young Communists.

To conclude the subject of Pierino's mamma, she is neither a beast nor is she an innocent. If we add up thousands of small selfish attitudes like hers, we get the total selfishness of a whole class, claiming for itself the lion's share.

It is a class that has not hesitated to unleash fascism, racism, war, unemployment. If it became necessary to "change everything so that nothing would change,"[9] it would not hesitate to embrace communism.

No one can know the precise mechanism—but when every law seems to cut to measure in order to serve Pierino and screw us, we have difficulty believing in change.

* * *

Career, culture, family, the good name of the school: you are using tiny sets of scales for grading your students. They really are petty. Too small to fill the life of a teacher.

Some among you have understood, but cannot find a way out. Always in fear of the sacred word. And yet, there is no choice. Nothing but politics can fill the life of a man of today.

In Africa, in Asia, in Latin America, in southern Italy, in the hills, in the fields, even in the cities, millions of children are waiting to be made equal. Shy, like me; stupid, like Sandro; lazy, like Gianni. The best of humanity.

[9] The phrase in quotation marks is from [Giuseppe di Lampedusa's] novel *The Leopard*. It is said by a Sicilian prince upon the arrival of the Garibaldi movement (1860). Later, he himself becomes a *garibaldino* and thus loses neither his money nor his power.

4 Preparing Girls and Boys for a Consuming-Producing Society

If the function of school racism-classism is to program the non-white and the poor for failure and, moreover, to convince them that they fail because of their own inadequacies, then the function of school sexism is to program girls for certain relatively powerless adult roles and, moreover, to convince them that these roles constitute their most cherished heart's desires. Both school racism and school sexism help children to grow up as deeply damaged human beings and to believe in the one case that the damage is their sin and in the other that it is their virtue.

Unlike the institution of school racism, however, which is so overt that one must be either very innocent or very arrogant to deny it, the institution of school sexism is barely recognized, even by many of its victims. Almost all racial-minority people and even many well-to-do whites suspect or understand how school programs nonwhite and poor children for failure. But very few women and fewer men understand how schools program girls to become poorer, less powerful, less respected, and less self-respecting adults than their boy classmates.

The mere facts of school sexism have been greatly obscured by myths about the "true nature" of women and men and girls and boys. Thus, a good deal of the literature on sexism in schools that has come out of the women's movement has had to devote itself merely to demonstrating the myriad ways in which schools discriminate between boys and girls to the latter's extreme detriment. (As many feminists are quick to point out, men are also damaged by sexism, just as whites are also damaged by racism. From the viewpoint of redressing old grievances, however, it seems logical and fair to concentrate first on the greater damage to the more oppressed class.)

Betty Levy's landmark study, here reproduced in its entirety, goes beyond such mere adducing of evidence. Enormous difficulties in discovering and overcoming school sexism are presented by popular uncertainties as to what are indeed the inherited or biological nonphysical differences between boys and girls. That is, most observers, when presented with discrimination between boys and girls, are inclined to say, "Well, there *are* basic born differences between males and females, always, in all cultures, and among all species." However, what these are and whether they are constant across cultures and across species the present state of our knowledge does not tell us for certain. Taking the history of the study of race differences as a guide, we might guess that two to four decades of scholarly work will begin to give us some better insights into these matters.

In the meantime, Levy's study begins to draw together the evidence we already have of how—regardless of born differences—nurturing practices create or enlarge sex differences. With respect to schools, this study demonstrates how specific school practices help to create certain specific and known traits generally regarded as typically (or genetically) female. It also draws our attention to a well-documented but little-analyzed phenomenon with respect to school learning and school behavior: Little girls are relatively good in school and learn relatively fast by comparison with little boys. (Evidence that the opposite is true in Germany and Japan would seem to throw doubt on the "natural development" explanation for this phenomenon.) We may speculate that, as in the case of analogous differences between low-status children and white middle-class children, bad behavior and slow learning versus good behavior and fast learning are related to susceptibility to alienation training; that is, alienation training "takes" better on girls and middle-class children than on boys and poor or nonwhite children.

Hank Ketcham unwittingly illustrated this part of the Levy article months before it was published.

"Decision of the Board of Education: No Freedom of Choice

. . ." tells about one girl who resisted blatant sex discrimination. " 'Now You See,' Said Mark" focuses on the primary-school reader as an instrument of sexist indoctrination and preparation of boys and girls for their destined roles in our consuming society.

"Fact Sheet on the Earnings Gap" demonstrates that instilling a self-image of impotence in girl children pays off in the market-place of prestige and money in which the adult "girls" earn their livelihood. And Chapter 7, "The Teachers: Fulcrum of the System," illustrates that, as most elementary teachers are women, instilling traits of passivity and compliance in girl children helps to reproduce in each new generation the sex-dominance patterns of the previous generation.

"IT'S EASY ENOUGH FOR YOU TO LEARN TO READ! YOU'RE NOT AS *BUSY* AS I AM!"

The School's Role in the Sex-Role Stereotyping of Girls: A Feminist Review of the Literature

by Betty Levy

The renewed feminist critique of traditional sex roles requires that we examine where and how these roles are learned. This article will review research studies, informal reports and speculative writings that bear on the school's role in elaborating and reinforcing damaging sex roles.

Developmental psychologists have tended to assume a "separate but equal" approach in their studies of sex roles. That is, implicit in most discussions of sex roles is the assumption that "girls learn their girl role" and "boys learn their boy role" in a relatively benign social context. There is little concern with the *content* of sex roles or the consequences of "appropriately" feminine and masculine characteristics for the psychological health, self-actualization, and achievement of women and men; the political and cultural realities of male-dominated society are ignored or minimized, and certainly left unchallenged. Most developmental studies, then, accept traditional sex roles as "given" and merely attempt to discover at what age "sex role appropriate" learning occurs. However, even within the context of "descriptive neutrality" (read "traditional sexism") certain findings are relevant to the present discussion:

1. Children learn the content ascribed to sex roles at an early age. The male-female distinction is clear to children beginning at about age two and is one of the earliest concepts they learn.[1] By the preschool years, children not only know which sex they are but know the behavior patterns, play preferences, and psychological characteristics expected of them.[2]

2. As children grow older their awareness of "appropriate" sex-role behavior increases and becomes more restricted and stereo-

From *Feminist Studies*, Vol. 1, No. 1 (Summer, 1972). Reprinted by permission. Notes appear on pp. 132-33.

typed.[3] However, boys are more aware of the female role than girls are of the male role, which suggests the presence of sex-role avoidance in boys.[4]

3. Both girls and boys increasingly value and prefer the male role. Fifteen of the twenty studies of sex-role acceptance reviewed by Oetzel[5] showed greater sex-role acceptance by males, supporting Brown's[6] suggestion that the wide latitude given to girls in expressing preference for masculine activities is due to the higher status awarded masculine activities. Girls are allowed to be tomboys; boys are censured if they are sissies. These studies also confirm Smith's[7] classic study of 100 boys and girls ages eight to fifteen who "voted" whether girls or boys possessed the greater degree of each of nineteen desirable and fourteen undesirable traits. He reported that with increasing chronological age both boys and girls develop a better opinion of boys and a progressively poorer opinion of girls. Kohlberg's review of early sex stereotypes indicated that both girls and boys learn to attribute more power and prestige to the male role: "At early ages (three–four) the father is not awarded more prestige than the mother, but by ages five–six he is. . . . Girls between the ages of five and eight do not show an increase in preference for same-sex objects and activities, whereas boys do."[8] What these studies do not tell us is *how* children learn to ascribe different values to male and female roles, and, ultimately, to view the female role as inferior.

4. Studies of adults reveal that both females and males think it preferable to be male and to have male children. A 1946 survey by *Fortune* magazine found that while 91 percent of the men would want to be males if they could be born again, 25 percent of the women would prefer to be male.[9] According to a 1955 Gallup poll, between five and twelve times as many women as men recall having wished they were of the opposite sex. Similarly, a mass of evidence demonstrates that American parents tend to prefer boys. More mothers of girls have post partum depression than do mothers of boys; pregnant women dream twice as often about male babies; mothers who have only daughters are happier about a new pregnancy than are mothers of sons; if the first child is a boy the interval before a second child is conceived is longer than if the first child is a girl; and the likelihood of having a third child is greater if the first two children both are girls than if they both are boys.[10]

5. The sex-role training of girls involves less tolerance for

aggressive behavior and greater permission and even encouragement of dependency.[11] Competence, independence, objectivity, logical thinking, self-assertiveness, and self-confidence all are stereotypically attributed to and reinforced in males, while emotional expressiveness, sensitivity to others, as well as incompetence, dependence, subjectivity, poor logic, submissiveness, and lack of self-confidence are stereotypically attributed to and reinforced in females.[12]

The remainder of this paper will discuss how schools function to reinforce these attitudes and behavior and thus perpetuate existing inequalities between the sexes.

Educational researchers and critics of the schools recently have demonstrated the contradiction between what schools *say* they do and what they *actually* do. The ostensible purpose of schools is to educate. Liberal reformers who accept this purpose at face value bemoan the fact that schools are "failing," i.e., not educating. Silberman[13] indicts the "mindlessness" of school personnel for the "grim, joyless and oppressive" classrooms. More sophisticated analysts move beyond the stated purpose of schools to examine their actual and multiple functions. In an important essay, Reimer writes:

> Schools in all nations, of all kinds, at all levels, combine four distinct social functions: custodial care, social-role selection, indoctrination, and education as usually defined in terms of the development of skills and knowledge. . . . It is the conflict among these functions which makes schools inefficient. It is the combination of these functions which tends to make the school a total institution . . . and which makes it such an effective instrument of social control.[14]

Reimer describes the institutional values of conformity, dependence on others for learning, and hierarchy or social stratification. The revolutionary Brazilian educator Freire asserts that there is no "neutral" education: education is either for "domination" or for "freedom."[15] Most schools, he contends, effectively "domesticate" and "pacify" the masses, since they transfer "prepossessed and predigested reality," divorced from both its origins and its uses. Illich[16] has focused on the "hidden curriculum" of the school, the structure of the school as opposed to what happens in schools. Friedenberg has noted: "In school . . . it is indeed true that the medium is the message . . . what is taught isn't as important as learning how you have to act in society, how other people will treat you, how they will respond to you, what the limits of respect that will be accorded to you really are."[17] Wasserman[18] contrasts the educational mythologies with the realities of education for oppression. She maintains that the current crisis in schools is created by the increasing incompatibility between the stated educational function and the unstated socialization, job selection, and indoctrination functions.

Looking more closely at how this incompatibility is revealed in schools, Jackson[19] describes the conflict between the demands of institutional conformity—i.e. between learning to be passive and to acquiesce to the network of rules, regulations and routines, and meeting the demands of intellectual scholarship. Holt[20] describes how the classroom discourages thinking and intellectual risk-taking. The reason why students "fail" at learning is because they "succeed" in mastering coping strategies to meet the institution's demands. Students trained in "answer-grabbing" and "teacher-pleasing" do not become critical thinkers. Silberman[21] empirically confirmed Holt's classroom observations and found a correlation between fifth graders' desire for teacher approval and their rejection of intellectual challenges. Other studies indicate that not only do children respond to institutional reward structures, but they often are more aware of institutional demands than they are of the requirements of learning itself. White,[22] for example, found that elementary school pupils have no "cognitive map of content" to help them perceive connections between subjects, but rather they have a "map of school experience"—that is, work and evaluation demands of the teachers. In a comparative study of elementary schools in four urban neighborhods, Leacock[23] found that children consistently reflected a stronger emphasis on "good behavior" than on "good work" when they were interviewed about what they thought their teachers wanted.

All students must learn to adapt to these oppressive demands of schools. Beyond this common socialization, however, are experiential differences of class, race, and sex. Rather than providing "equality of opportunity" for all students, schools in fact perpetuate existing inequalities in our society. Grannis[24] in a ground-breaking article, offers three models he believes typify American schools and describes the effects these different structures have on children's behavior and social-role training. In the "factory model" school, working-class children are taught in highly authoritarian, routinized, and rigid, hierarchically organized patterns that emphasize assignments, recitation, and rote learning. These children are socialized to accept monotonous factory and white-collar jobs. In the "corporate model" school, suburban middle-class children are taught in non-graded, team-teaching, highly "rationalized" instructional situations preparing them for the coldly task-oriented team and committee aspects of corporate life. The third model, the "family school," similar to the British infant school model in its concern for the whole life of the child, is said to typify only nursery schools. None of these models has been demonstrated to be "better" for raising students' achievement, but both the "factory" and the "corporate" models effectively perpetuate class differences by initiating pupils into a conception of work fitting their "proper place" in society.

Within schools, the two major mechanisms for perpetuating social distinctions are "tracking" and "teacher's expectations." In a thorough critique of urban schools, Rothstein[25] describes tracking, or the formal mechanisms by which certain types of students (particularly women, minority group and working-class students) are channeled into educational tracks, leading to dead-end and low-paying jobs. Rosenthal and Jacobson[26] introduced the concept of "teacher's expectations," of the interpersonal self-fulfilling prophecies that operate in the classroom and affect students' performance. Post-Pygmalion studies support the existence of this phenomenon and reveal the way teachers "expect" and then obtain differential performance from lower-class and minority-group students.[27]

In summary, schools promote an ideology of equality, but in reality they perpetuate inequality; schools profess that "learning" is their major purpose, but "teach" institutional conformity and non-thinking.

Most of the above remarks concerning the functions of schools are by now familiar and well worn. What the critics have failed to examine, however, is how the traditional demands of the schools function to perpetuate traditional sex roles. Elementary schools reinforce girls' training for obedience, social and emotional dependence, and docility. That girls on the whole like school better than boys[28] and perform better in most respects[29] may be due in part to the consistency of the sex-role demands of home and school. At the secondary school level, passive learning continues to be rewarded or no intellectual demands are made on girls; and it is expected that girls' education is chiefly a preparation for marriage and child-rearing. The prevalence of "role conflict" and decreased intellectual performance among many bright high school and college women is the result.[30]

The early socialization of girls towards obedience and approval-seeking predisposes them to accept more readily the school's demands of conformity to rules and "doing what you are told." Observations by Crandall et al.[31] of children during free play suggest that girls' more than boys' achievement in elementary school, but not in preschool, was more affected by their need for parent and teacher approval. Stein[32] tested Crandall's findings in a controlled reinforcement situation and found that while girls did not perform better if praised, they were more affected than boys by disapproval. Tulkin et al.[33] found that fifth- and sixth-grade "high-need-for-approval" girls were the most popular, whereas "high-need-for-approval" boys were the least popular. Furthermore, girls' awareness that they are less valued than boys also may contribute to their conforming, dependent behavior. Kohlberg[34] states that girls reach the "good-girl" stage of moral development earlier than boys, and stay there longer. He suggests that this is because girls are forced to distinguish between the "prestige of goodness" and the "prestige of power" in sex-role learning. Perhaps this means that girls learn that if they *have* to be a girl, they had better be a "good" one, since they have little else going for them.

"[The girl] internalizes a definition of maturity which is the early acceptance of quietness, obedience, and poise. Because these are character traits instilled in her from the time she is one, and because they correspond to the demands of the school system, she often does better in school. Which is why she's called more mature."[35]

The schools' emphasis on neatness, order, punctuality, and performance of often meaningless and monotonous tasks is an important part of the "domesticating" function of schools, particularly in the case of girls. Hartley has presented evidence that developmentally the traditional housekeeping aspect of the female sex role is the most thoroughly learned. Noting girls' imitation of domestic activities as well as their unhindered access to tools (both real and play) of the domestic trade at home and at school, he concludes: "The definition of this aspect of the female sex role seems to proceed without interruption and with continuous reinforcements, almost from the cradle on."[36] More recently, Poloma and Garland[37] presented evidence supporting a "toleration of domestication" hypothesis for married professional women; that is, even in dual-career marriages the woman has been so thoroughly trained in her domestic function that she puts her family role before her professional role, will often discontinue work because of family demands, and often does not perceive these choices forced upon her as discriminatory.

We need to know how the "domestication" of girls is strengthened in school. Do, in fact, teachers reward girls' docility and conforming behavior more than boys'? How do teachers respond to girls' needs for approval relative to boys'? What characterizes "mature" versus "immature" girls in the eyes of the teacher? How do teachers react to "inappropriately socialized" girls? What are the subtle ways in which girls are channeled into "feminine" interests and activities?

There is a triple aspect to sexist accounts of the effects of elementary schools on sex roles. First, there is more concern for what happens to boys than for what happens to girls. Second, female teachers are blamed for "feminizing" boys. Third, these biased studies rest on assumptions of inappropriately traditional sex-role stereotypes. Lest the charge of "sexism" appear too strong, the following representative quotation is offered: "Countless teachers, the overwhelming majority of whom are women, expect boy pupils to behave, react, and learn like girls. Even though frequently unaware of it, many of these women value neatness and cleanliness above individual initiative. They prefer conformity, mental passivity, and gentle obedience—at which girls excel—to the aggressive drive and originality of many boys."[38]

Sexton has decried the schools' "feminizing" influence on boys. She writes: "The school is too much a woman's world, governed by women's rules and standards. . . . The subject matter seems all too frilly and feminized. . . . Though the boy must learn to be his own authority, the school insists that he obey its authority. . . . This is not good preparation for real manhood."[39] By implication, the schools' "feminization" or "domestication" training *is* good preparation for "real womanhood." The fact that girls are being doubly trained—at home and at school—to be docile and conforming is not of concern. What is of concern is that boys might be treated badly in school, that is, "like girls." The fact that the school as an institution demands conformity and obedience of both sexes is not discussed. The fact that most schools are oppressive places for most children is not noted. Rather, female teachers are labelled the enemy in the destruction of male minds.

Evidence supporting the "inappropriate treatment of boys" hypothesis comes mainly from two sources. First are studies that claim that children perceive the elementary school as a "feminine" environment. Kagan[40] and Kellogg[41] showed that primary school girls and boys tend to label school objects as "feminine." This sex-typing was not a clear-cut trend, however, as boys labelled fewer objects "feminine" than did girls, and certain objects more frequently were associated with males than females.

Second, much evidence has been marshalled to demonstrate female teachers' discrimination against boys. A much-quoted study by Meyer and Thompson[42] found that sixth-grade boys received more disapproval or blame contacts from their teachers than did girls. Jackson and Lahaderne[43] found that boys received eight to ten times more prohibitory messages (order-keeping and mis-behavior-punishing messages) than girls. Yet, in three of the four classrooms observed, boys received more than their share of all types of interactions with the teacher. The researchers concluded that the teachers used instructional and managerial interactions with boys as "devious strategies for social control." In their review of the literature, Sears and Feldman[44] suggest that while boys, in general, receive more teacher disapproval in the lower grades than do girls, girls receive more approval for conformity, and interact less with their teachers. Thus, rather than being discriminated against, boys appear to be more intense or salient stimuli for teachers, and they receive more attention from them while girls either are ignored or rewarded for conformity and obedience.

Other recent studies support this hypothesis of boys' saliency in the eyes of the teacher. In contrast to earlier claims of female teachers' bias against boys during reading instruction, Davis and Slobodian[45] found that female first-grade teachers did *not* discriminate against boys or favor girls during reading periods. Good's and Brophy's recent findings[46] support the same conclusion. Moreover, Felsenthal[47] found that female first-grade teachers interacted more with boys in both positive and negative ways and tended to call on volunteering boys more than volunteering girls during reading instruction. Preliminary findings from the Columbia Classroom Environments Project[48] indicate that in second-grade classrooms, boys more than girls are "off-task" in daily activities, are more "controlled" by their teachers, but also receive more teaching time, more skill work, and more individual tutorial attention. Add to this Torrance's earlier finding[49] that teachers say they reward the creative behavior of boys three times as often as they do the creative behavior of girls and the "message" to girls becomes clear—be quiet, be good, be conforming; originality, self-assertion, and "center stage" activities are reserved for boys.

One study which indicated that nursery school teachers reward both girls and boys for traditionally "female" play activities was reported by Fagot and Patterson.[50] The so-called feminine behaviors included painting, art work, playing with dolls and the doll house, playing in the kitchen, and listening to stories; while so-called masculine behaviors included playing with building blocks and transportation toys, climbing, and riding tricycles. Observing three-year-olds in two nursery classes intermittently for a year, they found that teachers reinforced girls 363 times for sex-typed behaviors, and 353 of these were for "feminine" behaviors. They reinforced boys less for sex-typed behavior (232 times) but 199 of these were for "feminine" behaviors. However the boys' peer reinforcement apparently overcame the teachers' so-called feminizing influence since the boys did not become more "feminine" in their behavior preferences over the year. The researchers do not comment on the 3:2 ratio of sex-typed reinforcements given to girls or mention what effect the girls' peer group had on what apparently is a more intense sex-typing of female children.

Many studies have demonstrated that teachers discipline boys more harshly than girls,[51] and that the majority of teachers' "behavior problems" are boys.[52] Westbrook[53] confirmed earlier studies that indicated that teachers are more disapproving of extroverted behavior (impertinence, disobedience, interrupting, etc.) than of introverted behavior (fearfulness, shyness, sensitiveness). Yet, clinicians view introverted or withdrawal tendencies as being more serious.[54] Ullman[55] studied differences between girls and boys in school adjustment and observed that boys tended to act out while girls turned their conflicts on to themselves. He concluded that although teachers rate girls as being better adjusted, they do so uncritical of the standard of adjustment and unaware of the way in which girls are making their so-called adjustment. Interpretations of school adjustment research usually are along the lines of Sexton's concerns that boys are being "emasculated" by their female teachers,[56] rather than that girls, by being allowed and encouraged to turn their anger against themselves, perhaps are being less noticeably but more seriously damaged. Furthermore, a boy harshly yelled at from across the room may temporarily feel put down, but also may learn to defend and assert himself.

Bardwick[57] speculates that a boy learns in school that he can get attention and respect for non-conforming behavior, both from his teacher and his peers. Thus, teacher criticism, a seemingly negative response, may actually lead boys towards greater independence, autonomy, and activity. Spaulding found[58] that, compared to boys, a disproportionate number of teachers' negative remarks to girls concerned incorrect answers, a pattern that could only reinforce girls' sense of inferiority. If teacher criticism of girls is less harsh than criticism of boys, as Spaulding indicates, it may be even more difficult for girls to learn to fight back. The girl who is reassuringly (patronizingly?) told that everything will be all right, while the teacher supportingly (controllingly?) has her/his arm around her, is less likely to develop self-assertive behaviors that carry the risk of disapproval.

Other evidence indicates that even by the preschool years, boys tend to make more realistic achievement assessments than do girls.[59] Perhaps the criticism boys receive tends to be more task-oriented, helping them better to evaluate their skills. Girls may be receiving more general and more personal criticism. This latter type of criticism discourages what Minuchin[60] calls "self-differentiation . . . or . . . increasingly refined perceptions of one's patterns of strengths and deficits," and may lead to an oversensitivity to criticism and to doing tasks in order to gain social approval rather than to meet one's own standards.

One solution often proposed for the "feminization" of males is to place more adult male teachers in the primary grades. The evidence in support of this position is scanty. First, research on imitation learning and sex-identification has not shown a clear-cut trend for same-sex models to promote sex-typed behaviors. In fact, many researchers conclude[61] that the father, rather than the mother, is the major socializer of "sex-appropriate" behavior for both boys and girls. It is not at all clear whether the sex of the teacher-model has an influence distinct from cultural sex-role definitions and the institutional demands of the school which probably are shared and communicated equally by both male and female teachers. Comparing children in male-taught and female-taught kindergartens, Brody and Laosa found no evidence that the sex of the teacher was associated with girls' and boys' scores on sex-role measures, toy, game and occupation choice measures, sex-typing of school objects, or achievement strivings. They conclude: "The fears of Sexton and others about boys being 'feminized' seem clearly unfounded. There is no need to believe that female teachers cannot handle boys adequately simply because they are female, nor any reason to expect that the presence of a male teacher will have any dramatic effect on children of either sex."[62]

One way in which traditional sex roles *are* reinforced is through the authority structure of the school itself. Eighty-five percent of all elementary school teachers are women; 78 percent of all elementary school principals are men.[63] School children do not need to be taught the differential status of men and women—they learn it simply by attending school. It would be interesting to determine empirically what effect, if any, elementary schools that employ women and men on an equal basis in all positions, have on children's ideas of sex roles.

Another mechanism of sex-role reinforcement is segregated classes and activities. A number of primary-grade schools have been "experimenting" with sex-segregated classes. The teachers write glowingly of programs "specifically tailored to the needs of each sex." The all-boy classes emphasize large-muscle physical activity, team games, building, repairing and other tasks "ordinarily performed by fathers," arts and crafts with wood, rock, clay, and other "male" materials. The all-girl classes include activities such as "dressing up like mother and playing house," and playing with crayons, paper, and pasting materials. Although they noted that "in the mixed group which stressed masculinity, the girls seemed to enjoy the program as much as the boys," these informal reports did not discuss the varied needs of children or concern themselves with the rigid role definitions they impose on girls and boys by restricting their activities.[64]

Within unsegregated classes certain activities such as cooking and sewing are encouraged primarily for girls and other activities such as woodwork and mechanical work are encouraged primarily for boys. Physical education and playground activities frequently are sex-segregated. Even in "free schools" where there is no conscious attempt to sex-type, the policy of allowing children to "follow their own interests" usually results in condoning the pervasive sex-typed activities the children have learned outside the school. Effective "open classrooms," while basically non-interventionist, still require children to master basic skills. But intervening to require non-sex-typed choices and activities and more "sex-role-free" flexibility has not yet become one of "open classroom" concerns.

As children move through elementary school, certain subjects such as English come to be regarded as "girls' subjects" while math and science are perceived as "boys' subjects." Stein and Smithells[65] found that school children's sex-typing of these activities progressively became more rigid. The mechanisms by which this sex-typing occurs were not investigated in their study, but clearly they are of concern and should be studied.

There are a number of descriptive studies of sex-typing in elementary school reading materials. A 1946 study of third-grade readers found striking differences in the treatment of the sexes. Females were portrayed as "sociable and kind, but helpless, inactive, and uncreative" while males were portrayed as "the bearers of knowledge and wisdom."[66] More recently, a 1971 study, also of third-grade readers, reported a similar picture. The characteristics of the females in the stories reviewed closely resembled Jenkin's and Vroegh's[67] "most feminine woman imaginable"—appreciative, affectionate, charming, considerate. The range of occupations of the females is even more limited than the real restriction of women in the work force.[68] A thorough study of twelve elementary school reader series and award-winning trade books revealed a heavy preponderance of boys' stories "in which boys are portrayed as smarter than girls, with greater initiative and achievement" and girls often are portrayed as "younger sister ninnies" who have mishaps and need to be helped. Men assume a variety of roles in the stories and, if fathers, play creatively with their children. Women almost exclusively are portrayed as mothers and teachers. Mothers are "forever wearing aprons" and are cast in supportive, passive roles.[69] A recent survey of trade books for young children revealed "the general image of the female ranges from dull to degrading to invisible."[70]

Children's readers are not the only culprits. An analysis of mathematics textbooks in New York City school libraries revealed that even math problems are presented in social contexts which reinforce sex-role stereotypes. In one series, for example, women and girls shop, cook, sew, and get sick; while men and boys build things, drive cars, go camping, and earn money.[71] Sex-typing in elementary social studies books also has been examined,[72] and studies in other subject areas very likely would show that traditional sex-role stereotypes are imbedded in all school materials, songs, games, posters, educational films, and so on—all of which teach girls and boys "what's expected." As yet there are no studies of the effect of sex-typed school materials on the self-concepts, career aspirations, and achievements of girls.

The teachers' separation of boys and girls for seating, lining-up, hanging up coats and so on also calls attention to sex distinctions and sex roles (e.g., "Girls line up first."); the choice of class helpers also teaches sex roles ("Boys, move the chairs"; "Girls, water the plants"). The protocols of a microanalysis of a single urban classroom were filled with such comments. At one point the teacher requested a boy for a thumb-tacking job because "it's difficult for girls to climb up."[73] And after calling on three boys in a row who were unable to answer a question, the teacher asked, "Do I have to call on a girl?"[74] Such behaviors daily elaborate and reinforce traditional sex roles, yet no classroom observations studies have focused specifically on interactions of this type.

Studies of "expectancy effects" concerning how teachers' expectations of sex-role behaviors operate in the classroom have not been conducted. Specific areas that call for examination include differential expectations about the interests and competences of girls and boys, differences in disciplining them, and types of activities of girls and boys strongly rewarded or punished. Furthermore, we need to know how teachers differentially perceive and stereotype the same behaviors of girls and boys. Are there differences between girls and boys in behaviors represented by labels such as "withdrawn," "aggressive," and so on? How then do teachers *react* to these differences?

Although there have been many studies of elementary school children's sex-role conceptions and preferences, there are few data on whether or not they differentially perceive the same behaviors in girls and boys. How rigidly do children require compliance to traditional sex-role standards? How do children perceive the school demands on them for "sex-appropriate" behaviors? What is the association of level of cognitive development to stereotyping?

A few studies indicate that sex roles are not immutable but can be changed with a change in the school environment. Minuchin[75] compared 100 middle-class fourth graders in a "traditional" school and a "modern" school. She found that in the modern school, which had more flexible attitudes about sex roles, girls showed less concern for approval than in the traditional school. Modern school girls also were found to be as competent as boys in problem-solving, whereas in the traditional school the boys were better problem-solvers. Since sex differences in "need-for-approval" and problem-solving skills are not measurably great before elementary school, it is not clear to what extent these differences can be attributed to differences between schools. Joffee[76] reported a participant-observation study of a nursery school in which the general attitudes towards sex roles were a de-emphasis on sex-typed behavior and an accepting, relaxed attitude towards "violations" of traditional sex roles. There were no indications of sex or sex role in the activities or structure of the school—even bathrooms were shared. All the children knew their correct gender identity, but "there did not exist among the children any patterned recognition of appropriate sex roles; the children as a group did not perceive certain activities or modes of behavior as being the exclusive property of one sex." The only instances in which sex differences were invoked by the children were as reciprocal "last ditch attempts at behavior control"—that is, yelling "boys only" or "girls only" to maintain control of an activity, area, or toy.

Other exploratory studies are revealing. Chasen[77] found that after two months of a short daily reading program designed to raise career aspirations, preschool girls indicated more range of response to the question "What do you want to be when you grow up?" Selcer[78] found fewer sex-role stereotypes among children from women's liberation and non-mainstream families than among children from Orthodox Jewish families on three measures—toy preference, sex-role-stereotype questionnaire, and the question "What are the differences between girls and boys?" The free play behaviors of these children also indicated rigid sex-typed play in the Orthodox Jewish nursery school and relatively non-sex-typed play in the women's liberation nurseries. As more day care centers are created for young children and as feminists press for changes in primary education, more programs designed to expand role flexibility for girls and boys will be created. But the research validation of such programs has barely begun. We need to know much more about the effects of broad social changes in sex roles on the sex-role definitions, expectations and behaviors of girls and boys.

The same male-dominated authority structure, sex-segregated courses and programs and conventional sex-typing in textbooks, and the sex-role stereotyping of the teachers of elementary schools also is found at the secondary school level. Counselors guide female students into "feminine" occupations and tend to assume the girls desire marriage more than in fact they do.[79] A thorough documentation of the sex bias against women in New York City vocational and technical high schools and the misrepresentation of women in high school textbooks was reported by the New York City Chapter of the National Organization of Women.[80] There are more boys' than girls' high schools in New York City. There are more restricted programs and more restricted course offerings within programs for girls in both girls' and co-educational high schools. Two of the four specialized academic high schools only recently began to admit girls and that innovation occurred only after a court battle. As 14-year-old Alice de Rivera, who filed the court suit and won the right to attend Stuyvesant High School, said:

> Aside from being discouraged to study for a career, women are discouraged from preparing for jobs involving anything but secretarial work, beauty care, nursing, cooking, and the fashion industries. . . . This means that if a girl is seeking entrance to a vocational school she is pressured to feel that certain jobs are masculine and others feminine. She is forced to conform to the Board of Education's image of her sex.[81]

And that image is far from liberated. Nationally, more than half of the females in public vocational-education programs are being trained in home economics and about one-third in office practices.[82] Thus by completion of high school the tracking of female students is all but complete and inescapable.

The institutional sexism of high schools is supplemented and reinforced by the attitudes and behaviors of the teachers. A recent exploratory study by Aderer et al.[83] surveyed the sex-role attitudes and classroom behaviors of twenty secondary school teachers in and around New York City. A short form of the Broverman Sex-Role Stereotype Questionnaire—an 82-item bipolar list of traits (e.g., not at all aggressive—very aggressive)—was used to assess teachers' sex-role ideals, but the instructions were changed from the usual form, which asks the respondent to identify sex-role stereotypes to "What do you think an adolescent male or female *should* be like?" The teachers were asked to rate each trait on a scale of 0–70 according to how they thought an adolescent male and an adolescent female should exhibit that trait.

Results indicated that most of the teachers differentiated ideal behaviors by sex. Only 3 of the 19 respondents said all characteristics should be the same for both sexes. For the 16 other teachers, 9 of the 82 items were highly stereotypic (72 percent or more agreement), 21 items were moderately stereotypic (50–74 percent agreement), but no items were equalitarian (i.e., marked "same" for both males and females). The 9 items that were highly stereotypic were the more general characteristics mentioned on the questionnaire. Seventy-five percent or more of the respondents wanted adolescent males to be more masculine, dominant, independent, and assertive, and to be less emotional, ready to cry, and concerned about their appearance. They wanted females to be more feminine, submissive, dependent, unassertive, emotional, ready to cry, and concerned about their appearance. Except for "concern for appearance," the items that were desired for males were those generally considered more socially desirable characteristics.[84]

Classroom observations of these same teachers indicated that many of them acted out their sex-role stereotypes in the classroom. For example, a music teacher taught the boys how to tune their instruments, but tuned the girls' instruments for them. In an English class reviewing for exams, the teacher typically first called on a boy for the answer and then called on a girl for an illustration. When the class became noisy the teacher yelled at the girls for chattering. Although stereotyped in their ideals for adolescent male and female behavior, a few teachers did not treat boys and girls differently or give evidence of sex stereotyping in the classroom. Apparently, these teachers' attitude of "liberal professionalism" (i.e., treat everyone equally) in the classroom prevented our observation of their sex-role stereotypes in practice. These stereotypes are so pervasive and often so subtle (they are, in fact, a "nonconscious ideology")[85] that more sophisticated techniques of observation in and out of the classroom are required to measure students' perceptions of their teachers' attitudes and the effects of these attitudes on the students.

An additional instrument was administered to this same sample of secondary school teachers. Each teacher received brief individual statements about four students, and were instructed to describe how they thought the student would act and how they as teachers would discourage or encourage that student. For each statement, boys' and girls' names were alternated. Results indicated stereotyped responses for each statement. Teachers indicated they would treat a "withdrawn" boy more firmly than a "withdrawn" girl. A "withdrawn" girl would gently be encouraged to participate, whereas a "withdrawn" boy would firmly be made to "crack his shell" and become more assertive. Responding to a statement about a hypothetical "model student," teachers who were asked to describe a female "model student" tended to claim that she couldn't truly be intelligent but was probably "compensating" for something. No such comments appeared in the descriptions of the male "model student." If a student was presented as a "warm person who wants to help people," this characteristic in a girl often was seen as incompatible with academic ability and as implying specific vocational goals (teaching, nursing, social work). A "warm-and-helpful" boy was perceived either as a potential behavior problem because of his interest in others' business, or as potentially helpful academically to others. In other words, warmth and helpfulness—traditionally "feminine" characteristics—were perceived as having social-emotional consequences when displayed by girls and as having positive academic consequences when displayed by boys. Teachers responding to a "competent student interested in math and science" indicated they would encourage the student, if a boy, to build on that interest and encourage it in other areas; but if the student were a girl they expressed concern that she develop competences in areas besides mathematics and science to avoid becoming "lopsided." Despite the claims of our respondents that they "treated all students fairly and equally," the differential evaluation according to sex-role stereotypes was evident. That these responses appeared in such a small sample simply underscores their all-pervasiveness.

A recent study by Gaite[86] explores perceptions of ideal male and ideal female students. Teachers were given short descriptions of male or female students and were asked to imagine what these students' future lives would be like. Results indicated a greater and wider range of expectations for male students; teachers rarely expected females to be involved in anything other than marriage and child-rearing.

There are, then, a few studies documenting sex-role stereotypes in the "expectations" teachers have for their male and female

students. Intervention studies designed to change these expectations have yet to be attempted.

Concluding Remarks

The first phase of the renewed feminist wave of criticism, analysis
and polemic, seems to have peaked, and the difficult application of
feminist analysis to the traditionally male-biased social sciences
barely has begun. Studies of "sex-role socialization" typically have
accepted the *content* of sex roles as given and have attempted to
clarify the variables affecting the learning *process* along sex-role
lines. This objectification and reification of sex roles has prevented
our understanding of how sex-role learning is taught and elabo-
rated in patriarchal society. That "appropriate" sex-role learning
for girls, while functional to the maintenance of male-dominated
society, is detrimental to girls' psychological development has often
been acknowledged. But this fact has been overlooked in the over-
riding concern that schools might be "emasculating our boys."
There is not even a word in our language to represent the "castra-
tion" or "emasculation" of females. We need serious research into
how traditional sex-role stereotypes affect girls' learning and development and how schools continue to perpetuate and elaborate these
stereotypes. Most importantly, new educational environments must
be designed to eliminate restrictive sex-role learning so that girls
and boys can be free to explore their full human potential.

Notes

1. Jerome Kagan, "Check One: ☐ Male   ☐ Female." *Psychology Today*
   3, No. 2 (July, 1969) : 39–41.
2. Daniel G. Brown, "Sex Role Development in a Changing Culture,"
   Psychology Bulletin 55 (1958) : 232–242; William Ward, "Process of
   Sex-Role Development," *Developmental Psychology* 1, No. 2 (1969) :
   163–168.
3. Aletha H. Stein and Jancis Smithells, "Age and Sex Difference in Children's Sex-Role Standards about Achievement," *Developmental Psychology* 1, No. 3 (May, 1969) : 252–259.
4. Ruth Hartley and Frances Hardesty, "Children's Perceptions of Sex-
   Role in Childhood," *Journal of Genetic Psychology* 105, No. 1 (1964) :
   43–51; W. W. Hartup and S. G. Moore, "Avoidance of Inappropriate
   Sex-Typing by Young Children," *Journal of Consulting Psychology* 27
   (1963) : 467–473.
5. Roberta Oetzel, "Annotated Bibliography," in *The Development of*

Sex Differences, ed. Eleanor Maccoby (Stanford: Stanford University Press, 1966), pp. 223–322.

6. Brown, "Sex Role Development."
7. S. Smith, "Age and Sex Differences in Children's Opinions Concerning Sex Differences," *Journal of Genetic Psychology* 54 (1939): 17–25.
8. Lawrence Kohlberg, "A Cognitive-Developmental Analysis of Children's Sex-Role Concepts and Attitudes," in *The Development of Sex Differences,* ed. Eleanor Maccoby, pp. 105–106.
9. E. Roper, "Women in America, The *Fortune* Survey," part 1, *Fortune Magazine,* August, 1946.
10. Edward H. Pohlman, *The Psychology of Birth Planning* (Cambridge, Mass.: Shenkman, 1969).
11. Jerome Kagan and H. A. Moss, *Birth to Maturity: A Study in Psychological Development* (New York: John Wiley and Sons, 1962).
12. Inge K. Broverman, et al., "Sex-Role Stereotypes: A Current Appraisal," *Journal of Social Issues,* in press; A. C. Sherriffs and R. F. Jarrett, "Sex Differences in Attitudes About Sex Differences," *Journal of Personality* 35 (1953): 161–168; A. C. Sherriffs and J. P. McKee, "Qualitative Aspects of Beliefs About Men and Women," *Journal of Personality* 25 (June, 1957): 451–464.
13. Charles Silberman, *Crisis in the Classroom* (New York: Vintage, 1970).
14. Everett Reimer, *An Essay on Alternatives in Education* (Cuernavaca, Mexico: CIDOC Cuaderno No. 1005, 1970).
15. Paulo Freire, "Cultural Action for Freedom," *Harvard Educational Review,* Monograph Series No. 1, Cambridge, Mass., 1970, pp. 1, 6.
16. Ivan Illich, "After Deschooling, What?" *Social Policy* (September/October, 1971): 5–13.
17. Edgar Friedenberg, "What Do the Schools Do?" *This Magazine Is About Schools* 3, No. 1 (Winter, 1969): 33.
18. Miriam Wasserman, "School Mythology and the Education of Oppression," *This Magazine Is About Schools* 5, No. 3 (Summer, 1971): 23–36.
19. Philip W. Jackson, "The Student's World," *The Elementary School Journal* 66 (1966): 343–357.
20. John Holt, *How Children Fail* (New York: Delta, 1964).
21. Melvin L. Silberman, "Classroom Rewards and Intellectual Courage," in *The Experience of Schooling,* ed. M. L. Silberman (New York: Holt, Rinehart, and Winston, 1971).
22. Mary Alice White, "The View from the Pupil's Desk," *The Urban Review* 2 (1968): 5–7.
23. Eleanor Leacock, *Teaching and Learning in City Schools* (New York: Basic Books, 1969).
24. Joseph C. Grannis, "The School as a Model of Society," in *Learning of Political Behavior,* eds. N. Adler and C. Harrington (New York: Scott-Foresman, 1970), pp. 135–147.
25. Richard Rothstein, "Down the Up Staircase: Tracking in Schools," *This Magazine Is About Schools* 5, No. 3 (Summer, 1971): 103–139.
26. Robert Rosenthal and Lenore Jacobson, *Pygmalion in the Classroom* (New York: Holt, Rinehart, and Winston, 1968).
27. Ray C. Rist, "Student Social Class and Teacher Expectations: The Self-

Fulfilling Prophecy in Ghetto Education," *Harvard Educational Review* 40, No. 3 (August, 1970): 411–451; P. C. Rubovits and M. L. Maehr, "Toward an Explanation of the Rosenthal-Jacobson Findings." Paper presented at the American Educational Research Association, New York, February, 1971.

28. Philip W. Jackson, *Life in Classrooms* (New York: Holt, Rinehart, and Winston, 1968).

29. Eleanor Maccoby, "Sex Differences in Intellectual Functioning," in *The Development of Sex Differences*, ed. Eleanor Maccoby, pp. 24–39.

30. James J. Gallagher, "Sex Differences in Expressive Thought of Gifted Children in the Classroom," *Personnel and Guidance Journal* 45, No. 3 (November, 1966): 248–253; Matina Horner, "Fail: Bright Woman," *Psychology Today* 3 (November, 1969): 36–38; M. C. Shaw and J. T. McCuen, "The Onset of Academic Underachievement in Bright Children," *Journal of Educational Psychology* 51 (1960): 103–108.

31. V. Crandall and A. Rabson, "Children's Repetitive Choices in an Intellectual Achievement Situation Following Success and Failure," *Journal of Genetic Psychology* 97 (1960): 161–168; V. Crandall et al., "Parents' Attitudes and Behaviors and Grade School Children's Academic Achievements," *Journal of Genetic Psychology* 104 (1964): 53–66.

32. Aletha H. Stein, "The Influence of Social Reinforcement on the Achievement Behavior of Fourth Grade Boys and Girls," *Child Development* 40, No. 3 (1969): 727–736.

33. Steven R. Tulkin, John P. Muller and Lane K. Conn, "Need for Approval and Popularity: Sex Differences in Elementary School Students," *Journal of Consulting and Clinical Psychology* 33, No. 1 (1969): 35–39.

34. Lawrence Kohlberg, "A Cognitive-Developmental Analysis."

35. Sarah Spinks, "Sugar 'n Spice," *This Magazine Is About Schools* 3, No. 3 (Summer, 1969): 65.

36. Ruth Hartley, "A Developmental View of Female Sex-Role Definition and Identification," *Merrill-Palmer Quarterly* 10, No. 1 (1964): 7.

37. Margaret M. Poloma and Neal T. Garland, "The Married Professional Woman: A Study in the Toleration of Domestication," *Journal of Marriage and the Family* (August, 1971): 531–540.

38. Jack H. Pollack, "Are Teachers Fair to Boys?" *Today's Health* 46, No. 4 (1968): 21.

39. Patricia Sexton, "Schools Are Emasculating Our Boys," *Saturday Review*, June 19, 1965, p. 57.

40. Jerome Kagan, "The Child's Sex Role Classification of School Objects," *Child Development* 35 (1964): 1051–1056.

41. R. A. Kellogg, "A Direct Approach to Sex-Role Identification of School-Related Objects," *Psychological Reports* 24 (June, 1969): 839–841.

42. W. J. Meyer and G. C. Thompson, "Sex Differences in the Distribution of Teacher Approval and Disapproval Among Sixth Grade Children," *Journal of Educational Psychology* 47 (1956): 385–396.

43. Philip W. Jackson and Henriette M. Lahaderne, "Inequalities of Teacher-Pupil Contacts," *Psychology in the Schools* 4 (1967): 204–208.

44. Pauline Sears and D. Feldman, "Teacher Interactions with Boys and Girls," *The National Elementary Principal* 46, No. 2 (November, 1966): 31.

45. O. L. Davis and J. Slobodian, "Teacher Behavior Toward Boys and

Girls During First Grade Reading Instruction," *American Educational Research Journal* 4, No. 3 (May, 1967): 261–269.

46. T. L. Good and J. E. Brophy, "Questioned Equality for Grade One Boys and Girls," *Reading Teacher* 25 (December, 1971): 249–252.

47. H. Felsenthal, "Sex Differences in Teacher-Pupil Interaction during First Grade Reading Instruction." Paper presented at the Annual Meeting of the American Educational Research Association, Minneapolis, Minn., March, 1970.

48. J. C. Grannis, S. W. Kaminsky, and W. W. Furman, "Teachers' and Pupils' Roles in Variously Structured Classroom Settings and Subsettings: A Report from the Columbia Classroom Environments Projects." Paper presented at the Annual Meeting of the American Educational Research Association, Chicago, Ill., April 6, 1972.

49. E. P. Torrance, *Rewarding Creative Behavior: Experiment in Classroom Creativity* (Englewood Cliffs, N.J.: Prentice-Hall, 1965).

50. Beverly Fagot and Gerald R. Patterson, "An in vivo Analysis of Reinforcing Contingencies for Sex-Role Behaviors in the Preschool Child," *Developmental Psychology* 1, No. 55 (1969): 563–568.

51. R. L. Spaulding, "Achievement, Creativity, and Self-Concept Correlates of Teacher-Pupil Transactions in Elementary Schools." Cooperative Research Project No. 1352. Washington, D.C.: U.S. Department of Health, Education, and Welfare, Office of Education, 1963.

52. Frances Bentzen, "Sex Ratios in Learning and Behavior Disorders," *The National Elementary Principal* 46, No. 2 (November, 1966): 13–17.

53. A. Westbrook, "Teachers' Recognition of Problem Behavior and Referrals of Children to Pupil Personnel Services," *Journal of Educational Research* 63, No. 9 (May-June, 1970): 391–394.

54. G. A. W. Stauffer, Jr., "The Attitude of Secondary School Teachers Toward Certain Behavior Problems of Children," *School Review* 64 (1956): 358–362.

55. C. A. Ullman, "Identification of Maladjusted School Children," Public Health Monograph No. 7, 1952. Washington, D.C.: U.S. Department of Health, Education, and Welfare.

56. Patricia Sexton, "Schools Are Emasculating Our Boys."

57. Judith M. Bardwick, *Psychology of Women: A Study of Bio-cultural Conflicts* (New York: Harper and Row, 1971).

58. R. L. Spaulding, "Achievement, Creativity, and Self-Concept Correlates of Teacher-Pupil Transactions in Elementary Schools." Cooperative Research Project No. 1352, Washington, D.C.: U.S. Department of Health, Education, and Welfare. Office of Education, 1963.

59. V. J. Crandall, U. Natkousky, and A. Preston, "Motivational and Ability Determinants of Young Children's Intellectual Achievement Behaviors," *Child Development* 33 (1962): 643–661.

60. Patricia P. Minuchin, "The Schooling of Tomorrow's Women," *School Review* 80, No. 2 (February, 1972): 204–205.

61. For example, see Miriam M. Johnson, "Sex-Role in the Nuclear Family," *Child Development* 34 (1963): 319–333.

62. Jere E. Brody and Luis M. Laosa, "The Effect of a Male Teacher on the Sex-Typing of Kindergarten Children." The University of Texas at Austin, 1971, p. 47. Mimeographed.

63. Karen Branan, "What Can I Do About . . . Sex Discrimination?"

Scholastic Teacher (Elementary School Teachers' Edition), November, 1971, p. 20.

64. "Boys Are Different," Instructor (December, 1970), pp. 50–54.

65. Stein and Smithells, "Age and Sex Differences in Children's Sex-Role Standards About Achievement."

66. Irvin L. Child, Elmer H. Potter, and Estelle M. Levine, "Children's Textbooks and Personality Development," *Psychological Monographs* 40, No. 3 (1946).

67. Noel Jenkin and Karen Vroegh, "Contemporary Concepts of Masculinity and Femininity," *Psychological Reports* 25 (1969): 679-697.

68. Janice Pottker, "Female Sex Role Stereotypes in Elementary School Readers." Master's Thesis, University of Maryland, 1971.

69. *Dick and Jane as Victims: Sex Stereotyping in Children's Readers* (Princeton: Women on Words and Images. A Task Force of Central New Jersey NOW, 1972).

70. Elizabeth Fisher, "Children's Books: The Second Sex, Junior Division," *The New York Times Book Review* (May 24, 1970), p. 6.

71. "Sex Bias in the Public Schools," New York City Chapter of NOW, 1971, p. 19.

72. Jamie Kelem Frisof, "Textbooks and Channelling," *Women: A Journal of Liberation* 1, No. 1 (Fall, 1969): 26–28.

73. Louis M. Smith and William Geoffrey, *The Complexities of an Urban Classroom: An Analysis Toward a General Theory of Teaching* (New York: Holt, Rinehart, and Winston, 1968), p. 53.

74. *Ibid.*, p. 45.

75. Patricia P. Minuchin, "Sex Differences in Children," *The National Elementary Principal* 46, No. 2 (November, 1966): 45–48.

76. Carole Joffee, "Sex Role Socialization and the Nursery School: As the Twig Is Bent," *Journal of Marriage and the Family* 33, No. 3 (August, 1971): 467–475.

77. Barbara Chasen, "Sex Role Stereotypes: Self-Image of Pre-Kindergarten Boys and Girls in Regard to Doll Preference, Work Preference, and Sex Role Stereotype Questions." Unpublished paper, New York University, May, 1971.

78. Bobbi Selcer, "How Liberated Are Liberated Children?" *The Radical Therapist* 2, No. 5 (February, 1971): 14–15.

79. Robert Riordan, "Feminine Sex Role Concepts Among High School Counselor and Students," Ph.D. Dissertation, *Bibliography Abstract*, 1965.

80. New York City NOW, "Sex Bias."

81. Alice de Rivera, "On De-segregating Stuyvesant High," in *Sisterhood Is Powerful*, ed. Robin Morgan (New York: Vintage, 1970), p. 366.

82. *American Teacher*, November, 1971.

83. Alex Aderer et al., "A Survey of Secondary School Teachers' Sex Role Stereotypes and Sex-Typed Classroom Behaviors." Unpublished paper, Teachers College, Columbia University, January, 1972.

84. Inge K. Broverman et al., "Sex Role Stereotypes: A Current Appraisal," *Journal of Social Issues* 28, No. 2 (February, 1972): 59–78.

85. Sandra L. Bem and Daryl J. Bem, "Case Study of a Nonconscious

Ideology: Training the Woman to Know Her Place." Pittsburgh, Pa.: KNOW, Inc., 1970, p. 7.

86. A. J. H. Gaite,' "Teachers' Perceptions of Ideal Male and Female Students: Male Chauvinism in the Schools." Paper presented at the American Educational Research Association, Chicago, Illinois, April, 1972.

"Now You See," Said Mark

by Virginia Kidd

In 1969, California adopted a new line of textbooks for use throughout the state for children four to eight years old. The major line of first-grade texts is the Harper & Row Basic Reading Program. . . . During the fall of 1970, 376,500 students will enroll in the first grade in the California public schools, and most of them will now be taught to read from these books. I would like to examine in this letter the first-grade readers from this series designed for use in "usual" classrooms—not to judge whether they will teach "reading skills" but to show the implications of their rhetoric. These seem to me alarming.

The first observation to be made about the Harper & Row readers is something we all had realized about Dick and Jane in the even more popular Scott Foresman readers: once you start them, there is no escape. That is, the first book is about Janet and Mark and so are the second and the third. Janet and Mark and their ever-patient Mother and Daddy become the first grader's Everyman. There is only one world in these books—the world of Janet and Mark.

There are no extremes in the recurring world. The rhetoric is clear: a bland world is a good world. The attitudes of all characters are uniform; no one deviates from them. The same kinds of events recur regularly, and they never provoke criticism.

From a letter by Virginia Kidd to the *New York Review of Books,* September 3, 1970. Reprinted by permission.

Janet and Mark live in a plain house in a plain suburb. They go to the playground, they go on a picnic, they visit Grandma, they own a dog. They buy shoes in a building conveniently named "Shoe Store," and they give to the Red Cross. Mother wears clothing of another era. She still wears gloves to town and a dress on a picnic. (On one occasion she does don knee-length shorts. While it could be noted that she was at a swimming pool at that time, still we might generally agree that it represents an improvement over the skirt and blouse she wore in the speedboat.)

In keeping with modern trends, Janet and Mark have friends of different races. Negro children are easily recognizable in the playground. Mark's friend David is clearly dark but Janet still cheers the cowboy over the Indian, and it becomes evident that face colors could be changed indiscriminately without affecting the stories. Indeed, in one unforgettable instance a child changes color with just a flip of the page. While this can be passed off as simple inefficiency on the part of artist or printer, it may well be a reflection of the book's viewpoint.

The difficulty with this description of a world lies in its omissions. Janet and Mark never talk about school, paint pictures, take music lessons, write verse, or wonder about a God. There are no crises; their parents do not divorce, their grandmother does not move in, they do not wear glasses, their dog never gets pregnant, they're never embarrassed or ashamed.

They learn to behave in this way from their parents, who never quarrel, espouse political ideals, engage in artistic activities, hire baby-sitters, get sick, display mutual affection, or—most depressing of all—speak to each other. In 410 pages, Daddy and Mother say only two lines to one another: "I want a speedboat ride, Daddy," and "Look in the box, Mother."

The language of the reader steadily implies that there is only one sort of experience for all people, as is demonstrated clearly in Mother's speech when she talks of Mark's birthday party: "This is what he wants . . . and this is what all boys want." And again, when she describes the food for the party: "Just what all boys like! Just what all boys want!"

Mother's chief occupation, it is clear from the pictures, is washing dishes, cooking, sewing, ironing, and wearing aprons. (There are eighteen stories featuring women in the home; the woman wears an apron in twelve of them.) Daddy's chief occupation is coming home. Daddy is never seen wiping away Janet's tears or helping Mark clean his room; he plays ball with Mark. Mother never goes to work or drives the car; she helps Janet make a cake.

Janet and Mark continue this dramatization of sexual roles. The story of Janet's new skates illustrates the point clearly: Janet tries on the skates and falls.

> "Mark! Janet!" said Mother.
> "What is going on here?"

> "She cannot skate," said Mark.
> "I can help her.
> I want to help her.
> Look at her, Mother.
> Just look at her.
> She is just like a girl.
> She gives up."

Mother forces Janet to try again.

> "Now you see," said Mark.
> "Now you can skate.
> But just with me to help you."

Janet never makes a similar remark to Mark. The indoctrination of Janet, and through her the children of California, is clear.

Companion stories, featuring each child separately, continue the same viewpoint. Mark shows Janet his toys: parachute, rocket, space suit, helmet, gloves, and boots. He declares himself Mark the astronaut. Then it is Janet's turn. She shows her toys: playhouse, chairs, curtains, dolls, buggy, doll, bed dishes.

Within the text a "Just for Fun" section features animal stories. Even here, the text carefully follows along the same lines. Mother no longer looks like Jane Wyatt on "Father Knows Best." Now she is clearly a bear. But she is still wearing an apron and still drying dishes. Little Bear, given the pronoun "he," is a jolly sort, who spends "his" story looking for fun. Little Frog, given the pronoun "she," sits on a rock asking people what to do.

Certainly there are those who would accept the tradition which requires Janet to run from Mark's grass snake. What is to be criticized is the lack of options. Janet is never a potential artist, senator, scientist. Mark never will be an actor, professor, gourmet.

And Janet and Mark, like death and taxes, are with us always, and they act the same confining parts.

Janet and Mark are inveterate consumers. American business would be proud of them. The value of acquiring objects is illustrated in each of the preprimers, but it is the primer *Around the Corner* that most exactly demonstrates the value.

On page 29, Janet and Mark find a dime and reach one of the emotional climaxes of the book by quarreling over it. Mother, rather than reprimanding them, divides it, giving each a nickel. Janet's instant comment is: "Now we can get something." They leave immediately.

On page 41, Mrs. Long brings skates for Janet. Mark's first observation is "What do I get?"

On page 67, Janet expresses a desire to do something exciting. Mother's solution is to buy T-shirts and earrings.

The consumer impulse reaches its height on page 75, when Mark finds a pigeon. His friend David offers to buy it.

> "Will you give him to me?
> Will you give him to me for a nickel?"

Mark could conceivably give several replies at this point: you may have this pigeon as a present; you may have the pigeon if you will care for it; we must let the pigeon go free, etc. The reply given illustrates the viewpoint expressed in the book:

> "For a nickel!" said Mark.
> "What good is a nickel? . . .
> You can have my pigeon for a dime."

Notice that Mark is not selfish. Rather, both Mark and David are careful operators in a consumer society.

Janet's role as a consumer is similar. "I am going to have a birthday," she says. "You can get something for me." Daddy's reply?

> "Good for you," said Daddy.
> "Look out for yourself, Janet."

It is important to be aware of the dangers presented by rhetoric encouraging cultural uniformity. The most pointed warning about these books is to be found in the text itself. Laid out clearly, for all to see, is the deadly implication of the first-grade reader:

"What can I be, Mother?" said Little Lamb
"I want to be something new."

"What can you be?" said her mother.
"Someday you will be a sheep.
A sheep . . . just like me."

Little Lamb ran up and down
in the green meadow
Little Lamb was happy.

"Decision of the Board of Education: No Freedom of Choice . . ."

(Excerpts from the testimony of Laura Edelhart and her daughter Bonnie Cruz Sanchez in a case against New York City Junior High School 217)

THE WITNESS [Laura Edelhart]: I asked Miss Jones if my daughter could take metalworking or mechanics, and she said there is no freedom of choice. That is what she said.

THE COURT: That is it?

THE WITNESS: I also asked her whose decision this was, that there was no freedom of choice. And she told me it was the decision of the Board of Education.

I didn't ask her anything else because she clearly showed me that it was against the school policy for girls to be in the class. She said it was a Board of Education decision.

Q: Did she use that phrase, "no freedom of choice"?

A: Exactly that phrase, "no freedom of choice."

That is what made me so angry that I wanted to start this whole thing.

Q: [asked of Bonnie Cruz Sanchez]: Now, after this lawsuit was filed, they then permitted you to take the course; is that correct?

Reprinted from *Report on Sex Bias in the Public Schools,* Education Committee, National Organization for Women, New York City Chapter

A: No, we had to fight about it for quite a while.

Q: But, eventually, they did let you in the second semester?

A: They only let me in there.

Q: You are the only girl?

A: Yes.

Q: How did you do in the course?

A: I got the medal for it from all the boys there.

Q: Will you show the court?

A: Yes (indicating).

Q: And what does the medal say?

A: Metal 1970 Van Wyck.

Q: And why did they give you that medal?

A: Because I was the best out of all the boys.

THE COURT: I do not want any giggling or noises in the courtroom. Just do the best you can to control yourself or else I will have to ask you to leave the courtroom.

This is no picnic, you know. These are serious lawsuits.

Fact Sheet on the Earnings Gap

Women who work at full-time jobs the year round earn, on the average, only $3 for every $5 earned by similarly employed men. The ratio varies slightly from year to year, but the gap is greater than it was 15 years ago. From 64 percent in 1955, women's median wage or salary income as a proportion of men's fell to 61 percent by 1959 and 1960 and since then has fluctuated between 58 and 60 percent. Women's median earnings of $5,323 in 1970 were 59 percent of the $8,966 received by men. . . .

Another measure of the gap in the earnings of women and men full-time year-round workers is a distribution of these workers by earnings levels. For example, 12 percent of the women but only 5 percent of the men earned less than $3,000 in 1970. Moreover, 45 percent of the women but only 14 percent of the men earned less than $5,000. At the upper end of the scale, only 7 percent of

From Women's Bureau, U.S. Department of Labor.

the women but 40 percent of the men had earnings of $10,000 or more. . . .

The educational background of a worker often determines not only the type of work but also the level of job within an occupation for which he or she can qualify. However, women who work full time the year round earn substantially less than similarly employed men who have the same amount of education. Among workers who had completed only grade school or 1 to 3 years of high school, women's incomes in 1970 were only 55 percent of men's. Among those who had 5 years or more of college, the proportion was 65 percent. . . .

The previous figures do not necessarily indicate that women are receiving unequal pay for equal work. For the most part, they reflect the fact that women are more likely than men to be employed in low-skilled, low-paying jobs. For example:

- In public elementary and secondary schools, women were less than 20 percent of the principals; superintendents; deputy, associate, and assistant superintendents; and other central office administrators in 1970–71.
- Among professional and technical workers in business, women are concentrated in the class B and class C computer programmer positions, while men are more frequently employed in the higher-paying class A positions. Similarly, women are usually in the lowest category of draftsmen and engineering technicians.
- Among managers and proprietors, women frequently operate small retail establishments, while men may manage manufacturing plants or wholesale outlets.
- In the manufacturing of men's and boys' suits and coats, women are likely to be employed as hand finishers, thread trimmers and basting pullers, and sewing machine operators —jobs where their average hourly earnings are less than $2.70—while men are likely to be employed as finish pressers (hand or machine), underpressers, cutters, and markers— with average hourly earnings of $3.50 to $4.25.
- In the service occupations, women are likely to be cooks, nurses' aides, and waitresses, while men are likely to be employed in higher-paying jobs as bartenders, guards, custodians, firemen, policemen, and detectives.

Nevertheless, within some of these detailed occupations, men usually are better paid. . . .

MEDIAN SALARY OF FULL-TIME EMPLOYED CIVILIAN SCIENTISTS, BY SEX AND FIELD, 1970

Field	Median Salary		Women's Median Salary as Percent of Men's
	Women	Men	
All fields	$11,600	$15,200	76.3
Chemistry	10,500	15,600	67.3
Earth and marine sciences	10,500	15,000	70.0
Atmospheric and space sciences	13,000	15,200	85.5
Physics	12,000	16,000	75.0
Mathematics	10,000	15,000	66.7
Computer sciences	13,200	16,900	78.1
Agricultural sciences	9,400	12,800	73.4
Biological sciences	11,000	15,500	71.0
Psychology	13,000	15,500	83.9
Statistics	14,000	17,100	81.9
Economics	13,400	16,500	81.2
Sociology	11,000	13,500	81.5
Anthropology	12,300	15,000	82.0
Political science	11,000	13,500	81.5
Linguistics	11,300	13,000	86.9

SOURCE: National Science Foundation: "National Register of Scientific and Technical Personnel." 1970.

5 The Myth of Cultural Deprivation

One frequently hears or reads the statement that the home conditions, the rudeness of the parents, the field labour, the village games and so forth are the chief hindrances to school education. It may be that they really interfere with that school education, as pedagogues understand it; but it is time to convince ourselves that these conditions are the chief foundation of all education, and that they are far from being inimical and hindrances to the school, but that they are its prime and chief movers. . . . It seems strange that this coarse domestic life should have been able to teach the child . . . difficult things and should all of a sudden become unfit to instruct him in such easy things as reading, writing, and so forth, and should even become injurious for such an instruction.

—Leo Tolstoy, "On Popular Education," 1862

The myth that helps to conceal and sustain school sexism is that girls are born inferior.

The myth that helps to conceal and sustain school racism-classism is that the poor/dark children's parents are inferior. Their inferiority is most popularly formulated as "cultural deprivation."

The myth of cultural deprivation is a bizarre intellectual artifact, confusing two senses of "culture" in such a way that not dining with your family in a certain prescribed manner and not

appreciating a Beethoven quartet are equal evidences of deprivation. "Cultural deprivation" is a container for a variety of ster-
eotypical, shallow, and often contradictory notions about why
the children of the poor don't perform in school as the children
of the middle class do:

They come from "female-headed families" (itself a sexist
explanation for family inferiority).
They have no fathers.
They have too many fathers.
Their mothers don't talk to them enough, or talk to them in
"bad" English or in a foreign language.
They are over-, under-, or not "selectively" stimulated in
infancy.
There are no pencils or books in their homes.
They are not taken on trips to museums and zoos, or trips to
the country, or trips to the city.
They have too many responsibilities and cares in the home.
They don't know how to be responsible.
They are overdisciplined at home, or underdisciplined at
home.
And so on, and so on.

Some of these generalizations may refer to some poor and
poorly regarded children; others, to others. Some may be related
to facility in acquiring academic skills (specifically, language
and math skills). Others almost certainly are not. The one valid
generalization that probably can be made about these stereotypes is that all express in some measure the disapproval, contempt, or mere ethnocentricity of those who perpetrate them.
Ethnocentricity is manifest in the two best-respected of the
cultural-deprivation explanations: that the family structure of
poor, especially black, children is pathological, and that their
language is deficient.
The family-pathology argument was given great currency by
the publication in 1965 of a government report titled *The Negro
Family: The Case for National Action*, known as the "Moynihan
Report" after its principal author, Daniel Patrick Moynihan. A
good deal of literature refuting Moynihan's premise and labeling it racist appeared subsequently, including *Black Families in
White America*, by black sociologist Andrew Billingsley, who
wrote:

In every Negro neighborhood of any size in the country, a wide variety of family structures will be represented. This range and variety does not suggest, as some commentaries hold, that the Negro family is falling apart, but rather that these families are fully capable of surviving by adapting to the historical and contemporary social and economic conditions facing the Negro people. How does a people survive in the face of oppression and sharply restricted economic and social support? There are, of course, numerous ways. But surely one of them is to adapt the most basic of its institutions, the family, to meet the often conflicting demands placed on it. In this context, then, the Negro family has proved to be an amazingly resilient institution.

The deficient-language thesis has also received some strenuous and careful refutation, especially by linguists (meaning students of the structure of language). The selection by Joan C. Baratz is printed in its entirety, with full bibliography, in the hope that the material in it will be pedagogically helpful to teachers and future teachers of students who speak a black dialect.

Far away from the black youth of Harlem, Watts, or Chicago's West Side are the Oglala Sioux youth of Pine Ridge, South Dakota. Far away in miles and living in very different surroundings, but, meeting on a basketball court or in a "borrowed" automobile, they would probably understand one another very well. Because they are probably not far apart in the way in which their own cultures react to the impact of the culture of school, as it seeks to make of the young man not only a tool but a willing tool of a depersonalized, alienated world of work—and a tool that will always have a very lowly place in that world. Rosalie H. Wax, who writes of the Oglala Sioux, suggests that their bond with young blacks involves being rejected by, and rejecting, that school-work culture.

"The Chitling Test" stands cultural deprivation on its head.

Language and Cognitive Assessment of Negro Children: Assumptions and Research Needs

by Joan C. Baratz

The view of the black man as inherently inferior, an item of chattel rather than a person with human dignity, became a well-entrenched doctrine in American society. Even when the abolitionists were most vociferous in their insistence upon eliminating slavery in the United States (some 200 years after the initial importation of Negro slaves) they were not disputing the thought that the Negro was genetically inferior to the white man, but simply insisting that slavery was an immoral institution even if those held in bondage were inferior individuals.

The doctrine of genetic inferiority of the Negro was widely held and was responsible for many of the laws that created separate black and white communities after Emancipation. In fact, it was not until the 1954 Supreme Court decision concerning segregation in the public schools that the institutional tradition of regarding the Negro as genetically inferior was legally replaced by the idea that the Negro was not genetically inferior but rather that his behavior was pathological in the social sense, due to the history of slavery in this country.

The Professional Literature

The replacement of the genetic inferiority theory with the social pathology theory encouraged a great deal of research in the social sciences which was interested in describing Negro behavior in terms of how it deviated from the white norm. Thus an entire body of literature has been created that describes the Negro, not as he is, but in terms of how he does or does not conform to the modes of behavior that the white man has established as normative and appropriate. This body of knowledge (or, to look at it another way, this body of misunderstanding) might be termed the "myth of the Negro present."[1]

As Bernard (1966) has indicated, the use of white control groups

By Joan C. Baratz, Education Study Center, Washington, D.C. Reprinted by permission from *Asha*, Vol. XI, No. 3 (March, 1969).

to describe who the Negro is actually results in "studies of the white population with emphasis on Negro or non-white data as representing deviance from a white norm." This unhappy state of affairs has led the social sciences to create a picture of the Negro as a "sick white man." A man for whom we, the white society, should feel great compassion and no little amount of guilt, for we have infected him with his current "disease," but a man who nevertheless, no matter the reason why, is ill.

This mythical illness can be easily identified with a brief glance at the "professional literature." There are several prominent symptoms that are continuously diagnosed—disintegration or "lack of" family structure (Moynihan, 1965; Schiefelbusch, 1967), poor motivation (Katz, 1967), inability to delay gratification (Klaus and Gray, 1968), and underdeveloped language and cognitive abilities (Deutsch, 1965; John, 1963; Bereiter and Engelmann, 1966; Klaus and Gray, 1968). All these alleged symptoms need to be examined more closely, but the focus of this paper is on the premises operating in research on language and cognitive assessment of the Negro. The kinds of research assumptions that are present in the literature concerning language can also be found in regard to the myths about family structure, motivation, etc.

When reviewing the literature one finds three major professions concerned with describing the language and cognitive abilities of black children: educators, psychologists (mainly child development specialists), and linguists.[2] The educators were the first to contribute a statement about the language difficulties of these children, a statement that amounted to the fact that these children were virtually verbally destitute—i.e., they couldn't talk and if they did, their speech was deviant and filled with "errors." The next group to get into the foray—the psychologists—reconfirmed initially that the children didn't talk, and then added the sophisticated wrinkle that if they did talk, their speech was such that it was a deterrent to cognitive growth. The last group to come into the picture was composed of linguists who, though thoroughly impressed with the sophisticated research of the psychologist, were astonished at the naïvety of his pronouncements concerning lan-

---

[1] An obvious tribute to Herskovits' *Myth of the Negro Past* (1941), in which misunderstanding about the cultural background of Afro-Americans was first dealt with.

[2] Speech pathologists have been notably silent overall concerning language problems of subcultural groups. One can count on one hand the articles in our official journals concerning this topic.

guage. The linguist began to examine the language of black children and brought us to our current conceptions of the language abilities of these children—i.e., that they speak a well-ordered, highly structured, highly developed language system which in many aspects is different from standard English.

Assessing the Child's Language

We have a fascinating situation here where three professions are assessing the same behavior—the child's oral language production and comprehension—but with varying assumptions so that they see different things. However, it is not merely another example of the parable of the six blind men describing the elephant and asserting an elephant equalled that portion of the elephant that the blind man happened to be touching—for in the parable all men were partially correct, and an elephant could be adequately described in the sum total of their "observation." But when we look at the assumptions of the educator, the psychologist, and the linguist, we find that there are some premises held by one profession (psychology)—that, for example, a language system could be underdeveloped—that another profession (linguistics) sees as completely untenable, and even absurd. The educator worked under the assumption that there is a single correct way of speaking and that everyone who does not speak in this grammar book fashion is in error. (Indeed, although the psychologist may not recognize it, he tacitly adheres to this principle when he defines language development in terms of "correct" standard English usage.) This assumption is also untenable to the linguist who is interested in the structure and function of an utterance. To him the discussion of a hierarchical system that says a double negative such as *they don't have none* is inferior to a single negative, *they haven't any*, is meaningless. The linguist simply wishes to describe the rules of the system that allow a speaker of that system to generate a negative utterance—or any other complex structure—that is considered grammatical and is understood as intended by the users of the system.

Let me briefly review the linguistic research on the assessment of language abilities of Negro children and then look back at the assumptions of the psychologist that led him astray and allowed him to build an elaborate, mythological body of literature concerning the linguistic incompetence of black children.

The linguist takes as basic that all humans develop language.

After all, there is no reason to assume that black African bush children develop a language and black inner city Harlem children do not! Subsumed under this is that the language is a well-ordered system with a predictable sound pattern, grammatical structure, and vocabulary (in this sense, there are no "primitive" languages). The linguist assumes that any verbal system used by a community that fulfills the above requirements is a language and that no language is structurally better than any other language; French is not better than German, Yiddish is not better than Gaelic, Oxford English is not better than standard English, etc.

The second assumption of the linguist is that children learn language in the context of their environment—that is to say, a French child learns French not because his father is in the home or his mother reads him books, but because French is the language that he hears continually from whatever source and it is the language that individuals in his environment respond to.

The third assumption that the linguist works with is that by the time a child is five he has developed language—he has learned the rules of his linguistic environment.

Rules of the Linguistic Environment

What are those rules and how have they been determined? By using ghetto informants, linguists such as Stewart (1964, 1965, 1967, 1968), Dillard (1965, 1967), Bailey (1965, 1968), Labov (1967), Labov and Cohen (1967), and Shuy, Wolfram, and Riley (1967) have described some of the linguistic parameters of Negro nonstandard English. Differences between standard English and Negro nonstandard occur to varying degrees in regard to the sound system, grammar, and vocabulary.

Although Negro nonstandard has many phonemes similar to those of standard English the distribution of these phonemes varies from standard English. For example /ɪ/ and /ɛ/ may not be distinguished before nasals, so that a "pin" in Negro nonstandard may be either an instrument for writing a letter or something one uses to fasten a baby's diaper. Sounds such as /r/ and /l/ are distributed so that *cat* may mean that orange vegetable that one puts in salads—standard English *carrot*—as well as the four-legged fuzzy animal, or a "big black dude." The reduction of /l/ and /r/ in many positions may create such homonyms as *toe* meaning a digit on the foot, or the church bell sound—standard English *toll*. Final clusters are reduced in Negro nonstandard so that *bowl* is used to describe either a vessel for cereal or a very brave soldier—standard English *bold*.

These are but a few of the many instances where Negro nonstandard sound usage differs from standard English. It is no wonder, then, that Cynthia Deutsch (1964) should find in her assessment of auditory discrimination that disadvantaged black children did not "discriminate" as well as white children from middle class linguistic environments. She administered a discrimination task that equated "correct responses" with judgments of equivalences and differences in standard English sound usage. Many of her stimuli though different to the standard English speaker, i.e., *pin-pen*, are similar to the Negro nonstandard speaker. She attributed the difference in performance of disadvantaged children to such things as the constant blare of the TV in their homes and there being so much "noise" in their environment that the children tended to "tune out." However, black children make responses based on the kind of language they consider appropriate. In the same way that *cot* for sleeping and *caught* for ensnared, or *marry* for to wed, *Mary* for the girl, and *merry* for to be happy are not distinguished in the speech of many white people (so that they would say on an auditory discrimination test that *cot* and *caught* were the same), *pin* and *pen* are the same in the language of ghetto blacks. The responses that the black child makes are on the basis of the sound usage that he has learned in his social and geographical milieu, and do not reflect some difficulty discriminating—just watch how fast he picks out the scamper of a rat from the "noise" in his environment!

The syntax of low income Negro children also differs from standard English in many ways (unfortunately the psychologist, not knowing the rules of Negro nonstandard, has interpreted these differences not as the result of well learned rules, but as evidence of "linguistic underdevelopment"). Some examples of the differences are provided below:

1. When you have a numerical quantifier such as 2, 7, 50, etc., you don't have to add the obligatory morphemes for the plural: *50 cent, 2 foot*.
2. The use of the possessive marker is different. For example, the standard English speaker says *John's cousin*; the nonstandard Negro speaker says *John cousin*. The possessive is marked here by the contiguous relationship of John and cousin.

3. Conditional is expressed by word order change rather than by *if*. Standard English: *I asked if he wanted to go.* Negro nonstandard: *I aks did he want to go.*
4. The third person singular has no obligatory morphological ending in nonstandard so that *she works here* is expressed as *she work here* in Negro nonstandard.
5. Verb agreement differs so that one says *she have a bike, they was going.*
6. The use of the copula is not obligatory: *I going, he a bad boy.*
7. The rules for negation are different. The double negative is used. Standard English *I don't have any* becomes *I don't got none* in Negro nonstandard.
8. The use of ain't in expression of the past: Negro nonstandard present tense is *he don't go*; past tense is *he ain't go.*
9. The use of the *be* to express habitual action: *he working right now* as contrasted with *he be working every day.*

These are but a few examples of the rules that the nonstandard speaker employs to produce utterances that are grammatical to other speakers in his environment.

Baratz and Povich (1967) assessed the language development of a group of five-year-old black Head Start children. They analyzed speech responses to photographs and to CAT cards using Lee's (1966) developmental sentence types model. A comparison of their data and Menyuk's (1964) restricted and transformational 'types of white middle class children was performed. Results indicated that the Negro Head Start child is not delayed in language acquisition—the majority of his utterances are on the . . . transformational levels of Lee's developmental model. His transformational utterances are similar to those described above—he has learned the many complicated structures of Negro nonstandard English.

Assessment by the Psychologist

Language Development
But how has the psychologist assessed language abilities of Negro children that led him to conclude erroneously that the black child has an insufficient or underdeveloped linguistic system? The psychologist's basic problem was his assumption that the development of language meant the development of his own form of standard English. Therefore, he concluded that if black children do not

speak like white children they are deficient in language development. His measures of "language development" were measures based on standard English (Bereiter, 1965; Thomas, 1962; Deutsch, 1964; Klaus and Gray, 1968).

The illogical aspects of the psychologists' assumptions are evident if one realizes that using their criteria for "language development" one would have to say that a French child of five was linguistically underdeveloped because he did not speak standard English! Clearly in future assessment procedures the psychologist must distinguish between the questions: (1) has this child acquired language? and (2) has this child acquired competence in standard English? Only then can he make valid statements about the black child's linguistic abilities.

Language and Cognition

But what other faulty notions does the psychologist appear to be using to assess language and cognitive ability of black children? Perhaps one of the most blatant has been a confusion between hypotheses concerning language and ones concerning cognition. For this reason, superficial differences in language structures and language styles have been taken as manifestations of underlying differences in cognitive ability.

For example, Bereiter and Engelmann (1966) hold as one of the cardinal cognitive needs of the child the learning of conditionality as measured by the use of *if* constructions. They assume that the absence of *if* by a child indicates an instance in which the concept of conditionality is absent. However, Stewart and other linguists have described the fact that, in some nonstandard dialects of English such as Negro nonstandard, conditionality may be expressed by the use of a word order inversion rather than with the vocabulary item "if." Thus, conditionality is expressed in the statement *I ask Alvin did he want to go* by changing *he* plus verb to *did he* plus verb, even though in standard English the same kind of conditionality would be expressed with *if* as in *I asked Alvin if he wanted to go.*

Different usages of vocabulary items may lead to confusion on the part of the examiner so that he feels the child is lacking in a particular concept. For example, the Peabody Picture Vocabulary Test has an item that asks children to identify *building*; the correct response being the picture of men constructing an edifice. However, in Negro nonstandard vernacular *building* is used only as a noun (one *makes* an edifice) so that the child will not respond to that item in the expected way. (There are other aspects about the PPVT which are culturally biased against the black child.)

The literature on cognitive abilities of black children comes mainly from two sources. One is the attempt of many child psychologists to adopt Basil Bernstein's postulates on differences in language styles between lower and middle class English speakers, and to concretize these hypotheses into categories of language behavior that directly imply restrictions in cognitive ability. Interesting as are Bernstein's ideas about language style differences of various socioeconomic groups, the relationship of particular linguistic usages to conceptual ability has yet to be determined. In fact, the preceding case of the confusion of the concept of conditionality with the presence or absence of the word *if* is an illustration of how misled one can become when relating specific speech forms with cognitive processes. Bernstein's writings appear to deal more specifically with the sociolinguistics of style variation than with the psycholinguistic implications of cognitive functioning.

The second problem with the cognitive assessment literature is that there has been a tendency to take Piaget's cognitive development formulations as a total definition of cognition, and to equate cognition with rationality. As Greenfield and Bruner (1966) have pointed out concerning cross-cultural studies of Piagetian psychology (in which I believe we can include the American studies with black ghetto children) the main effect has been to depict developmental lag through a tacit acceptance of white control group norms. Bruner et al. (1966) have several illustrations of cases where the experimenters' recognition of cultural differences affected the child's abilities to perform the task. In one instance involving a conservative task, the child was asked, "Why do you say they are different?" He could not answer the question. Then it was discovered that the use of "do you say," though grammatically correct, was inappropriate to that culture. When the child was asked instead, "Why are they different?" he answered the question immediately. The psychologist must take cultural differences of black ghetto children into consideration in the course of his assessment of their cognitive ability.

Environment and Language

The last assumption of the psychologist that I wish to deal with briefly is the widespread notion that "some environments are better than others for stimulating general language and cognitive growth" (Deutsch and Deutsch, 1968). This assumption is, I believe, an attempt to deal with the psychologist's confusion of language development and the acquisition of standard English, which was discussed earlier. His confusion causes him to think he must explain a "language deficit." According to these researchers, one set of factors that is most detrimental for language and cognitive development involves the following "inadequacies" of the ghetto mothering patterns:

1. The ghetto mother is so taken up with survival ("subsistence behaviors") that she is too exhausted to talk to her children. Such a notion tells us more about the psychologist's lack of knowledge about the ghetto mother than it does about her actual role. It also assumes that there is a minimal amount of language that must be present for language to be learned and that Negro mothers don't give this to their children. Subsumed under this is the notion that language is only learned from one's mother (and that, of course, it can only be transmitted when there is a father in the home!). Also underlying such statements about the mother's role is the assumption that she is verbally immature (Ralph, 1967), i.e., the language learned from her is underdeveloped.

2. It is presumed that the mother of a black child does not know how to stimulate or reinforce her child so that learning can occur. Subsumed under that assumption is the idea that such things as reading a book and singing to a child are essential behaviors for language to develop. The discussions on the inadequate reinforcements of verbal behavior on the part of the ghetto mother presume that she encourages "passive, withdrawn behavior in her children" (Schiefelbusch, 1967) and that verbal ability is not highly valued in the ghetto community. One need only to look at the anthropological literature concerned with language behavior to find dozens of attestations of the importance of verbal skills— "rapping, playing the dozens, signifying, etc." to the ghetto community (Hannerz, 1968; Newman, 1968; Abrahams, 1964; Kochman, 1968).

The assumptions that the psychologist uses in assessing language and cognitive skills of the black ghetto community appear to have evolved because of misconceptions of what language is and how it functions. He has constructed elaborate ecological and psychological explanations of differences in language behavior which can be understood much more simply in terms of how linguistic and cultural systems operate. The assumptions have been used "after the fact" to erroneously explain data. The assumptions themselves have no observational-experimental base.

Clearly what the psychologist and speech pathologist need is some sense of the ghetto child's culture: how he organizes his world, what his language system is, what his learning patterns are, how they are similar to those of children in middle class white cultures, how they are different, and how these differences interfere with the child's learning in a society that uses white cognitive styles and linguistic patterns as a basis for instruction and assessment of ability.

References

Abrahams, R., *Deep Down in the Jungle*. Hatboro, Pa.: Folklore Associates (1964).

Bailey, B., Linguistics on non-standard language patterns. Nat. Coun. Tchrs. English paper (1965).

Bailey, B., Some aspects of the impact of linguistics on language teaching in disadvantaged communities. *Elementary English*, 45, 570–79 (1968).

Baratz, J. C., and Povich, E. A., Grammatical constructions in the language of the Negro preschool child. ASHA Convention (1967).

Bereiter, C., Academic instruction and preschool children. In Corbin, R., and Crosby, M. (eds.), *Language Programs for the Disadvantaged*. Champaign, Ill.: Nat. Coun. Tchrs. English (1965).

Bereiter, C., and Engelmann, S., *Teaching Disadvantaged Children in Preschool*. Englewood Cliffs, N.J.: Prentice-Hall (1966).

Bernard, J., *Marriage and Family Among Negroes*. Englewood Cliffs, N.J.: Prentice-Hall (1966).

Bruner, J. Oliver, and Greenfield, P., *Studies in Cognitive Growth*. N.Y.: Wiley (1966).

Deutsch, C., Auditory discrimination and learning: social factors, *Merrill-Palmer Qu.*, 10, 277–96 (1964).

Deutsch, C., and Deutsch, M., Brief reflections on the theory of early childhood enrichment programs. In Hess, R., and Bear, R. (eds.), *Early Education Current Theory, Research and Action*. Chicago, Ill.: Aldine (1968).

Deutsch, M., The role of social class in language development and cognition. *Amer. J. Orthopsychiat.*, 35, 78–88 (1965).

Dillard, J. L., Negro children's dialect in the inner city. *The Florida Foreign Language Reporter*, 2 (1967a).

Dillard, J. L., The Urban Language Study of the Center for Applied Linguistics. *Linguistic Reporter*, 8, 1–2 (1967b).

Greenfield, P., and Bruner, J., Culture and cognitive growth. *Int. J. Psychol.*, 1, 89–107, 1966.

Hannerz, U., What ghetto males are like: another look. In Szwed, J., and Witten, N. (eds.), *Negroes in the New World: Problems in Theory and Method.* In press.

Herskovits, M., *The Myth of the Negro Past.* N.Y.: Harper (1941).

John, V., The intellectual development of slum children. *Amer. J. Orthopsychiat.,* 33, 813–822 (1963).

Katz, I., The socialization of academic motivation in minority group children. *Nebraska Symposium on Motivation,* Univ. Nebraska Press (1967).

Klaus, R., and Gray, S., The early training project for disadvantaged children: A report after five years. *Monogr. Soc. Res. Child Dev.,* 33 (1968).

Kochman, T., Language in the ghetto. Midwestern Anthropological Assoc., Detroit (1968).

Labov, W., Some suggestions for teaching standard English to speakers of non-standard urban dialects. In *New Directions in Elementary English.* Champaign, Ill. (1967).

Labov, W., and Cohen, P., Systematic relations of standard rules in grammar of Negro speakers. Project Literacy #7 (1967).

Lee, L., Developmental sentence types: a method for comparing normal and deviant syntactic development, *J. Speech Hearing Dis.,* 31, 311–30 (1966).

Menyuk, P., Syntactic rules used by children from preschool through first grade. *Child Dev.,* 35, 533–46 (1964).

Moynihan, D., *The Negro Family: The Case for National Action.* U.S. Dept. Labor, Washington, D.C. (1965).

Newman, S., The Goucher, Midwestern Anthropology Assoc., Detroit (1968).

Raph, J., Language and speech deficits in culturally-disadvantaged children, *J. Speech Hearing Dis.,* 32, 203–15 (1967).

Schiefelbusch, R., Language development and language modification. In Haring, N., and Schiefelbusch, R. (eds.), *Methods in Special Education.* N.Y.: McGraw-Hill (1967).

Shuy, R., Wolfram, W., and Riley, W., *Linguistic Correlates of Speech Stratification in Detroit Speech,* Final Report, Co-op. Res. Project 6, 1347, U.S. Off. Ed. (1967).

Stewart, W., Urban Negro speech: sociolinguistic factors affecting English teaching. In Shuy, R. (ed.), *Social Dialects and Language Learning.* Champaign, Ill.: Nat. Coun. Tchrs. English (1964).

Stewart, W., Foreign language teaching methods in quasi-foreign language situations. In Stewart, W. (ed.), *Nonstandard Speech and the Teaching of English.* Washington, D.C.: Center for Applied Linguistics (1965).

Stewart, W., Sociolinguistic factors in the history of American Negro dialects. *The Florida Foreign Language Reporter,* 6, 3ff. (1967).

Stewart, W., Continuity and change in American Negro dialects. *The Florida Foreign Language Reporter,* 7, 1ff. (1968).

Thomas, D., Oral language sentence structure and vocabulary of kindergarten children living in low socio-economic areas. *Dissertation Abstracts*, 23, No. 3, 1014 (1962).

The Warrior Dropouts

by Rosalie H. Wax

Scattered over the prairie on the Pine Ridge reservation of South Dakota, loosely grouped into bands along the creeks and roads, live thousands of Sioux Indians. Most live in cabins, some in tents, a few in houses; most lack the conventional utilities—running water, electricity, telephone, and gas. None has a street address. They are called "country Indians" and most speak the Lakota language. They are very poor, the most impoverished people on the reservation.

For four years I have been studying the problems of the high school dropouts among these Oglala Sioux. In many ways these Indian youths are very different from slum school dropouts— Negro, Mexican-American, rural white—just as in each group individuals differ widely one from another. Yet no one who has any familiarity with their problems can avoid being struck by certain parallels, both between groups and individuals.

In slum schools and Pine Ridge schools scholastic achievement is low, and the dropout rate is high; the children's primary loyalties go to friends and peers, not schools or educators; and all of them are confronted by teachers who see them as inadequately prepared, uncultured offspring of alien and ignorant folk. They are classified as "culturally deprived." All such schools serve as the custodial, constabulary, and reformative arm of one element of society directed against another.

Otherwise well-informed people, including educators themselves, assume on the basis of spurious evidence that dropouts dislike and voluntarily reject school, that they all leave it for much the same reasons, and that they are really much alike. But dropouts leave high school under strikingly different situations and for quite different reasons.

Published by permission of Transaction, Inc. from *trans*action, Vol. 4, May 1967. Copyright © 1967 by Transaction, Inc.

Many explicitly state that they do not wish to leave and are really "pushouts" or "kickouts" rather than "dropouts." As a Sioux youth in our sample put it, "I quit, but I never did *want* to quit!" Perhaps the fact that educators consider all dropouts to be similar tells us more about educators and their schools than about dropouts.

On the Reservation

The process that alienates many country Indian boys from the high schools they are obliged to attend begins early in childhood and reflects the basic Sioux social structure. Sioux boys are reared to be physically reckless and impetuous. One that does not perform an occasional brash act may be accepted as "quiet" or "bashful," but he is not considered a desirable son, brother, or sweetheart. Sioux boys are reared to be proud and feisty and are expected to resent public censure. They have some obligations to relatives; but the major social controls after infancy are exerted by their fellows —their "peer group."

From about the age of seven or eight, they spend almost the entire day without adult supervision, running or riding about with friends of their age and returning home only for food and sleep. Even we (my husband, Dr. Murray L. Wax, and I), who had lived with Indian families from other tribal groups, were startled when we heard a responsible and respected Sioux matron dismiss a lad of six or seven for the entire day with the statement, "Go play with Larry and John." . . .

Sioux boys have intense loyalties and dependencies. They almost never tattle on each other. But when forced to live with strangers, they tend to become inarticulate, psychologically disorganized, or withdrawn.

With most children the peer group reaches the zenith of its power in school. In middle class neighborhoods, independent children can usually seek and secure support from parents, teachers, or adult society as a whole. But when, as in an urban slum or Indian reservation, the teachers stay aloof from parents, and parents feel that teachers are a breed apart, the peer group may become so powerful that the children literally take over the school. Then group activities are carried on in class—jokes, notes, intrigues, teasing, mock-combat, comic book reading, courtship—all without the teacher's knowledge and often without grossly interfering with the learning process. . . .

We marveled at the variety and efficiency of the devices developed by Indian children to frustrate formal learning—unanimous inattention, refusal to go to the board, writing on the board in letters less than an inch high, inarticulate responses, and whispered or pantomime teasing of victims called on to recite. In some seventh and eighth grade classes there was a withdrawal so uncompromising that no voice could be heard for hours except the teacher's plaintively asking questions or giving instructions.

Most Sioux children insist they like school, and most Sioux parents corroborate this. Once the power and depth of their social life within the school are appreciated, it is not difficult to see why they like it. . . .

Day School Graduates

By the time he has finished the eighth grade, the country Indian boy has many fine qualities: zest for life, curiosity, pride, physical courage, sensibility to human relationships, experience with the elemental facts of life, and intense group loyalty and integrity. His experiences in day school have done nothing to diminish or tarnish his ideal—the physically reckless and impetuous youth, who is admired by all.

But, on the other hand, the country Indian boy is almost completely lacking in the traits most highly valued by the school authorities: a narrow and absolute respect for "regulations," "government property," routine, discipline, and diligence. He is also deficient in other skills apparently essential to rapid and easy passage through high school and boarding school—especially the abilities to make short-term superficial social adjustments with strangers. Nor can he easily adjust to a system which demands, on the one hand, that he study competitively as an individual, and, on the other, that he live in barrack-type dormitories where this kind of study is impossible.

Finally, his English is inadequate for high school work. Despite eight or more years of formal training in reading and writing, many day school graduates cannot converse fluently in English even among themselves. In contrast, most of the students with whom they will compete in higher schools have spoken English since childhood.

To leave home and the familiar and pleasant day school for boarding life at the distant and formidable high school is a prospect both fascinating and frightening. . . .

For the young men there is the chance to play high school basketball, baseball, or football; for the young women there is the
increased distance from overwatchful, conservative parents. . . .

[The High School in Town]

Many country Indians drop out of high school before they have
any clear idea what high school is all about. In our sample, 35 percent dropped out before the end of the ninth grade and many of
these left during the first semester. Our first interviews with them
were tantalizingly contradictory—about half the young men
seemed to have found high school so painful they could scarcely
talk about it; the other half were also laconic, but insisted that
they had liked school. In time, those who had found school un-
bearable confided that they had left school because they were
lonely or because they were abused by more experienced boarders.
Only rarely did they mention that they had trouble with their
studies.

The following statement, made by a mild and pleasant boy,
conveys some idea of the agony of loneliness, embarrassment, and
inadequacy that a country Indian newcomer may suffer when he
enters high school:

> At day school it was kind of easy for me. But high school was
> really hard, and I can't figure out even simple questions that
> they ask me. . . . Besides I'm so quiet [modest and unaggres-
> sive] that the boys really took advantage of me. They borrow
> money from me every Sunday night and they don't even care
> to pay it back. . . . I can't talk English very good, and I'm
> really bashful and shy, and I get scared when I talk to white
> people. I usually just stay quiet in the [day school] class-
> room, and the teachers will leave me alone. But at boarding
> school they wanted me to get up and talk or say something. . . .
> I quit and I never went back. . . . I can't seem to get along
> with different people, and I'm so shy I can't even make
> friends. [Translated from Lakota by interviewer.]

. . . for these young men, an essential part of having friends was
"raising Cain"—that is, engaging in daring and defiant deeds forbidden by the school authorities. The spirit of these escapades is
difficult to portray to members of a society where most people no
longer seem capable of thinking about the modern equivalents of
Tom Sawyer, Huckleberry Finn, or Kim, except as juvenile delin-

quents. We ourselves, burdened by sober professional interest in dropouts, at first found it hard to recognize that these able and engaging young men were taking pride and joy in doing exactly what the school authorities thought most reprehensible; and they were not confessing, but boasting, although their stunts had propelled them out of school.

For instance, this story from one bright lad of 15 who had run away from high school. Shortly after entering ninth grade he and his friends had appropriated a government car. (The usual pattern in such adventures is to drive off the reservation until the gas gives out.) For this offense (according to the respondent) they were restricted for the rest of the term—they were forbidden to leave the high school campus or attend any of the school recreational events, games, dances, or movies. (In effect, this meant doing nothing but going to class, performing work chores, and sitting in the dormitory.) Even then our respondent seems to have kept up with his class work and did not play hookey except in reading class:

> It was after we stole that car Mrs. Bluger [pseudonym for reading teacher] would keep asking who stole the car in class. So I just quit going there.... One night we were the only ones up in the older boys' dorm. We said, "Hell with this noise. We're not going to be the only ones here." So we snuck out and went over to the dining hall. I pried this one window open about this far and then it started to crack, so I let it go.... We heard someone so we took off. It was show that night I think. [Motion picture was being shown in school auditorium.] ... All the rest of the guys was sneaking in and getting something. So I said I was going to get my share too. We had a case of apples and a case of oranges. Then I think it was the night watchman was coming, so we run around and hid behind those steps. He shined that light on us. So I thought right then I was going to keep on going. That was around Christmas time. We walked back to Oglala [about 15 miles] and we were eating this stuff all the way back.

This young man implied that after this escapade he simply did not have the nerve to try to return to the high school. He insisted, however, that he would like to try another high school:

> I'd like to finish [high school] and get a good job someplace.

If I don't I'll probably just be a bum around here or something.

Young Men Who Stay in School

Roughly half the young Sioux who leave high school very early claim they left because they were unable to conform to school regulations. What happens to the country boys who remain? Do they "shape-up" and obey the regulations? Do they, even, come to "believe" in them? We found that most of these older and more experienced youths were, if anything, even *more* inclined to boast of triumphs over the rules than the younger fellows who had left. Indeed, all but one assured us that they were adept at hookey, and food and car stealing, and that they had frequent surreptitious beer parties and other outlaw enjoyments. We do not know whether they (especially the star athletes) actually disobey the school regulations as frequently and flagrantly as they claim. But there can be no doubt that most Sioux young men above 12 wish to be regarded as hellions in school. For them, it would be unmanly to have any other attitude. . . .

The impulse to boast of the virile achievements of youth seems to maintain itself into middle and even into old age. Country Indians with college training zestfully told how they and a group of proctors had stolen large amounts of food from the high school kitchen and were never apprehended, or how they and their friends drank three fifths of whiskey in one night and did not pass out.

Clearly, the activities school administrators and teachers denounce as immature and delinquent are regarded as part of youthful daring, excitement, manly honor, and contests of skill and wits by the Sioux young men and many of their elders.

They are also, we suspect, an integral part of the world of competitive sports. "I like to play basketball" was one of the most frequent responses of young men to the question: "What do you like most about school?" . . .

The unself-conscious devotion and ardor with which many of these young men participate in sports must be witnessed to be appreciated even mildly. . . .

Unfortunately, we have seen little evidence that school administrators and teachers recognize the opportunity to use sports as a bridge to school.

By the eleventh and twelfth grades many country Indians have left the reservation or gone into the armed services, and it is not always easy to tell which are actual dropouts. However, we did reach some. Their reasons for dropping out varied. One pled boredom: "I was just sitting there doing anything to pass the time." Another said he didn't know what made him quit: "I just didn't fit in any more. . . . I just wasn't like the other guys any more." . . .

Different as they appear at first, these statements have a common undertone: They are the expressions not of immature delinquents, but of relatively mature young men who find the atmosphere of the high school stultifying and childish.

The Dilemma of Sioux Youth

Any intense cross-cultural study is likely to reveal as many tragi-comic situations as social-scientific insights. Thus, on the Pine Ridge reservation, a majority of the young men arrive at adolescence valuing *élan*, bravery, generosity, passion, and luck, and admiring outstanding talent in athletics, singing, and dancing. While capable of wider relations and reciprocities, they function at their social best as members of small groups of peers or relatives. Yet to obtain even modest employment in the greater society, they must graduate from high school. And in order to graduate from high school, they are told that they must develop qualities exactly opposite to those they possess: a respect for humdrum diligence and routine, for "discipline" (in the sense of not smoking in toilets, not cutting classes, and not getting drunk), and for government property. In addition, they are expected to compete scholastically on a highly privatized and individualistic level, while living in large dormitories, surrounded by strangers who make privacy of any type impossible. . . .

Working Class Youth

How does our study of the Sioux relate to the problems of city dropouts? A specific comparison of the Sioux dropouts with dropouts from the urban working class—Negroes, Puerto Ricans, or whites—would, no doubt, reveal many salient differences in cultural background and world view. Nevertheless, investigations so far undertaken suggest that the attitudes held by these peoples *toward education and the schools* are startlingly similar.

Both Sioux and working class parents wish their children to continue in school because they believe that graduating from high school is a guarantee of employment. Though some teachers would not believe it, many working class dropouts, like the Sioux dropouts, express a generally favorable attitude toward school, stating that teachers are generally fair and that the worst thing about dropping out of school is missing one's friends. Most important, many working class dropouts assert that they were pushed out of school and frequently add that the push was fairly direct. The Sioux boys put the matter more delicately, implying that the school authorities would not really welcome them back.

These similarities should not be seized on as evidence that all disprivileged children are alike and that they will respond as one to the single, ideal educational policy. What it does mean is that the schools and their administrators are so monotonously alike that the boy brought up in a minority social or ethnic community can only look at and react to them in the same way. Despite their differences, they are all in much the same boat as they face the great monolith of middle class society and its one-track education escalator.

An even more important—if often unrecognized—point is that not only does the school pose a dilemma for the working class or Sioux, Negro, or Puerto Rican boy—he also poses one for the school. In many traditional or ethnic cultures boys are encouraged to be virile adolescents and become "real men." But our schools try to deprive youth of adolescence—and they demand that high school students behave like "mature people"—which in our culture often seems to mean in a pretty dull, conformist fashion.

Those who submit and succeed in school can often fit into the bureaucratic requirements of employers, but they are also likely to lack independence of thought and creativity. The dropouts are failures—they have failed to become what the school demands. But the school has failed also—failed to offer what the boys from even the most "deprived" and "underdeveloped" peoples take as a matter of course—the opportunity to become whole men.

S. M. Miller and Ira E. Harrison, studying working class youth, assert that individuals who do poorly in school are handicapped or disfavored for the remainder of their lives, because "the schools have become the occupational gatekeepers" and "the level of education affects the kind and level of job that can be attained." On the other hand, the investigations of Edgar Z. Friedenberg and Jules Henry suggest that the youths who perform creditably in high school according to the views of the authorities are disfavored in that they emerge from this experience as permanently crippled . . . human beings.

In a curious way our researches among the Sioux may be viewed as supporting both of these contentions, for they suggest that some young people leave high school because they are too vital and independent to submit to a dehumanizing situation.

A Note on the Study

In studying the adolescents on Pine Ridge we concentrated on two areas, the high school and a particular day school community with a country Indian population of about 1,000. We interviewed somewhat less than half the young people then enrolled in the high school plus a random sample of 48 young country Indians. Subsequently, we obtained basic socio-economic and educational data from all the young people who had graduated from the day school in 1961, 1962, and 1963. We interviewed 153 young people between the ages of 13 and 21, about 50 of whom were high school dropouts. We used many approaches and several types of questionnaires, but our most illuminating and reliable data were obtained from interviews conducted by Indian college students who were able to associate with the Sioux adolescents and participate in some of their activities.

While "country Sioux" or "country Indian" might loosely be considered a synonym for "full-blood," I have avoided the latter term as connoting a traditional Indian culture which vanished long ago and whose unchanging qualities were a mythology of white observers rather than a social reality of Indian participants. In any case, I use "country Indian" to refer to the people raised and living "out on the reservation (prairie)" who participate in the social and ceremonial activities of their local rural communities, as opposed to those persons, also known as Indians, who live in Pine Ridge town and make a point of avoiding these backwoods activities.

Further Reading Suggested by the Author

Formal Education in an American Indian Community by Murray L. Wax, Rosalie H. Wax, and Robert V. Dumont (The Society for the Study of Social Problems, Spring 1964). A detailed study of the Pine Ridge reservation and of the problems of children and the federal schools.

Blue-Collar World: Studies of the American Worker edited by Arthur B. Shostak and William Gomberg (Englewood Cliffs, N.J.: Prentice-Hall, 1964). See articles by S. M. Miller on problems of schools and lower class youth that are markedly similar to those in this article.

The Dignity of Youth and Other Atavisms by Edgar Z. Friedenberg
(Boston, Mass.: Beacon Press, 1966). Essays exploring the interrela-
tionship of youth and the school system.

The Chitling Test

Those schooled in psychometrics have known for some time that
traditional tests of intelligence are discriminatory. White, urban,
verbal, middle-class people score as relatively more intelligent.
The tests do not measure special aptitudes and nonverbal skills
of rural, ghetto, lower-class types—people who don't know and
don't need to know the difference between "exoteric" and "eso-
teric." There have been various, but not very successful, attempts
to develop a test of innate abilities that doesn't penalize poor
Negroes and farm boys.

There is a test, however, which does not purport to be fair, but
which is intended as a rebuke to all the others. Devised by Adrian
Dove, a social worker in Watts, it is called the Dove Counterbal-
ance Intelligence Test. It is currently making the rounds among
VISTA volunteers and other white young people who work in
the ghetto and who want to know their "ghetto IQ" and whether
they are "culturally deprived." The test consists of 30 multiple
choice questions of which the following are samples:

• Which word is out of place here? (a) Splib (b) Blood (c)
Grey (d) Spook (e) Black.

• A "handkerchief head" is (a) a cool cat (b) a porter (c)
an "Uncle Tom" (d) a hoddi (e) a "preacher."

• Cheap "chitlings" . . . will taste rubbery unless they are
cooked long enough. How soon can you quit cooking them to eat
and enjoy them? (a) 15 minutes (b) 2 hours (c) 24 hours (d)
1 week [on a low flame] (e) 1 hour.

• Hattie Mae Johnson is on the county. She has four children
and her husband is now in jail for nonsupport, as he was unemployed and was not able to give her any money. Her welfare
check is now $286 per month. Last night she went out with the

biggest player in town. If she got pregnant, then, nine months from now, how much more will her welfare check be? (a) $80 (b) $2 less (c) $35 (d) $150 (e) $100.

• "Hully Gully" came from (a) "East Oakland" (b) Fillmore (c) Watts (d) Harlem (e) Motor City.

The answer is (c) in each case.

6 Curriculum: Grim Competition, Alienating Language, and the Mythology of Imperialism

Your life at school you probably take for granted. You don't know yet what requirements you must fill as an adult. The men and women who are in charge of your work at school do know. Without your realizing exactly why you study certain subjects each year, your teachers are directing your preparation for adult life and the job you will hold.

> —Thomas Gordon Lawrence et al., Your Health and Safety (New York: Harcourt, Brace & World, 1963), a junior high school book for "slow" classes

The curriculum of our schools, commonly viewed as the sum and substance of the "knowledge" you have to acquire to be certified as a legitimate adult, is in fact a recipe concocted of myths about our society wrapped in alienating words and served up in a spirit of cut-throat competition.

The competition, which prevails at every school level and in every aspect of the curriculum, is nowhere so fierce as in athletics. Mike Spino's "Athletics: The Competition for Community Love" describes how market-place values alienate young men from what might be among their freest, least alienating activities—physical play. An aspect of market-place athletics not dealt with by Spino (for whom "adolescent" means male adolescent) is that adolescent women come to regard physical play as a largely male prerogative which they have been created to admire and encourage (not even openly to envy). Thus, by experiencing sports only vicariously, through men's bodies, women are alienated from the activities and pleasures of their own. The champion complex in sports, as elsewhere, reinforces training for market-place competition, contempt for losers, and the relegating of women to the passive role of cheerleaders and morale-supporters.

"Speling" suggests how the printed word can alienate the learner from himself and the real world. Oral language represents and describes perceptions of reality. It also creates and continually molds relationships among its users (people talking to each other). Written language is a representation of oral language. When written language or isolated and meaningless written words come to determine human fate, a frightening "reification" is in process. This reification is performed by the ten or twenty "hostile strangers" of the grade school's most revered ritual—the weekly spelling test.

In writing about alienation, Marx refers to the phenomenon that the worker's product comes to stand apart from him and confront him as a hostile and alien power. So words, which, when they are his own, assert and create the child's growing humanness, in school are put to him by the teacher as the embodiment of the world of power, for him to subdue or be subdued by. It is no wonder that those children for whom the nonverbal realities of life are most pressing (the children of the poor and despised) are least able to accommodate to the alienating force of the senseless or hostile written word.

Knowles and Prewitt's contribution suggests some of the myths about black U.S. citizens and dark citizens of the world that most nonblack U.S. citizens and a few black ones believe in. With regard to the United States, they are: that slavery was relatively unimportant until it became a cause of the Civil War; that integration is the sole strategy of blacks for overcoming oppression; that the situation of blacks in the United States is getting better all the time; and so forth. With respect to Africa (and this also holds true to some extent for the rest of the non-Western neocolonial world), the myths are: that Africa did not exist in history until it was "discovered" by Europeans; that its peoples were, and maybe still are, uncivilized, primitive, proto-human; that it took Westerners to teach these people how to be civilized and how to govern themselves; and that the European-

American role toward them is that of the benevolent, disinterested bringer of good.

Knowles and Prewitt refer to the textbooks' "inability to acknowledge the historical and present disparity between our stated ideals and our institutional practice." A more accurate statement might be that the myths purveyed by the textbooks— in other words, the heart of our social studies curriculum— portray the oppression of minorities at home and of technologically backward peoples abroad as if the oppression were nonexistent, unwitting, or in the interests of the oppressed.

Thus the myths both conceal and justify an oppression that can be shown to serve the interests of the oppressor. The interests are the perpetuation of a national and world system of domination which we can call imperialism.

Although native U.S. working men and women, especially white ones, benefit from the world position of U.S. capitalism, they are also among its victims. "Myths About Work and Labor" demonstrates how standard textbooks mystify working people's relations to the processes of production and falsify their great historic struggles for freedom. Thus the books conceal from white boys and girls the hardships and struggles of their ancestors which might help them to identify in sympathy and understanding with the hardships and struggles of their dark brothers and sisters at home and abroad.

Nowhere is the mythology concealing historical policies of extermination and present policies of oppression more romantic or more insidious than with regard to native Americans. The degradation of whole peoples to the status of a bad joke, as reported in ". . . Not One Indian Child . . . ," eats away the self-respect of the child who is the butt and rots the humanity of the child who is the snickerer. If the Battle of Waterloo was won on the playing fields of Eton, the extermination of the people of Vietnam was begun in the schoolrooms of America.

In these selections, we see that racism, which, like sexism, is often justified or criticized as arising out of human nature or ignorance, is in fact fed and watered by the standard curriculum of compulsory public schools.

Athletics: The Competition for Community Love

by Mike Spino

Almost every adolescent wants to be a touchdown hero, or high scorer on the basketball team. Yearly, thousands of students bounce balls, select bats, and run laps with an enthusiasm shared in no other school subject or discipline. Because of this degree of involvement, many people carry with them, their whole lives, values developed in these activities. It is my hope in describing the events that led to my own understandings that I can help those who, in their love of sport, are being used as pawns in a meaningless, educationally unrewarding game.

I grew up in a small New Jersey suburb which is located ten miles from New York City. The school was similar to most. The entire year was full of athletic seasons and games. What did these activities mean to the athletes? It wasn't really scoring the baskets, winning the praise; it was more subtle, an easier thing to damage. I was shaping an image of myself, my worth and value as a human being, to feel, be aware—and care about others.

I can remember spending hour upon hour shooting baskets in the half-light of our neighborhood court. I had many fantasies about myself. I would spend days working these images over in my mind. Sometimes I would spend an afternoon playing and daydreaming an entire season. I wanted something good and beautiful for myself and the kids I played with—and we should have been able to continue constructing our visions. Perhaps, then, my athletic education might have been different. As it was, we were forced to hate and play against each other.

One incident stands out. Once, during an early season basketball game, my best friend broke his ankle. I was glad—happy that the competition for community love was lessened. I would go to football games, and feel jealous every time someone was praised. It wasn't the adulation that angered me, it was the nature of the spectators' behavior. Their vicarious thrills, stored-up anxiety, and resentment at living half-lives were dumped into the air with screams and shouts to further pit athlete against athlete, totally consuming them.

According to the season, a clique of athletes "ruled" the school, only to be followed by other groups until the year exhausted itself and everyone was let out to either await the summer, or find other organizations to rule. I can remember the day after the annual Thanksgiving Day football game. The basketball team was having morning practice. Through the windows would peek a crew of football players. They would come into the gym and make some awkward moves, already feeling unneeded in the new role of non-heroes. If you were a graduating athlete, June was likely to be a time of brutal realization. Some won scholarships but most looked unsuccessfully for high-paying jobs, only to meet the Fall with a melancholy and crumbling image. . . .

Athletic activities as confrontations with the environment, enabling us to earn a sense of self-mastery by handling and overcoming stress, should be the learning experience. Instead, athletics has become a pragmatic business of winning regardless of what it does to the total feeling, thinking person. Beauty to most coaches means a scored basket or a fast run, even at the price of personal expression or development. They exist in a brutally ordered world, propagated by sex symbols and relegated to commodity selling. To them, winning is success, losing is failure. Profit is either made or lost, business is in the black or the red. . . .

Sensitive students by the dozens are being forced to organize physical activities outside established teams. These youth, who are in most instances honest and idealistic, cannot reconcile their enforced behavior on playing fields with the beginning attempts to find themselves. They refuse to sacrifice their identity to the goddess of victory—and suffer greatly. In their isolation, they present small obstacles to coaches familiar with the techniques of labeling "undesirables." The students who look and dress differently, or have personal human problems, are the first to be turned away. Throughout the United States, the length of one's hair is becoming an issue. Coaches are taking sides for and against school and societal innovation. Will the students have personal rights or will the coaches have dictatorial privileges? Our most important educational decisions may emanate from the hair debate.

Athletic contests and games present an optimum environment for people trying to come to terms with personal inconsistencies and problems. The best athletic environment should mean one in which people experience joy while learning about themselves through physical struggle. Joy means individual awareness and concern for others. . . .

What I am suggesting is a change in ethics. Coaches seem to have forgotten why men engage in sport. Every training run is considered money in the bank, and each basketball practice is followed by a hundred practice throws. These activities ready a man to push a key-punch or open a bank account but have no relationship to joyous experience.

SUPPOSE coaches were told that their seasons were to be judged on a per capita joy ratio. At first there would be chaos. Without a solid base for measurement the athletes would feel lost, insecure. Slowly, they might begin to recall the original thrills of a child's physical life. Runners might gallop like horses. Basketball could again become the ballet of short steps and graceful leaps. The grim animalism of modern sport would pass.

Speling

by Gloria Channon

The teacher was dictating a list of three-letter words to a fifth grade class: *"Can."* A boy raised his hand. "Which *can* do you mean—*can* of beans or *can* I go?"

The classroom was in a middle-class school; the boy was reading on grade level. His question was not as foolish as it may at first appear. He had observed that the meanings of words vary with their context, and that sometimes these variations have different spellings. He had observed that the sounds of words vary: sometimes *can* is pronounced *k'n*.

But in spite of his quite sophisticated observations, he had not learned to relate the variations of the spoken language with their written symbols. Until he learned that relationship, he would be hampered in both reading and writing. For the reading-writing process to be effective, the first hurdle has to be overcome: the eye must learn what the ear has learned. One of the most direct ways to help him learn this is through spelling instruction—but not through the spelling curriculum in widespread use today.

In the search for more effective techniques, we tend to concentrate on the major areas of the curriculum: reading, math, science.

From *The Urban Review*, Vol. 3, No. 3 (January, 1969), published by the Center for Urban Education, New York, N.Y. Reprinted by permission.

Largely ignored is the teaching of spelling, an isolated compulsive ritual which takes place almost daily in every classroom throughout the elementary school years.

Year in, year out, we as parents have watched our children march in the dull lockstep of Pre-test (Monday), Alphabetize (Tuesday), Buddy-test (Wednesday), Sentences (Thursday) and Re-test (Friday); and we have seen the words learned so grimly and with such effort die in use on Saturday like Solomon Grundy, to be buried on Sunday in the cluttered, inaccessible deeps of the child's mind. . . .

Let us look at the prescription in current use in the New York City Public Schools, the curriculum bulletin for spelling.

The basic premises of the program are:

1. That spelling should be taught with regard for the child's pattern of growth in language, in relation to his vocabulary needs
2. That spelling is not taught until the child has gained a considerable sight vocabulary (usually the end of first grade or beginning of the second)
3. That spelling is viewed primarily as a tool and adjunct of writing, and that the words taught have been selected from a frequency count of words used by children in their writing

The 5,000 words selected by frequency-count studies are distributed over ten levels, related—supposedly—to children's age and interest. Thus *rock* appears at level 3, and *rocket* at level 10.

The simplest spelling pattern in English is Consonant + Vowel + Consonant: *cat*. To write or read dozens and dozens of words of this pattern, the child needs to know 18 regular consonant sounds and five vowel sounds. But I have found repeatedly that only two or three children in a New York City fifth or sixth grade class will be able to write a list of 40 words of this pattern correctly, or read them without hesitation and error. I am not talking now of the ability to "read" the meaning: I am talking of the ability to "read" the sound. Without the latter ability, the former will be so constricted as to be almost useless anywhere, except in the shelter of the controlled vocabulary readers.

Reading has not developed the word-attack skills of children so that they will be able to deal with any regular three-letter word they may meet. But why hasn't spelling done the job?

Look at the frequency–word-list distribution of three-letter words in the bulletin:

LEVEL	PATTERN Consonant + a + Consonant
1	cat can had man ran (am, an, at)
2	bad fat hat sat
3	bag cap gas mad rat
4	Jan. pan sad
5	map tag
6	dam fan lad lap mat nap pal pat rag Sat. tan
7	ham jam tap
8	—
9	pad ram vat
10	—

The following do not even appear: dad, cab, jab, rap, sap, wag, gag, nag. . . .

Select any sound-spelling pattern that you wish, and you will find the same random spread. And at each level the words are taught in lists of ten or twenty, often selected at random by the classroom teacher, so each time a word is encountered it is encountered as an isolated singular word, one more hostile stranger to be learned all by itself and added gradually and we hope permanently to the other 4,999 hostile strangers on the list. . . .

One of the most maddeningly illogical aspects of the frequency spelling list is its complete disorder. It presents *spices* before *spice*, *frightened* before *fright*. Inflections, suffixed words, plurals, compounds, all jumbled together until it is no wonder that a child, taught *nice* before *ice*, taught *exciting* at level 5 and *excitement* at level 6 and finally *excite* at level 10 will sometimes respond with astonishment when told that there is a relationship of structure and meaning among many words. . . .

To use the idea of frequency count as a basis for teaching spelling (and reading) is to misread the nature of both. Spelling is simply the agreed upon arrangement of letters to represent the sounds of the language. Reading and writing are simply the skills needed to manipulate with some understanding the written symbols of the spoken language.

Teachers often seem to assume that reading is more important than speaking. We forget that writing was developed primarily to extend the spoken language in time and space. We forget that nothing very meaningful has happened until the words, whether received by the ear or the eye, are reacted to by the brain. We place high value on the silent classroom and do not check constantly to see that what is being understood by the child is what we want him to understand. We tend to treat what is written as a special and higher form of language, to be divorced from speech and from sound as quickly as possible. Children will often read in the exaggerated, overstressed phrasing they picked up from teachers reading "with feeling" the sterile unnatural prose of the primers. At the other extreme, children come to associate flat, robot intonations with reading to such an extent that when they are asked to dictate a story they will automatically fall into word-calling and the staccato syntax of primers. Reading, at its most elementary, is the ability to recognize the sounds of the language in their written forms. At a higher level, it is the ability to reproduce those sounds in phrases and sentences, in the accepted and understandable intonation patterns of grammatical speech. Ultimately, reading is the ability to understand the levels of meaning embedded in the sentences and to respond to them.

We might fruitfully compare the reading process with the speaking process. The infant learns to abstract significant sounds from the continuous flow of language and to use some of those sounds as his first words; then he learns to string the isolated sounds into sentences of increasing length and complexity; finally, he learns to express and to understand complicated ideas. Our so-called disadvantaged children have followed this process; even our verbally advantaged children have.

Too often the skills needed for reading are taught as though they were but one skill. A large part of remedial instruction then becomes a sorting out of the skills and treating them separately: e.g., sounding out new words, and then understanding what is meant by those sounds. Many children do learn to read and write without having the separate skills formally dissected for them. But they seem to have developed their own rules of thumb for translating the written words into recognizable sounds. (The converse— translating sounds into written words—is not so successfully developed.) Often these children are the ones who have been raised in a "verbal environment." Anyone who has overhead (as I have) a conscientiously articulate mother talking to her three-year-old in front of the penguin enclosure at the Coney Island aquarium will know what I mean by a verbal environment. The children of this environment have an extended vocabulary to draw on, and a mindset, inculcated from infancy, which seems to say that no real experience exists until it has been translated into words, pinned down like so many lexical butterflies to be kept forever and re-examined from time to time. . . .

How, then, should we develop our spelling curriculum, so that it will serve us most efficiently in writing and reading? First of all, we will base our lessons on the sound patterns of the language. Each lesson will contain many variations on a single theme. Many of the words will be in the child's speaking or hearing vocabulary, but some will not. They will be spoken and listened to, written and looked at, compared and contrasted, in isolation and in context. The small number of truly "irregular" words (*any, many*) that don't seem to fit any pattern will be introduced one or two or three at a time, clearly identified as exceptions.

Second, the spelling lesson will use the spoken language as much as the written one in learning the sounds. It will use the sounds the child makes as the basis for learning. It will train the child to listen to how *he* says the word, how the teacher says it, and how it looks when written down. It will not drive the child into uncomfortable, inadequate silence when he does not "say the word right." One of my boys, in the middle of a spelling lesson based on *st* words, said, "Las' year my teacher use' to holler at me saying mos'. Boy, I use' to get mad. She always said *mos'* herself." The spelling program will work to increase his sensitivity, and his teacher's, to the sounds people make, and to identify those sounds in speech and writing.

Third, the spelling lesson will encourage the child to be orderly in his thinking. If he errs on the side of logic (*fossul*) he will see that his mistake was not the result of stupidity or ignorance. He must accept, as we all have, the arbitrary standard spellings of the language. But he will learn to avoid the confusion and noncommunication of a word like *frangloss*. And he will bring the liberating orderly skills to the printed page and to his own writing.

Fourth, meaning will not be approached primarily in the scavenger hunt through the dictionary, but in an analysis of structure, in the observation of words and sounds, of roots and compounds and affixes and inflexions. He will make discoveries about the language, even from a foolish game like writing your name backwards. (Seth discovered that there was no approved English way of pronouncing his name backward: *Htes*. He is now less likely to spell *either* as *eihter*.)

Fifth, spelling will encourage the teacher to stress constantly the sound-sight relationship. She will encourage the children to become sound-detectives, imitating instead of ridiculing each other's speech, looking for clues to sounds in strange words, flexing their multisyllabic muscles.

And last, it will free more of the time allotted to *reading* to be used in working with ideas, with enriched vocabulary in context, with the subtleties of sentence structure and emotional or factual content.

Let us take some of the time devoted to a search for excuses for our failure to look at our own contributions to it. Instead of finding more complicated and tortuous descriptions (dyslexia, disadvantaged, language deprivation!), let us change the conditions in which the failure occurs. A doctor may satisfy some inner need of the patient by labeling a cold as an upper respiratory infection, but he is not curing it. Although in idle daydreams we envision a whole nation of teachers radically and sensibly reforming, in one generation, the spelling of English, we know that such a goal is unrealistic. But we know too that the goal of literacy is not an impossible dream.

The Miseducation of White Children

by Louis L. Knowles and Kenneth Prewitt

In their treatment of racial matters, American history textbooks present an idealized and distorted picture of the national state of affairs. In the past the general public (most teachers and school administrators included) has either been unaware of the "great lie of silence," as Mark Twain put it, or has chosen to let half-truths remain as educational content. Although there recently have been efforts to correct errors and to include the black American in textbooks, these efforts still fall far short of a fair treatment. The new texts, although less overtly racist than the old, are marked by the same inability to acknowledge the historical and present disparity

From Louis L. Knowles & Kenneth Prewitt, Editors, *Institutional Racism in America,* © 1969. Reprinted by permission of Prentice-Hall, Inc., Englewood Cliffs, N.J.

between our stated ideals and actual institutional practices. This lack of a self-critical perspective extends to the treatment of other societies, particularly the nonwhite, non-Western, nonindustrialized cultures, which are evaluated in terms of their acceptance or rejection of white American values.

The treatment of American minority groups in traditional textbooks has been abominable, with publishers catering to the "Southern view." A study by the Anti-Defamation League covering the twenty-four major secondary school U.S. history texts in 1949 and again in 1961 showed that the treatment of Asiatic and Spanish-speaking minorities had improved steadily if slowly, although there was still much distortion in the 1961 texts. However, the position of the Negro in texts over this period had not changed; he remained "invisible."[1]

A study of the texts used in California public schools in 1964 showed the same results: "While the authors of the books must know that there are Negroes in America and have been since 1619, they evidently do not care to mention them too frequently. In one book there is no account of slavery in the colonial period; in a second, there is not a single word about Negroes after the Civil War; in a third (composed of documents and substantive chapters), the narrative does not mention Negroes in any connection."[2] . . .

Since 1963 the pressure of the civil rights movement has brought a rash of new "integrated" textbooks. These "multiethnic" texts are less overtly racist and include more Negro history and some treatment of the civil rights movement and of black people's position in contemporary America. Yet the texts fall short of an accurate statement of white individual and institutional racism and of the life and struggles of the black people throughout the history of America. . . .

A shortcoming even more serious than the inconsistent and superficial treatment of black people in American history is the misleading optimism which pervades coverage of racial matters. The authors of the new books assume that assimilation of blacks into the present American society is possible and desired by both blacks and whites. In accord with this assumption the authors

---

[1] Lloyd Marcus, "The Treatment of Minorities in Secondary School Textbooks" (New York: Anti-Defamation League, 1961), pp. 38–48.

[2] Kenneth M. Stampp *et al.*, "The Negro in American History Textbooks," unpublished paper accepted unanimously by the California State Board of Education on March 12, 1964, p. 2.

minimize individual racism, ignore institutional racism, and exaggerate white support for the black struggle. In addition, they fail to mention any black political or cultural forces that assert an ethnic or cultural identity of their own or that are directed toward any other goal than assimilation into white America.

The new texts emphasize what whites have done in the civil rights movement, but they play down the extent and violent nature of white opposition to the struggle for equality. Thus, the books stress legislation, the area in which whites have done most of their work for civil rights. But the legislative loopholes and the nonenforcement of civil rights laws are largely ignored. Furthermore, the texts do not recognize the problems which legislation alone cannot solve, problems such as unemployment, police brutality, or lack of access to positions of power. . . .

Even the history text *Land of the Free*, which was commended by the AFT pamphlet[3] for its treatment of the civil rights movement, exaggerates the role of whites, particularly the federal government.[4] The text implies that the "important advances" which have theoretically been made came about through action by the federal government which would have occurred without the demonstrations. . . .

In dealing with the civil rights movement, *Land of the Free* emphasizes the Supreme Court decision on school integration in 1954 and the work of Martin Luther King (the only black named as a leader of demonstrations). There is considerable space devoted to the programs of Booker T. Washington, but only passing reference to W. E. B. DuBois, a founder of the NAACP, who came much closer to demanding full human rights for black people. DuBois's demands were unacceptable to the whites in power. His forthright attack on American racism is as repugnant to the whites in control of textbooks today as it was during his lifetime. Militant organizations such as CORE and SNCC and the black separatist movements of Marcus Garvey, the Black Muslims, and Malcolm X are entirely ignored. Thus the text brings the struggle for black liberation into the American system by stressing white participation and government support, while failing to recognize any leaders or groups which asserted black identity or demanded more than white

[3] Irving Sloan, *The Negro in Modern American History Textbooks,* 2d ed. (Washington, D.C.: American Federation of Teachers, AFL-CIO, 1967).

[4] John W. Caughey, John Hope Franklin, and Ernest R. May, *Land of the Free* (Pasadena, Calif.: Franklin Publications, 1967).

America was ready to allow. This approach does not convey the severity of the oppression or the bitterness of the struggle for self-determination; it also leaves the white student without an awareness of the rapidly growing trend toward black consciousness and self-rule in the black community.

Coverage of the culture of black people is negligible. Only those areas are covered which have influenced the tastes and values of white America. For example, in *Land of the Free* blues are not mentioned at all, and jazz is mentioned only insofar as it was popular in mainstream America in general in the 1920's. The text mentions no black musicians or athletes, presumably because the California Curriculum Commission has ordered that books should help pupils to refrain from attempts at stereotyping. Admittedly, a discussion of black musicians and athletes alone would not be adequate coverage of black culture, but their exclusion has not been balanced by the inclusion of black authors, artists, and social thinkers. Stereotyping is not remedied by reducing the amount of information but by increasing its volume and scope.

The "ethnocentrism" of white American society affects not only the way our textbooks treat whites and blacks in America, but also how they treat the history and culture of other peoples. The attitudes that one's own race, nation, and culture are superior to all others may be natural but nevertheless very dangerous beliefs. American textbooks generally treat European cultures as basically the same as our own with the addition of the accumulated ornaments of antiquity. However, when dealing with areas beyond the white, Western world, the authors change their approach significantly.

The treatment of people of color in nonindustrialized countries, even in the new textbooks, denies the existence of fully integrated cultures based upon values and institutions different from our own. An anthropologist from a major university who had just received the edited version of a fourth-grade monograph on a South Sea Island culture remarked that "as usual, the editors have cut everything that was actually different from American culture." He commented further that he always had to tone down cultural differences when writing and that publishers, hoping to sell their books widely, cut out most of what was left.

Let us take the elementary school children in California schools as an example. They are exposed to African culture in the regular curriculum only through two short chapters in the seventh-grade

Eurasia[6] and, if their school has purchased them, through two supplementary books—one a seventh-grade supplement to *Eurasia* entitled *Africa*.[7] The brevity of coverage would be partially excusable if the material were fair. But a survey of *Eurasia* and *Africa* shows how our racism, ethnocentrism, and paternalism are interwoven.

Eurasia begins: "Until about sixty years ago, Africa was often spoken of as the Dark Continent." The rest of the chapter makes it clear that, thanks to white efforts, this name is becoming less appropriate. The history of Africa in both this and the supplementary text is the story of how Europeans "discovered" and developed Africa.

In *Africa* there is not a single discussion of a traditional African culture that gives a sense of different values and another way of life from that in America. The very categories into which the discussion of African life is divided do not allow for other than an ethnocentric presentation. Following a single chapter on the races and ecology of African people, the headings for the rest of the book are "Farming and Grazing," "Natural Resources," "Industry," "Transportation," "Cities of Africa," and "Education and Health." Thus the book deals almost entirely with technology and economy, the most important factors in American eyes and the dimensions of society in which Africa suffers most by comparison.

Despite the fact that anthropologists and historians now document the existence of highly organized civilizations with complex legal systems in sub-Sahara Africa for the past fifteen to twenty centuries,[8] *Africa* suggests continually that Africans did not know how to govern themselves until Europeans instructed them: "As more Africans became educated and learned about life in the rest of the world, they came to believe that they would have better lives if they could govern themselves. . . . In some parts of Africa, the people do not yet know how to govern themselves in a peaceful, orderly way. . . . The British government has worked hard to train the people in its colonies for self-government."[9] These passages continue the stereotype of the Dark Continent to which benevolent Europeans brought the gift of enlightenment.

[6] Robert M. Glendinning, and Marguerite U. Hley, *Eurasia: Lands and Peoples of the World* (Boston: Ginn, 1958).

[7] William D. Allen, *Africa* (Sacramento: California State Department of Education, 1964).

[8] Basil Davidson, *The Lost Cities of Africa* (Boston: Little, Brown. 1959).

[9] Allen, *op. cit.*, pp. 53–54.

There is no recognition of the rights of African people. These books discuss colonization without one word as to what Africans felt about this usurpation and exploitation of themselves, their resources, and their cultures. The struggle against European domination and the process of gaining independence are mentioned only with the doubtful comment that where tribes have had little contact with the outside world, "they are greatly puzzled by the changes and often resentful of coming foreigners."[10] It is not asked why foreigners are invading the territory.

Western influence is lumped together under the heading of "modernization" and is implicitly considered good: "Since 1900 great changes have taken place in Africa, and changes are continuing rapidly today. People from other continents are penetrating to all parts of Africa. They are bringing with them modern ideas and modern ways of living and working."[11] The books do not admit the exploitation of African labor and resources and the destruction of native culture that have accompanied foreign modernization. In *Africa*'s single attempt to pay homage to traditional craftsmen, the handmade goods are admitted to be "beautiful," but "craftsmen cannot produce the things needed for a modern way of life."[12] The implication is that the acquisition of a European way of life is the only acceptable social goal, and therefore the craftsmen must be replaced.

Given the assumption that modernization has first priority and the fact that Africa's people "do not have the money or equipment to build dams, power plants, industries, schools, hospitals, and other things that they must have to become modern nations,"[13] it follows that Africans must be dependent on the paternalism of white Western nations. In this view, just as the Africans needed Europeans to show them how to govern themselves, they now "need" Europeans to show them how to build up their countries. Thus the texts prepare the way for a very favorable presentation of current white paternalism toward Africa. "People in other parts of the world are trying to help the nations of Africa. Britain, France, and other former colonial powers are lending money and sending engineers and other skilled workers to Africa. The United Nations, the United States, and the Soviet Union are also giving

---

[10] Glendinning and Hley, *op. cit.*, p. 324.

[11] *Ibid.*, p. 315.

[12] Allen, *op. cit.*, p. 116.

[13] *Ibid.*, pp. 54–55.

aid."[14] Pictures show European foremen instructing African laborers. The greater part of *Africa* is spent in discussing the dams, schools, industries, and roads which white men have either built or shown Africans how to build.

Underlying the treatment of nonwhite cultures in *Eurasia* and *Africa* are the assumptions that white values and forms of government are by nature good and must be shared with the less fortunate nonwhites of the world. Africans are presented not as having a *different* culture and way of life from white Americans, but as having *no* culture worth saving. Africans may be seen as "good" only when they have adopted the "modern" white way of life. Until then people of color should be grateful to whites for their generosity in helping them to become "white." The presentation in the new texts is merely a continuation of the old "white man's burden" notion in more subtle form. But the use of "modern," "Western," and "European" in place of "white" does not change the fact of underlying racism. Through books such as these, American schoolchildren today are acquiring the same sense of white superiority to other cultures that their parents and grandparents learned from lessons about "savages" and the "Dark Continent." In a manner similar to the new American history textbooks, *Eurasia* and *Africa* carry on the racism of their predecessors in a form that is less overt but just as false and dangerous.

[14] *Ibid.,* p. 55.

Myths About Work and Labor
by Will Scoggins

G. K. Chesterton, noted early-twentieth-century essayist, supposedly said that Times Square at night would be the most wondrous sight in the world for a man who couldn't read. So it might be said, with less exaggeration, that the United States as portrayed in high school social studies textbooks would seem very near

From Will Scoggins, *Labor in Learning: Public School Treatment of the World of Work,* Institute of Industrial Relations, University of California, Los Angeles, 1966. Reprinted by permission of the publisher.

paradise for a man who was blind to economic and social facts. . . .

In searching the textbooks on the subjects of Section 7 (a) of the National Industrial Recovery Act and the National Labor Relations (Wagner) Act, items 11 and 12, I had in mind the importance of the historical context in which these profoundly precedent-making acts, which encouraged collective bargaining, came about. For instance, it seems inconceivable that an author should simply state that in 1883 Congress enacted the Pendleton Civil Service Act without pointing out that the "spoils system" had been a part of political life so long that the very words had become popular parlance, that abuses had existed for three-quarters of a century in government employment, that a President of the United States had just been assassinated by a disappointed spoilsman, and that the Civil Service Act was a public-policy reaction to these disturbing events. Only in this context does the Act have meaning to the student living in the comfort of present-day recognized merit rating in public employment.

These labor acts must also be described in relation to more than a century of organized management's intense opposition to organized labor. As late as 1917, the Supreme Court was still upholding the enforceability of "yellow-dog" contracts, still standing as a firm ally of management against the ambitions of labor. "Blacklisting," company unions, labor spies, use of Pinkerton and Baldwin-Felts private detectives and strikebreakers, or even the use of public law-enforcement officers and National Guardsmen were still hampering the organization of workingmen until the passage of the N.R.A. legislation. The student should know that these laws were passed to correct practices widely offensive to the civil rights of employees. The government was insuring, under law, the right of employees to bargain collectively with their employers, and to select their bargaining representatives without interference from the employer. Bragdon and McCutchen, in *History of a Free People* (p. 602), put it thus:

> Once the New Deal was launched, labor's rights to organize received even more protection. Section 7 (a) of the *National Recovery Act* provided that every N.R.A. code should guarantee the worker's right of collective bargaining and forbid employers to interfere with the formation of labor unions. Section 7 (a) encouraged a rapid revival of unionism. Be-

tween May and October, 1933, the American Federation of Labor gained 1,500,000 new members.

This treatment implies that congressmen were not only yielding to the pleading of workers; they were looking with a broader vision to the United States itself, and they saw that the existing labor-management anarchy was in fact detrimental to the whole nation. Title I, Section 1, of the National Labor Relations (Wagner) Act states with precision the reasons for the passage of that law:

> The inequality of bargaining power between employees who do not possess full freedom of association or actual liberty of contract, and employers who are organized in the corporate or other forms of ownership association substantially burdens and affects the flow of commerce, and tends to aggravate recurrent business depressions, by depressing wage rates and the purchasing power of wage earners in industry and by preventing the stabilization of competitive wage rates and working conditions within and between industries.

. . . Most textbooks associate the capitalist system, in its older and perhaps purer laissez-faire definition, with the "American way," and deal severely with any proposed or accomplished changes in that system. In Muzzey and Link's *Our Country's History* (p. 705), one finds a full-page engraving, done in a most artistic way, showing a giant monument before which parade George Washington and the valiant Revolutionary Army. The monument rests upon a giant stone entitled, "Fundamental Belief in God." Above this stone is a slightly smaller one, but still part of the base, called "Constitutional Government Designed to Serve the People." On the monument itself, headed by the American eagle and entitled "Political and Economic Rights Which Protect the Dignity and Freedom of the Individual," one starts to read what is obviously the Bill of Rights—the right to free speech and press, the right to trial by jury, and so on, down the line. But suddenly one reads, "the right to own private property, the right to go into business, compete, make a profit, the right to bargain for goods and services in a free market, the right to freedom from arbitrary government regulations and control," and one realizes that something has happened here to the Bill of Rights. . . .
Strikes are usually portrayed as exceedingly violent and accom-

plishing nothing. Unions, as political activists and instigators of social-economic legislation, are adequately described by only two of the eighteen U.S. history textbooks and by only one-third of the government-and-problems books. Even an adequate definition of such words as "injunction." "arbitration," "closed shop," etc., is seldom given in the books. Although more care is exhibited in describing the labor-management laws now existent, little is said of the historical background, or the need, for such legislation. Collective bargaining, which has established a system of industrial jurisprudence in most of American industry, whether organized by a union or not, is ignored by well over half of all books. Little is said of automation, and what is said suggests that a technological marvel is in the offing, with little hint of accompanying labor dislocations. Social Security, although generally better handled than most other items of this study (perhaps because it is easier to chart with lists of benefits), still seems a bit paternalistic to some authors. Possible extensions of such legislation, or precedents set by other democratic countries, are usually ignored or dismissed as socialistic. Workmen's Compensation and state disability insurance are barely mentioned in most U.S. history books and adequately handled by only a minority of the government-and-problems books. Progressive taxation is treated with childish naïveté.

If this study were to end with the perusal of textbooks, the question of what is being taught to prospective employees of America about labor and the economy would have to receive a rather unsatisfactory answer. The answer would be unsatisfactory not so much because of a lack of information, but because . . . what is included in the textbook so often invites, encourages, and even demands an anti-labor position from the reader. . . .

Not a single labor topic, except industrial versus craft unions, was adequately described or explained in the majority of the textbooks. Not a single U.S. history text did more than mention the political activities of unions, both historically and presently— despite the fact that the very educational institution the student now occupies is, at least in part, a result of such activities. Only two history texts went beyond mentioning the all-important labor-management practice of free collective bargaining. None told the student about the public employment service, a service he will most likely have need of shortly after graduation. None told him of disability insurance. None made a case for public assistance programs.

By a perusal of today's textbooks, few students will be diverted from the "great man" theory of history. George Washington launched the nation, Madison was the "father of the Constitution," Jackson gave the masses the right to vote, Lincoln freed the slaves, F.D.R. saved the nation during the Depression, and, if you please, Samuel Gompers created the American labor movement. The history of the nation is portrayed as the work of earlier-day Matt Dillons and men from U.N.C.L.E., who single-handedly stood against hosts of wrong and, naturally, triumphed. There is little to indicate that collective action or mass pressure may often have forced the "great man" to act in the manner now considered great to keep his elected office. And there is most certainly very little which will apprise the student of the techniques employees have historically used to become members of the middle class, a class to which most high school students seem to aspire.

The teacher of the social studies, who works from these textbooks, is himself a highly mobile product of the lower middle class who has achieved middle-class comfort and laid claim to professional status. He has done the first by hard work at more than one job and the second by presumption. His formal education in industrial relations is almost nonexistent, and he regards any acquaintance with labor unions as vaguely damaging to his image. He sees himself as mildly liberal but associates the concept with Jefferson rather than with Walter Reuther. His teen-aged charges often baffle and enrage him. He despairs of breaking through their peculiar adolescent barriers and their comfortable complaisance. He has little faith in himself, and even less in his colleagues, to rouse his students to high-minded idealism. He is tired.

In summary, this study has revealed serious shortcomings in the textbooks' treatment of the labor movement and social-economic security legislation. Textbooks overgeneralize; they distort the import of labor's role in the history of the American success; they may even exaggerate that success itself in the hope of satisfying ardently patriotic boards of education; they may be too fervent in their proclamations of the middle-class ethic of accumulation and consumption. But, even so, they do contain some basic facts. The student can learn something of labor's past and even of labor's present; he can learn the details, if not the spirit, of such relatively noncontroversial subjects as the Social Security Act.

What is also most distressingly missing in the classroom is not just the basic information. It is the will to teach the subject of labor and the will to learn it. The liberal teacher, tired and sometimes even cynical, too often believes that labor has reached the "dry rot" stage, that its evangelism is gone, its earlier promise of a brighter tomorrow largely fulfilled. The conservative teacher, circumspect and sometimes even suspicious, more often believes that labor is "too big" and a dangerous threat to the economic stability of the nation. And both men are apt to believe that the presently alleged misdoings of James R. Hoffa are representative of the American labor movement today.

"There Is Not One Indian Child Who Has Not Come Home in Shame and Tears"

by Rupert Costo and the American Indian Historical Society

In our contact with the whites, we have always and without fail asked for one thing. We wanted education. You can examine any treaty, any negotiations with the American whites. The first condition, specifically asked for by the Indian tribes, was education. What we got was third-rate, left-handed, meager, miserly, unqualified training, with the greatest expenditure of federal funds and the least amount of actual education for the Indian himself. . . .

The American Indian Historical Society has been working in the field of education for four years. We were only a small group of dedicated Indians to begin with. Now we have the added strength of the Ad Hoc Committee which is bringing this work still further forward. The Society began its program with a period of investigation as to what was being taught about Indians in the schools. On the elementary level, we found general misinformation in the textbooks, teachers largely unprepared, instructional material generally lacking, and an overwhelming lack of information about the Indian today. On the high school level, we found outright slanders against Indian people in the books. . . .

As evidence I submit the August edition of *The Indian His-*

From *The Study of the Education of Indian Children,* Hearings before the Special Subcommittee on Indian Education of the Committee on Labor and Public Welfare, United States Senate, Government Printing Office, 1969. Statement of Rupert Costo, American Indian Historical Society and Chairman Cahuilla Indian Tribe, and Exhibit on "Land of the Oaks," submitted by the American Indian Historical Society. Reprinted by permission of the American Indian Historical Society.

torian which contains a criticism and evaluation of seven state-adopted textbooks in detail. . . . There is not one Indian in the whole of this country who does not cringe in anguish and frustration because of these textbooks. There is not one Indian child who has not come home in shame and tears after one of those sessions in which he is taught that his people were dirty, animal-like, something less than a human being. . . .

"LAND OF THE OAKS"

by JAMES HARLOW

☆

Published 1953 by Oakland Unified School District	EVALUATION	Reprinted 1955 and 1959. Edition 1959 here Evaluated

Submitted by the American Indian Historical Society, an All-Indian educational, cultural, and historical organization. . . .

GENERAL: This book contains no factual material concerning the American Indian in the Oakland area. No sources are quoted. No references are given. No evidence is submitted to support the propaganda material contained therein. It purports to be a departure "to some extent, from the usual social studies textbook in that it is light and conversational in approach; it deals with the anecdotal and humorous phases of local history, as well as the factual; and it is colored in places so as to secure more dramatic reading." (Preface)

This statement appears to be a plea for the reader's indulgence as to any possible errors contained in the book. The approach is not merely "light." It is facetious in the extreme. Such an approach is ill suited to such a subject as the Indians of America as to their role in our history. Especially when it is tinctured with outright misinterpretation of Indian life and history. To display prejudice is bad enough. But to try and be funny about it adds insult to error.

Page 16:

a) "They [the Indians] liked the land for the same reason the animals had. The weather was warm and comfortable. There was plenty of food for everybody."

The comparison between Indians and animals is degrading to the Indians as a people, as a race, and as individuals.

All human beings have "animal" instincts and needs. Yet textbooks do not make such comparisons about other peoples. . . .

b) "The Digger Indians liked to take life easy."

There was no such tribe as Digger. This is a term of insult and ought not to be used.

Indian life was not "easy," nor was the native lazy. He worked hard and well, and had a highly organized life, or he could not have survived in decency, in that type of society and in that environment. . . .

Page 18:
a) "When winter came and the cold winds started to blow, they covered their bodies with big gobs of mud. They left the mud on all winter, only replacing from time to time what had fallen off."

This is a misinterpretation of Indian customs. Generally, the body was covered with mud in certain ceremonies, in certain rituals, in an effort to hide from the white man's depredations, and as a cleansing agent. At no time was "mud" utilized to keep the body warm, nor was it ever left on the body for any length of time.

East Bay Indian tribes, like all others in California, were expert tanners. They had available to them, and freely utilized, all types of skins. They owned blankets of rabbit fur, otter, and skins of other furred animals. They hunted local game for this purpose as well as for food, and they traded for other furs with distant tribes. . . .

Page 21:
a) "It seems like an awfully complicated way of taking a bath, but it was probably better than no bath at all."

The steam bath is an Indian invention now utilized by the whole world. Indians had streams and lakes in which to bathe and they did, as often each day as time permitted.

b) "If there was any trouble with a neighboring village, the men marched off to battle."

This is another oversimplification of Indian history and culture. It is so simple it is wrong. Only as a last resort did the East Bay Indians resort to "battle." And then first of all, in the event of any "trouble," they called a council and discussed the matter. . . .

d) "At the same time she had to keep an eye on at least a half dozen little Indians who were forever dropping off cliffs, getting lost, or catching whooping cough. In her spare time, mama had to make enough acorn flour to last through the winter."

> Indian children were highly disciplined, highly knowledgeable about the woods and their country. They never had whooping cough, which is a white man's disease. Acorn flour is made to last only for the next cooking. Only the acorn NUTS were stored, and they could be stored for as long as two years. The Indian ingenuity in constructing their storage bins might have been of far more interest to the students than this silly attempt at humor. . . .

Page 22:
a) "The Indians could neither read nor write."

> No people in that state of society had writing. The word "could" leads to misconceptions. Neither could 99% of the Spaniards read and write, and THEY *had* writing. The '49'ers are estimated to have been 75% illiterate. . . .

Page 23:
a) "If an Indian got sick, he was almost sure to die, since little was known about the proper treatment of illness and injury."

> The Indian knowledge of medicinal herbs and plants is too well known by naturalists and scientists to make comment on this inaccuracy. Indians had a longer life-span than the white man has today. They had few, if any, diseases. They had a knowledge of treating the special conditions which might threaten their health—such as accidents, eating improper foods, or poisonous snake bites. They had a superb knowledge of botany. Diseases introduced by the white man, however, were of such a virulent nature that Indian methods were incapable of treating them. . . .

Page 25:
a) "Communication and transportation. The Indians didn't bother much with either of these important things."

The trade routes of the California and other Western Indians are too well known to give citations confirming that they had long and well-established routes—taking them hundreds of miles to other tribal lands for purposes of trade and ritual. Settlers who stole Indian land and made war upon our people have good reason to know the Indian system of communication, which was superb for that day and under those conditions. . . .

Page 28:

a) "They never tried to make their villages more beautiful. They never bothered to learn newer, better ways of doing things."

They had the whole country FILLED with the beauty of God and nature. Their hills, clean and MAINTAINED by themselves, were beautiful to behold. Their meadows, streams, valleys, and forests were the most beautiful in all the world. They LIVED and thrived in all this beauty. They appreciated it, loved it, preserved it, cared for it, cherished it, and enhanced it. Care of the forests, streams, and meadows is an Indian art only now receiving appreciation. Conservation was an Indian mode of life only now being considered as the most effective method of preserving our remaining natural beauties. See what we have made it possible for you to HAVE—and look what you have done with it!

7 The Teachers: Fulcrum of the System

There is probably no group of people who have been more honored and more scorned, more praised and more blamed than schoolteachers (except perhaps mothers). Measured against grandiose visions of inspired devotion, subjected to the harsh demands of a heavy institution, and confronting daily the hopes and disappointments of scores of rebellious or sullen, highly energetic people, it is no wonder that teachers are the objects of an insane public ambivalence.

The teachers, some of whom even share the grandiose visions, do not establish the terms of their daily confrontations. But it is difficult to recognize their powerlessness because they often use the little power they do have—over individual children in the classroom—in such fierce and arbitrary ways. Often they blame the children for their own powerlessness or for the souring of their visions, just as the children and their parents blame them for the turning of hopes into disappointments, adding to the system of oppression in which they are all caught a system of mutual recrimination.

To understand these systems, we need to examine (1) the role that society expects teachers to perform, (2) the relations of power in which teachers operate, and (3) the teachers' internalization and propagation of the myths that give legitimacy to the relations of power and their role. The selections in this chapter are intended to provide an introduction to these analytic tasks.

Lee Rainwater's "The Revolt of the Dirty-Workers" uses a shocking analogy to dramatize the repressive role society imposes on the teacher. Teachers and others won't like the analogy, which recalls Hannah Arendt's formulation the "banality of evil." This means that the evil one does is so ordinary a part of one's day and one's life that one ceases even to recognize it. (The anti-heroes of the White House, trained to team obedience in the high schools of suburbia, are a prominent contemporary example.) But it is only through the shock and distress of acknowledging the evil in which one is implicated that one can begin to overcome the damage done to one's own and others' humanity.

This, in a way, is the main point of "Letter to My Sisters in School." Taken together with the selections in Chapter 4, it may help readers to scrape through the layers of blame and recrimination against teachers, often specifically against women teachers. It suggests that, if they are to stop doing society's "dirty work," women teachers have to heal the wounds inflicted by the dirty work that was done against them.

Among the contradictions of schoolteaching is the fact that, despite the difficulties, low status, and harsh demands of the job, the profession is considered desirable by many people, including those who are likely to be excluded from the more prestigious professions and those who feel they have a special mission to help others in their ethnic group. But the system tends to function so as to exclude precisely these people from employment as teachers. Much publicity has been given to the exclusion of blacks from the teaching profession in cities where black children constitute a large proportion of the school population. "Chinese and Public School Teaching" demonstrates that even among a people whose culture predisposes the children to take to school easily, the adults of the culture are excluded from teaching their own children in the public schools.

The other selections demonstrate the weak position of teachers as individuals and as groups in the schools' higher levels of power. Another contradiction appears here. Many people who identify with the children in their struggles against teachers have been supporting abolition of teacher tenure, stricter accountability for teachers' performance, and more power for supervisors over teachers. In most cases—as the news reports suggest—the teachers who are victimized by the general weakening of teacher power are precisely the ones who are the most conscientious and the staunchest in defense of their students, while often the teachers who are most willing to do the assigned "dirty work" remain secure in their jobs.

Job insecurity in the 1970's increases the likelihood that teachers will perform in conventionally ineffective ways—that is, will fear to cut through the vine of contradictions that chokes the classroom. The so-called teacher surplus is a product of national policy of the 1960's (see "How Tracking Works," pages 61–74) and the fiscal crisis of the public realm of the 1970's (see Chapter 8).

Nevertheless teachers are the fulcrum of the system, and their complicity is necessary to its continued functioning. Though they are relatively powerless when they support the system, they can—together with the students and parents with whom they are now caught in a circle of blame—endeavor to break out of that circle in order to change the system. Chapter 11 explores some possibilities for such change.

•

The Revolt of the Dirty-Workers

by Lee Rainwater

Schoolteachers, social workers, and policemen in a number of major cities have recently gone on strike, or resigned en masse, or taken mass sick leaves. These events bring to mind the works of Everett C. Hughes, the man who established the investigation of work, occupations, and professions as a major area of social research. In "Good People and Dirty Work," Everett Hughes analyzed some of the societal and social-psychological factors in Germany that fostered the mass murder of concentration-camp victims. He was particularly concerned with the link between the cadre that actually carried out the dirty work and the Germans in general who were "ignorant" of and silent about what went on in the concentration camps. As in much social-science research,

Published by permission of Transaction, from *transaction*, Vol. 5, November 1967. Copyright © 1967 by Transaction, Inc.

Hughes was able to use an extreme, almost unique social event to advance our understanding of much more common processes. The German murderers raised much more general questions about how societies go about handling situations in which repressive action is considered necessary but few citizens are willing to do what they want done.

The Germans' anti-Semitism made them feel that "something must be done about the Jews," which in turn led them to covertly delegate to the S.S. the task of doing that something. It then became important to the Germans to fuzz over the gory details, to conceal from themselves, as well as from others, exactly what was being done. Hughes suggested that this is a typical way societies deal with out-groups:

> The greater their social distance from us the more we leave in the hands of others a sort of mandate by default. . . . Perhaps we give them an unconscious mandate to go beyond anything we ourselves would care to do, or even to acknowledge. I venture to suggest that the higher and more expert functionaries who act in our behalf represent something of a distillation of what we may consider our public wishes, while some of the others show a sort of concentrate of those impulses of which we are, or wish to be, less aware.

This shameful work that nevertheless must be done is, then, (morally) "dirty work."

It is easy to see the same processes operating in the deeply felt American ambivalence toward the police. But the process operates much more broadly. In our world, there is a large out-group—a separate nation of ghetto Negroes whom most white Americans feel must be controlled and confined. Yet those same white Americans are deeply ashamed and uncertain about *how* Negroes are controlled and confined, and they prefer to conceal from themselves much of the detail of how the doers of the dirty work actually go about their assigned tasks.

As the urban ghettos have grown, so has the cohort of functionaries who receive the covert assignment to "keep the colored out of our way." In the process, many institutions officially designed to further well-being and opportunity have become perverted into institutions of custody and constraint. Social-welfare workers find that their profession, designed to help, has been perverted into one designed to spy and to punish. More dramatically, the schools have become custodial institutions in which less and less learning takes place. To conceal their failure, year in and year out the schools promote students who have learned less than they should. The proliferation of policemen in schools, of special schools for "incorrigible" children, and the like testifies to the prison-like functions that undergird the educational rhetoric and increasingly calls into question the national ideology that "education" cures all ills.

Americans are, in general, indifferent to the welfare of their public functionaries—witness the notoriously poor prestige and salaries of these functionaries. This indifference has been so great that those recruited for many public-service jobs tend to be people who are not the main breadwinners of their familes, or who regard public-service work as temporary, or who are motivated more by a desire for security than by the usual American expectation of affluence. And, in the same way, society's indifference has served to blunt the drive of public-service workers for equitable compensation and for a reasonable recognition of their right to collective bargaining.

As the ghettos in this country grow, a new dimension is added, a dimension of silence and ignorance about exactly what these functionaries are expected to do, and how in fact they do carry out society's covert orders to control and cool out those who must be excluded from ordinary society. If the teachers, social workers, and cops were ever to spell out in detail what their duties are in order to justify their wage demands, they would threaten the delicate balance preserved by silence about their assigned dirty work—no one wants to learn that they are striking for "combat pay."

But the dirty-workers *are* striking—for increased pay, of course, but also for other demands that are more directly related to the dangers of dirty work, and to the disrespect society insists on giving to those who do its tacit bidding. The New York teachers, for example, openly and directly challenged the implicit understanding that it is more important for them to be custodians than for them to be teachers.* It is gradually dawning on all of these public servants that both their official public tasks (to educate, to protect

---

* This is doubtless a reference to strikes by the New York City United Federation of Teachers for smaller classes and improved learning facilities, not to the strike against community control of schools, which occurred after this article was published.—Ed.

the citizens, to look after the welfare of the dependent) and their covert tasks (to control Negroes and make them as invisible as possible) are impossible to achieve.

The dirty-workers are increasingly caught between the silent middle class, which wants them to do the dirty work and keep quiet about it, and the objects of that dirty work, who refuse to continue to take it lying down. Individual revolts confront the teachers with the problems of the "blackboard jungle," the police with the problem of "disrespect for law and order," and the welfare workers with the problem of their charges' feigned stupidity and real deception. These civilian colonial armies find their right to respect from their charges challenged at every turn, and often they must carry out their daily duties with fear for their physical safety.

Equally ominous for the dirty-workers is the organized Negro challenge to their legitimacy. Not only must they cope with individual resistance to their ministrations, but also, more and more, with militant and insistent local civil-rights groups that expose their failures and tax them with their abrogation of their professional responsibilities to teach, to protect, to help.

It is encouraging that those expected to do the dirty work are rebelling. But it is really too much to expect that they will admit their own individual culpability, at least as long as the rest of us won't. Even so, the more the teachers, the police, and the welfare workers insist on the impossibility of their tasks, the more that society at large, and its political leaders, will have to confront the fact that our tacit understandings about the dirty work that is to be done are no longer adequate.

Of course there are dangers, too. The police are our internal hawks, and they might win—and there are also hawks among schoolteachers (they want unruly children kicked out of school) and welfare workers (who want to escalate the attack on welfare chiselers). As dangerous in the long run, perhaps, are the doves— the teachers and the social workers who want to save the ghetto through education and casework (or that form of neighborhood casework called "community action"). Should either the ghetto hawks or doves carry the day, their victory could become the basis for a new tacit understanding about dirty work, one that would save the country from paying the price it is apparently most reluctant to pay—the price of providing economic resources and open, decent housing to Negroes, so there is no longer a ghetto that requires dirty-workers.

High School Students Have More Rights than Teachers

by Gael Pierce

Think the title is an exaggeration? Since the U.S. Supreme Court's landmark decision of *Tinker* v. *Des Moines Independent Community School District*, students have established certain rights by legal processes that teachers do not now enjoy. Some of these rights are:

A. While student dress and hair length are now up to student discretion, teachers must submit to arbitrary whims of each school principal as to whether they can grow beards, wear miniskirts, or go without neckties.

B. Many schools have open campuses for students, but many teachers (the professionals) must still ask permission and sign out before they are permitted to leave school during their free period. While the principal doesn't ask the student his reason for leaving, he must approve the request of a teacher to depart (having one's hair fixed is not an adequate reason).

C. Students are allowed to express political and controversial opinions. The basis for the *Tinker* decision was the wearing of black bands as a gesture of mourning for the dead in Vietnam. The U.S. Supreme Court held that: (1) school officials do not have absolute authority over their students; (2) students in school as well as out of school must be considered as "persons" under the Constitution and are protected by its rights; and (3) if the state (or the local school district) regulates expression of a student's view or speech, it must show constitutionally valid reasons for doing so. The decision stated that the state (and hence the local school district) must respect the rights of students. While students have won these rights by confrontation, no teacher could get away with discussing the legality of marijuana or the benefits of free love ... and keep his job.

D. In California, the state board of education appointed a 16-year-old junior high school student to serve on the board. Although she is a nonvoting member, have you ever heard of a teacher sitting on a board of education?

E. The Sequoia school district in California involves students

Reprinted from *American Teacher* (AFT, AFL-CIO), February, 1972.

in the teacher-selection process. Has any teacher or teacher organization been asked or been able to set up standards as to teacher qualifications? Do they have any voice in the teacher-selection process?

F. Rights that the schools must respect in regard to students are those involving free speech and expression, petition, conscience, due process, and equal treatment under the law. This is not true of teachers. In addition, where a local school district interferes with the free exercise of an individual student's rights for reasons not constitutionally sound, the officials of that district may be subject to personal suit. Teachers have nowhere near that protection, even though they come under the same Constitution.

What is the lesson to be learned? That students are willing to fight for the redress of their grievances, to face confrontations with the school administration, and to carry their confrontation to the Supreme Court . . . and teachers are not?

Margaret Mead, in her book *Culture and Commitment: A Study of the Generation Gap*, said that we have faced three cultures: one a postfigurative, in which the parents taught the children; another a cofigurative, in which the parents and young learned together; and a third a prefigurative, in which the young taught the parents. She believes that we are now in the prefigurative, and, if the student achievement of constitutional rights within our school system is an example, then we adults should learn from the children.

Teachers in News and Letters

Threat to Teachers Who Discuss War

SACRAMENTO. Legislation to allow firing of teachers who digress from their regular subjects to discuss the war was approved 46–13 by the Assembly yesterday.

Assembly Speaker pro tem Charles Conrad (Rep-Sherman Oaks), introduced the legislation in response to Vietnam Moratorium days last October and November.

It allows suspension or dismissal of public school teachers who either dismiss classes or deviate from their regular topics. Conrad said the initial action would be at the direction of the local school superintendent.

(*San Francisco Chronicle*, June 12, 1970)

You Can't Teach That
by Michael Mead, President, Local 1846,
American Federation of Teachers

Recently the Board of Education in Island Trees, Long Island, ordered the entire instructional staff to submit copies of all curriculum guides in all courses, titles of all films, filmstrips, slides, and copies of all textbooks used in courses K–12 in the school system.

At first glance this seems to reflect an appropriate interest by the board in the kinds of educational materials currently in use in the program. But when examined in perspective, it might take on a much different meaning.

In some districts the board's "curiosity" has turned out to be a subtle, but clearly discernible form of censorship, designed to make teachers conform to the political, religious or social views of one or more board members. Such boards of education have attempted to make all learning in their districts "teacher proof" by usurping the duties of the State Education Commissioner, the superintendent, the administration and the faculty, all of whom have been mandated by law to work together to create meaningful courses of study. Boards of education which attempt to impose a curriculum based on the possibly narrow-minded or prejudiced views of a small group of people remove from the student's school life the most American of all experiences—variety.

(*United Teacher*, February 27, 1972)

Daly City Teachers' Rights Fight

The Jefferson Elementary School District in Daly City has become a focal point of public school teachers' drive for rights accorded workers in private industry.

At issue is a provision for binding arbitration of grievances.

The provision is part of a settlement package approved by the school board last September after a two-day teachers' strike.

But now the school board has ordered the San Mateo County District Attorney—its counsel—to ask the courts to break the arbitration clause.

The Jefferson board cited a Los Angeles Superior Court judge's ruling in October that allowing binding arbitration of grievances is an "invalid delegation of authority" by a school board.

The right to binding arbitration has special significance for teachers.

Some observers say teachers would surrender their right to tenure—which has come under heavy attack in recent years—if they had other protections, such as binding arbitration, against arbitrary dismissal by school boards and administrators.

(*San Francisco Chronicle*, January 2, 1971)

What Teachers Can Expect from Their State Legislatures: Forecasts from 28 State Capitols

WASHINGTON, D.C. Tax reform, state financing of education, parochiaid, teacher tenure and retirement, performance contracting, and More Effective Schools, and anti-injunction and collective-bargaining bills have been considered this year by a majority of the state legislatures, some of which have finished their deliberations and will not meet again on such matters for as long as two years.

In an effort to discover what is new in legislation in the states— a matter of vital importance to all citizens, and particularly public employees and teachers—the *American Teacher* presents a state-by-state report of the situation in 28 states, covering the bulk of AFT membership. Additional reports will appear later.

"Teachers are being made the whipping-boys for a taxpayers' revolt," said Henry Winkels, lobbyist for the Minnesota Federation of Teachers. "And the battle cry," he reported, "is tenure." He characterized as "gesturism" the consideration by Minnesota legislators of a host of anti-teacher bills which he believed would not be favorably acted on in the long run.

In Washington State, Federation representative Stan Bloom reported, "The big thing now is tax reform; taxes are quite complicated and regressive, but the legislature's not dealing with it at all."

Perhaps the clearest example of what Winkels and Bloom were talking about came in the New York State Legislature early in April, when the Assembly, pushing against a budget deadline, at 1 A.M. threw a sop to bloodthirsty delegates who needed something in return for their vote to slash the state budget. What they got was an increase of from three to five years in the probationary period for teachers, and complete elimination of tenure for new supervisors in the school systems. Albert Shanker, president of the United Federation of Teachers, AFT Local 2, said, "The passage of this measure proves more than ever the absolute necessity of the union and our 80,000 members and families getting deeply involved in politics. Since so many vital matters affecting our well-being, our rights, and our conditions of employment grow out of legislative action, we must play a stronger role in the elections."

In some states, such as New Jersey, state bodies of service to public-employee bargaining are in danger, because of money shortages. In others, such as Maryland, funds which would normally go to the public schools will be going, if not stopped by voter and court challenges, to private and parochial schools in the state. . . .

The Colorado legislature's 1971 session ended April 28. It meets next January only to consider the budget and the governor's items. At this session, it passed an "Educational Accountability Act," funded with $40,000, for all state school districts to establish "goals" to be measured with "tests and other means," and a Performance Program Budget Evaluation System act covering six pilot programs now, and mandatory for all the state's 181 districts in 1973. A bill to abolish tenure for all future teachers and for strikers and an "ethics" bill were killed. Three Colorado Federation of Teachers members of the House education committee helped scuttle the latter, which would have revoked certification of striking teachers. Said Rep. Dennis Gallagher, CFT member at Regis College, Denver, "The legislature should be half as concerned about bankers." Other Federation legislators are Wayne Knox, CFT president and Adams City District teacher, and Paul Hamilton, former teacher now developing a black-studies program for Denver schools.

(American Teacher, May, 1971)

●

A man teacher in Ontario wrote giving permission for the publication of some letters he and his students had written. The letters, which were about how the students felt teachers discriminated between boys and girls, were very constrained in tone.

February 18, 1973
Please feel free to use the letters my students wrote. I would appreciate your concealing their names, my name, and our school's name. My status is not all that great with the administration and the next few months are critical for my permanent contract.

A woman teacher in a small community in Washington wrote about her attempt to get answers to the same kinds of questions about boys and girls.

February 22, 1972
A weird thing happened to me while trying to gather information for your article. I made a special trip to the high school

at dismissal time one day to interview some high school women. I found several in the hall who were happy to chat with me in a deserted classroom briefly. They talked of class scheduling, dating customs, and sports programs. They also felt that the old stereotypes were as harmful to boys as they were to girls. . . . As I was leaving, I was cornered by the principal, my principal, for whom I had worked reasonably happily for three years, who demanded to know what I was doing, then told me he heard what I was doing, and don't . . . do it again without first clearing it with him. . . . There were all kinds of things, I thought later, I could have said, but I was so flabbergasted I didn't say anything. Mostly there was a fine sense of outrage that I should be talked to like that.

A friend wrote a newsy letter.

May 17, 1971

You ask, "How are things?" Just came from a board meeting. The issue: a statement made to the school board by the executive director of the local organization of CTA [Classroom Teachers Association]. About 12 tenured teachers were reassigned to other schools. In giving reasons for the transfers the teachers were told poor performance, that sort of thing. However, in a survey made by [the CTA] the evaluation procedures of the district have been violated. Some teachers had never been evaluated, some not in 21 years, others in varying years. So lack of due process, violation of teachers' rights, and violation of evaluation procedures were taken up.

A popular, hardworking teacher was fired after one year in a school.

I did not come to Union Springs to be a political organizer. I came to teach. But I refused to be the teacher that both the administration and students expected me to be. I had rejected the role of cop and socializer not out of any revolutionary commitment, but out of my need to relate to my students. This same need made me reject the labels "lower tract," "non-college-bound," "slow learner" that were placed on my students. My refusal to play the traditional teacher role was linked to my refusal to accept them as inferior because they had been treated as such. By breaking down their stereotypes of themselves and of me, I also helped them break down their self-confining images of the world around them.

One letter I received from a female student indicated the achievement as well as the limitations of my work at Union Springs: "Up until you came to us, I'm sure no student knew where he or she stood in school. They didn't know the powers they had. Now we know them and are trying to use them as best we can. It's going to take time to get organized, but the way things are going now, I'm sure the time will come. I remember the time I was accused of smoking. The principal told me that I had no alternative but to admit I was smoking. I told him that I wasn't and that he could get the Supreme Court on it if he wanted to, but he couldn't prove it. That was the first time I really used the power I had and I won. It doesn't seem like much power when it was all over, but I can still remember looking at his face and noticing that his smirk was gone and that he really looked afraid of me. I don't know if you realize it or not, but that small power has affected almost every kid in school and I think that's why you were fired."

(Patricia Michaels, "Teaching and Rebellion at Union Springs," *No More Teachers' Dirty Looks*, Vol. 1, No. 2. Reprinted by permission.)

Chinese and Public School Teaching
by Lonnie Chin

. . . Although acutely aware of the many barriers, Chinese have regarded education as a major avenue for progress in American society as well as being innately valuable. Therefore, as we look into the employment of Chinese teachers in San Francisco, it would be appropriate to mention briefly the history of discrimination and segregation of Chinese in education.

Reprinted by permission from *Chinese-Americans: School and Community Problems,* published by Integrated Education Associates, School of Education, Northwestern University, 2003 Sheridan Road, Evanston, Illinois 60201. The author represented the Association of Chinese Teachers in making this statement before the California Fair Employment Practice Commission, December 10, 1970.

The Chinese had been systematically and officially excluded from education until a court ruling established an Oriental school in 1885. . . . Chinese [students] now make up about 14% of San Francisco's total [school] population.

It is conservatively estimated that 100 Chinese from San Francisco graduate from colleges and universities around the Bay Area with teaching credentials. If that has been the pattern since 1960, we would have 1,000 qualified Chinese teachers. If we add another 500 teachers from 1950–1960, we would have a total of 1,500 teachers. With qualified Chinese teachers coming from other parts of the state, country and world, the number would be bolstered even higher. . . .

It is instructive to note that although there has been additional hiring of Chinese teachers since 1965, the additional hiring has not been great. In 1965, in the elementary division there was a total of 88 Chinese teachers (4% of total number of teachers in San Francisco), in the junior high division there was a total of 24 Chinese teachers (2%) and in the high school division there was a total of 23 Chinese teachers (2%).

Discriminatory practices are often very subtle and nebulous, but very damaging in their effect upon society. A most heinous disservice to minorities is the self-righteous rationalization and also stereotyping that is perpetuated, such as: Chinese students should not have Chinese teachers, Chinese are not good teachers because they have an accent, they lack initiative, they are too soft-spoken, bilingual teachers are not effective in any subject. These kinds of attitudes serve to discourage and stagnate whatever ambitions, talents and potentials Chinese teachers may have and do not support continuing professional growth and effectiveness.

As a consequence, many Chinese students are deprived of teachers who can share their common background and can offer empathy, concern, warmth and expertise for their intellectual, emotional and social maturation. This sensitivity to and understanding of the students' linguistic and cultural heritage and special problems is crucial in nurturing self-esteem, a sense of intellectual curiosity, an openness and responsiveness to the world and increasing responsibility.

Mature and rational people would agree that discrimination and prejudice against people because of race, religion, color or creed is detrimental to society and not conducive to harmonious relationships. As members of the FEPC, you must believe this. As an official governmental body, it is your assigned duty and moral responsibility to vigorously root out and eradicate unfair employment practices.

Letter to My Sisters in School

by Miriam Wasserman

> Women and children are always mentioned in the same breath ("Women and children to the forts!"). The special tie women have with children is recognized by everyone. I submit, however, that the nature of this bond is no more than shared oppression. And that moreover this oppression is intertwined and mutually reinforcing in such complex ways that we will be unable to speak of the liberation of women without also discussing the liberation of children, and vice versa.
>
> —SHULAMITH FIRESTONE

I am addressing this communication to women teachers, but I believe and wish that some men teachers as well as some men and women supervisors will read it. The objection will be made that men teachers share the problems of women teachers. That is so; they do share many of the problems of women teachers. But not the problem of being a woman. The objection will also be made that women supervisors can be as harsh as or harsher than men supervisors. That is so, too. The ways in which women handle authority in a male-dominated society is another problem, and we ought to talk about that sometime. But in this letter I am addressing myself to one problem, which is a big enough problem involving enough people to make it a legitimate subject in itself. That is the problem of being a woman schoolteacher.

I should like to add that I am writing mainly to white women teachers, because I am a white woman teacher and believe I have some understanding of our common experiences. I think that the problems of Third World women teachers overlap but are not at all identical with those of white women teachers. I should like to see some discussion of these differences and similarities.

From *The Teacher Paper,* Vol. 5, No. 2 (December, 1972). Reprinted by permission.

Finally, I wish to say that like any other letter writer, I like to receive answers.

I think we should try to understand some of the causes of our discontent. People say, and we believe, that we are well off and should be happy. But often we are not, and then we feel guilty because we are not. I think we should try to stop feeling guilty and begin to take account of ourselves and our lives—so that we may become stronger women, and also stronger and better wives, mothers, friends, daughters, more comradely colleagues, and more effective teachers.

Among any group of women teachers, each is unique, different from the others in age, style, personality, family status, background, interests, and race. I think many of us barely perceive how, for the system, our femaleness overrides the individual differences—overrides them because sex, like race, is a determinant of one's status in the system. As we are teachers, and women, our differences are irrelevant to our status at the bottom of the school hierarchy. (Who—except themselves—cared much about the individual differences among the slaves?)

We are reminded of our low status a dozen times a day: by the double standard of name calling ("Marjorie!" "Yes, Mr. Stubbs."); by our invisibility at male-dominated committee or department meetings, so that we are almost compelled to be the ones who get up to pour the coffee, simply to remind ourselves that we exist; by the children's sense that the real authority in the school—in our very classroom—is the (usually male) principal; by the high-level conferences of the (predominantly male) authorities and experts to which parents may be summoned and at which we and the child are the conspicuously absent subjects of the discussion. (As Shulamith Firestone points out, the devaluing of children goes along with the devaluing of women.) To these customary humiliations, we customarily respond with outward indifference or good grace, although the next hour or the next day some of the hot lava of our buried resentment may pour out on the children. Then we become "bitchy" and hate ourselves for that. (Self-disrespect seems to reinforce and perpetuate itself; disrespecting ourselves makes us act in ways that make us disrespect ourselves more.)

Our troubles lie not so much in the fact that some men may be "chauvinist," although that surely doesn't help. More fundamentally, however, it is a matter of the system being rigged. The rules by which the school game is played are sexist just as surely as they are racist, although the strategy and the consequences of racism and sexism are, of course, different.

First, we should observe that teaching below the university level is a predominantly female profession and a low-status profession—the two being associated in a reciprocity of cause and effect. Historically this has been so for a long time. In the nineteenth century the salaries and status of schoolteachers were so low, writes one educator, that the profession appealed only to "young girls, effeminate boys, spinsters, former clergymen, unemployed mechanics [i.e., common laborers] and retired ship captains." (Here it may be seen how the low status associated with us rubs off on the men in the profession, except for those who are upwardly mobile within the system.)

Salaries reflect the low status. In one recent year, the average public school teacher earned $7,000 a year, the average college-educated male earned $12,000, and the average physician earned $35,000. Now, can you imagine that if the average doctor were a woman and the average schoolteacher a man, the doctors would be earning five times as much as the teachers? . . .

The system is rigged in that the lowest-status jobs in it are reserved for females. It is also rigged in that college-educated women have almost no place else to go. About a third of all women professionals are teachers. . . . The lower one's status in society, the fewer one's vocational options, and schoolteaching is one of our major options. . . .

Last night I was rereading Sylvia Ashton-Warner's beautiful *Spinster*, a novel that tells us more about ourselves and what's wrong with us and the schools than a hundred dull foundation reports and romantic reformers' philippics. Miss Vorontsov, a brilliant and tender teacher, is on her way to school, having first prepared herself for the day with a half-tumbler of brandy.

> My song stops. So does my step. . . . If only I had done all that inspectors had told me in the past—whenever they wanted me to, in the way they wanted me to and for the reason! If only I had been a good teacher, an obedient teacher and submissive! . . . Yet it can't be too late. True, the mistakes have all been mine. . . . Plainly the inspectors are all good men and all I need to do is to co-operate. Slowly I will recover my lagging professional status and prove myself a thoroughly useful force in the service. Then maybe this Old Man Guilt will release my throat and I'll be one with the other at last.

Even in faraway New Zealand, even inside that strong and gifted woman teacher, is the quivering little girl judging herself by the judgment of some looming authority figure. And so does the frightened, guilt-ridden, desperately wanting-to-be-good little girl we all once were corrode our womanhood. They say we castrate little boys, i.e., destroy their manhood. But they barely notice how we collaborate with the authorities in the destruction of little girls' and our own womanhood.

And the authorities are usually men. While 67 percent of all teachers are women, 85 percent of the principals are men. They say women don't become supervisors and administrators because: (1) Women are just in teaching for a little while, until they get married or have babies; then they want to devote themselves full time to their families. (2) Even women who work after marriage and children are "fulfilled" by their motherhood and wifehood; they don't really want or have time for a career, only a "little" job. (3) Most women wouldn't be able to be authoritative supervisors over men; alternatively most men can't work well under most women. (4) Women are naturally not ambitious the way men are.

The arguments are more or less specious:

(1) The average woman teacher has a longer career than the average man teacher. While 24 percent of the women teachers have been in teaching for twenty years or more, only 15 percent of the men teachers have.

(2) A conscientious teacher works as many hours and has as much emotional investment in her work as a conscientious principal. That makes her "job" into a "career," although without the status and salary of a career.

(3) This argument simply means that most men don't like to take orders from women, because they consider women to be their inferiors. When more women achieve higher status and more power, they will no longer be considered inferior—either by the men or by themselves. And the men will learn to work under them (the way whites are learning to work under blacks—once considered out of the question by most whites).

(4) We don't know very much about how women and men "naturally" are, because our natures are so overlaid with culture and training. If our expectations of little girls, big girls, and women were different, then girls and women would be different. Ambition is a social, as well as possibly a biological, trait. We have been taught and trained *not* to be ambitious.

We have also been taught *not* to be strong, self-respecting, loyal to our peers. What we have been taught to be is good (obedient). We have been taught, moreover, that to be good is: to "do our own work," not to share, not to cooperate, to hide. And so we guard and hide ourselves like a stubborn virgin guarding and hiding her maidenhead. Shamefully we close our rooms, as we close our souls, to our sister teachers, lest they pry out our missteps, our misde-meanors, our misgivings. Over coffee or lunch we report only our triumphs, or else the terrible transgressions committed by those awful children who are not good like us—as if they were our own bad-boy classmates of fifteen or twenty years ago.

And now comes the pinch. There is a breakdown in the system in which women and children are supposed to be good and men are supposed to be strong. Everywhere the children are refusing to be good. And a lot of the men, and also a lot of women who are not teachers, are saying, "Oh, the trouble is that women teachers aren't strong. What we need are more strong men in the schools."

And they're right—though wrong. Because what we need is not for us to meekly step aside to make room for strong men but to become strong ourselves. Strength is not a male attribute. It is a human attribute. Male strength, traditionally conceived, implies, depends on, and creates female weakness. But human strength is the collective overcoming of the weaknesses of us all.

A system built on people's weakness can last only as long as people agree to be weak. We have to give up being weak, even if that means that we have to give up being good. The system will be stronger, or we will create a new system, and new people—women and men, and children and adults. That act of creation will be a struggle for us. And once we begin to struggle we will be less discontent.

8 The Fiscal Crisis: Where School and Economy Intersect

School reformers often ignore or conceal with lofty rhetoric the thickety areas where school and economy intersect. But it is precisely in those thorny places that the crises and the contradictions of both are most stubbornly entangled. So the easy saying "If we had the money, we could solve all those problems" is about the equivalent of the German aphorism "If my aunt were a bus, she'd have four wheels." (Incidentally, the obverse, "There is nothing to be done, because we have no money," is equally foolish, and another demonstration of that alienation that divests human beings of power and bestows it on things.)

The corporate economy requires an ever expanding educational sector, which, however, the corporate economy will not spare the funds to support. So the fiscal crisis experienced by the school system in the early 1970's is a function of the contradiction between the economy's need to absorb surplus labor via the educational apparatus and the economy's inability to divert sufficient funds from private profit-making to meet this need. "The Political Economy of Youth" is a tightly reasoned explanation of the way the educational apparatus serves the economy. The reader who is willing to struggle against the natural terror of things economic and devote care to it will almost certainly be rewarded with gratifying insights into his own career as a student, as well as into the meaning of the inflationary spiral of educational expectations.

Daniel Patrick Moynihan was a counselor to Presidents Nixon and Johnson. His "Can Courts and Money Do It?" provides some insights into the rationale for the national educational policy of fiscal retrenchment. Moynihan seems to be arguing that spending more money on schools below the college level (1) will not significantly alter the traditional differential between the school performance of the poor and that of the middle class but (2) will subject low-income and middle-income taxpayers to strains that they may well resent. Profits cannot be diverted from the private sector to support the public sector (schools): "Taxes on the rich just aren't that important," he says. Also not important is justice in fact; there needs only to be an illusion of justice: The Texas school decision "will strike most persons as adhering to a principle of fairness. We need this in our society more than we need educational achievement [of the poor]."

Moynihan seems to propose a course that would divert funds now being spent on teachers' salaries at the elementary and secondary levels to educational research and development (bureaucratic and high-status professional salaries) and possibly to community colleges and vocational training. This policy would foster employment of higher-status educational personnel at the expense of lower-status ones (researchers and junior-college teachers over elementary and secondary teachers) and more years in school rather than more effective elementary and secondary schooling for low-status students. The inflationary spiral in education would thus be perpetuated with no alteration in the relative positions of the various social classes.

Next, the New York State United Teachers and the National Education Association respond to the federal government's fiscal policy, protesting the deterioration of the school situation and the mounting unemployment of teachers.

Finally, the generalizations and analyses of the preceding are exemplified by the layoff of thirteen teachers from a vocational school in Oakland, California, and the near bankruptcy of the school system of Detroit, Michigan. That the center of the auto empire of the world should be unable to afford minimal education for the next generation of auto workers is a neat example of the central contradiction of the fiscal crisis.

The Political Economy of Youth*
by John Rowntree and Margaret Ellinger

First, the economy is dominated by the defense and education industries; *second*, these two industries are particularly adapted to the task of absorbing surplus manpower in the economy; *finally*, this surplus manpower is young and economically exploited.

A. The Growth Industries: Defense and Education

Table I reveals the growth in the relative size of the public sector since 1940.[1]

TABLE I. THE U.S. ECONOMY, 1940–1965

Year	1940	1950	1965
Public expenditure as a per cent of GNP	18.4%	21.5%	26.0%
Government civilian employees:			
(number in millions)	4.5	6.4	10.6
per cent of the labor force	8.0%	10.0%	14.0%

Further analysis shows that this growth was concentrated in defense and education, whose share of public expenditures, GNP, and employment is so large and growing so rapidly that these industries have come to dominate the U.S. economy.

* Reference footnotes in the original have been eliminated for space reasons.—Ed.

[1] Unless otherwise indicated, the data presented here have been calculated from standard sources—Statistical Abstract of the United States, Census of Population of the United States, etc. To keep our historical perspective and to avoid the problems of the statistical short run, we have generally brought our data only up to 1965. Our case does not depend on the current war spending and we do not want to confuse our analysis of the long run problems of the U.S. economy by introducing data affected by this particular war.

In statements regarding the data the word "adult" as in "adult population" or "adult labor force" will refer to all persons 14 years old and over, unless otherwise noted.

Reprinted for this edition by the kind permission of *Our Generation,* a new left quarterly, 3934 St. Urbain, Montreal 131, Canada. This essay first appeared in *Our Generation,* Vol. 6, Nos. 1–2, under the title "Youth as Class—The Political Economy of Youth," by John and Margaret Rowntree.

. . . The Department of Labor's estimate that total defense employment was 7 million jobs in 1962 means that about 1 in 10 employed workers was directly employed by the defense industry.[2] If the indirect effects could be measured, the total employment effect would of course be much larger.

The education industry has also grown dramatically. The Council of Economic Advisers notes that education spending has been increasing 10½% a year for the last decade, in a period in which total economic growth has been less than 4% a year. The Council calls it "one of the major U.S. growth industries" and calculates direct spending in 1966–67 as $49 billion, "nearly 6½% of GNP."[3] Clark Kerr draws on the work of Princeton economist Fritz Machlup and concludes that "The production, distribution and consumption of 'knowledge' in all its forms is said to account for 29 per cent of gross national product, . . . and knowledge production is growing at about twice the rate of the rest of the economy."[4]

Table II shows the significant increase in direct employment in education, narrowly defined, in the fifteen year period 1950–65.

TABLE II.   PUBLIC EDUCATIONAL EMPLOYMENT, 1950–1965

Year	1950	1965
Governmental employment in education, number (in millions)	1.723	3.974
1950–65 increase (in per cent)	130%	

While total employment in the 1960–65 period increased by only 21%, the public educational employment increased by 130%. The increase in public educational employment in the 15 years accounted for about *one out of every six new jobs created* in the U.S. economy. . . .

Our *first* point, then, is that in the last 25 years the U.S. economy has been changing from a goods-producing private economy to a government-supported economy producing war and knowledge. The defense and education industries, very narrowly defined, now account for more than one-sixth of actual GNP. *Further*, these industries have become increasingly interrelated and should be viewed as a single industrial complex. Our second argument goes much farther and argues that the true (and astounding) importance

[2] U.S. Department of Labor, *Report on Manpower Requirements* . . . . 1966, p. 19.

[3] Council of Economic Advisers, *1967 Annual Report*, p. 143.

[4] Clark Kerr, *The Uses of the University*, 1963, pp. 87–88.

of the defense-education complex can only be seen by going beyond
its share of GNP to its very important role in *absorbing surplus
manpower*—especially young manpower.

B. Surplus Absorption

The important economic role of the public sector and, in particular,
the defense-education complex can only be understood when the
economic aggregates are viewed in manpower-utilization as well
as income-generation terms. Table III makes the comparison.

TABLE III. MANPOWER IN THE PUBLIC SECTOR, 1950–1965

Year	1950	1965
Percentage of national income of government origin	9.8%	13.5%
Percentage of civilian labor force employed by government	10.0%	14.0%
Government civilian employment:		
number (in millions)	6.4	10.6
per cent of adult population[a]	5.8%	7.8%
Government civilian employment, armed forces on active duty, and adult student population:		
number (in millions)	16.7	31.9
per cent of adult population	15.1%	23.5%

[a] Recall that adult refers to those 14 years and over.

The increase in the public sector is relatively insignificant when
measured by the change in the percentage of civilian government
employment either in the labor force or in the adult population.
However, if we examine the growth in total "socialized" manpower, including adult students and members of the armed forces
as well as the conventionally designated civilian employees of
government, we see not only that total "socialized" manpower
utilizes 23.5% of the nation's adult manpower, but also that this
percentage has grown spectacularly, a change of 8.4% of the
adult population in 15 years. Thus, when we go beyond the data
on national income originating in the public sector and the data
using a narrow concept of employment (i.e., excluding students
and military personnel), we see that the public sector has been
exceedingly successful at "utilizing" adult manpower.

Furthermore, this real growth of the public sector took place
primarily in two industries—*defense and education*. While civilian
government employment during 1950–65 increased only 2% as a
proportion of adult population, students and military personnel

during the same period increased by 6.4% as a proportion of adult population. (Together the change was 8.4%.) These defense and education industries are particularly suited to absorb workers almost indefinitely, and the workers they absorb are primarily young. In 1965, almost three-quarters of the armed forces were under 30 and 56% were under 25.[5] Almost all students are under 35, and about 95% are between the ages of 14 and 24. The task of absorbing the surplus of the U.S. economy has therefore increasingly fallen on the shoulders of young people.

The education industry has a seemingly unlimited capacity to absorb manpower by enrolling it in school. This form of socialized investment takes up the slack left by the failing private sector of the economy by reducing the labor supply and by absorbing vast quantities of resources for teachers, buildings, etc. Ironically, however, investment in education increases the productivity of the labor force, simply compounding the problem of surplus disposal in the future. This increasingly difficult problem is being "solved" in two ways: extending the years of schooling; and training students for unproductive labor. . . .

These data reveal the tremendous importance of the total defense and education industries in "using" the increase in laboring manpower between 18 and 64 years of age during the 15 year period, 1960–65. . . .

. . . Is the defense-education complex the *necessary* method of surplus absorption in the administrative imperialist state? Obviously the U.S. economy has failed to provide an alternative method of absorbing its tremendous productive capacity. But more than this, as Table IV reveals, the very dynamism of the economic system has arisen from the government-sponsored defense-education complex. Recent U.S. history should cause even the most stouthearted Keynesian to doubt the private sector's ability to generate new employment independently. Even in the 1960's, with the much discussed tax cuts, the war on poverty, and the war in Vietnam,

---

[5] In addition, an ever increasing number of young men have labored in the military. Almost half (46% in 1967) of young men have served in the armed forces by the time they reach the age of 26. Even this figure underestimates the impact of military life in the United States, because it does not include the reserve forces. In 1965, for example, the standing army was 2.7 million, but the reserves comprised another 2.6 million, 1 million of whom were paid for drill training. Throughout the remainder of this study we deal *only* with the armed forces on active duty.

TABLE IV. UTILIZATION OF 1950–1965 INCREASE IN
LABORING POPULATION, 18–64 YEARS OLD[6]

Increase in school enrollment[a]	3.68	24%
Increase in armed forces	.96	6%
Total increase in students and military	4.64	31%
Increase in defense employment (civilian)	2.25	15%
Increase in educational employment	3.19	21%
Total increase in defense and education	5.44	36%
Increase in private employment and government employment not directly related to defense or education (inc. unemployment)	4.92	33%
Total increase in laboring population	15.0	100%

[a] All categories include only persons 18–64 years old.

during the longest economic expansion in history, from 1961 to the present, the growth of the U.S. income and employment has been founded on a rapid and continuous expansion of the defense and education industries. . . .

C. Exploitation of Youth. . . .

Although being a student is called investing in one's human capital, and although much is made of the high returns on the educational investment, no one stops to consider whether this investment

[6] These data must be interpreted carefully. First, we use an unusual definition of "laboring population." We include civilian labor force and military personnel plus student enrollment minus, to avoid double counting, enrolled students who are in the labor force. Breaking our rule of treating 14 year olds as adult, we laboriously took out 14–17 year olds and 65 year olds and older in order to treat only the laboring population of ages 18–64. We felt that, given the biases of most "adult" readers, it was enough to treat students as workers without also confusing the facts in this case by treating ages 14–17 as adult. High School has, after all, become so much a part of U.S. society.

Our estimate for the total increase in the 18–64 laboring population still contains an element of double counting, but we think it a defensible estimate with a 1% margin. The increase in civilian employment in the defense industry includes the change in private employment directly resulting from defense purchases based on . . . [a] 1962 estimate. . . . The increase in private employment directly resulting from educational purchases of goods and services was conservatively estimated at 750,000 jobs, about 1% of the 1965 labor force; these jobs are primarily involved in school construction and supplies. Our point is well made, however, even with this element of conservatism.

is truly voluntary, or in fact coerced.[7] No positive proof can be offered that students are coerced; we can, however, show that they are exploited. Since school is a full-time but unpaid job, most students work part-time or not at all, living on loans or support from their families. Professor Theodore Schultz estimates that 55% of the costs of a college and 43% of the costs of a high school education are foregone income. The Council of Economic Advisers' foregone earnings estimate of $20 to $30 billion, viewed above as an indicator of absorbed surplus, can also be seen as an index of exploitation. This estimate implies that, for all students 16 and over foregone earnings amount to about 40 to 60% of their "investment in human capital." This is roughly $2,000 per student 16 and over. These estimates are minimums, reflecting how little choice students, like soldiers, really have: they must stay in school (and be exploited), or face exploitively high unemployment rates and/or low wages.

[7] Recall the slogan "A college education is worth $100,000" in extra income earned over a lifetime. Gary Becker has estimated in "Underinvestment in College Education," *Proceedings,* American Economics Association, May, 1960, that, between 1940 and 1955, the return on investment in a college education was 12.5% before taxes. These returns, much celebrated by liberals and blithely promised by the economists, should be viewed with caution. First, they are an average of data with great variance; second, they imply that anyone who gets his schooling will get his return as if the labor market were competitive, while in fact it is notoriously monopolistic. In particular, returns from an investment in a college education are associated with one's economic and social background. A much more reasonable interpretation of all the "returns to education" data is that the number of years of schooling necessary to maintain the social status to which one was born has increased significantly. This is but another demonstration of our thesis: the system's exploitation is focused on the young, who are excluded from the labor force for more years than were their parents, and who must pay ever more dearly for the same social position.

For a brilliant attack on the "returns to educational investment" literature, see Chapter 4 of Fritz Machlup's *The Production and Distribution of Knowledge in the United States*; Machlup also brings forth strong data to support his thesis that the U.S. education system has tremendous waste built into it and to support his program to reduce the high school leaving age from the current 18 to about 14 or 15. What Machlup does not recognize is that the system at the broadest level thrives on the waste, which absorbs surplus.

It should be noted that our conclusions above regarding the progressively increasing use of education as surplus absorber is not affected whether education really increases the productivity of labor (in constant supply) or merely increases the productivity of a smaller labor force due to the growing school enrollment.

In spite of the massive diversions of young people from the labor force into school and the military forces, unemployment rates among the young remain much higher than among older workers. . . .

Discriminatory exploitation of the young works perhaps the greatest hardship where it reinforces other discriminatory handicaps and is particularly severe for black youth and for young women. Blacks experience the worst job discrimination; as a whole, non-white unemployment rates are typically twice the unemployment rates of the white labor force. This ratio persists among the young; thus, in 1965, while whites between 16 and 19 years experienced a 13.4% unemployment rate, non-whites between 16 and 19 had a 26.2% unemployment rate. In 1964, median income of non-white families was only 56% of the median income of white families. In the face of such discrimination, it is not surprising to find a large number of blacks in the professional military—the major U.S. institution that really gives "equal pay for equal work." This "equality" of exploitive wages and inhuman work reveals equality in the United States today for what it is and has no doubt fostered the rise of black power politics led by young blacks who are the most oppressed by the administrative imperialist system.

Young women also experienced multiple discrimination, first because they are women and second because they are young. Young women in the present period are in transition between roles, often finding satisfaction in neither. If they seek to leave behind the traditional role at home, they enter a job market in which they face severe discrimination (the median income of women is about one-third that of men, largely because so many are forced to work part-time). No consideration is given to the ways in which they differ from men. Yet an increasing number cannot withdraw from the unfair competition and stay at home, because this traditional role is being eroded by the exploitation of the young men whom they marry. Women married to young men see them excluded from adulthood. An increasing portion of young marriages takes place while the husband is in the armed forces or in school. The couple's parents or the young wife provides the support. Exploitation of the young has in this way narrowed the traditional escape of women into the home. Increasingly, therefore, we should expect to see women playing an important role in the formation of youth class-consciousness.[8] . . .

[8] For an excellent discussion of the role of radical women, see "The Look Is You," *New Left Notes,* March 18, 1968.

D. Summary

What are our conclusions? Increasingly, young people are laboring in the two dynamic "socialized" sectors of the administrative imperialist system. If they venture outside army or school they meet unemployment rates two to five times the average. The young are being exploited and are undergoing impoverishment.

Can Courts and Money Do It?
by Daniel Patrick Moynihan

Two years ago, writing in the *Times*'s annual education supplement, I contended that "the crucial phase in solving a problem is the process by which it comes to be defined." I distinguished between two kinds of problems in the area of social policy. First there are those that involve the aggregation of sufficient support in the political system to bring about a change in public policy. Second there are those in which social goals are fairly well agreed upon but where administrators lack the knowledge to achieve them. I called the first political problems, the second knowledge problems.

It is fairly clear—is it not?—that much of the 1970's is going to be taken up with efforts to solve knowledge problems in the fields of education, and to do so in a context of political problems that are equally unsolved. This trend became more or less fixed in late December, 1971, when a special panel of three federal judges—in the aftermath of similar cases in California and Minnesota—declared the method of financing the Texas school system unconstitutional because of unequal expenditures as between different school districts. The judges ordered the Texas Legislature to devise a new system that will meet the equal protection provisions of the 14th Amendment. One may sympathize—as I do—with the court's decision without having to suppose that the judges had the slightest awareness of the knowledge problems they were raising, nor yet of the political problems they were bringing about by ordering the Legislature to do something which on its own it was clearly averse to doing.

Let us list just a few of these knowledge problems.

The first has to do with the effect of expenditure, equal or unequal, on education. The evidence seems to be that there is so little effect as for practical purposes to be naught, or at least for the matter to be judged, in judicial terms, de minimis. This month Frederick Mosteller and I will publish the results of four years of reanalysis by a score of social scientists of the data of the Equal Educational Opportunity Survey on which the Coleman Report (James S. Coleman, 1966) was based. Our findings confirm those of the original report. If anything, they diminish further the extraordinarily weak influence which school "inputs" such as per pupil expenditure seem to have on educational "outputs." One contributor concluded that given the state of our knowledge the least promising thing we could do in education would be to spend more money on it. On quite different grounds Kenneth Boulding has suggested that education may indeed be a "pathological sector" of the economy in which increased investment brings no greater, or conceivably even lesser, returns.

I would take it for granted that the federal judges ruling in the Texas case knew little of such matters and cared less. They confronted an inequity in the expenditure of public funds to provide a basic public service, and ordered the Legislature to do something. The effect of the order, almost certainly, will be to raise educational expenditures. The only certain result that will come from this is that a particular cadre of middle-class persons in the possession of certain licenses—that is to say, teachers—will receive more public money in the future than they do now.

Who will provide this money is not clear: it could come from heavier taxes on the poor and the working classes, or it could come from heavier taxes on the middle class itself (taxes on the rich just aren't that important). That is to say, it could involve a shift in resource allocation up the social scale, or it could redistribute resources within a particular social-class level. No one knows.

Other questions arise, of which the most important has to do with the constitutionality of unequal expenditure designed to compensate for whatever it is that makes for weaker educational achievement among children of the poor. It was precisely for this purpose that federal aid to education was begun in 1965. The stereotype of rich districts in the suburbs and poor ones in the central city persists, but studies by Robert J. Havighurst and others suggest that compensatory programs are reaching their targets and that there are now many instances of fiscal imbalance in the opposite direction of the one traditionally assumed.

Others deny this and the argument will go on, but it would appear we have to face the possibility that the constitutionality of compensatory programs is open to challenge.

Serious Questions

I would wish to repeat that the Texas school decision seems to me to have been just, if only because it will strike most persons as adhering to a principle of fairness. We need this in our society more than we need educational achievement. Still, there remain serious questions which the judiciary ignores at the risk of being judged incompetent, and which the rest of us can avoid only by the exercise of high irresponsibility. In a word, the emergence of knowledge problems in fields such as education has quite transformed the standards of acceptable political conduct.

To extend a concept which Chris Argyris has applied to business management, it may be said that with each new year the amount and kind of information that a legislator or political executive—now including the President himself—may be held responsible for increases. This is not quite so much a burden as might at first appear. A good deal of what a President, or other such political executive, must know consists of nothing more than awareness of what is not known. Two or three Presidencies back, a Chief Executive could be excused if he allowed diplomats or military men to persuade him that nations in Southeast Asia could be transformed into viable bastions against Communism or something like that by the introduction of modern weapons technology. No one then (or now) knew how to bring about such a transformation, but the President was not then required to be aware of this. Henceforth he will be, which is to say that he may not allow others to pretend to knowledge that does not exist.

Obviously this can be a relief to all concerned. On the other hand there are fields in which positive knowledge is increasingly demanded of political executives, the President included. Of these none has come forward in so demanding a way as the field of education.

If a political executive does not know, he has to set in motion an effort to learn, and to devise other ways to cope in the interval. Especially as the courts are becoming more active, it becomes crucial that what is known and not known in education be more carefully delineated. Perhaps this misstates the possibility. It may only be that different degrees of confidence can be assigned different propositions about what education is, and how it occurs.

But some such sorting out must take place.

With just this in mind, in March, 1970, President Nixon proposed to Congress the establishment of a National Institute of Education. The object was to bring "big" science to bear on education, especially the problem of low achievement among students from low-income families.

Institute of Education

Congress was silent for almost a year, but by the end of 1971 legislation to establish a National Institute of Education had passed both the House and Senate. In one form or another we should expect that such an institution will begin in 1972.

With this we can at least tell that a period of serious research and development in education will follow.

The National Science Foundation estimates $162.4 million was obligated for research and development in education in the fiscal year 1972. But we don't seem to get much for it. Testifying before the Select Subcommittee on Education of the House of Representatives, Sheldon White of Harvard noted of Project Head Start that when it began "there was no pre-school program in the country which had shown that it could produce large and lasting benefits to children's subsequent success in school."

We went ahead anyway and most would agree that we ought to have done so. But isn't it beginning to be time we began getting an answer to that question? Or is it that the question has been answered and everyone feels the need to keep quiet?

Hence a final point: Educational research, like all social research, is threatening. It can and does produce unwelcome information. I for one would be willing to bet that the more we learn about formal schooling the less we will come to value it. Rather than spending more money on early education, for example, we are likely to conclude that the transition we manage least well in our society is that of the young person leaving the world of school for the world of work, and that accordingly much more resources should be applied to this period in individual development rather than the much earlier one.

We are entered on a decade in which the elementary and secondary school population will not grow at all, but in which the labor force will increase by one-quarter. This will be the largest such increase since the late nineteenth century. We have no institutions for managing it. Or at least we have few. It would be terrible if for that reason we decide instead to continue to concentrate our efforts where there are large and threatening institutions. To do so would likely lead to a social imbalance which by transforming a knowledge problem into a political one will perhaps at last impress upon us that both matter and neither will go away.

Nixon Budget Spells Trouble for Schools

WASHINGTON, D.C. (UTP News Service). While it is very difficult to unravel and compare President Nixon's simultaneous revised fiscal year 1973 and fiscal 1974 education budget requests which went to Congress January 29 along with his overall $268.7 billion federal 1974 budget, one thing is very clear: the hatchet job on education funds portends bitter battle between the President, Congress, and the education lobbyists.

Not only did the President propose a reduced "hold the line" $5.2 billion overall 1974 education budget for the Office of Education, the National Institute of Education (NIE), and the new Assistant HEW Secretary's office which would cut a number of existing programs, but he also submitted a revised 1973 education budget calling for $5.4 billion as opposed to his original $6.1 billion request last year.

While cuts in the 1974 budget, therefore, are listed as $208 million when compared with the 1973 revised budget, they would actually be closer to $900 million in proposed presidential cuts between the two years. In addition, many of the new funds which have been added to the education budget for NIE have come from programs formerly funded under the Office of Economic Opportunity (OEO), which is slated to be disbanded under the President's new budget. NEA specialists also say that much of the 1974 funds, a mix of money and loans, is the same as funds that have not been spent in 1973.

From *The New York Teacher*, February 4, 1973.

There has been no action on the 1973 Labor-HEW budget, which includes education funds, since it has been twice vetoed by the President as inflationary. Education funding, now in the middle of the 1973 fiscal year which began July 1, 1972, has been maintained under a continuing resolution under which education formula grant allocations are based on either 1972 budget levels or the President's original 1973 budget request—whichever is less. Congressional education committees, however, say that education programs under the language of the resolution which was signed by Nixon should be funded at a higher level of either the first House-passed or first Senate-passed version of the fiscal year 1973 bill.

For the first time that NEA legislative and budget specialists recall, the President has reduced education funds in the previous year's budget by two different means: rescissions, or negative appropriation actions, which request amendments to the appropriation acts already passed by Congress to withdraw unneeded funds; and budget amendments, which involve a revision of the President's original budget request when a final appropriation has not yet been made by Congress.

Through these two methods, the President has asked for a $126 million decrease in his original 1973 budget proposal which would reduce programs in Indian education, higher education, education professions development, educational development (career education), Title I ESEA for educationally deprived children, vocational education curriculum development, educational activities overseas, and strengthening state departments of education.

The issue of such impoundment of funds and the related battle of who controls the pursestrings—Congress or the President—is shaping up as one of the key issues in the current session of Congress.

While cutting both 1973 and 1974 funds predominantly for public education as part of a program to hold down the budget, the President on the other hand has proposed another program which is guaranteed to anger public school educators: tax credits for parents of private and parochial school youngsters. The program, which will cost the U.S. Treasury $600 million a year in revenues, would provide tax credits for half the cost of tuition and fees up to $200 per child in such schools to parents earning $18,000 or less.

As last year, there is again expected to be some strong Congressional resistance to enacting special education revenue sharing.

NEA has been opposed to the proposal because it offers no additional funds to the schools in the long run. The battle between the administration and Congress on this matter will heighten this year because the entire Elementary and Secondary Education Act (ESEA)—most of which the administration has pegged to go into special revenue sharing—is up for renewal July 1.

Biggest cuts in the 1974 budget are in elementary and secondary education programs, impact aid, environmental education, vocational education, and follow-through (which will be phased out in 1978). No federal funds have been proposed for creation of experimental and innovative programs under ESEA Title III, improvement of state education agencies under Title V, Aid to Libraries (all federal aid to libraries has been cut), environmental education and nutrition and health projects, and direct operating subsidies to colleges and universities.

An Appeal to the Honorable Richard M. Nixon
by the National Education Association

OFFICE OF THE PRESIDENT
NATIONAL EDUCATION ASSOCIATION

October 2, 1972

The Honorable Richard M. Nixon
President of the United States
The White House
Washington, D.C. 20500

Dear Mr. President:

The National Education Association is appealing to you to help transform a serious national problem—the unemployment of a record 111,000 prospective beginning school teachers—into an unprecedented opportunity for the nation's nearly 50 million public school students. We believe the large supply of qualified teachers, many of whom must mark time while education deteriorates, can and should be utilized in bolstering and improving education. I am confident I speak for our 1.2 million members in deploring the waste of talent in a field closely tied to the well-being of our nation's children and to the welfare of all America.

A critical level has been reached in the number of unemployed teachers. The 111,000 newly qualified 1972 college graduates who have been unable to locate jobs as teachers follow last year's 100,700 professionally jobless graduates and the previous year's 54,800. Thus, over the last three years approximately one-quarter million newly qualified teachers have been unemployed as professionals.

Twenty-six states reported in a recent NEA survey that they had a "larger" excess of applicants this year than last and four others indicated a "much larger" excess, while none reported a smaller supply. On the average in the nation's largest school systems, there were nine applicants for each teaching position this year, and the unemployment rate among new college graduates prepared to teach now exceeds 7 per cent compared to 1 to 2 per cent each year prior to 1968. Unfortunately, the teacher unemployment situation is only part of the much broader problem of unemployment and underutilization of human resources in the professions generally.

While qualified persons search unsuccessfully for teaching jobs, the birthright of children—a good education—remains in serious jeopardy. Many teaching and support positions in local schools have been eliminated. Subjects like art, music, and physical education, frequently the keys to academic or occupational success, have been casualties of "economy measures." In some schools, the sizes of reading, math, English and other classes, including elementary school classes, have become unmanageable.

Many of the teacher strikes, which have been considerably more numerous this fall than last, reflect teachers' deep concern for this erosion of quality education.

Good teachers still are, as ever, the key to children's learning. The record supply of qualified educators offers unusual opportunities to prevent or reduce overcrowded classrooms, raise the quality of education for disadvantaged children, individualize instruction and curriculum, make kindergarten programs universal, improve general education, and spur other advancements.

The NEA survey showed that less than 6 per cent of the children enrolled in 63 of the nation's largest school districts are in those that indicated the enlarged teacher supply was being used to improve school staffing and programs faster than the relatively slow normal pace of the past. In fact, nearly half of the children enrolled in 20 reporting states are in school districts where "financial conditions are slowing, arresting, or reversing normal progress toward improved school programs and staffing."

If every school achieved what we consider, in our professional judgment, is a minimum standard of quality in educational staffing, there would be no so-called teacher surplus. In fact, there would be a shortage of 660,000 teachers. This standard would encompass improving teacher qualifications, eliminating oversize classes, and expanding the number of children who have access to educational programs and services such as kindergarten and special education.

Underutilization of qualified teachers rarely stems from a district's unwillingness to provide better education for its children. Rather, the lack of improvement despite the availability of professional talent results from the financial plight of a large and growing number of districts throughout the nation.

The fact that only a relatively few communities—the more affluent ones—have the money to take advantage of these new opportunities underscores the inequality of education today.

The NEA believes the major road to substantial improvement of all the schools is a much greater financial contribution by the federal government. We have proposed, in our National Standard of Education, that the federal contribution be increased from the present inadequate 7 per cent to one-third of the education dollar by 1976, the bicentennial of our nation's founding.

We offer our help in finding ways to tap the abundant pool of professional teaching talent, which we believe would be a stride toward making the nation's hopes and dreams for a better America come true.

Enclosed is a copy of the preliminary report on teacher supply and demand prepared by the NEA Research Division.

Sincerely,
(Mrs.) CATHARINE BARRETT
President, National Education Association

Bankruptcy Proceedings

Detroit Schools Face Fund Crisis
by Jerry M. Flint

DETROIT, June 3. Detroit's school system has reached the brink of bankruptcy and school officials are talking about "survival" plans that for practical purposes would end the educational function of the schools.

From *New York Times*, June 4, 1972.

The plans, for example, envision opening schools in mid-December next fall instead of September or running on four-day school weeks. Other stringency measures involve eliminating about a third of the school days, plus layoffs of a major portion of the teaching staff and severe curtailment of the school programs.

The Detroit schools, state tests show, are already providing less than adequate education for 291,000 children in the system, two-thirds black.

The Detroit school crisis is symbolic of the total urban crisis. The Governor, state education officials, and federal and state judges call for "equal educational opportunity," but Charles Wolfer, Detroit School Superintendent, says that no state or federal body is attempting to save the city's already "unequal" schools from collapse.

Some school board members are recommending that the system start the schools in the fall and close them when the money runs out in early spring. They maintain that this is the only action that is likely to bring legislative or court intervention.

The crisis is tied to school financing.

This year's Detroit school budget is about $270 million, but revenues will fall about $38 million short. Thus the schools will have to dip into next fall's funds.

In addition, Detroit residents voted down a continuation on $28 million in present school taxes as well as voting down a request for an extra $28 million. Generally, Detroit's taxpayers pay higher taxes than in most suburbs. But in the suburbs most of the taxes go for the schools while in Detroit most of the taxes go to cover city costs.

The school board will require about $295 million to maintain the present programs in the next school year.

The federal courts are indirectly involved because a federal judge, Stephen Roth, has ruled that Detroit's schools are segregated and made it clear he would combine city and suburbs in some kind of metropolitan school district. Some form of busing could be part of the plan. But it is unlikely that suburban parents would or could be made to send their children into a school system that is eliminating much of its instruction.

There are various suits in the courts to end the property tax as the basis of school support in Michigan, too, and voters are to face the issue of shifting the school tax burden to an income tax this fall. But these are long-term solutions and not likely to end the present crisis.

"On This Sad Note ... Wish You the Best"

OFFICE OF THE PRINCIPAL
OAKLAND TECHNICAL HIGH SCHOOL

July 13, 1971

Mr. Leo R. Croce
Associate Superintendent, Region I
Oakland Unified School District
1025-2nd Avenue (Ethel Moore Annex)
Oakland, California 94606

Dear Leo:

Needless to say, when you cut a school teaching staff by twelve positions the heart of a program is almost eliminated. The twelve people I am losing are the ones I recruited and who helped stabilize the school. Just two short years ago Tech was rocked by dissension and student turmoil. Although we have not eliminated all the problems, we were on the road to becoming the high school Tech has the potential to be. Our program for next year was creative and imaginative—what now?

Unfortunately, when cuts must be made on a seniority basis, the young, eager teacher is eliminated. Every school needs the mature, experienced teacher, but it also should be balanced with new ideas; we had finally attained that position. We worked very hard to hire teachers who represented the racial composition of the school—all is back as it was with these cuts. We have some teachers who are unhappy at Tech because of progressive change. Wouldn't it be better to put them at a school where they would fit and be able to make their kind of contribution?

I need your help and advice on the following problems:

(1) We were given two periods to do our attendance work on our Tab machine. These have been cut. Tech has a tremendous absence rate and we need to do all we can to improve. This cut severely hampers our efforts. We need one additional position just for attendance and programming—can we expect it?

(2) Our E.S.L.* program has doubled in size, yet we still have only 3½ positions. We need another teacher added to this staff. This program should have a budget for equipment, supplies and books.

* English as a Second Language, for non-English-speaking students.—ED.

We're in trouble, Leo—from a good high school we become a mediocre one. I am sure the staff and I will do all we can, but the future looks dim. Our students are great and I'm sure we will have a quiet year, but will it be a year of good education? The students, parents, staff and I stand ready to help in any way we can to get the money needed to restore and upgrade our program. Let us know what we can do.

Sincerely,
/s/
Principal

OFFICE OF THE PRINCIPAL
OAKLAND TECHNICAL HIGH SCHOOL
July 13, 1971

TO: All Teaching Staff, Oakland Technical High School
FROM: Principal
SUBJECT: Consolidation of Teaching Staff

We have received official word to reduce our staff by eleven positions. After discussions with teacher representatives and central administration we have been advised that all changes must be made on a seniority basis. Needless to say, we will lose many teachers we consider essential to our program, and since we have made an effort to increase our minority teaching staff, we will lose teachers who represent our student population. With the above restriction as our basis, we have been forced to cut the following teachers:

[Here follow the names and departments of thirteen teachers, some on half-time.]

We will still need to cut another position, but we are going to start the school year with an extra position in the hope that our enrollment will allow us to keep it.

It goes without saying we have to drastically curtail our creative program to one of less imagination. I wish I could offer encouragement, but it seems all our work of the past two years has been eliminated with these cuts.

If any position opens or we are allowed to keep more teachers we will naturally select from the teachers eliminated by the consolidations.

I am sure the total staff joins me in thanking the departing teachers for their hard work and enthusiasm and in hoping that they may . . . rejoin us at Tech in the very near future. . . .

On this sad note it is hard to ascertain what our school year will be like. We will mail you copies of your schedule within a couple of weeks. I hope your summer is enjoyable and wish you the best.

Sincerely,
/s/
Principal

9 Bureaucracy and the Permanent Record

Bureaucracy is the swathing of events and processes in smothering layers of paper. Soon the packaging comes to be more significant than the event.

Thus, in schools, administration takes precedence over teaching; the correct completion of attendance files is more important than the children who are in attendance; and the destruction of a piece of paper is more dastardly than the destruction of a child.

Periodically in the history of U.S. schooling, great public attacks have been mounted against bureaucracy—"downtown," "pencil-pushing bureaucrats," "supervisors who haven't seen the inside of a classroom in twenty years," and so forth. Everyone agrees, except the bureaucrats, who manage to wait it out until the word shall again become the "operative" reality.

The word supersedes the deed. The word is the deed. The children, confronted weekly with their twenty hostile strangers, understand this better than anyone.

For the stubborn persistence of bureaucracy is more than the stubborn persistence of the bureaucrats. Michael B. Katz's "Bureaucracy and the Industrial Order" analyzes bureaucracy as central to the school's function of molding the children of the poor to the needs of an economic order that keeps poor the children of the poor. Desexualization, compulsory attendance, contempt for the children's homes, and racist scorn are all inherent in the bureaucratic mission. To some, it looks like progress that the urban poor Katz describes were those very immigrant Irish, German, Polish, Jewish, and Italian urban poor whose descendants today are the bureaucratic missionaries among the black, Puerto Rican, and Chicano urban poor.

How the bureaucratic swathing chokes the humanity of teachers and children alike in a church-related residential school for Indians in the Yukon is described in A. Richard King's "The Bureaucrat, the Martyr, and the Artificial Self." The alienation of the adults, who sustain their egos by sucking up to the sources of power, and of the children, who re-create theirs to meet Whiteman's strange rituals, is more sharply focused than, but not so different from, the human situation of the teachers and children we are more familiar with. And the role of Christian ethics in concealing and exculpating the damage being done to all of them is analogous to the role of the democratic myth in the schools we all know.

But there is an internal contradiction: The economic order is dependent on school bureaucracy, but school bureaucracy is, indeed, troublesome and inefficient, and it does interfere with academic learning. The grand-jury committee irritably comments on some aspects of this contradiction, without, however, recognizing it for what it is.

The gathering dangers of the elevation of the word are proposed by the reports of the prestigious Russell Sage Foundation and the Black Teachers Caucus on *The Permanent Record*. What these important files look like and how students feel about them are shown in the next two documents. A most interesting aspect of the junior high school dean's dossiers is the fitting of the punishment to the crime: In general, crimes against the system (including against the flag) are graver than crimes against other students. Authority and symbols of authority outweigh fraternity.

The vulgar but sensitive students of Monroe High confronted the system's hostile words with their own hostile acts. "It is a fantasy," wrote the students, "to believe that a human being's knowledge can be measured with numbers and letters." Perhaps they also perceived that beyond the fantasy is the nightmare—the nightmare of a world in which human beings serve merely as a kind of organic fodder for files and computer tapes, in which body counts signify more than bodies, and words and images released into the air have a power surpassing the power of flesh and blood.

Bureaucracy and the Industrial Order

by Michael B. Katz

In the nineteenth century, as now, the controversy over the shape of education reflected a debate over the shape of society. Thus the analysis of organizational models, of alternative proposals, provides direct insight into the key value conflicts within American culture.

. . . I shall try . . . to demonstrate a connection between bureaucracy and social class. Bureaucracy is not a neutral form; it represents the crystallization of particular social values. In America those values have expressed and worked for class interests. . . .

For a complex variety of reasons . . . schools came to be perceived as the key agencies for uplifting the quality of city life by stemming diffusion of the poverty, crime, and immorality that were thought to accompany urban and industrial development. As Henry Barnard phrased the problem: "The condition and improvement of her manufacturing population, in connection with the education of the whole people, is at this time the great problem for New England to work out." . . .

In that setting, the first problem of the schools became, very simply, to ensure the regular attendance of all children upon a prolonged, systematic, and carefully structured formal education. Within the city, "so unfavorable" were the "surrounding circumstances," so "numerous . . . the temptations in the street, from the example and teaching of low-bred idleness" that school attendance should begin at the age of five. In fact, the incompetence of the urban poor as parents implied the need to exchange the natural for an artificial family setting:

> No one at all familiar with the deficient household arrangements and deranged machinery of domestic life, of the extreme poor, and ignorant, to say nothing of the intemperate —of the examples of rude manners, impure and profane language, and all the vicious habits of low bred idleness, which abound in certain sections of all populous districts—can

From Michael B. Katz, *Class, Bureaucracy, and Schools: The Illusion of Educational Change in America* (New York: Praeger Publishers, 1971). © 1971 by Praeger Publishers, Inc. Reprinted by permission of Praeger Publishers.

doubt, that it is better for children to be removed as early
and as long as possible from such scenes and examples.

As might be expected from their image of the urban poor, school
reformers held that the "primary object" in removing the child
from the influence of the parent to the influence of the school
was "not so much . . . intellectual culture as the regulation of the
feelings and dispositions [and] the extirpation of vicious propen-
sities." . . . Under the influence of a surrogate mother, a female
teacher, the process should continue until the age of twelve, at
which time working-class children might safely leave school to
receive the rest of their character training in the practical business
of earning a living. The matter of school attendance, warned
Barnard, was not to be taken lightly. Should its neglect continue,
society would reap its "retribution" for the "crime of neglected
childhood." . . .

That task assumed special importance in relation to industrial
society. The values to be instilled by the schools were precisely
those required for the conduct of a complex urban society—for
example, the importance of time. Expressed as the problem of
irregular and tardy attendance, the problem of instilling a sense
of time into children and their parents obsessed school committees.
Aside from the real problems caused by a lack of that sense, the
great stress on time indicates a concern that extended beyond the
schoolroom. One writer, to make that concern explicit, pointed to
the parallel behavior required of the schoolboy and the working
man. . . . The connection was unmistakable; schools were training
grounds for commerce. What had been "instilled in the mind of
the pupil" became "thoroughly recognized by the man as of the
first importance in the transaction of business."

The problem of time haunts developing societies; it is at the very
heart of the transformation of agrarian habits, which do not emphasize precision and promptness, into habits consonant with city life
and large-scale manufacture. Every society since the Industrial
Revolution began has had to develop a mechanism for changing
the behaviors appropriate in a traditional society into those called
for by modernity. America handled that problem, the problem of
industrial discipline, like so many others, through the schools.
Industrialists, in fact, have not been hesitant about stating what
they have wanted. That was clear, to take two instances, in the
responses that Horace Mann and George Boutwell received in
1841 and 1859 when they asked manufacturers about the value of
educated labor. One wrote that knowledge was secondary to

morality, and that educated workers showed "more orderly and respectful . . . deportment," plus a greater willingness "to comply with the . . . regulations of an establishment." During labor disputes, the same experienced capitalist wrote, "I have always looked to the most intelligent, best educated and the most moral for support." It goes without saying that it was "the ignorant and uneducated . . . the most turbulent and troublesome" who acted "under the impulse of excited passion and jealousy." The association of virtues was significant: Education, morality, and docility were all equated; they formed a trinity marking a properly schooled man. If there be any doubt on that point, consider the words of another manufacturer, who praised the "diligence and . . . willing acquiescence" of the educated who, working their way into the confidence of their colleagues, exerted a "conservative influence" in times of labor trouble, an influence "of great value pecuniarily and morally." The common school made company men. . . .

Thus, the first generation of urban schoolmen began by rejecting democratic localism* and argued for carefully structured systems of education. Fully developed plans for systems of schools and elaborate architecture, curriculums, and pedagogy mark the reports and appeals of Mann, Barnard, and their contemporaries. Their goal was to uplift the quality of public education by standardizing and systematizing its structure and content.

All their plans had certain characteristics in common, most important among them centralization. This had two principal components: first, the modification and eventual elimination of the bastion of democratic localism, the district system, whereby each section of a town or city managed its own schools with a great deal of autonomy. . . . The ultimate remedy was the replacement of the district by one central board of education. In most cases, however, that was politically impossible, and reformers consequently turned to an interim measure, the establishment of high schools. In Massachusetts, for example, both the law and practical considerations required the high school to be a town school, administered by the town-school committee and siphoning off students from all the districts into the one central institution. It was thus an administrative device for undercutting the power of the districts.

The grading of schools formed the second and related component of centralization. In the district system, children of all ages were taught in one room by one teacher. That is precisely what

* A system of school governance whereby the adult members of local communities set up and control the schools their children attend.—ED.

school reformers wanted to end. As Barnard put it, one of the principal "conditions of success" for a system of public schools was a "classification of scholars" that brought "a large number of similar age and attainments, at all times, and in every state of their advancement" together within classrooms under the exclusive charge of the same teacher. Reformers argued that graded schools yielded enormous increases in educational efficiency and effectiveness, and their blueprints featured carefully designed sequences of schools of which a high school formed the apex.

An emphasis on supervision accompanied centralization. The opponents of democratic localism argued eloquently for state boards of education with paid secretaries and, at the local level, for superintendents of schools. . . . Like the grading of schools, a superintendent would improve educational efficiency and, in addition, would increase the honesty of school operation to a degree that would more than compensate for his salary.

The stress on paid, full-time supervision spilled over into arguments for professional expertise. The emphasis on teacher training and the development of normal schools became an intimate aspect of the bureaucratic strategy. The case for normal schools shared an important assumption with the argument for professional supervision: that education had become a difficult and complex undertaking whose conduct and administration required individuals with specialized talents, knowledge, and experience. . . .

Professionalism and system, like the obsession with punctuality, reflected industrial values. . . . Unlike traditional societies, with well-defined roles and rigid social structures, societies that are modernizing require a commitment to competence. It is necessary to call forth and reward achievement if specialized and technical tasks are to be performed. The transition from a pre-industrial society requires a shift in the basis of social valuation from ascription to achievement. That became one function of public education, as schoolmen again attempted to facilitate economic change through the transformation of social attitudes.

. . . It became a key function of the schools to teach the substitution of higher for lower pleasures, which, from one point of view, represented a systematic attempt to diffuse sexual repression throughout society. "Passionate" and "sensual" became two of the most pejorative words in educational discourse. "Those, whose minds and whose hearts have been properly trained and disciplined by education, have control over their passions. Having cultivated a taste for simple and innocent pleasures, rather than a love for vicious excitement, their desires are awakened by objects higher than any gratification merely animal." In their objectives for education, schoolmen thus reflected a peculiarly Victorian combination of sexual and status anxiety that forms one of the least lovely aspects of nineteenth-century culture. Whether that came from their own discomfort at suspecting mass indulgence in pleasures that they themselves had painfully renounced or from a desire for social control, it was apparent that the traits of character schoolmen found necessary to fit the working class for upright urban living represented an idealized Victorian middle-class portrait of itself. It is apparent, too, that public school represented an attempt to effect a massive and permanent desexualization of society.

Herein lies an irony: Schoolmen who thought they were promoting a neutral and classless—indeed, a *common*—school education remained unwilling to perceive the extent of cultural bias inherent in their own writing and activity. However, the bias was central and not incidental to the standardization and administrative rationalization of public education. For, in the last analysis, the rejection of democratic localism rested only partly on its inefficiency and violation of parental prerogative. It stemmed equally from a gut fear of the cultural divisiveness inherent in the increasing religious and ethnic diversity of American life. Cultural homogenization played counterpoint to administrative rationality. Bureaucracy was intended to standardize far more than the conduct of public life. . . .

What is less obvious, although closely related, is the racist implication of such a point of view. If an attitude that considers one group to be different from, and inferior to, another in some basic and essential fashion can be labeled racist, then we are forced to the conclusion that racist sentiment scarred the origins of public education. For it is in precisely those terms—difference and inferiority—that school people perceived lower-class children. . . .

It was partly to deal effectively with the problem of the urban poor that bureaucracy developed as the mode of organizing urban schools. The racism thus integral to bureaucratic structure became even more deeply entrenched, because it early acquired a functional utility as a defense of bureaucratic failure. In 1876 one

commentator related an alleged decrease in the standard of educational attainment to the altered background of students. . . .

> A very large proportion of the pupils in our cities and popu-
> lous towns come from homes utterly destitute of culture, and
> of the means and the spirit of culture, where a book is never
> seen, and reading is with the adult members a lost art, or one
> never acquired. There are schools in which four-fifths or
> more of the children are of this class. I at one time had under
> my supervision a school in which ninety-nine percent of the
> children were of foreign parentage, and hardly one of the
> whole from a home level with the lowest status of native-born
> intelligence. In such minds a sunken foundation must be laid
> by months or years of unpromising toil before any portion of
> the work begins to appear above the surface. It seems almost
> impossible to give them a conception of either the uses or the
> pleasures of knowledge, or to lead them to that primal
> exercise of judgment by which two ideas are compared or
> combined. Even the simplest object-lessons are often unin-
> telligible to them. Instruction can hardly be conveyed to them
> in terms which they can understand, and in what they attempt
> to learn, memory derives no assistance from association. A
> person of exceptional skill and patience might hope out of a
> single such block in the lapse of years to carve a statue; but
> what shall we think of the sculptor who is compelled every
> day to make some strokes of the chisel on forty or fifty of
> them?

What, indeed, but to excuse his failure? That this essentially
racist excuse for educational failure is reminiscent of current discourse about cultural deprivation is not an accident, for the current
notion is but a continuation of the old: a well-developed bureaucratic strategy for explaining educational disaster by reference to
the inferiority of the pupils.

    . . . compulsory education followed inexorably upon the demise
of democratic localism. . . . Thus, in 1851 Massachusetts passed
the first general compulsory-education law. A serious confrontation
with the realities of nonattendance in that state and others had
forced school promoters to recognize the logic of their long-
standing position. . . .
Both compulsory education and the imposition of bureaucratic

reform upon reluctant communities rested on an assumption contrary to the one at the heart of democratic localism . . .: Social change flows from the top down—always and inevitably. The function of government is to lead and to educate, not to acquiesce in public whims.

. . . bureaucracy retained the notion of a central monopoly and systematized its operation through the creation of elaborately structured schools and school systems. [Also] bureaucracy continued, and even strengthened, the notion that education was something the better part of the community did to the others to make them orderly, moral, and tractable. Unfortunately, the embodiment of that idea in compulsory, bureaucratic monopolies has continued to characterize American education.

The Bureaucrat, the Martyr, and the Artificial Self

by A. Richard King

For the children, the residential school constitutes a social enclave almost totally insulated from the community within which it functions; yet Mopass School reflects in a microcosmic but dismayingly faithful manner the social processes of the larger society. Two distinct domains of social interaction exist independently: Whiteman society and Indian society. Where these domains overlap, they do so with common purposes shared at the highest level of abstraction —but minimal congruence of purposes, values, and perceptions, at the operating levels of interaction. The Whiteman maintains his social order according to his own perceptions of reality. The Indian bears the burden of adaptation to a social order that he may perceive more realistically—and surely he perceives it with a different ordering of reality—than does the Whiteman. From his perceptions, the Indian finds it impossible to accept the social order and, at the same time, impossible to reject it completely. He therefore creates an artificial self to cope with the unique interactive situations.

In the residential school, the Whiteman staff and teachers are the end men of huge bureaucratic organizations (church and national government) that are so organized as to provide no reflection of the local communities. These employees derive their social, economic, and psychological identity from the organizations of which they are members. They validate their identities by effective job performance in organizational terms. The inherent authoritarianism in bureaucracies intensifies as one moves hierarchically downward until at the lowest level one finds maximum reliance upon power sources for authority and minimal local or individual autonomy. Since these employees are the end of the authority chain—there are none below them in the organizational structure to receive transmitted directives—only two outlets are available for reactions to the cumulative authoritarian input. One outlet is the children of the school; the other is interpersonal aggression in seeking closer identification with the nearest source of power.

The criteria for effective job performance are based more on adult relationships than on relationships with the children. The children of the school are little more than components to be manipulated in the course of the day's work. At best, they reflect the employee's ability to control; at worst they are a distractive element to one's psychological equilibrium, which is much more dependent upon relations with other adults. No job at the school is defined in terms of *outcomes*, expected or observable, in the children. As is common in bureaucracies, "Don't rock the boat" is the operating criterion for effective performance. This is literally translated as meaning one should not create or point out problems that upset the routine.

Since all the members of the school adult population are deviant or marginal individuals, both in their total society and within their bureaucracies, their jobs and their social status are precarious. A considerable degree of anxiety about job security prevails; there is a tendency to perceive a threat in any unusual situation or comment. A strong dependency is fostered, which intensifies the need for authoritarianism which, in turn, has been initially responsible for the situation. The net result is continual factionalism with frequently shifting alliances as a result of newly perceived threats from all directions. The goal of the factional alliance is to cement identity with a power source or to protect against those who seem to have closer identification with those sources. The alliances themselves thus become salient realities in the adult school life. Concerns about the consequences of interactions among school adults often assume dimensions so far removed from any Indian School purposes as to seem ridiculous, were they not so tragically effective in dissipating energies that could be directed toward the education of children.

An ideal among the non-Indian adults of the school (which is completely incomprehensible to Indians) is the modified martyr syndrome. *Seeking* martyrdom as an overt behavior is a far different order of behavior and personality organization than *enduring* martyrdom. The seeker often has surrendered himself to a situation in which higher status is unobtainable through the usual channels, yet he is driven by a need for such status. His loss of autonomy and lack of real purpose in life creates intense inner concerns about self-justification, much of which can be somewhat smoothed out if public identification as a near-martyr can be achieved without one's having to endure actual martyrdom. To achieve such identification, one must suffer publicly; not *too* much suffering, but preferably a controllable, constant amount and in a manner that can be shared and observed. The martyrdom-seeker is a difficult person with whom to work or live, since he is forced to reconstruct all reality to fit the self-justifying fantasy role that has developed in his imagination. He is often identifiable as the person who states that his purpose is "to help people *less fortunate than myself*" or "to show them how to live a better life," rather than making a frank acknowledgment that he is involved in work at which he feels he can achieve maximum personal gratification. None of the non-Indian personnel of the residential school was willing or able to admit that the job he had was the best job he could hope to get, carrying with it more physical comfort and higher status than anything he had previously known.

Children find the adult society of the school impenetrable, although they are at first inclined to be attracted toward it. A special order is developed among the Indian children, based on patterns brought from home experiences and the necessary adaptations they must make at school. Friendship associations, the few free activity choices permitted, and the children's communication system all reflect the Indian adult society of the total community in its adaptation to the Whiteman adult society.

The school children become uniquely adept at personality analysis, since their major task is to cope with the demands of shifting adult personalities. But this analysis is limited to their needs as the children pragmatically perceive them in specific situations. The children have no understanding of the concepts of martyrdom, for example. Much less do they understand why these seemingly well-paid, comfortably housed adults have such complex emotional problems among themselves. To maintain an equilibrium within their own peer group and in their relations with the impersonal adult society, the Indian children adopt the mechanism of creating a school self that functions only within the school boundaries. If this artificial self is not consciously developed, it is at least partially recognized and consciously controlled. The children sustain themselves with the conviction that their "real self" is not this person in the school at all.

Thus, long before the end of experiences at the residential school, the fundamental barriers between Whiteman and Indian are firmly developed, not so much by a conscious rejection on the part of the Whiteman as by a conscious rejection on the part of the Indian child. The sterile shallowness of the adult model presented by the school Whitemen serves only to enhance—and probably to romanticise—memories of attachments in the child's primary family group, and to affirm a conviction prevalent among the present adult Indian generation that Indians must strive to maintain an identity separate from Whitemen. . . .

An inevitable conclusion is that the organized purveyors of Christianity bear the brunt of responsibility for the nonfunctional adaptation of Indians in today's Yukon society. This conclusion is not an indictment of any church, or of the good and conscientious people who have made contributions by way of church responsibilities. It is, rather an assertion that Canadian society has forced upon the churches collectively, both by default and by actual direction, a function that the churches are incapable of performing. In a sense, the Christian churches have been the Whiteman's scapegoat—the buffer instruments with which he hoped to assuage his collective guilt and polish his tarnished conscience.

Christianity was "given" to the Indian by means of the churches and church schools, as a primary acculturative pathway. In all of the contact period and down to the present time, churches were the chosen instruments for "dealing with" Indians. To Indians, church people were the Whitemen most genuinely interested in them; and church people appeared to have a status in Whiteman society that guaranteed acceptance in that society if one identified with the Whiteman's church. Yukon Indians accepted Christianity so wholeheartedly that, within two generations, they had abandoned basic cultural patterns in a matter seldom before known to anthropological science. Language, technology, and custom became archaic overnight. Their very name identities and attendant patterns of ceremony and tradition were totally abandoned in favor of Christian identification.

Unfortunately, their newly acquired morality concepts proved to be unrelated to political and economic power in the Whiteman's society; or, at least, related in a manner not clear to Indians. Christian morality is not a set of precepts by which White businessmen do business or White workingmen labor or White social leaders accumulate prestige and wealth. Christian morality is the Whiteman's symbolization of a set of ideals which *he* recognizes as unattainable, but which he supports by means of an institutionalized social appendix called a church because this set of ideals acts as a source of forgiveness which compensates for the complexity of his individual rationalizations of self-interest and his acquisitive motivations. The subtle complexities of guilt-sin-forgiveness-salvation which have been developing among Whitemen for nearly two thousand years have not been easily transferable to Indians within only a few generations.

The Whiteman was—and is—willing to give his idealized moral order to the Indian. Indeed, he is quite insistent about it! He was not—and he is not—willing to give political and economic power to *anyone* if he can keep it for himself. To the Indian, whose indigenous individualistic morality was very similar to that of the Whiteman's—minus the superimposed Christian ideals—the new morality introduced by the Whiteman seemed a wonderful protective device for the stabilization of society, representing a great advancement for man. But the disillusion of finding that the "new morality" was only verbalization, and not a set of functioning precepts for living, has proved bewildering and disintegrative. Indian attitudes have shifted from eagerness to be a part of that society to eagerness to get what one can *from* that society.

Such an attitude is reinforced by the would-be martyrs who come with a missionary zeal. Whereas the true missionary is seldom concerned with direct self-gratification, the deviant, misplaced "missionaries" feel themselves to be self-sacrificing bearers of truth and light to a shadowed place of sinful error. This becomes an essential motivation and a broad justification for such inadequate individuals, perverting the intent of their institution and their society. These individuals are incapable of recognizing any validity in another belief system. With these people controlling the school, there is no possibility of consulting with Indian adults or of treating Indians as equals in the planning of educational experiences for the children. They seldom demonstrate a truly internalized set of values or guiding concepts. Such people often originate in culturally deprived segments of their own society and bear scars from compensating for their own origin. Understanding neither themselves nor their own purposes, much less the institutional purposes of their church, government, or society, the core of the residential school operating personnel can fall back upon only the pecking-order mechanisms of very primitive social organizations. Inherent in their closed belief systems are perceptions of hostility everywhere, a universe in which one must fight for the slightest recognition, a population with base and sinful motivations, and the capacity to achieve ultimate personal gratification only by the means of identifying oneself with the highest possible authority.

Report of Committee #2 of the 1972 Grand Jury

The school system is a collection of people performing various functions with few leaders. . . .

There are more administrators and support personnel employed by the system than there are teachers with direct classroom assignments. At the same time that student enrollment declined in San Francisco, the ratio of total personnel to students increased. Because the Administrators are tenured, if they fail as a Principal they are then transferred to the Central Office or some non-sensitive job. . . .

The Principals are the backbone of the educational system. Most have little respect for the bureaucracy at the Central Office. They have to go along with the system on the surface since the power of money and personnel transfers is controlled by the Central Office.

There is little on-site training for teachers to handle current student problems. Solutions are largely left to the individual teacher with little guidance from the Central Office. The teachers' organizations are unwilling to have their members judged or blamed for current conditions; their feeling is that lack of leader-

Reprinted from the *Interim Report of the 1972 Grand Jury: Board of Education, San Francisco Unified School District.*

ship among the administrators must be solved before questioning the actions of teachers. . . .

The financial resources and expenditures of the school system are in a crisis. The public is rejecting tax increases and the main source of funds, the property tax, might shrink drastically in November. Last spring the teachers bargained with the Central Office in good faith, accepted the word of the staff as to money available with misgivings and now find that the Central Office and Board were ignorant of their own financial situation.

The San Francisco Grand Jury recommends that the Board in its role as the policy maker should:

1. Develop an effective set of goals and philosophy for the school system—a master plan. . . .
9. San Francisco spends more money per pupil than all other large cities except New York. We cannot be proud of the results. Unless the new Board can accept fiscal responsibility, and demand it from the Superintendent we will suggest that an alternate budget procedure be adopted. This budget represents over ⅓ of the property tax.
10. Take immediate steps to reduce the number of administrators by eliminating the job themselves. . . .
11. Demand a program for this fall that will have teachers and supplies where they are needed and are effective. Insure that this program includes teaching the children to read and comprehend at an early age. Insure that the special programs required for individual student needs are available. . . .
16. Many studies have been made by the in-house groups and outside consultants regarding the organization of the administration. We urge that the Board utilize these reports, eliminate most of the Central Office positions and have the certified personnel go back to the school and teach. . . .

This report was prepared by the members of Committee #2, August 3, 1972.

Hostile Words and Hostile Acts

Permanent Records
by the Russell Sage Foundation

Schools typically maintain extensive and intimate information about pupils and their families for legitimate educational purposes including instruction, guidance, and research. Necessarily, the collection and maintenance of any information about a pupil or his family constitutes a potential intrusion on privacy. At the same time, society, by its approval of our educational institutions, legitimizes such intrusions, at least in those cases where the information collected can be demonstrated to be necessary for the effective performance of designated educational functions.

There are clear indications, however, that current practices of schools and school personnel relating to the collection, maintenance, use, and dissemination of information about pupils threaten a desirable balance between the individual's right to privacy and the school's stated need to know. Specifically, we may point to the following examples of potential abuse:

Information about both pupils and their parents is often collected by schools without the informed consent of either children or their parents. Where consent is obtained for the collection of information for one purpose, the same information is often used subsequently for other purposes. For example, information collected by a counselor for use in guiding students is sometimes released, without consent of students or parents, to a college or employer for use in selecting students.

Pupils and parents typically have little or, at best, incomplete knowledge of what information about them is contained in school records and what use is made of this information by the school. For example, teacher or counselor evaluations of a pupil's character and personality traits may be incorporated into the pupil's permanent record, without parental knowledge, and used subsequently as a basis for a college recommendation.

Parental and pupil access to school records typically is limited

From *Guidelines for the Collection, Maintenance and Dissemination of Pupil Records: Report of a Conference on the Ethical and Legal Aspects of School Record Keeping* (New York: Russell Sage Foundation, 1970). Reprinted by permission.

by schools to the pupil's attendance and achievement record (including standardized achievement test scores). For example, intelligence test scores, personality data, and teacher and counselor reports are usually withheld from both parents and pupils.

The secrecy with which school records usually are maintained makes difficult any systematic assessments of the accuracy of information contained therein. Formal procedures permitting parental or pupil challenges of allegedly erroneous information do not exist. An unverified allegation of misconduct may therefore, for example, become part of a pupil's permanent record.

Procedures governing the periodic destruction of outdated or no longer useful information do not exist in most systems. Moreover, the cumulative nature of most record-keeping systems makes a fresh start difficult or impossible for most pupils.

Within many school systems few provisions are made to protect school records from examination by unauthorized school personnel. Thus, for example, a teacher may usually obtain access to a pupil's record file, whether or not the pupil is a student of his, and without demonstrating a legitimate need for the information.

Access to pupil records by nonschool personnel and representatives of outside agencies is, for the most part, handled on an *ad hoc* basis. Formal policies governing access by law enforcement officials, the courts, potential employers, colleges, researchers, and others do not exist in most school systems. For example, in many school systems a police official may obtain access to a pupil's record file.

Sensitive and intimate information collected in the course of teacher-pupil or counselor-pupil contacts is not protected from subpoena by formal authority in most states.

It is our opinion that these deficiencies in record-keeping policies, taken together, constitute a serious threat to individual privacy in the United States. These deficiencies also interfere with the effective functioning of our educational institutions in that school administrators, if they are to continue to obtain information necessary for the effective performance of their duties, must maintain the good will of their clients who voluntarily supply such information. We therefore hope that school authorities will review their current record-keeping policies . . . and, where appropriate, revise them in such a way as to strike a balance between the need for educationally relevant information about children and the protection of individual rights to privacy.

Documents from the Dean's Files*
by the Teachers and the Boys' Dean of P. Junior High School

Humphrey, Rupert
12/2. Brings food to class. *Two swats.* 2/19. Called me a knot-headed chump. *Called parent. He is to apologize.* 2/25. Doing math with dice. *30 minutes detention.*

Mitchell, James
4/21. Popping pencils. *Lines.* 5/5. Cutting, nonstrip. *2 swats.* 9/30. Excessive tardiness (7 times). *3 swats.* 2/18. Continually roaming halls. *1 day discipline [in the dean's office].* 2/23. Defiance. Came to library without pass and refused to leave after several requests. *30 minutes detention.* 3/1. Rude and smart. *30 minutes detention.*

Ray, Chuck
2/1. Late to fifth period. *Warned.* 2/6. Smoking. *1 day discipline.* 2/27. Teasing a girl. *Warned.* 3/27. Late to first period. *Warned.* 5/17. Fight in yard with Dwight S. *2 swats and parents notified.* 5/29. Threw objects in room. *Swat.* 10/9. Spitting out of bus window and defying teacher during field trip. *Parent contact and severe detention.* 12/3. Throwing a ball. *Warning.* 1/7. Throwing metal type at a student with four other boys. *1 day discipline.* [Note that this is a less severe penalty than was awarded for "spitting out of bus window and defying teacher."] 2/17. Playing cards. *Counseling and severe detention.* 3/3. "I hate this school. I hate these teachers. I don't have to do anything." *Fail, detention, lines, counseling.* 3/13. Walking out of detention and slamming the door. *1 day suspension.* 4/28. Nonstrip and class cuts and in building without permission. *30 minutes detention.* 5/7. Hitting Ray S. and chasing students during lunch. *2 days suspension and mother phoned.* 5/12. Throwing metal objects at student, teacher. *Deten-*

---

* Roman type indicates the offense; italics, the punishment. Punishments increase in severity approximately as follows: warning, counseling (harsher scolding, which may be accompanied by finger jabs and threats of still harsher punishments or may include the advice to apologize), "lines" (copying so many lines from a book), swats (about the same as counseling, depending on number administered; preferred by many students to detention), detention, suspension, parent notification. The last may precede a recommendation for court action. Chuck Ray's file is about five times as long as is shown here.—ED.

tion, counseling. 5/20. "I don't care what you like." "Nobody's starting nothing." "You can't tell me what to do." *1 day suspension. To return with father.* 5/26. Accused of taking money from Jerry F. *Search.* No money. *Warned.* 9/24. Eating pollyseeds. *30 minutes detention.* 10/3. Late for class. Hitting girls. *30 minutes detention.* 1/5. Play-fight in class. Refused swat. *1 day suspension. To return with parent.* 1/7. *Parent contacted.* 1/12. Disturbed class. "I'm not pledging that motherfucking flag." *Counseling and severe warning and 30 minutes detention for two days.* 4/2. Threw a fork at Jimmy B. *½-hour detention.* 10/14. Kicked a girl, who had to go to hospital. *To apologize.*

"Used Against Blacks," Dossiers on Students Hit

Those cumulative folder files the school kept on each student—from kindergarten through high school—are being used to the detriment of black students and should be abandoned in San Francisco by the end of this school year.

That was the recommendation yesterday of parents and teachers attending a conference called by the San Francisco Black Teachers Caucus.

The folders amount to dossiers on each student—containing grades, teachers' comments, records of behavior problems and disciplinary actions—and can reflect the teacher's racial bias, the conference charged.

"The folders for blacks are at least a half inch thicker than [for] whites," claimed Yvonne Golden, a San Francisco high school teacher and chairman of the conference.

Joel Mitchell, chairman of the United Black Caucus, cautioned that in the future information from such folders will be available to police agency computer data banks.

The conference recommended the folders be replaced with a small card with only enough space for identification of the students, listing serious medical handicaps and a notation that the youngster passed or failed a class.

> (*San Francisco Sunday Examiner and Chronicle,*
> February 25, 1973)

Monroe Mindfuck
by Students of Monroe High School

One year ago, on February 7, 1971, the student files at Monroe High School in Rochester, New York, were destroyed. Ironically, they were destroyed in the school's own incinerator. . . .

Why did this happen? Who would ever want to burn files, smash windows, and urinate on the girls' dean's desk? They seem like acts of violence by "immature troublemakers."

But on the other hand, why keep student files to use as a threat tactic and measure students' "progress" and "personal development"? It is fantasy to believe that a human being's knowledge can be measured with numbers and letters. It is impossible to do this on a piece of paper, to have educators read this, and attempt to "know" the student and be able to satisfy his/her needs. This is the reason for destroying Monroe's files.

If one could experience the regimentation, tension, and feeling of inferiority that exist within the walls of what educators call "school," one would soon realize that learning is a rare occurrence in these institutions; and learning experiences do not occur in the classroom—they happen at lunch, in bathrooms, and on school grounds. Why? Because then students do not feel the overhanging threat and pressure created in the classroom. They can feel spontaneity, and can look inside for who they *really* are and what they *really* like.

If this society is to survive and continue, it must stop producing neurotic machines and start helping people to create and build a world in which they can live as individuals. In conclusion, the action at Monroe High was only a beginning. Its purpose is to help students lose their fear of the power structure and give them confidence in themselves, even to spread this idea. . . .

MONROE MINDFUCK*

We burned all but 78 transcripts. We burned many of the school psychologist's papers. (He had sent information that students told him in confidence to their parents and the principal.) We messed up the main guidance office, pissed on the girls' dean's desk, and burned two flats. . . .

Everyone in the group has to agree on what you want to do, how you want to do it, and why. This usually involved a lot of brainstorming and brilliant but impractical ideas. At one point we wanted to steal the transcripts, some 48 file cabinet drawers full, and send them back to the students they belonged to. (Can you imagine getting your transcript in the mail and reading what your kindergarten teacher, not to mention your school psychologist,

* Copies of this letter, accompanied by transcripts, files, and other materials, were sent to FPS in an unmarked envelope.

thought of you?) You have to decide what files . . . you want to get, and whether you want to burn them, pour blood, shit, glue, or paint on them, or whether to dump them in the school pool. You have to plan for contingencies, like what to do if you get caught, getaway routes, what to tell your parents, going underground. Most of all, you have to plan exactly what you are going to do when you get inside—just like "Mission Impossible." And you will need to discuss publicity after the action, and write a statement explaining what you did and why. It took us about four months to do all this plotting and planning.

(FPS, Issue Number 18; reprinted by permission of Ann Arbor Youth Liberation.)

10 Institutional Reform Strategies

In a surprising number of recent cases, educational needs have been defined by the very firms selling goods and services. . . . John Henry Martin, superintendent of schools in Mount Vernon, N.Y., exclaimed, "The center of gravity for educational change is moving from the teachers' college and the superintendent's office to the corporation executive suite." And fitting his actions to his words, Martin resigned as superintendent of schools to take a top executive position with the Responsive Environments Corp.

—American Teacher, *October, 1970*

Institutional reform strategies are usually introduced and managed by bureaucracies and thus helpfully enlarge the bureaucratic tumor. Attempting to deal with one or another symptom of the school crisis without regard for its contradictions, they usually also aggravate other symptoms. Pressures then build up from other sectors of the school or beyond-school world that compel modification or abandonment of that strategy. Other strategies are tried, or the same one in another place. (To a student of schools, it seems remarkable how little awareness policy-makers or victims in one state or city or school have of what is going on next door, how universal their most significant experiences are, and how widespread is their belief in their uniqueness.) And so the crisis continues, and mounts, with the reform strategies making their own new contributions. (This is transparently so in the case of desegregation-busing.)

The confusing variety of books, legislation, programs, proposals, and packages is aimed at two symptoms of the school crisis in particular. They are: the mutual antipathy between school and its lower-class (and/or nonwhite) clientele, and growing resistance to alienation training by middle-class children.

Lower-class children hate school, behave badly, and don't learn properly. School punishes them, first because they are lower class, and then because they hate school, behave badly, and don't learn properly. Of these three, their most outrageous offense is hating the punishing school. Note the harsh penalties against Chuck Ray for his statements "I hate this school" and "I'm not pledging that motherfucking flag." Equivalent punishments for not learning would be considered barbaric by most school personnel.

This complex of symptoms has traditionally been dealt with by increasing punishment—stricter rules, more rigid classrooms, "stronger" (more authoritarian) personnel, truant officers, detentions, policemen, hall guards. The remedies are brutal, patently counterproductive, and often expensive. A new wave of programs is being tried, based on more subtle techniques of control. We might call it "efficiency teaching." It includes computer-assisted instruction (CAI), behavior modification, programed learning, and teaching machines. Less openly oppressive than the old way, it is more agreeable to many educators.

These classroom techniques are a latter-day development of the combination of cost-cutting and corporate style that characterized early twentieth-century reform, as described in Raymond E. Callahan's "Education and the Cult of Efficiency." From the point of view of the business world, they are an improvement over those earlier reforms in that they may also produce corporate profits. In addition, this strategy of reform, which is deemed to require a good deal of research and development, also provides, if not profits in the strict economic sense, support for considerable numbers of research and academic personnel, whose prestige and salaries exceed those of teachers and lower supervisors. Thus, an interesting aspect (contradiction) of this strategy is that, while seeking to reduce school class bias against students, it increases class differentiations among education personnel, putting the classroom teacher down lower and lower as more and more layers of experts are laid on.

This problem, as well as the implications of these kinds of programs for the children, is dealt with in "The Experiment at Banneker School." The particular program employed there, performance contracting, seems at this time to be going out of style. This is not so much because of the kinds of objections raised in Francine Moscove's piece as because performance contracting turned out not to provide the profits its proponents had hoped for. Efficiency teaching, however, goes on under other arrangements. So the poor provide profits twice: once as a source of low-literacy, low-paid workers and again as customers for various remedial teaching packages.

Efficiency teaching is one variant of a style of reform called compensatory education, meaning more books, equipment, teachers, audiovisual aids, trips, and other cultural activities for low-status children to "compensate" for the disadvantages of their economic oppression—a handicap advantage, as it were. In one way or another, much compensatory education is federally sponsored. "'Sesame Street': An Educational Dead End" and "Compensatory Education" discuss its effects and implications.

A debate that has been boiling along in the school pot for several years now is "compensatory education *versus* integration." To many, desegregation and then desegregation-busing have come to seem the cure for the school crisis—and to others they seem to be the cause of it. Again, this strategy addresses one symptom of the crisis with little regard for all the others or for the contradictions inherent in itself. These are analyzed in "The Contradictions of Busing."

Efficiency teaching, other forms of compensatory education, and desegregation are addressed mainly to the issue of tracking. They reflect, perhaps, some concern for the fiscal crisis, but little for the problems of bureaucracy, teacher oppression, and alienation training. Side by side with the business-style philosophy of reform is a philosophy of reform that stems from the cherished humane, democratic tradition of free-enterprise capitalism, and that does address these problems, especially alienation training. It is the "free the children" movement, whose grandfathers were John Dewey and Sigmund Freud.

The open classroom, British infant-school style, and free-school or alternative-school movement are in this tradition.

There is a great deal of variation within the movement, as well as some borrowing from it by efficiency-teaching advocates. Addressed in principle to all children's oppression, the free-the-children movement has tended in fact to be most realized in schools for so-called advantaged children. To a certain extent, this movement, which may reduce the alienation training of its largely middle-class clients, leaves untouched or even aggravates class divisions, the fiscal crisis, and even sometimes, perversely, the oppression of teachers. (The last because most of the reformers are nonteachers whose writings tend to encourage the myth that the faults of the system are created by the deficiencies of its adult victims.) The confusions and sentimentality of the proponents of this strategy are dealt with in " 'Freedom Works': The Theory of Radical School Reform." What happens when adults react sentimentally to school oppression without taking responsibility for creating new social values is described in "Summerhill—Some Are Hell." That particular free school did indeed almost get itself together during the two years after the piece was written, but it soon succumbed to the fiscal crisis of the free-school world. Its story properly belongs more than halfway into the next chapter, which deals with people re-creating themselves and their world.

•

Run, Computer, Run
by Anthony Oettinger

> Come, Dick. Come, Jane.
> See Spot run.
> Run, Spot, run!

To pick up almost any current magazine or to listen to eminent researchers and educational spokesmen is to be persuaded that, thanks to the wonders of modern technology, the necessary educational revolution is just around the corner. But is it?

Excerpted by permission of the publishers from Anthony G. Oettinger, *Run, Computer, Run: The Mythology of Educational Innovation* (Cambridge, Mass.: Harvard University Press). Copyright 1969, by the President and Fellows of Harvard College.

The introduction of technology into education is an age-old process alternately exhilarating and depressing. The vastness of prevailing ignorance about both education and technology is matched only by the acrimony of debate about the value of educational technology, a debate blighted by a persistent confusion of ultimate promise with immediate possibility. Scientists or engineers who believe that quick but expensive technological remedies are all that's needed to cure education confront businessmen and school board members at ease with the status quo and anxious only to keep both the budget and the kids in line. Teachers are helpless in the middle.

We cannot ignore the fact that technology *does* offer us hitherto undreamt of possibilities. At the same time, there is merit in the common-sense conclusion that buying some gadget or following some fad *today* might only waste money.

That is one reason why it is vital to distinguish carefully between the long-range promise of educational technology and the technology that is ready for immediate delivery. One purpose of this essay is to sharpen this distinction and to examine the causes of prevalent confusion. . . .

When a President and Congress set great store in education as a weapon of social reform, agencies like the U.S. Office of Education or the National Science Foundation are put under great pressure to produce immediate results. But when a program must be successful by definition, the need for a good show often overwhelms scientific objectivity; after the curtain falls, little remains either of practical value or of added insight. It may be politically expedient, when poverty is In, to seek support of educational technology on the ground that it will solve the problems of our inner cities and then to use it as a Trojan horse for wheeling in needed reforms. If this leads to demands for an immediate return on investment, however, and if failure to produce this return is both probable and verifiable, then the expedient is really not good strategy. Ideas that are promising as objects of research and honest experiment tend to give birth. through artificial dissemination, to broods of depressing fads. There is then the danger that an angry reaction will kill the promise along with the fads.

Here is an example: In March 1968, the U.S. Office of Education sponsored a conference titled "An Educational System for the Seventies" (fashionably shortened to "ES '70"). The tenor of the conference was typical of the state of thinking in much of the education establishment. I do not want to make too much of this happening—in fact, my point is that not much *can* be made of it—but it will serve the purposes of my argument better than any straw man imagination could conjure up.

Note, for instance, the implicit suggestion in a *preconference* announcement that ES '70 already had a concrete existence: "It is hoped that the conference will serve these objectives: 1) to get consultative thinking from various groups about priority goals and outcomes for *ES '70* [emphasis added] in their subject matter area; 2) to provide practice in articulating desired student outcomes in terms of behaviors, values, attitudes, transfer to life situations, citizen role; 3) to provide cross-group communication and efforts at integrative thinking in exploring the realities of *the organic curriculum* [emphasis added]; 4) to provide a limited yet critical exposure of the organic curriculum to secondary school leadership, teachers, and policymaking citizen groups."

A basis for belief in the concrete existence of ES '70 and of *the* organic curriculum was supplied in a document accompanying the statement of conference objectives and claiming that "various elements of the educational process, such as team teaching, programmed instruction, flexible scheduling, computer-assisted teaching, and individualized curricula have recently been examined by researchers *and judged to be important additions to current practice* [emphasis added]."

This belief was further supported, with an air of authority and finality, by the statement that an "overall plan, the first phase of which is almost completed, will identify all of the activities that must be completed before the total new curriculum can become operational." The very next sentence, however, said that "these activities can roughly be classified as research, development, or demonstration," meaning that no one really knew what to do next.

This uncomfortable inconsistency was clarified by the following much more illuminating words from a preconference report on secondary education in the United States:

> Educational researchers have made significant findings about the learning process, curriculum innovation, and educational technology. Yet, it is distressing when one considers the implementation of these findings. Even with a rapid escalation of federal research funds for education, the return on this investment has been inconsequential. In short, it seems that a massive and radical redesign of the secondary education program is imperative. To bring this about, a coordinated

planning and development effort, involving a variety of social institutions, is necessary.

This paragraph raises very interesting questions: *Have* researchers indeed "made significant findings about the learning process . . . and educational technology?" *Why* is there a "time lag" between initial research findings and their implementation? *Has* the return on investment of federal research funds for education been "inconsequential," and if so, *why*? Are "significant findings" at hand to justify a "massive and radical redesign" of education programs?

These questions—the reworded *assumptions* of ES '70—are so important, in fact, that the future of education, and therefore of education research, rests on their answers. And, education itself is of such a magnitude that even minor changes, if extended throughout the system, entail a commitment of major economic and social resources and affect all of society. *Changing education policy is comparable in impact to changing national defense policy.*

Many have therefore thought it appropriate to apply to education an intellectual tool strongly identified with defense policy, namely systems analysis. Scientific methods, in recent years rechristened as systems analysis, can indeed help us understand something of the complexity of American education on the national scale. In the simplest language, the systems analyst says: "It is better to see the whole problem than just a part of the problem." In education, we must recognize that the proper sphere of explicit quantitative analysis is still severely limited. Beyond that sphere, as within it, a scientific viewpoint is merely an aid to clear thinking. It does reveal quickly that technology alone cannot fix education, because it makes us see clearly that the schools and the polity are so tightly intertwined as to preclude any change that is resisted by any one of the multitude of participants in the educational enterprise. Where every partner has veto power, none alone can proceed toward change. The prevalent notion that the possession of technological devices is sufficient impetus to change is thus revealed as an illusion. . . .

Take, for instance, an experiment conducted in elementary schools. Widely described as promising, it has addressed itself to reaching measurable universal goals through processes created by mass production and applied by mass production at custom-tailored rates to pupils grouped by the level of their attained "behavioral objectives" rather than by their chronological ages. The teachers in this experiment behave like machines. Though they are successful in some respects, their work is washed out by the leveling influence of the unexperimental high school. This experiment again does not represent an important addition to current *general* practice. Nonetheless, the pressure for quick returns on investment has increased the number of participating schools from 23 to 88, with 1,000 more innovation-drunk schools clamoring to take part. By diverting resources into premature dissemination, these pressures for quickie cure-alls threaten to stop further progress with this promising form of mass production while imposing on pupils and taxpayers yet another change in form without change in substance. . . .

There is a tendency nowadays to equate educational technology with inert *devices*. Devices are important, but worthless without people and processes. It should go without saying that a system intended for human use should be adapted to humans and not vice versa. Beyond that rather obvious but often ignored point, the system should be *transparent* in the sense that the system should not obscure the student's view of the subject. Few of the multitude of systems based on devices from chalk to television are now transparent enough for service in the schools. . . .

Enter the computer. The promise seems immense; hence the excitement is great. Like books or tutors, computers can serve any goals. They are indifferent to how the processes they apply are created. The man-made programs that control computers can embody universal or particular goals; they can either be mass produced or hand-tailored on the spot. Like a book, a computer can perform for either a group or a lone individual. . . .

The prospects are exciting indeed. But, although computers may revolutionize possibilities, they alter the facts of life not at all. When we go to schools where computers are actually in use, we find them serving as expensive page turners, mimicking programmed instruction texts. Yes, computers have practically infinite branching capabilities, but this matters little when we are unable to foresee more than a very few of the most common possible learner responses. Restricted to narrow ranges of preordained alternatives, the learner is constrained to answer in the program's terms. Computers are being used simply to churn out masses of data of doubtful value. Moreover, even with computers, the facts of life reassert themselves in the shape of cost, amount, reliability, maintenance, complexity, comfort, standardization, integration, and content. In short, much lead time is still between us and the reduction of experiments to practice. We shall see that time and again in the brief history of computing, glowing experimental results have lost their meaning in the translation from pilot study to useful operating size. Much of what computer-aided instruction and learning needs is still in the laboratory. Costs are high though decreasing, and hopes for personnel savings are largely illusions. Even computers are subject to all the usual social problems.

If we want real technological change—not just the appearance of it—we must, as in all enterprises, invest money in better ideas and better people. The scale of investment is bound to be large. With 46.5 million pupils expected in public elementary and secondary schools by 1975, each additional dollar to be spent on one child translates into $46.5 million on a national scale. Given this massive multiplier and the knowledge that ideas, people, and money have little effect if used inefficiently, it is clear that when and how resources flow are decisive for economically efficient progress.

Some policies are therefore suggested as more conducive to efficient progress than current ones. We must support promising ideas longer than either private or government programs now permit. We must support risk-taking and [must] cushion failure. All partners in the educational enterprise must share the dangers, the costs, and the credit or blame attendant on changing technology. Though we may want *technological* change, we must, nonetheless, chart our course by *human* judgment.

Education and the Cult of Efficiency

by Raymond E. Callahan

The study of various aspects of the actions administrators took between 1910 and 1929 in applying business and industrial values and practices to education [would reveal] that, regardless of the motivation, the consequences for American education and American society were tragic. And when all of the strands in the story

From Raymond E. Callahan, *Education and the Cult of Efficiency* (Chicago: University of Chicago Press, 1962). © 1962 by The University of Chicago.

are woven together, it is clear that the essence of the tragedy was in adopting values and practices indiscriminately and applying them with little or no consideration of educational values or purposes. . . . But to understand the full impact of the business influence this concern for economy has to be placed in its historical context. It is clear in retrospect that part of the tragedy was in what proved to be the unfortunate timing and sequence of events. First, by 1910 a decade of concern with reform, stimulated by the muckraking journalists, had produced a public suspicious and ready to be critical of the management of all public institutions. Second, just at this time Taylor's system was brought dramatically before the nation, not with a mundane label such as "shop management" but with the appealing title of "scientific management."* Very quickly the alleged mismanagement of the railroads was transferred to the management of other institutions, especially public institutions. By 1912 the full force of public criticism had hit the schools. Third, by 1912 the prestige of business and of businessmen was again in the ascendency and Americans were urging that business methods be introduced into the operation of government and were electing businessmen to serve on their school boards. Fourth, and of basic importance, was the fact that the "profession" of school administration was in 1910 in its formative stage, just being developed. If America had had a tradition of graduate training in administration—genuinely educational, intellectual, and scholarly, if not scientific— such a tradition might have served as a brake or restraining force. As it was, all was in flux.

These facts must be coupled with an understanding of the great force of public opinion (especially opinion marshaled by the profit-motivated popular press), on the one hand, and on the other, the almost pathetic vulnerability of public school administrators. The situation was one of a "profession" of school administration, vulnerable to the pressures of the community and with no solid tradition behind it to counteract these strong pressures, being

---

* Also called the Taylor system, after Frederick W. Taylor, an engineer whose ideas for cost-cutting in manufacturing and corporate management swept the country in the early decades of the twentieth century. School administrators sought to apply to the process of education its principle of getting greater productivity from human labor. Many still do: Recently a defense witness in a hearing against a teacher whose dismissal was sought was asked by the teacher's supervisor whether the teacher couldn't well have reduced the lining-up-for-recess time from five to three minutes, with a resulting 40 per cent increase in efficiency.—ED.

criticized for inefficiency at the very time when the community's most influential group, the businessmen, were adopting for this very problem a new panacea, the panacea of scientific management. No wonder that schoolmen sought to emulate the efficiency of business and use whatever methods business had used to attain it, and no wonder that "scientific management" appeared in the forefront of these methods. Its appearance, however, was an unhappy one for our educational system. For instead of approaching the study of administration through the social sciences, school administrators applied the "science" of business-industrial management as they understood it. . . .

The persistence of the unfortunate patterns in educational administration in the 1960s, with all of the harmful educational consequences that they have entailed, is partly a result of the diffusion of ideas and practices from the leaders in administration in the age of efficiency through their students in the schools and colleges of education down to the present time. But their strength in the 1960's is also due to the fact that the same societal factors which were responsible for their adoption in 1919–29 are still operating in the 1960's. The legacy from the age of efficiency has not been limited to school administrators and education.

As a result of their graduate training administrators have developed a kind of protective coloration that has enabled them to keep their jobs. . . . But the basic facts of life so far as educational administrators in the public schools are concerned are much the same in 1960 as they were in 1912. They are still vulnerable to public opinion and to all kinds of pressures, and their perennial problem is how to get enough money to operate the schools from a nation that is reluctant to spend money in the public sectors of the economy. Since 1957, for example, superintendents have been under great pressure to emphasize science, mathematics, and foreign language and they have responded quickly to that demand. They are also being urged, often with the hope of economizing, to introduce new panaceas such as teaching machines and educational television. Unfortunately their training does not enable them to understand the *educational aspects,* advantages and limitations, of these devices; so if they are adopted it is apt to be for public relations purposes. In American education it is important to be able to say that one's school system is abreast of the latest developments.

Administrators are also under pressure as they were in the efficiency era to apply business and industrial values and practices to education. One of the most prominent manifestations of this pressure was an article which appeared in *Fortune* in October, 1958, entitled "The Low Productivity of the Education Industry." The author conceded that it was more difficult "to put a firm figure on the value of the output" in education than it was in industry but he said there was "still something to be learned from the cold figures on quality." "For the schools," he said, "no less than the automobile industry, have an inescapable production problem." The schools were no different from General Motors, for their job was to "optimize the number of students and to minimize the input of man-hours and capital." The main point of the article was to show that whereas the productivity per worker had increased in the steel industry and others, the productivity of the education industry had declined. Like Spaulding,* the author could reach no conclusion as to the difference in the quality of education (in this instance between 1929 and 1958), but the per-pupil costs were easily available, so they were used as the "most relevant measure of productivity." For this unfortunate state of affairs, the author had a happy solution—introduce new techniques such as television, audio-visual aids, teaching machines, teacher aids, and more efficient utilization of buildings and classrooms—this last, incidentally, was entitled "scientific pro-gramming," a label which somehow did not occur to school administrators in the age of efficiency. The author's crowning achievement, however, was his recommendation that schools could improve their efficiency by hiring management consultants— the modern term for efficiency experts. *"The schools,"* said the author seriously, *"have just begun to discover scientific manage-ment."* (Italics mine.)

Of more importance in forcing the continuation of the emphasis on the financial accounting aspects of education is the chronic problem of inadequate support. In most school systems in the United States there is an annual financial crisis. Each year unless a major publicity campaign is carried out (and this some-times entails having teachers ringing doorbells to solicit votes) there is a possibility that, at best, school programs will be cur-tailed and, at worst, . . . the schools will be closed or placed on a double shift basis. . . .

* Frank Spaulding, superintendent of schools in Newton, Massachusetts, and Minneapolis, Minnesota, in the early decades of the twentieth century and a leading exponent of scientific management in education.—ED.

Did the American people get what they deserved for forcing their educators to become bookkeepers and public relations men instead of educators? I think they got more from their educators than they deserved. Inadequate as most of our public schools have been as measured against an absolute standard of excellence, they could have been much worse if a great many teachers and administrators had not been dedicated to their country and its children. . . . Educators and especially the leaders in administration have to accept part of the responsibility, of course. Many joined the loudest critics, jumped on the various bandwagons and outdid themselves in bowing to the dominant pressures. Others capitulated too easily. But many worked patiently and silently to provide the best education possible. At the mercy of every arrogant editor, every self-seeking politician, and every self-righteous protector of the public money, they and their families had to believe strongly in what they were doing or they would have left the field. They deserve our sympathy and our gratitude. The tragedy in education was part of a greater tragedy in American society.

The Experiment at Banneker School

by Francine Moscove

Last September [1970], when Behavioral Research Laboratories* came to Gary [Indiana] to organize an experimental educational project at Banneker School, it immediately became the center of a controversy in which the State Board of Education, the Gary Teachers' Union, the school board, the parents, the media and others became involved. Since that time each group has questioned the program in its own way and using its own criteria. Sometimes the criterion was self-interest, sometimes it was a question of legality, but more often the controversy has raged around the question of what is best for our children. And the ultimate criteria

---

* Behavioral Research Laboratories (BRL) is a private, profit-making education consulting and development corporation located in Palo Alto, California.—ED.

From Francine Polsky Moscove, "The Experiment at Banneker School," Gary, Indiana, Writers Workshop Pamphlet No. 3, May, 1971.

for judging this program should center around the question of what is best for the children.

Programmed, or behavioral, learning is a machine- and book-oriented system of learning. The underlying rationale is that, given the proper machines and books, a child can progress at his own pace through a series of graduated materials. In a typical programmed situation, the child works with materials that are question and answer–oriented. The book or machine poses a question and the child selects what he believes is the "correct" answer. Then the child checks the answer to see if he got the "right" one. If the answer is "right," the child goes ahead to the next problem. If the answer is "wrong," the child is directed to another branch that helps him correct his mistake, and this branch eventually leads him back to the main section of the program. The emphasis in such materials is on "right" and "wrong" answers. There can be no room for interpretive or creative answers. The underlying assumption is that there always is a "right" answer. So in addition to teaching a certain body of material, the program also teaches an attitude toward learning. The answers, of course, are determined, not by the child or the teacher or the group, but by whoever "programmed" the materials. In an age when education is becoming more interpretive than prescriptive, when learning how to learn is the direction being taken in education, the attitude that one answer is right while another is wrong could be detrimental to the intellectual attitude they will need in later life when the ability to choose from a whole field of possible answers will be vital. There is the possibility that programmed learning could inhibit an attitude of intellectual inquiry.

One of the purposes of primary education is to help a child become socialized, to help him learn to function well in groups, to get along with other people. In a behavioral system, all the emphasis is placed on directing the child's attention to a book or machine. The child spends a great deal of time working with materials, rather than with people. What the effects of socializing children to machines and books are we don't know yet, since this type of educational system is new. But the importance of socialization with people taking place at an early age is obvious. It is in early childhood that people learn their attitudes and begin to form behavior patterns that stay with them all their lives.

In addition to an attitude of intellectual inquiry and socialization, we want our children to learn about their culture. . . .

In a programmed learning situation . . . the program developers alone determine what the children learn. We would hope that the people who develop materials for young children are intelligent men of good will who care that our children learn the many truths that make up the world and not what they consider to be "The Truth." But can we assume this? What kind of men are involved in behavioral learning? Who are the people who developed the program? Where have their interests been in the past? What were the outcomes of other projects that are, in some ways, similar to BRL's program at Banneker? Is their primary goal the education of our children? In order to examine these questions, the following interviews, statements, information and insights are presented.

First, I would like to examine interviews with two men who are intimately connected with the program at Banneker School. The first interview is with Otha Porter, who is an administrative assistant for School City of Gary and whose job it is to maintain close contact between the Banneker program and School City. Then I would like to examine portions of an interview with Donald Kendrick, who is the Resident Manager of Banneker School and who works for BRL.

One of the points that School City has made about BRL is that they "guarantee" the learning of the children for the same price that the schools are now spending. My inquiries on this came near the beginning of the interview:

Q. It's costing you the same thing to run the school for a year?
A. It's costing us the same to run the school, approximately $800 per student.
Q. Are they spending $800 per child?
A. Well, I imagine they will come pretty close to it, but that's their business.

According to information obtained from Vern Charlson, Director of Special Services at School City, the cost per pupil of education in Gary which is given to parents of out-of-district pupils is, for grades 1–6, $669.13 per year. According to an article in *The American Teacher,* BRL thus earns a profit of $150,000. In any case, there are no public figures available as to what BRL spends per child.

276 Institutional Reform Strategies

Q. How are they going to determine whether or not a child is up to grade level?

A. We have an independent evaluator, company name is Center for Urban Redevelopment (CURE). Bernard Donovan, the former Superintendent of New York Schools, is president of that company. . . .*

Q. Who are the teacher's aides and what kind of training do they have, and how are they used in the classroom? How do they function?

A. We don't refer to them as teacher aides in that program. They are Learning Supervisors. You see, our teachers are Curriculum Managers and Assistant Curriculum Managers.

Q. What's the purpose of changing the traditional names of the teachers?

A. Because we've changed the function of the people. They more or less monitor learning, rather than involve themselves deeply in it, you see, just because you are working with, for the most part, programmed materials.

Q. When the behavioral learning approach is perfected, will the teacher become obsolete?

A. I don't think the teacher will become obsolete. Maybe teachers as we know them today, their function and all will be a thing of the past. And, I'll tell you, there are several things that are going to make a change. Number one, if we forget about education, let's just talk about money. As long as the expenditure of education remains somewhat constant, recognizing that it will rise each year . . . we won't be able to afford a professional person for a group of thirty youngsters. I mean, forget about education as such. I mean, that's pure economics. That is as I see it. When you stop to think with me, suppose tomorrow we were able to pay all teachers between eighteen and twenty thousand dollars, well, we would have to reduce our professional staff significantly.

Q. I see, and then there would be increased use of aides?

* In performance contracting, typically one private corporation delivers the learning "system" and another evaluates the delivery and the results. Often the delivery corporation and the evaluating corporation operate together over several contracts. This arrangement may well raise questions regarding the evaluator's disinterest in the results of the evaluation. Bernard Donovan is one of a number of top-level school administrators who have moved from the precarious world of school politics in the tumultuous 1970's to the world of private or corporate consulting, systems delivery, or school publishing.—Ed.

A. But, what we might say, we might say, "O.K., we'll have this professional person making eighteen, twenty, or twenty-five thousand dollars, and assign this person one-hundred kids." And then, this person is going to direct the activities of a semi-professional person. And then those activities, then there might be another level of people working with these kids that we call para-professionals, because we just won't be able to afford it. We might end up with the superteacher concept. This person might spend more time diagnosing learning problems and prescribing treatment, in an educational sense, and operating more or less as a true professional rather than as a technician. And with programmed materials I can see greater use made of hardware and software and some of the modern things that we don't know. And it will be for pure, purely economic reasons.

There are a few attitudes implicit in Mr. Porter's views that I would like to mention. The first is that a teacher becomes a "true professional" rather than a "technician" by being removed from the classroom and becoming a diagnostician. This is an attitude widespread in educational circles; the farther one becomes from the classroom, the more "professional" one becomes. . . .

Another assumption here is that diverting spending into "para-professional" aides and into hardware and software (machines and books) is an educationally sound way of spending money. It seems to me that by the time the "superteacher" is paid and all the aides are paid and all the money is spent on machines and books, the same expenditures, if not more, will be made. The only difference is that the money spent on teachers' salaries will be diverted to the companies who produce the materials. . . . I realize the schools' desperate need to save money, but will this, in fact, happen? And if, after all these new machines are paid for, all the new programmed books are purchased, and all the aides are paid, and the "superteacher" receives his or her $25,000 per year, and money is saved by some sort of unbelievable manipulation, what about the child at the bottom of this educational superbureaucracy?

Q. But aren't you shaping the purposes of education by, if you teach a child in a behavioral manner from first grade through college or twelfth grade, aren't you shaping what education is?

A. It depends on what the priorities of education are, if they

teach or you can measure behaviorally, you know, I guess
you can identify that on paper now. Sometimes people
guess wisely and they'll know the answer that people are
seeking. But that's education, that's the mark of an educated person, too.

Q. You mean knowing how to take tests?

A. Yes. No, knowing how to give the answer that they think
the person in charge is seeking.

Q. Where does creativity come in?

Mr. Porter's implication is that the "mark of an educated
person" is knowing how to give the person asking the questions
the "right answer." If the educational bureaucracy decides that
the most important thing for our children to know is how to
give "right answers" then the schools will, if they succeed, turn
out children who value responding "correctly" to a stimulus
rather than children who value intellectual inquiry.

The necessity to teach to a test puts a great deal of pressure
on the teacher to deal only with factual materials and encourages
him to leave out conceptual learning. In the average classroom,
the teacher is free to balance out the situation with varied
lessons. . . . But where teachers are constantly aware that at the
end of each lesson there lies a quiz or test, they are put under
enormous pressure to conform to the demands of the test.

BRL may be the first company to take over an entire school,
but it is not the first company to involve itself in a public school
system. One interesting predecessor of the BRL project [was] the
involvement of Dorsett Educational Systems in the Texarkana
Schools. The company was contracted to run a reading and math
program in the school. The program was funded by a $270,000
federal grant and concentrated on students in grades 7–12. Minnie
Berson in her column, which appeared in the *Journal of Association for Childhood Education* (March, 1971), states: "In May,
1970, when pupils were being tested for achievement, some
admitted familiarity with the standardized test items. An independent auditor concluded that pupils had been taught 'to the test.'"
Lloyd G. Dorsett, the contractor, agreed that the experiment had
been "slightly contaminated," blaming "the misguided efforts
of a harried and pressured head programmer." (Nina McCain,
"Education's Cure-All a Profitable Gimmick?" *Boston Globe,*
September 30, 1970.) In another report on the same project in
the November, 1970, issue of *American Teacher,* Miles Myers

states, "Texarkana's program began October 15, 1969, and early evaluations reported phenomenal results. But a recent audit established that Dorsett's teaching machines were programmed to teach some of the questions that appeared on the evaluation test. Lloyd Dorsett, head of the company, reported that the irregularities were caused by an 'overanxious programmer' no longer with the project, and that only 6.5% of the test results were involved." (The programmer turned out to be Dorsett's sister, who plaintively explained: "I did everything I could to see that the company made money on the project.") Myers goes on to say, "Dr. Dean C. Andrews, whose Regional Educational Service Center, Magnolia, Arkansas, has been hired to evaluate the Texarkana project, claims that between 30 and 60 percent of the test results may be invalid. Whatever the results, it is quite clear from this experience that the profit motive does not guarantee a deep commitment to improving a child's education."

. . . Another interview—this time with Donald Kendrick, the man who is in charge of the Banneker project for BRL—may give us some insights into the question. This interview appeared in the *Journal of the Association for Childhood Education* in March, 1971, and was conducted by Minnie Perrin Berson. The goals and values of the company were reflected in the people who were chosen to represent it.

Q. We would like to know something of the in-service training you did with the staff to prepare them for this program.

A. Retraining a staff is difficult in concepts and methodology. We say, "Throw away everything you've done, because it's not going to be useful any longer. You are no longer the dictator in the classroom. The child learns *by himself*, so you get out of that problem. The *system* teaches."

Q. How is the center administered?

A. My staff (BRL employees) and I administer the school. We're going to establish, in this center, a program improving learning. All the students will read and do math well.

Q. How?

A. By using BRL-Sullivan and AAAS Allyn and Bacon materials. Materials make things happen.

Q. That's it?

A. The teachers come in a couple of weeks before school starts and we train them.

Q. Who trains the staff?

A. The representatives of the book companies whose books we use.

Q. What about human relations?

A. Competence is the most important thing.

Q. Mr. K., what is your background?

A. Oh, I was afraid you'd ask me. Lockheed Missiles. I'm a systems analyst. I view things analytically. Keep out emotions. The idea is, "Let's fix this and the children will come out different." When people have needs, the relationship disrupts. If you want more money, it interferes.

Q. But we hear that the teachers have threatened to strike and the aides, who are community parents, are ready to walk out at Banneker.

A. You're always going to have tensions. Industry says, "We want a job done." This is the difference. You don't have to love the guy next to you on the assembly line to make the product. He puts in the nuts, you put in the bolts, and the product comes out. Teachers can hate me and still get children to learn.

It seems that we adult humans are to become automatons on an assembly line conveyor belt down which roll our children. We need only to take orders, put in the nuts and bolts, ignore each other, and our children will come rolling off the conveyor belt like so many pieces of assembled machinery and into the waiting bins of society to be checked for imperfections, sorted and put to use until they wear out and are discarded. Of course, once the "system" is perfected, worn out machines will be replaced more rapidly and the "system" we call society will never be without the parts to keep its huge industrial machine in order. As Mr. Myers said in relation to the Texarkana project, "It is quite clear from this experience that the profit motive does not guarantee a deep commitment to improving a child's education."

Michael Harrington makes an interesting point in his book concerning dangers of the "social-industrial complex." He states, "America might unwittingly hire business to build a new urban civilization on the basis of the very money-making priorities which brought the old civilization to crisis." He also quotes Charles Silberman, author of *Crisis in the Classroom*, saying industry and government are "likely to transform both the organization and content of education, and through it, of American society itself." In other words, industry could use its influence in our schools to serve its own ends. Ultimately, the specifications of the contracts that they make with the public schools could be developed by the company, rather than by the school system. Then the industries would be in a position to dictate content to the schools as well as organization. And ultimately we might find ourselves in a position in which the school system would be designed to fit the needs of industry, the buildings themselves adapted to the machinery that industry would produce and the entire focus of education switched to suit the needs of industry rather than the needs of the children. Just as there was enormous pressure to build the SST [supersonic transport plane] because of the government money that was being poured into private interests, there will be enormous pressure to put government money into the schools to increase corporate profit. General Motors can't seem to make a safe car. Can it educate our children? General Mills's cereals are full of "empty calories." What will it do for our children's minds? General Electric has contributed to the pollution of our lakes. Can it suddenly care enough about the "public" to ignore its own need for profits in relation to our schools? If industry can serve "in the public interest," it certainly hasn't exhibited a need to do so in the past.

"Sesame Street": An Educational Dead End

by Frank Garfunkel

"Sesame Street" reaches an estimated 6 million children six days a week on 190 stations. It is clearly being promoted as—and is understood by the public to be—a break-through in educational television programming for young children. In this light, underlined by its producers' plan to evaluate its educational impact by achievement tests, the program should be carefully studied so its educational values can be understood. For surely the form and content of such a widely acclaimed educational television program can easily become a yardstick used by parents in assessing both preschool and school programs.

The typical hour-long program consists of between 25 and 30 separate segments, of which 10 to 15 sequences—10 to 20 min-

From *The Red Pencil*, Vol. I, No. 3 (June, 1970). Reprinted with the permission of *The Red Pencil*.

utes of program time—use animation to present numbers and letters. These number-letter segments often are repetitious, while other segments are generally unrelated. The continuity of number-letter material—not to mention the daily "sponsorship" of the program by numbers and letters—makes it quite clear that they are priority content.

These number-letter sequences, presented in the short trigger-happy bursts so typical of TV commercials, are tailored to promote memorization and, at the same time, minimize understanding. Memorization becomes *the* device for learning *the* important material.

The content of nonnumber-letter sequences is heavily weighted toward definitions and labels. Children and the program's "Muppet" puppets are constantly told the right answers—the correct way to do things, the parts of the body, who and what make particular sounds, names of animals. Rarely is a child on the program heard to ask "why" or "how." Any questioning is usually done by either adults or Muppets, during or immediately after a staged display of stupidity reminiscent of Laurel and Hardy.

It does, however, reflect an educational philosophy that distinguishes work from play and presumes that knowledge can be imparted piece by piece—and that children first learn pieces of knowledge and then use those pieces in problem solving. The assumption is that the former is independent of the latter.

In observing Head Start, kindergarten, and first-grade children watching and discussing the program, I have found that despite some day-to-day variations, numbers, letters, Muppets, and stupidity stand out in their impressions.

As you may have suspected, I think the image of "Sesame Street" as a unique, vanguard educational experience is a mirage. When I add up all of its numbers and letters, explanations and examples, documentaries and animations, I do not discover a "major departure from the past." For the most part, the episodes are a disjointed collection of tidbits. Some of the program is rather clever and much of it holds the attention of preschool children. But adults are in control and children do what they are told.

The claim that "Sesame Street" is a major educational or media innovation is preposterous. The values implicit in the form and content—strictly "The Three Rs" with a mixed bag of dressing—are traditional.

This is not to imply that children are not actively responding—many certainly are. But why are they responding and what kind of response is it? These are crucial questions. I have been struck by the similarity between these responses and those to TV commercials—an almost compulsive attachment to attending and repeating without regard to meaning or relationship.

Television commercials, of course, are designed to mesmerize, to make viewers memorize slogans *without* questioning facts or assumptions.

To bombard such different children with what has to be least-common-denominator stimuli, and to do so in a manner which stifles real probing or spontaneity, is to continue what mass communications, textbooks, standardization, and rubber stamps have begun. The more massive the audience, the more unobjectionable its content must be to greater numbers of people. The more extensive the claims regarding the program's educational value, the more its material has to be straight instruction without subtlety.

This leads to a simple but fundamental proposition. Certain tasks cannot be delegated to television or other mass media because they cannot be accomplished in an impersonal mass context. Direct, creative instruction of preschool children is one of those tasks. Yes, "Sesame Street" could be improved—but that is not the point. Simply put, a single massive source of direct instruction is necessarily antagonistic to the development of thinking in young children. Thinking involves seeing, choosing and influencing—interaction. Just as there is no choice to be had from a textbook, there is even less for a four-year-old confronted by a television package designed for 6 million children.

Compensatory Education

President Nixon Speaks

The educational aspects of the Equal Educational Opportunities Act are an integral part of this Administration's perspective on

From *The Effectiveness of Compensatory Education: Summary and Review of the Evidence* (Washington, D.C.: U.S. Department of Health, Education, and Welfare, 1972).

social policy. In his first message on Poverty in 1969, the President told the Nation about the negative preliminary results of the Head Start program and he added:

> This must not discourage us. To the contrary it only demonstrates the immense contribution the Head Start Program has made simply by having raised to prominence on the national agenda the fact—known for some time, but never widely recognized—that the children of the poor mostly arrive at school age seriously deficient in the ability to profit from formal education, and already significantly behind their contemporaries. It also has been made abundantly clear that our schools as they now exist are unable to overcome this deficiency.

In August, 1969, the President submitted the Family Assistance Program to the Congress. A major underlying assumption of the President's welfare reform initiative was that schools could only contribute a part of the resources needed to help poor children and that improved achievement for these children was more related to family income. This perspective was very much shaped by the findings of the Coleman Report.

A consistent theme of educational policy has been the search for reforms which would help poor children. In 1970, the President stated that:

> The most glaring shortcoming in American education today continues to be the lag in essential learning skills in large numbers of children of poor families.
>
> In the last decade, the Government launched a series of ambitious, idealistic, and costly programs for the disadvantaged, based on the assumption that extra resources would equalize learning opportunity and eventually help eliminate poverty.
>
> In some instances, such programs have dramatically improved children's educational achievement. In many cases, the programs have provided important auxiliary services such as medical care and improved nutrition. They may also have helped prevent some children from falling even further behind.
>
> *However, the best available evidence indicates that most of the compensatory education programs have not measur-*

ably helped poor children catch up. [Emphasis in the original.]

At that time the President concluded that "more of the same," whether in programs called compensatory education or in regular school practices, simply would not provide the effective help needed by poor children. A major part of the reform which the President proposed was establishment of a National Institute of Education, which is to provide a federal basis for stimulation of educational innovation and the discovery of programs and practices that can be effective.

Similar themes were repeated in the President's recent message on the Equal Opportunities Act—routine compensatory and school programs are not enough; there is a need for innovative concentrated compensatory efforts focused on basic learning skills in order to help poor children.

Once again the Congress has before it a proposal intended to help millions of poor children—we know that the problems are too great to wait for our completely certain knowledge. Responsibility requires that we make our best efforts on the basis of the knowledge before us.

Federal Money: Whom Is It Helping?

This study examines what has happened to Title I in the four school years since the Elementary and Secondary Education Act (ESEA) was passed. This is not an evaluation of compensatory programs, but a report on how Title I money has been spent and how Title I has been administered at the local, state, and federal levels.

Since passage of ESEA, Congress has appropriated $4.3 billion for the benefit of educationally deprived poor children—black, brown, white, and Indian children. Because most of these children attend inadequately financed and staffed schools, the windfall of federal appropriations no doubt brings many improvements to these schools that these children never had. To hear the educational profession and school administrators talk (or write), Title I is the best thing that ever happened to American school systems. Educational opportunities, services, and facilities for poor

From *Title I of ESEA: Is It Helping Poor Children?* Reprinted with permission of NAACP Legal Defense and Educational Fund, Inc., 10 Columbus Circle, New York, New York 10019.

children are provided. Some poor children are now well fed and taught by more teachers in new buildings with all the latest equipment, materials, and supplies. Early evaluations of academic gain have not been so optimistic. Some school systems report that, despite the massive infusion of federal dollars, poor children are not making academic gains beyond what is normally expected. Some report moderate academic gain in programs, and some report real academic improvement.

Despite these reports, the almost universal assumption about Title I is that it is providing great benefits to educationally disadvantaged children from low-income families.

We find this optimistic assumption largely unwarranted. Instead we find that:

1. The intended beneficiaries of Title I—poor children—are being denied the benefits of the Act because of improper and illegal use of Title I funds.
2. Many Title I programs are poorly planned and executed so that the needs of educationally deprived children are not met. In some instances there are no Title I programs to meet the needs of these children.
3. State departments of education, which have major responsibility for operating the program and approving Title I project applications, have not lived up to their legal responsibility to administer the program in conformity with the law and the intent of Congress.
4. The United States Office of Education, which has overall responsibility for administering the Act, is reluctant and timid in its administration of Title I and abdicates to the states its responsibility for enforcing the law.
5. Poor people and representatives of community organizations are excluded from the planning and design of Title I programs. In many poor communities, the parents of Title I–eligible children know nothing about Title I. In some communities, school officials refuse to provide information about the Title I program to local residents.

An HEW audit of Milwaukee, Wisconsin, disclosed that in fiscal year 1967, $21,605 was spent on salaries for school personnel not involved in Title I projects, such as the swimming coach and teachers assigned to general teaching duties.

Attala County, Mississippi, constructed two lagoons for sewage disposal, costing $16,000, with Title I money and installed an intercom system costing $1,750.

An HEW audit of Louisiana school districts covering Title I expenditures in fiscal year 1966, the first year of the program, found that 23 parishes (counties) "loaned" equipment costing $645,624 to schools that were ineligible to participate in Title I programs. The auditors noted that much of the "loaned" equipment was "set in concrete or fastened to the plumbing." Much of the equipment had been at ineligible schools since its acquisition.

No educational effort can truly succeed apart from the community in which the students live. The Office of Education recognizes this and requires that each local district provide for the maximum practical involvement of parents in the design, planning, operation, and evaluation of Title I programs. Some appropriate vehicle for community involvement, such as a Title I advisory committee, must be established by school systems, with at least half of the committee composed of parents and representatives of community agencies serving the poor community. The Title I program itself should include activities and services in which parents may be involved.

. . . An observer of the New York City school system writes:

> Evidence . . . suggests that the Board of Education at least partly disregarded the spirit and intent of the Federal law. It used traditional organizational strategies—delaying the formulation of a program until it was too late for any citizen review; informing the board members on the program at the last possible moment; maintaining a façade of consultation through citizens' groups in the form of "democratic ceremonials" while refusing to invite them in on any joint planning basis. And it did this despite a Federal law and an increasingly enraged citizenry who were opposed to that style.

. . . [P]rivate citizens, including interviewers for this study, were denied access to project applications. Some school officials even refused to provide specific information on the number of children participating and how federal money had been spent.

A Waukegan, Illinois, school administrator told our interviewer that the administration knew "everything" and thus he saw no need for community involvement.

In Tucson, Arizona, a principal was asked about community involvement and responded, "We don't need that kind of involvement."

A principal in Oxford, Mississippi, told our interviewer that parents "play no part" in the Title I program, but that since he himself was a parent any decision he made would be sufficient for other parents.

An Even Chance

Indians have a unique claim on the U.S. government for the support of their children's education. That claim is based on treaties signed by Indian nations and the U.S. government and on laws passed by Congress which provide funds specifically for the education of Indian children.

Almost every treaty signed with an Indian tribe commits the federal government to provide education for Indian children. Congress made its first appropriation for Indian education 170 years ago. Since that time, it has provided funds for the education of Indian children in mission schools, federal boarding schools, and public schools.

Today, two-thirds of all American Indian children attend public schools. While they have a special claim to federal support, Indian children are entitled to the same educational opportunities as other children. They have a constitutional right to equal protection under state and federal laws, and as state citizens to state aid for public schools. Those rights and the reality of public education that they are in fact provided are two quite different things.

Estimated Indian School Age Population (1968)	240,700
Estimated Indian Public School Enrollment (1968)	177,463
Estimated Number of Indian Children as	
Johnson-O'Malley Enrollment (fiscal year 1968)	62,676
Indian Enrollment in Schools Operated	
by Bureau of Indian Affairs (fiscal year 1968)	51,558

They are also entitled to benefits from three federal financial programs—Impact Aid, Johnson-O'Malley, and Title I of the Elementary and Secondary Education Act. These commit over $66 million annually for the support of Indian children in public schools.

Impact Aid provides the largest source of money for Indian children ($27.9 million in fiscal year 1969). The number of

From *An Even Chance: A Report on Federal Funds for Indian Children in Public School Districts.* Reprinted with permission of NAACP Legal Defense and Educational Fund, Inc., 10 Columbus Circle, New York, New York 10019.

children whose parents live and/or work on Indian reservations determines how much Impact Aid money a district will receive. Indian children frequently "earn" more for their district than non-Indian children who are ineligible for federal assistance.

Title I of the Elementary and Secondary Education Act of 1965 provides money to school districts with high concentrations of low-income children. It is intended to assure "something extra" for children designated as educationally deprived. Because of severe poverty in Indian communities, and because Title I [funds] must be spent on those with the greatest educational needs, Indians are especially qualified for Title I assistance. Since the amount of Title I funds allocated per child in the Title I formula is $148, and if we assume that, conservatively, there are 150,000 Indian children in public schools who meet the Title I eligibility criteria, then Indian students are entitled to receive approximately $22 million from Title I.

The Johnson-O'Malley Act, passed by Congress in 1934, provides $16.4 million (in fiscal year 1969) for Indian education. Money under that act is to be spent only for Indians.

Indian children bring millions of federal dollars each year into public school districts. Indian students are counted three times, under three different statutes, in order to make a school district eligible for federal funds. These funds are supposed to support both the basic educational program in Indian schools and special programs designed to meet the unique needs of Indian children.

This is the legal framework. But what really happens to the money? How are Indian children faring in the public schools? How well has the American government honored its historic commitment to Indian children?

By every standard, Indians receive the worst education of any children in the country. . . . One reason for this failure lies in the misuse of federal dollars intended to benefit Indian children. That is the heart of our story. Those dollars have been used for every conceivable school system need *except* the need that Congress had in mind.

Some examples of this misuse:

- The Tucson Elementary School District in Arizona, which enrolls 460 Indian students, illegally spent $1.3 million of Title I funds as general aid to the entire district in the belief that it was wrong to spend it just on poor children. . . .
- In Pierre Independent School District in South Dakota, one

school listed in the Title I project application as eligible to receive funds, had not a single poor child in it, although that district has 152 Indian students.

- In Wakpala, South Dakota, school taxes were lowered, and per-pupil expenditures dropped $30 from one school year to the next. To counteract this drop, school officials included every student in the district in the Title I program, or approximately $66 per child.
- The Bennett County High School District in Martin, South Dakota, which has 40 educationally deprived Indian children, spent some of its Title I funds on golf sets, tennis rackets and balls, and archery bows and arrows.
- The Johnson-O'Malley Act provides $2 million annually for free school lunches for needy Indian children, yet Navajo parents have been known to sell their sheep and pawn their jewelry in order to pay the lunch bill sent home by school authorities.
- In many public schools eligible children are required to declare each day, "I am poor" in order to get their lunch. They are made to stand in separate lines; they are given different tickets; and in many unsubtle ways are branded as second-class citizens. Their crime? Asserting their federal educational entitlement.
- School officials do not spend available federal money on Indian language and history classes—the programs Indians most want— in the almost unanimous belief that the purpose of education is to wipe out Indian culture and language and replace it with the "superior" culture of white middle-class America. . . .

What we have found out about Indian education in the course of this study is not new, especially to Indians. The history of education for American Indians is a history of reports, studies, task forces and more studies. They all make the same sharp criticism and similar recommendations. . . .

Indians have good reason to be cynical about another report. As one Indian woman whom we interviewed said: "What will change from this interview? Or will it be put on a shelf?" We hope that this report provides the tools for change, and that it can and will be used by Indian parents and tribes to bring about that change. . . .

The misuse of federal funds designed to help Indian children is a real issue in Indian communities. Land has been stolen from Indians. Indian parents now see federal funds being stolen from their children.

The Contradictions of Busing

by Miriam Wasserman and BARTOC

Busing-antibusing, segregation-desegregation are cover issues. Beneath all the rhetoric are the real issues of school racism, oppression, and a crisis that is beginning to affect all members, even the most privileged, of our school population and . . . that arises out of the social functions schools in America perform. . . .

In a school system that serves important racist functions, segregation is merely the tip of the iceberg of racism. Desegregating the schools (whether by busing or in some other way) is a possible tactic for dealing with that minor part of school racism that is expressed as segregation. But it is not the only, or even the most important, tactic for dealing with racist and oppressive schools, and it is not a principle. . . .

The Contradictions of Busing

We at BARTOC are taking a strong stand *against antibusing*, although not necessarily and not unequivocally for busing. The apparent contradiction of our position grows out of the following contradictions of busing itself:

1. One of the fundamental educational theories underlying integration (desegregation) is itself a racist theory.
2. Desegregation by court or bureaucratic order probably does not significantly improve the academic achievement of minority children.
3. Many Third World students, parents, and communities are opposed to desegregation and/or busing.
4. The strongest opponents of desegregation-busing are likely to be white working-class parents and communities whose own children are among those most victimized by the racism-classism of our society and our schools.

1. The racist rationale of an anti-racist policy . . .

Clearly the decision in *Brown* v. *The Board of Education* was an anti-racist decision that was necessary and appropriate in 1954.

But the theory behind the decision—that black children need to sit next to white children in order to learn as well (or almost as well) as white children—was a racist one, which eventually blossomed out into the theory of cultural deprivation. . . .

However, while recognizing that the current ideology of desegregation is racist, we still feel that there may be valid reasons for supporting desegregation in particular situations. We haven't even begun to create a theory and a practice of multiracial education. And we have barely begun to consider whether or not desegregation might not be an appropriate educational tactic for overcoming some of the disadvantages, for example, of the mystified, racist, mainstream children who will constitute the majority of the next generation of adults.

2. Desegregation and the academic performance of minority children

The theory of cultural deprivation is not only based on racist assumptions, but there are strong indications that in practice, its inferences seem not to work out. Although much of the research on the effect of court-ordered or bureaucratically administered desegregation on minority children's academic performance has not been carefully done and has yielded inconclusive results,[1] so far it appears that in no case has moving minority children from segregated to desegregated schools and/or classrooms improved their performance enough—according to the standards by which performance is currently recognized and measured—to enable them to equal or surpass their white or middle-class schoolmates.

Even if desegregation or busing for racial balance should become national policy and even if that should help minority children to improve their school performance, they will still remain at the bottom of the school heap and end up with the worst jobs—or no jobs at all. . . .

3. Minority group opposition to desegregation and busing

Desegregation can help to overcome powerlessness, but it can also serve as a tool to further exploit that powerlessness by undermining the sense of identity and solidarity students may have developed in their old schools, as the following cases demonstrate.

[1] Pat Lines, "Race and Learning: A Perspective on the Research," *Inequality in Education,* Harvard Center for Law and Education, No. 11.

Throughout the Deep South the black teachers and black principals who have formed the backbone of the black middle class are being fired as black students are integrated into white schools with mainly white staffs. And large numbers of black students in integrated schools are being unceremoniously suspended and expelled on the flimsiest of pretexts.

In North Carolina, Lumbee Indians are seeing native teachers fired as Lumbee, lumped together with blacks as "nonwhites," are desegregated into white schools. The Lumbees have long been opposing an HEW desegregation plan and are sitting in at their traditional schools, keeping their children away from the newly assigned schools and filing a federal suit asking that the plan be blocked.

In San Francisco, half the schoolchildren due to be bused out of Chinatown in September, 1971, were instead sent to freedom schools created and maintained with the help of their parents. San Francisco's then Superintendent of Schools Thomas Shaheen, regarded by these parents as the symbol of pro-black busing and integration, was chased out of a meeting in Chinatown and down the street to his car. "Chinese parents have always been quiet and docile," said a young male teacher at one of the freedom schools. "This is the first time there's been real grass-roots political action." Interestingly, the media in San Francisco gave plenty of attention to the boycott by 3,000 Asian schoolchildren, while virtually ignoring the fact that about an equal number of white schoolchildren were also boycotting the desegregated public schools and attending parochial schools or little neighborhood basement and living-room schools. . . .

In Detroit, Michigan, city and business leaders are seeking a partial desegregation plan not, it appears, to achieve racial balance, but to break up all-black schools in which local forces are beginning to press for community control. . . .

In Gary, Indiana, the National Black Political Convention, meeting just before Nixon's announcement of his antibusing policy, proposed and even adopted apparently contradictory positions on busing: they denounced segregated schools but opposed busing for racial balance. One resolution read in part: "We condemn racial integration of schools as a bankrupt, suicidal method of de-segregating schools based on the false notion that black children are unable to learn unless they are in the same setting as white children. As an alternative to busing of black children to achieve racial balance, we demand quality education in the black community by controlling our school districts and a guarantee of an equal share of the money."

Transporting the racism around the city by bus will not make it disappear; it will only turn up with new faces in new places. Black and other antiracists understand that desegregation which is done *to* them, *for* them, *at* them, is done in the same way as any other social policy in a racist system. Only when desegregation, or some other antiracist social policy, is achieved *by* and *through* them (which does not preclude the support of others) does it begin to overcome their powerlessness as the victims of racism.

4. White opposition to desegregation and busing . . .

Poor and working-class white parents know that their children are disadvantaged in school compared with the children of doctors, business executives, college professors. They also know that they are advantaged compared with the children of blacks, Mexican-Americans, Puerto Ricans. Therefore, they perceive desegregation or busing for racial balance as something that will wipe out that small advantage—which they feel is all they have to pass on to their children. They also perceive court-ordered desegregation or bureaucratically administered desegregation as a manipulation of their lives and fates by remote figures who do not know their struggles and are not concerned with their needs. They see the little space they have to move around in getting littler and littler.

Some of the whites who oppose busing prefer their children to go to a neighborhood school; are afraid of the violence, drugs, and lack of discipline, which they associate with the children of the poor or the children of blacks; and are racial bigots who are being offered political and ideological leadership by other racial bigots (some at very high levels in the nation, indeed). But the significant factor in the opposition to busing by poor and working-class whites—whether in Pontiac or in New Orleans—is not that *they* are racist but that the *situation* is racist. What matters most is not the parent who fights to retain her or his child's small advantage in the world and who may feel hate or contempt or fear for the black child who is competing with hers or his, but rather the school system and the social system of America, which have thrown the working-class white child into cutthroat competition with the black or Chicano or Asian child for a place in tomorrow's job market.

The Politics and the Contradictions of Antibusing

Nixon's antibusing policy* inflates and capitalizes on the contradictions and weaknesses of desegregation as a response to racist schools, and it shamelessly exploits the racist expression of deep discontents and immediate hardships. . . . his legislative program constitutes a retreat from the policy of desegregation that the Executive Branch has at least claimed to support since *Brown* v. *The Board of Education*. In addition to attacking the Fourteenth Amendment, on which *Brown* and subsequent desegregation decisions have been based, he also attacks the principle of separation of powers, a cornerstone of the democratic myth of America. Former Supreme Court Justice Arthur J. Goldberg, testifying before the House Judiciary Committee on May 4, 1972, said, "To acquiesce in the removal of jurisdiction over busing would be to alter the substance of established constitutional law, to surrender the citadel of equal justice and to breach the separation of judicial and legislative powers."[2]

In fact, a revitalized and revamped racist school policy may temporarily relieve Richard Nixon's problems, but it will not relieve working-class and poor whites' problems. It will not relieve their more fundamental and enduring economic and social hardships. Moreover, it will not even reduce their children's school disadvantages.

The . . . fiscal crisis in the United States is profoundly affecting all public services, including public schools. The Nixon Administration's response to the crisis of public education is not to support schools more generously, but to open them up to big-business experimentation. Throughout the country, big business and school administrators influenced by big business are submitting "culturally disadvantaged" children—including the children of poor and working-class whites—to computer-assisted and other rigid, mechanized, behavioristic teaching programs in classes that are steadily becoming larger and that are often under the supervision of very low-paid teachers (called "aides" or "paraprofessionals," some of whom have teaching credentials but cannot find jobs as "regular" teachers).

---

* This piece was written in the spring of 1972, and the reference is to Nixon's re-election-oriented antibusing legislative program. The analysis holds, however, for antibusing policy in general—ED.

[2] See also I. F. Stone, "Moving the Constitution to the Back of the Bus," *New York Review of Books,* April 20, 1972.

Thus, although antibusing may indeed help the children of poor and working-class whites maintain their present slim edge over the children of nonwhites, it must be seen as part of an educational trend which is even more damaging to their very humanity than present conventional education. And their disadvantages compared with the children of the more well-to-do are likely to be increased as wealthy suburban schools and university town schools seek the more humane "free school" and "open classroom" solutions to the school crisis.

Guidelines for Radicals and Antiracists

The contradictions of busing cannot be resolved in the context of a society and a school system that operate on racist-classist principles. But we are here today in this system, and we must deal with it.

The foregoing analysis suggests the following as possible courses for radicals with respect to the issues of busing, desegregation, and racism.

We should oppose racist antibusing policies in elections, courts, and schools. In local electoral or educational politics, this might mean that radicals should make alliances with liberals on the busing issue. It does not mean, however, that desegregation busing should be treated as an issue requiring a consistent, inflexible position. . . .

Where desegregation busing is not a local or state issue, we should probably not expend energies in trying to bring about desegregation but rather should concentrate on the substantive issues of school oppressiveness and divisiveness. Thus, it would be quite possible and even logical in some communities to take an open stand against Nixon's national antibusing policy and at the same time concentrate locally on community control, students' rights, teacher unionism, ethnic studies, minority hiring, etc.

Busing-antibusing is a phony issue only to the extent that we see busing versus antibusing as the real problem and the choice of one or the other as a real solution. The real problem is a school system that helps to perpetuate the relations of an oppressive and hierarchical society by acting out the relations of oppression and hierarchy.

The real problem is not who are in what school and how they got there, but how the people in any school relate to one another and what and how they learn from and teach one another.

"Freedom Works": The Theory of Radical School Reform

by Allen Graubard

The theory of radical school reform is not really a "theory," in a respectable philosophy-of-science sense. It would be more accurate to talk about a cluster of attitudes, assumptions, and interpreted experiences (not always consistent or clear) about the nature of children, the evaluation of the effects of dominant school techniques, and the relation of educational questions to larger social, political, and economic issues.

The theory of radical school reform and the new schools movement ("movement," like "theory," understood in a very loose sense) is expressed in a number of recent books. A relatively small number of these writings have been very widely read and discussed for the past several years. Works like John Holt's *How Children Fail* have been extremely important in inspiring people to action. The free school development sprang up almost from scratch so far as actual experience was concerned. Very few people who organized schools had actually seen or worked in a free school, so that what they had to go on was a concrete sense of what was wrong with public schools and an abstract hope of how marvelous "free learning" would be. In this situation the books of radical school reform became a prime source of inspiration and support. One often finds in talking to free school people about how they got started that they say things like: "We read John Holt and then called a meeting," or "A friend gave me copies of *Summerhill*, Herb Kohl and Joseph Featherstone's articles on the British infant schools, and then I talked to some other parents." . . .

The corpus of new schools literature can be divided into four basic genres. (Some works overlap genres and some are difficult to classify. I have not attempted to be comprehensive in this listing, but I have included the most widely known and I feel the selection is fairly representative.)

(1) Critical analyses of the structure and function of the public school system—Paul Goodman, *Compulsory Mis-education;* Jules

From Allen Graubard, *Free the Children: Radical Reform and the Free School* (New York: Pantheon Books, 1972).

Henry, *Culture Against Man;* John Holt, *How Children Fail* and
The Underachieving School; Edgar Friedenberg, *Coming of Age
in America;* Miriam Wasserman, *The School Fix: NYC, USA;* Paul
Lauter and Florence Howe, *The Conspiracy of the Young;* Ivan
Illich, *Deschooling Society;* The Schoolboys of Barbiana, *Letter
to a Teacher.*

(2) Personal accounts of experiences of teaching in public
schools and of sometimes attempting to try out free education
ideas—Jonathan Kozol, *Death at an Early Age;* Herbert Kohl, *36
Children;* James Herndon, *The Way It Spozed to Be* and *How to
Survive in Your Native Land;* Nat Hentoff, *Our Children Are
Dying.*

(3) Personal accounts of doing new schools—A. S. Neill,
Summerhill; George Dennison, *The Lives of Children;* Sylvia
Ashton-Warner, *Teacher;* Elwyn Richardson, *In the Early World;*
Peter Marin, "The Open Truth and Fiery Vehemence of Youth"
(much anthologized).

(4) What could very loosely be called theory into practice,
either in new schools or in public school classrooms—George
Leonard, *Education and Ecstasy;* Neil Postman and Charles Weingartner, *Teaching as a Subversive Activity;* Herbert Kohl, *The
Open Classroom;* John Holt, *How Children Learn* and *What Do
I Do Monday?;* Carl Rogers, *Freedom to Learn;* Robert Greenway
and Salli Rasberry, *Rasberry Exercises;* Joseph Featherstone,
articles on British Infant Schools contained in *Schools Where
Children Learn;* Jonathan Kozol, *Free Schools.*

Although these works (and others I haven't named) are often
listed together as a kind of united front against the authoritarian
system of public school education, there are substantial conflicts
among them, and these conflicts reflect the tensions of theory and
practice within the new schools movement....

The most widely known example of the free school is, of
course, Summerhill in Suffolk, England. Neill's book about the
school and its philosophy has been read by millions of people,
and the school, now fifty years old, has had countless visitors.
Although Neill has never claimed to speak for a movement, and
although many people involved in the new schools would disagree with much that he says (especially his explicit Freudianism),
Neill's conceptions of "freedom" and of "free children" express
definitely and clearly an important part of the core assumptions
of many new schools. Also, the emphasis on the *inherent* nature

of the child and the image of social change through the development of happy free children by means of a free school environment are an important strain in free school thought.

Neill states boldly what is derogatorily called the "romantic" view of children: "My view is that a child is innately wise and realistic. If left to himself without adult suggestion of any kind, he will develop as far as he is capable of developing."

. . . Neill's simple answer to the question of how happiness can be bestowed is "Abolish authority. Let the child be himself. Don't push him around. Don't teach him. Don't lecture him. Don't elevate him. Don't force him to do anything." . . .

Neill's conception of the function of education emphasizes the effect of freedom on the child's personality. The hope (and claim) is that free children will be self-motivated, integrated, able to seek out the learning they need in order to pursue interests that are truly their own, and, when they become adults, capable of choosing a way of life and work on the basis of considerations flowing from inside, rather than being ruled by externally imposed standards and goals. . . .

The most widely read of the recent radical reform writers is John Holt. His first book, *How Children Fail,* was truly startling, portraying in a vivid and concrete way the schools' effect of creating stupidity. Somehow, although almost everyone sees or experiences what Holt describes, no one had been able to see so clearly the process of how children fail and present it so convincingly, and the book deeply affected many people. In this and later books, especially *How Children Learn,* Holt also expresses some considerations of the good approach to education, a formulation of some principal themes of the "freedom" approach to learning. He writes, "When they learn in their own way and for their own reasons, children learn so much more rapidly and effectively than we could possibly teach them."

Holt's image abstracts from the social and cultural world in which the natural child becomes a real individual child. The description of the child expresses what *should* be—concerning the expression of interest and intelligence, curiosity and self-motivation; and it is implied that it *can* be—when bad interventions don't happen (which always happen, to some degree). For example, Holt says that children "learn out of interest and curiosity, not to please or appease the adults in power." But it would seem that what he means is that children *ought* to learn out of interest and curiosity, that, as in other areas of human activity, some motivations are morally superior and are related to morally preferable situations in other areas in life. It is clearly true that children often learn—quickly and deeply—in order to please adults in power. Love is complicated, and children are naturally motivated to gain the love (and approval) of relevant powerful adults. It would be very difficult to isolate pure "interest" from the complexity of other motives like desire for approval or a good self-image. (This, of course, applies to adults too.) Thus, if one child notices how pleased a parent is by his "self-motivated" interest activities, like learning to read or making a pot, or, later on, reading history or physics books, and he also notices that he can surpass his sibling by doing it, I think it would be natural to find the child working hard, learning fast, retaining well.

None of this is to say that what might be called "intrinsic interest" can't be part of what happens. But it is true that the natural child, like the natural person, appears purely only as a concept, while real children are always a mixture of the pure natural capacities and the effects of a particular world—a family, parents and siblings, a history of experience, responses from adults, the effects of a complex cultural environment which creates motives or at least warps the so-called natural motives. Even in Holt's terms, there is a crucial ambiguity in "giving children as much help and guidance as they need and ask for and then getting out of the way and trusting them to do the rest." In the ideal conception, nature will lead them to ask for what they need, but with real children what they ask for and what they need may not be identical, and often it will be necessary for adults to make judgments. . . .

The idea of a "nature," modified badly by unnatural external pressures, can be misleading in that it can misrepresent the meaning of culture. Cultural norms, social personality traits, and typical value clusters are not accidental shapings added on to an essential human nature, at least not in any interesting sense. The human being is always a cultural creature, and always part of a particular culture. . . .

In the introduction to *Teaching as a Subversive Activity*, Postman and Weingartner summarize in brief the list of complaints about public schools, in a revealing way:

The institution we call "school" is what it is because we made it that way. If it is irrelevant, as Marshall McLuhan says; if it shields children from reality, as Norbert Wiener says;

if it educates for obsolescence, as John Gardner says; if it does not develop intelligence, as Jerome Bruner says; if it is based on fear, as John Holt says; if it avoids the promotion of significant learning, as Carl Rogers said; if it punishes creativity and independence, as Edgar Freidenberg says; if, in short, it is not doing what needs to be done, it can be changed; it *must* be changed. It can be changed, we believe, because there are so many wise men who, in one way or another, have offered us clear, intelligent, and new ideas to use, and as long as these ideas and the alternatives they suggest are available, there is no reason to abandon hope.

This passage is revealing in several ways of the kind of reform spirit I am attempting to describe. First, there is that ubiquitous reformist "we." There is no mention of class structure or class interest, no sense of the dominant historical considerations in the development of public education which help explain the forms and purposes of the school system. The important social, political, and economic ways in which the system is successful are not discussed. The standard complaints are listed without qualification (for example, public school may shield children from some reality, but as in the working of the "hidden curriculum," there is an abundance of significant reality in the school); these complaints are given punch by citing as eclectic a bunch of authorities as one can find from McLuhan . . . to Gardner. . . .

No explanation is given of why the schools are as bad as the authors claim they are, other than that "we" made them that way. Also, almost all of the specified defects have to do with the effect of the dominant school methods on creativity, intelligence, and originality. The authors see the old education as creating "passive, acquiescent, dogmatic, intolerant, authoritarian, inflexible, conservative personalities who desperately need to resist change in an effort to keep their illusion of certainty intact." This seems to me a curiously superficial characterization in the face of the obsessive American search for a certain sort of change and newness—moving to new places, the "democratic-relativist" attitude which makes it very bad taste to appear dogmatically certain or not agree that one person's opinion is as good as anybody's.

The "super-reformism" of this perspective consists in the great scope of the claim concerning the fantastic effects that will result from a particular *educational method change*. Postman and Weingartner find this elixir of "new kinds of persons" in "new ideas" —which turn out to be a pretentious gimmick called the "inquiry method," theoretically (so to speak) grounded in a pastiche of bad philosophy and pretentiously phrased common sense taken from McLuhan and general semantics. (The inquiry method seems to be the idea that teachers should teach by asking good questions which they themselves don't know the answers to, and letting the curriculum develop from that.)

George Leonard's *Education and Ecstasy* does not focus on talking to teachers as *Teaching as a Subversive Activity* does, and is even more sweeping in its pretensions and its vision, but it offers the same conception of a fantastic transformation to be wrought by changes in education proper. Leonard, a former *Look* magazine editor and Esalen Institute vice-president, offers a similar critique of public schools, similarly ignoring any analysis of the social and historical roots and functions of the system. His vision is learning as the goal of life but learning that will be constant ecstasy, helpfully defined as "ananda, the ultimate delight." (If this doesn't help, try the idea that solving a mathematical problem and making love are experiences in the same order of things, sharing common ecstasy.)

His gimmick is a combination of groovy technology, brain-wave controls, teaching machines, and encounter groups. Postman and Weingartner claimed for their "inquiry method" that, "like the locomotive, light bulb, and radio, its impact will be unique and revolutionary." Leonard, approving Friedenberg and Goodman for their cries against dehumanization (although never confronting the social and poltical dimensions of their critique), faults them for not seeing the marvelous opportunities for unlimited transformation. He writes, "Distrusting science, they often fail to credit recent experimental work in human learning that shows real reform is practical, not visionary." (It should be noted that the terms "practical" and "visionary" have no connotation of limits imposed by political power, class interest, indeed, the state of our knowledge of psychology, but only of electronics technology and what Leonard extrapolates wildly from some highly questionable biological and psychological experiments which he reports uncritically, unknowledgeably, and breathlessly.)

. . . The superiority of libertarian schools rests, as [George] Dennison points out, on the morality of the issue and on our restrained sense of how much better the situation would be, rather than on the perfection of it. In fact, as with an issue like starvation in America, the real problems of educational reform are social, political, economic, and ideological. The constraints on having the reasonably good learning situations that are possible are deep-rooted in the needs of the particular social, economic, and political structures of our social order. Therefore, the fundamental issue for educational reform is the understanding of and struggle with the hindrances to putting into effect the not terribly complicated or cosmic or new radical reform ideas which have been around for a good while. . . .

Summerhill — Some Are Hell

by Jane and BARTOC

Most free schools are started with the best of intentions. So was the one at which I taught last year in P. It was a school for five- and six-year-olds; parents and teachers decide on policy jointly at the school's biweekly meetings. We met a number of times before school opened in order to discuss the philosophy of the school. Noble-sounding ideas were the order of the day: we were going to provide an atmosphere where our children could explore the world as their needs and desires dictated; we were going to remain subtly in the background while our children played and learned in patterns created by their own natural rhythms; we were going to contribute to the revolution in the schools by providing alternative modes of humane education. We decided to begin with no rules or structure; these were to emerge organically if and when they were needed.

The first week was delightful and we were all so proud of ourselves. The children seemed calm and friendly. They were excited about all the new equipment, their new teachers, their new friends. Little did we realize that our kids were calm on the outside and sizing up the situation on the inside. By the second week, all hell broke loose. By 10 A.M. each day the school looked

From *No More Teachers' Dirty Looks,* Vol. II, No. 1. Published by BARTOC. Reprinted by permission.

as if a herd of elephants had stamped on through. The paints were all over the floor; books were written in with magic markers; the brand-new microscope lay disassembled on the table; oil paint had been thrown in the fish bowl; Louisiana and Maryland were missing from our new United States puzzle. Our casualties included one black eye, one busted lip, and a hamster lost in the supply room. As one child sat down to lunch, he found his Dr. Seuss lunchbox filled with sand instead of a peanut-butter sandwich.

It's not that the teachers weren't aware of the need for order of some sort. When we told the kids to pick up their mess they'd screech, "Shut up. This is a free school and I don't hafta do anything I don't wanna. You told me so on the first day."

We couldn't even get enough quiet to describe the fabulous field trips we'd planned. When we did manage to get some kids interested in a project, it was sure to be disrupted by our cootie-catcher brigade, a group of six or seven boys who spent all day using our 89¢ art paper to construct various sizes and shapes of machines which caught cooties off of unpopular people—meaning, naturally, everyone not in the brigade.

Chaos, destruction, and physical injury weren't the only problems. We had hoped to change basic attitudes in our school simply by allowing children to interact in a free environment. Yet racism and sexism were as rampant in our school as in any public school. At our Halloween party we had four brides, six nurses, one bunny rabbit, and two stewardesses among our girls; the boys were adorned in monster, doctor, astronaut, and scientist costumes. The boys still did woodworking while our girls did mosaics or played in the Wendy corner. When a black kid visited our school he was called stinky by two of our kids, and when an Indian visited our school one kid said he wasn't really an Indian because he didn't scalp anyone while he was there.

We tried to deal with all of these problems at our parent-faculty meetings. But when someone suggested that we search out minority children to enroll, it was described as tokenism or as unfair to discriminate by color. When someone suggested the need for rules about the legitimacy of destroying a scientific instrument (our microscope), another person would scream, "Stop! That would be laying a trip on our children. If they're catching cooties all day or breaking equipment it's because we failed. The children are bored. We don't have enough for them to do here." And so we would all rush out and bring in bigger and better projects, all the while feeling guilty that we weren't John Holt or Herb Kohl.

Somehow we managed to muddle through the year without any serious physical injuries; the psychic ones were more serious. Since then I've gotten to know other free schools and done quite a lot of thinking about what went wrong with ours. I've noticed that most free schools have one thing in common: their founders band together as a reaction against the negative aspects of public schooling. Like those in my school, many free school people's violent reactions against the horrors of public education enable them to do away with such things as testing, rote learning, and regimentation. But what also happens is that along with the hatreds of public school oppressiveness, people have deep fears which hinder the development of new ideas. What I've seen happen is that free school people become so adamant about the rules and structures of the public school that they consider all structure to be detrimental to the development of children. Instead of an attempt to differentiate sensible rules from repressive ones, or an order that makes children feel secure from one that hinders their growth, most free schools (like mine) begin by throwing out all structures.

Another thing that happens is that free school people become terrified of their so-called liberated children. They haven't really discussed what freedom means, and so their own children's testing of their newfound paradise scares them. The adults don't like what they've created but aren't conscious enough to change it.

That seems to be the crux of the problem: free school people need to be more conscious of where they came from and where they want to go. They need to band together, not only because of the things they hate, but because they share certain values. This means knowing what sorts of human beings they want to create. It also means giving up the notion that children will just naturally change for the better. Children come to the free school with capitalism's values in their heads; they've learned sexism, racism, extreme competitiveness, obedience to authority, etc. from TV, from their storybooks, from the kids down the street, not to mention from their schools. My school failed because it left its children structureless and unguided, thus insuring their retention of their old consciousness. If free schools really want to challenge the school system, the adults must create a new set of values in themselves and in their children with as much seriousness as they criticized the old.

11 Education for Social Change

Think about the kind of world you want to live and work in. What do you need to know to build that world? Demand that your teachers teach you that.

—Peter Kropotkin, 1842–1921

A contradiction of its own courses through the argument of this book: The internal contradictions of school and society block the effectiveness of all reform strategies and even prevent the final solution of simply exterminating the offending institution. Are we then to abandon ourselves, our children, and our children's children to a mad descent into a mis-culture which we cannot perpetuate because we have lost the human capacity to socialize the young?

This is, in fact, the route the school crisis seems to be taking. Children are being socialized by their slightly older peers in accordance with some weird abstractions of messages from the media and the drug culture, distorted by their continuous and purposeful rejection of all school messages, including the skills they would need to surpass the alienation of both media and school. Meanwhile the few children who are accepting the alienation training are being socialized to run the world as part of the winning Team.

This argument may make it appear that there is nothing to be done. On the contrary, there is everything to be done. And everyone has a part in the doing.

Reform strategies are instituted and conducted by people who have, or have access to, money and power (by which are meant the present sources of power). Radical strategies can be instituted by anyone—or by anyone who is willing to take risks.

If institutional strategies for change are fraught with contradictions, radical, grass-roots strategies are fraught with risk. Radical change requires that people change their roles and relationships, and doing this produces both inner and outer insecurity. (You are no longer quite sure of who you are in the classroom and teachers' lounge and principal's office. And, moreover, you can lose your job.) But at some periods in history and in confrontation with some degrees of injustice and inhumanity, many quite ordinary people are willing to take such risks.

The cast assembled in this chapter consists of people who are in one sense quite ordinary; they have no special credentials, degrees, or expertise entitling them to a place in the history of social change. But here they are.

Some of these writers tell parts of their own stories. Of others: John Schaller was himself a high school student when he began the task of organizing a high school underground press news service. Ellen Lurie was a New York City "school mother" who worked with a group of other school mothers in an organization called the United Bronx Parents. Stokely Carmichael was a former student at Howard University and a field worker in Lowndes County, Alabama, for the Student Nonviolent Coordinating Committee (SNCC). Jane Stembridge was also a SNCC field worker. Patricia Michaels was a substitute teacher who worked with a small group of other teachers to try to understand how schools function and to create change in their own classrooms and schools.

At one level or another, every one of the experiences presented in this chapter involved a process of demystification and de-alienation. The demystification lay in the students' and teachers' together openly addressing, rather than conventionally concealing, the world of power in which they operated. The de-alienation lay in their regarding that learning task not as an arduous chore performed by the former at the behest of the latter but as essential to all their deepest needs. So, Stokely's class discovered that the definition of "correct" and "incorrect" grammar is a function of the power relations of society. The rebellious high school journalists found that they could move the principle of freedom of the press out of the civics text into their lives but that their rights would never be secure without continuous struggle. The endangered substitute at Folsom High helped her students to understand how the powers used against them had corrupted their very sense of themselves and their rights. The nursery school children began to understand how society was creating their ideas about "girlness" and "boyness."

Every one of the experiences, too, shows how the very conditions of oppression can give rise to demands for knowledge and skills to overcome the oppression. So that learning wells up out of the oppression and overcomes it.

We may say that these isolated, fragmentary attempts to deal with the school crisis are too few to be significant. The institutional reform strategies are far more extensive—but thin. The radical strategies are small in scale—but heavy. They expose the system and use the exposure to change the system. True, a few radical teachers, parents, or students here and there will not reverse the schools' downward drift. But they will provide a means by which the significant skills of our culture can be passed on without almost irreparable damage to the moral being of the learners, and in which groups of students, teachers, and parents can begin to free one another by freeing themselves. And they will help to create a growing body of people who, in rejecting the alienation, eagerly embrace, instead of also rejecting, genuine learning. These are the people who alone will be able to challenge the alienated automatons of the winning Team.

Institutions do not change themselves. Injustices do not right themselves. Pyramids of power do not fall from the top. Great social change occurs when ordinary people begin to look at the social world and together make the decision to be its subjects rather than its objects.

Up Against the Blackboard: A History of the High School Underground Press

by John Schaller

It was the need for coverage of important issues and the irrelevancy of most official school papers that in 1965 and 1966 inspired the first wave of the high school underground press. For the most part, these early papers appeared in major urban areas on the coasts and were often influenced by, though not duplicates of, the larger community and college underground papers.

Technology also had an effect on the growth of these papers. High school students had access to new printing methods and processes that had been unavailable to previous generations. Two were of special value. The electrostenciling process, which makes a mimeograph stencil from a layout of typescript, drawings, headlines, and photographs, made it possible to prepare impressive-looking mimeographed papers with a minimum of money or skill. And the widespread availability of low-cost photo-offset printing meant that, for as little as $50, students could print up a four-page tabloid newspaper, using only an electric typewriter and a few simple layout tools. The increasing use of office copying equipment, electric typewriter, and instant lettering also helped. By the spring of 1968, there were high school underground papers in scores, probably hundreds, of cities.

It was in that year that the movement took its biggest jump. Through the McCarthy and Kennedy campaigns, high school students across the country became involved in politics and the antiwar movement. The Chicago convention, whether experienced in person or vicariously through television, convinced many students that it was time to start doing something concrete about the problems they felt, and, when school started in the fall, papers began to sprout.

These papers varied as much as their publishers, ranging from a moderate liberal tone through left-wing satire to a firm Marxist-Leninist line. For the most part, their editors came from among the college-bound students of well-to-do suburbs, college towns, and the middle-income neighborhoods of large cities.

Through many articles in newspapers and major magazines, the high school underground press became a recognized phenomenon. Media coverage helped spread the movement further, encouraging students with the thought that "if other kids can start their own paper, so can we." Yet the subjects of this media publicity, as they read the articles about themselves, frequently found only an assortment of misquotations, sensationalism, condescending titles ("Revolutionaries Who Have to Be Home by 7:30" read the headline in one major daily), and outright lies. And they may well have wondered if the big professional newspapers, though more sophisticated than the school papers, were any better.

Meanwhile, faced with a situation that college had not prepared them for, administrators were reacting in various ways. In most schools, officials tried to suppress the papers in some way that would not create a sensation or stir up student interest in the issue, but few succeeded. Intimidation of active students, lectures about how they were endangering their chances of success in later life, threats of unfavorable reports to college admissions departments, and parent-dean conferences were among the most common tactics. When these failed, as was often the case, the school fell back on the strategy of suspending or expelling the students involved, and sometimes even calling in the police to make arrests. Other schools skipped the first step and started directly with the suspensions, expulsions, and arrests. Usually, the students resisted even this, and some went completely underground, so that no one knew who published the paper.

Occasionally, students managed to fight back and initiated legal suits against their schools for invasion of their First Amendment rights. The most significant of these court actions was undertaken by Ray Scoville and Arthur Breen, who, in February, 1968, were expelled from a Joliet, Illinois, high school for distributing a publication called *Grass High*. Administrators complained that the paper encouraged students to disobey certain school rules, and objected to a statement in it that "Oral sex may prevent tooth decay." Although the expulsions were at first upheld in court, the Seventh Circuit Court of Appeals ruled in April, 1970, that the school had violated the First Amendment rights of Breen and Scoville, and said that freedom of the press in public schools could not be restricted unless it could be shown that such action was necessary to prevent substantial disruption. The court referred to the 1969 *Tinker* v. *Des Moines School District* case, in which the U.S. Supreme Court had ruled that, in order to suppress a student's freedom of expression, a school must show that such expression would "materially and substantially interfere with the requirements of appropriate discipline" in the school. The Supreme Court, coming as close as it ever has to actually dealing with the issue of censorship in the public schools, refused to review the *Scoville* v. *Joliet* case, and the school paid nearly a thousand dollars in damages to the two students involved.

Yet, as significant a precedent as this case may have been for legal scholars, it meant nothing to high school students elsewhere. School administrators, fully aware that few students had the time, resources, and legally required parental backing to take a case to court, continued to do as they pleased, regardless of court rulings. Thus, the only students who have significantly benefited from the *Scoville* case have been those few who have been able to initiate court suits against their schools.

It was during this period, also, that students started developing ways to communicate with others who were publishing papers. In the fall of 1968 the High School Independent Press Service (HIPS) was formed in New York City, operating out of the offices of the Liberation News Service. HIPS sent out weekly packets of news and graphics to as many as two hundred underground papers, but after ten issues it had fallen over a thousand dollars into debt, and it folded the spring after it began. To fill the gap created by HIPS's demise, the Cooperative Highschool Independent Press Syndicate (CHIPS) was formed in May of 1969, first as a Chicago-area organization but soon becoming nationwide in focus. CHIPS made it possible for students to exchange their publications with each other, and also reprinted articles. When the new school year began in the fall of 1970, a news service named the Free Press Service (FPS) formed as an offshoot of CHIPS, filling much the same purpose as the defunct New York HIPS had, sending graphics and articles to the high school underground press. In addition to these nationwide organizations, regional groups formed in cities and states both in the United States and in Canada.

By 1970, the underground press movement had spread not only geographically across the United States but also into the lower grade levels. Junior-high students had their own papers in such places as Santa Barbara, California (*The Star Spangled Revolutionary Press*), Chicago (*The Plot*), and even Omaha, Nebraska (*Hiram*), while at least one group of elementary school students published an underground paper. Some papers were expanding their circulation and becoming citywide. The *New York High School Free Press* and the *New York Herald Tribune*, probably the best known of such papers, eventually reached press runs of 20,000 to 40,000. Dozens of other papers grew to circulations of 4,000 to 5,000, with actual readerships even larger than that.

Nous, published by students in Denver, Colorado, was one such paper. The first issue, in November of 1969, consisted of six mimeographed sheets with a cover price of a nickel. Although it was thought of as an "underground" paper, and four students were suspended for distributing the first issue, the content of the first *Nous* was hardly radical. That issue contained a description of the metaphysical origins of the publication's name; two short articles, about inflation and integration; a page of original poetry and artwork; and a mild student's bill of rights, calling for freedom of speech, press, and dress.

During the 1969–70 school year, *Nous* was printed about once a month. Distribution took place in five of the nine Denver public schools, as well as five or six suburban schools. By May, 1970, when its seventh issue came out, *Nous* was more political. It had begun to emphasize what students themselves were doing: There was a walkout at Northside because the administration was harassing a militant Chicago organization; at another school the student council president led 500 students in a protest against a biased drug-education seminar being held for parents; students at South tried to abolish the Confederate flag as the official school symbol; and 150 students were suspended from Kennedy High after a walkout over students' rights. The paper also started taking a stronger stand on certain national issues. For example, it supported the Earth Day demonstrations and printed several articles about ecology but simultaneously ran a cartoon denouncing Nixon for using the "nice safe pollution issue" to keep people from thinking about the war.

In the fall of 1970, *Nous* began its second year of publication with an $1,800 budget from Model Cities and a drastically different appearance. What had happened, as coeditor Nancy Morris put it, was: "The Model Cities Youth Department wanted a communications medium for the city's 'target area' schools. And since they didn't really know how to get their own paper together, and since a typical Model Cities 'youth' is about 26 years old, they figured they'd take the paper that already existed, and use it." In return for putting a short Model Cities plug into each issue, the *Nous* staff got enough money to print the paper offset, double its size, reach twice as many schools, and give it away free. Most of the staff was new, the two coeditors being the only carry-overs from the previous year, and the paper continued getting more politically oriented. The staff kept busy not only working on *Nous* but also helping other papers to form, starting a Denver high school student union, and supporting an under-age candidate for the school board. Nevertheless, *Nous* folded at the end of that year. Most of the staff, including the two coeditors, graduated, and no one took the initiative to keep it going the next year. The student union, and many of the other papers in the area, also collapsed then or during the following year.

Except for its circulation—most papers distribute only five hundred to a thousand copies in one or two schools—*Nous* was similar to the several thousand other independent underground student papers that have been published. Their contents cover a wide range of subjects. A satire on school life, student-council news, new course proposals, a long treatise about the Vietnam war, poetry, a declaration that "we do not recognize and will not accept the school's authority over us" signed by ten students, and an article condemning the school for trying to interfere with freedom of the press—all this made its way into one issue of a typical paper, and resulted in suspensions for the ten rebels.

Nous lasted two years. This was not unusual; a few papers are published continuously for twice this long, but most live out their complete life cycles within a single school year. Although a few meet premature and violent deaths at the hands of parents or school officials, the cause is usually neither so dramatic nor so clear-cut. It is more often a combination of student-body apathy and an accompanying loss of enthusiasm among the staff. Even those editors who never lose interest in the paper eventually graduate. New papers frequently start in schools where this happens, but they face the same problems and often follow life cycles similar to their predecessors'.

Student newspapers face other problems also. Realizing that they have to become more relevant if they are to survive, the official, school-sponsored papers have gradually been improving, frequently being able to take advantage of the relaxed publication codes pioneered by the underground papers. In some schools, more politically oriented students are getting on the staff of the school paper, pushing it to, and often beyond, its administration-defined limits. Another problem arose when the general level of political protest in the country started to decline. There are fewer and fewer demonstrations and moratoria, and students who once got energy from feeling like a part of a larger movement have been feeling their spirits dampened. Since 1971, the number of papers has been declining.

What will happen in the future is hard to guess; possibly, the number will continue to decrease during the next several years, eventually leveling off to several hundred papers scattered nationwide. The students who publish them will continue filling many of the same basic functions—threatening the adults who control their lives and challenging other students to question more of what they are told.

An important accomplishment of the high school underground press is that it has created for future students the option of starting their own paper, an option that was absent in the past. Whether future students will continue publishing large numbers of papers or will find other means of gaining control over their own lives, the high school underground press has had its impact. There will be no going back to the high school of the 1950's.

Our School: Struggling and Strategizing Along

by Vicki Wirth Legion

The Central West End of St. Louis is a hodge-podge neighborhood, an area of decaying greatness. Two blocks south of our school begins an enclave of huge old mansions, gated and guarded —the private streets. Ringed around the mansions is a strip of nice town apartments, then some large old rambly houses like the one I live in, mixed in with a few apartments of students and hip white folks. Also, within a block, starts the black ocean—the ghetto crumbles northward and then into some pretty rough territory.

Our school was made by a group of people fittingly diverse for this neighborhood. My brother and I, as suburban high school kids, had done tutoring and recreation work in the area, working

From *Outside the Net*, No. 4 (Winter–Spring, 1972). Reprinted by permission.

from one of the few churches, Trinity, that wasn't just shrinking from the "nasty" changes taking place around it. A new minister at Trinity was a dynamic guy who wanted to see the church *used*—so little kids, teenagers, and mothers started to keep the place alive all day every day. I came back to the neighborhood from college full of doubts about the place of white people working in programs for black people. But I was eager to work with the kids I had known as a suburban volunteer, and I finally decided "theory is gray, the tree of life is green," and took a job in a summer program and moved in.

That was how I got to know some of the mothers better. We worked in the same program, screamed at and played with the children together, and kept meeting each other around the only air conditioner in the little building.

At the end of the summer I didn't want to leave. A crazy idea about establishing a school—a real school for some of the kids— didn't seem so crazy to us once the minister gave us encouragement. The mothers were motivated by years of disappointment and frustration at the permanently appalling state of the public school in the area. I was motivated by all the critiques of urban education I had read.

New School Seeds

The Jefferson Elementary School—where most of our kids went— is one of the biggest baddies of them all in St. Louis. In June of 1967 the older children in the school had hung the aged principal from the flagpole outside his office window by his suit, and for a while it looked as if Jefferson were no longer a successfully repressive environment. The parents had been working for years to have the principal removed. But the School Board had a different remedy for the state of ongoing breakdown: in June of 1968 police with riot guns and dogs attended the final day of school to "maintain order."

The mothers had already had the idea for a new kind of school planted in their minds the year before. In the summer of 1968 Mrs. P. and Mrs. B. had been approached by some of the wealthy liberals of the Central West End. They wanted to start a good school for all the children in the area, they said. Would the mothers join a united effort of all colors and classes in the neighborhood to raise money for such a school? Mrs. P. and Mrs. B. were excited by the idea: all their protests to the School Board over the principal had been ignored, and the after-school tutoring program they had worked on was patently inadequate to meet the needs at hand. So Pauline and Rosie sent their children to the private streets to pose on the back of the Shetland pony owned by children of the "other half" of the alliance. James's and Reggie's black faces duly appeared on the money-raising brochure for the new school, and Pauline and Rosie carried the brochure from door to door, raising money.

Wealthy people in the Central West End knew that their enclave could not survive without at least one "quality" school, for now even the parochial finishing schools had moved to the suburbs. So they gave. The new school accumulated an endowment of a million dollars, and at last it was ready to open its doors.

A delegate from the new school's fund-raising committee came back to the black mothers' group that had worked to help raise money. He was very sorry, he said, but getting under way was more costly than they had imagined, and tuition had had to be set high this year. For those who could not pay $1,000 tuition, he recommended waiting a couple of years, when the new school would hopefully be able to give substantial scholarships.

Of course not one of the mothers could even dream of paying $1,000 to send one child to school for a year. They were angry—very angry—about that decision. Perhaps it was the anger from that final betrayal that supplied the audacity necessary for embarking on a project as ambitious as starting their own school. Father Robertson, the priest of Trinity, went about finding space in a bigger church. A friend and I wrote up the outline for a proposal to present to foundations.

(Rereading that initial proposal after two years provides a measure of the distance I have moved. Now technical inexperience and political naïveté fairly scream at me from those first brave words. In one section of the proposal, I talked about the philosophy of education that I wanted to guide my role as teacher. It was a litany in free-schoolese: "freedom to learn . . . offer meaningful subject matter in meaningful ways . . . students can be trusted to want to learn . . . teacher as a resource person . . . do real-life problem solving.")

From Rhetoric to Reality

When school actually started, we moved from free school rhetoric to what is, I think, a very common free school reality. We found that while we knew a lot about what we didn't like about the kind of education we rejected, we were fairly helpless

to make a place we *did* like out of our school. The words of
Kohl, Kozol, Holt, etc. at that point didn't give us many ideas
on what *did* make learning happen. It became very painfully
apparent that a vacuum occupied only by "nice people" didn't
lead to creative investigation and involvement. The first days of
school took place in a room bare of equipment and supplies,
with fourteen children coming out of six years of ghetto education, and a couple of young teachers who had never realized how
long a school day was. Those first few days of no structure were
unbearably chaotic for us and, I imagine, the kids. ("Where's
the principal?" they kept asking. "We need a principal.") Before
long I was sitting up late each night writing up lessons that I
hoped would take up a lot of time. "I look to the ditto machine
from whence cometh my help."

Gradually we recruited some good volunteers (out of the
usual majority of duds). Seven or eight young people working
very hard to bring a lot of material in, plus a VW bus that kept
busy taking us all out into the city, made the school a pretty
good place to learn, even the first year.

Someone put a book about the British infant schools and the
integrated day into my hands. There was something very honest
about the book. The people who wrote it had been through a
twenty-year process in Leicestershire of moving toward a natural
way of helping children learn and grow. They talked about all
the problems you were likely to run into. They gave dozens of
practical ideas that had worked in their groups over the years.
It was exactly the kind of help that was so scarce in the American
free school literature. They talked about what kinds of cheap
equipment made a lot happen and how to put junk to all sorts
of new uses. I felt they *knew* how hard it was to do the job we
had set ourselves.

The teachers at our school have put an immense amount of
energy into finding ways of allowing and encouraging the kids
to do good work. We have achieved some degree of success
with the school.

How Does Our Good Little School
Fit into the Larger Context?

As we said in our initial proposal, "We are not trying merely
to create one small experimental school for a few children in the
community." The school's controlling board of people from the
neighborhood was thought of as the nucleus of a well-organized,

confident, and experienced parent group that could demand to influence significantly the schools in our community and that could move from its experience to demand that the public School Board begin to make the kinds of changes necessary to provide high quality education for *all* children in the city. We presented our initial thoughts on why our public schools were so bad: "The locus of decision-making power resides in a centralized board and an administrative bureaucracy. Parents, students, and community leaders have little influence over the schools in their community. We believe that the inability of these groups to influence their educational environment is a basic cause of the inadequacies of urban education."

The solution? My scenario, at least, looked like Paul Goodman's mini-school proposal: a school on every block, schools in storefronts and vacant apartments and churches—each one made by the people around it.

What about the problem of making the dream come true? We didn't talk about that in the proposal, or among ourselves, for that matter, but I recall the vague notions that were floating around in my head. "First we'll make a good school," I thought breezily. Then, in my imagination, the blinking light from our successful venture would challenge the public schools into a fight. They would try to shut us down, on one pretext or another. In the process of fighting for the life of our school, many new parents in our neighborhood and around the city would be drawn into the struggle. We would sit in the local public school, start a freedom school on every block, and eventually demand control of the school monies in our district. Jefferson School would become a community center serving a solar system of mini-schools. Other areas of the city would be inspired by our success and whew! The Revolution.

It's clear that we cheerily overestimated the political strength and educational skill we had upon opening. But we also grossly overestimated the threat that our alternative school would present to the system. Our good little school, it seems, is in no danger at all of perishing in battle. Unless we aggressively organize for good education for all the children in the city, it seems as though we will die a living death instead in the sweet embrace of approval and insignificance. "Westminster Neighborhood School offers Unique Educational Opportunities," read the Sunday supplement feature story, flanked on either side by pictures of happy black and white children.

So now we began to ask ourselves, "How can we avoid just

doing the Man's work for him?" Here we are running a good school for the kids of the most active and discontented parents in the area—so much the *less* heat on Jefferson. The first year we had fifteen kids, this year thirty, and maybe if we hit every foundation in the region, next year we can have forty-five. I worry that each year we will bust ass scrounging money, begging donations, and learning how to be better Board members or teachers, while the public school, only one block away, rumbles on to Armageddon. In the meanwhile, we provide good public relations for the Danforth Family (Ralston Purina aristocracy), which funds us, and lend credence to the popular belief that American society *is* doing right by "Those People."

I suppose what I didn't understand before is that our school is no threat to Jefferson School because we're really *not* competing at doing the same job. The task that our local public school has been designed for is that of equipping the children who go there to assume their place in society. Because the children who go to Jefferson are black and generally poor or lower class, they need to be taught to accept the role America will assign them. Aside from the violence three years ago, Jefferson is succeeding at that job: the children *do* sit in rows seven hours a day; they *do* say "yes, sir" and "yes, ma'am" (at least when the principal brings a visitor around). And they prove again and again, on those standardized tests every June, that they really aren't fit for those "better" jobs. As the Superintendent said in a special report, "That the average achievement test scores of big city [read, "poor" or "black"] pupils are below national norms after the first year of school is not surprising. For whatever reasons, human beings differ in their capacities to perform, and learning is one kind of performance."

If the children are not fit to learn, what *are* they fit to do? The superintendent's report provided an answer. On the front cover, on the *front cover,* of the report appeared these statements, telling what the kids would be good for:

Working for Ralston Purina is not "chicken feed." It's $1.60 per hour, a summer job and a chance for permanent employment after graduation.

Standard Oil Company—Learn everything from A to Z about filling station operations in the work-study program at the filling station on 12th and Morrison.

Southwestern Bell—Learn and earn at Southwestern Bell

Telephone Co. Boys work as framemen; girls work as telephone operators in the work-study program with McKinley High. Many extras provided.

A Contradiction

Our school, or any alternative school, bumps right into this giant contradiction: what parents and teachers want for the children is the ability to think creatively and independently, to work for their own reasons, for the satisfaction they get from the job at hand. But what the kids have to be able to do instead, to get by in our country, is the exact opposite. Your livelihood and your children's welfare depends on saying "yes, ma'am" and "yes, sir" and giving the answers the boss wants to hear.

Unless we can clearly name this contradiction, and recognize where it comes from, it can reach into the life of a school and tear it apart. In many cases, I think, the contradiction appears in the form of tensions between parents and teachers—it certainly did in our school. The parents wanted the children to be excited about learning, but grew very nervous when it seemed that that tended away from "order" and regimentation. There were many crises of anxiety the first year that couldn't even be assuaged by high scores on the standardized tests. (After lengthy discussions back and forth, teachers acceded to the parents' strong wishes to give standardized tests.) I think the parents had a sound initial instinct that "making it" might depend as much on sycophantism as on achievement—and sycophantism the kids were *not* learning at school. (With time and struggle, and the good offices of a very progressive university professor whom the parents trusted very much, the mothers moved consistently and courageously in the direction of placing more and more trust in the children's own learning processes. For their part teachers have grown more and more respectful of the seriousness of the students' survival needs.)

Then, as the big kids in the school get closer to public high school, and start vividly to remember what it's like in the meat grinder, the anxiety grips even them. We have had the short-lived "People for Geography" movement, where the students demanded and received public school geography tests. (Although no one made it much farther than the first list of exports and imports.) Or the Democrats for Coercion Movement, wherein a majority of the class voted that they wanted to be forced to come to classes.

Crosswinds like these can tear our hopes apart, and I imagine that many a school has gone down in that struggle—teachers convinced that parents are reactionary and materialistic; parents convinced that teachers are wild and irresponsible. It's easy to forget that the contradiction comes from *outside* the school. Parents are *not* crass for insisting that the children must be able to grow up and earn a living. (In fact, what little relief one can get in a city must be bought—a machine to make your air breathable, a yard for the children, a trip away.) The teachers are *not* irresponsible for wanting to work in a way that will help a younger person be excited about what she or he is doing *now*. The present conflict between these two sets of legitimate concerns is a measure of the sickness of our country under its present economic system.

So I, at least, don't know how the school fits into the larger context or where it will go from here. Our struggle with the public school hasn't materialized yet, and I doubt that it ever will unless we become more aggressive. And which of us in the school can now find the energy and courage and imagination to make the school a ground to fight from instead of a corner to hide in? And if we do have something good here, something good for thirty or forty-five children, wouldn't it be crazy or irresponsible to risk blowing it in a fight that we're likely to lose? I don't know. I'm stuck on all these questions. I think it's time for me to leave St. Louis for a while, for a place where I can gather materials on these questions, but I'm sure gonna keep my ear to the ground and listen for rumblings from that direction.

Much love, dear school . . . much strength!

How to Organize Parents to Beat the System
by Ellen Lurie

Choose specific tangible issues which are important to parents.

Don't be abstract, vague or intellectual. Select nitty-gritty demands —the more specific the better.

Go after several things at once, including a number of easily

From Ellen Lurie, *How to Change the Schools: A Parents' Action Handbook on How to Fight the System* (New York: Random House, 1970). Reprinted by permission.

won issues. Parents will be encouraged by their success and will then gain the strength and self-confidence to tackle the more difficult problems.

Get things which parents want right now. If there are also some long-range demands (e.g., a new school), be sure you are also fighting for some immediate help at the same time (e.g., repair of the broken toilets at once).

Parents must develop their own list of grievances and demands.

No outside group, no matter how dedicated or concerned, can do this job. Don't let anyone tell you what you should be demanding. One of the main reasons parent campaigns fail is that they are not really "parent" campaigns at all. The principal or some teachers have manipulated some parents into fighting for a particular program, and this sort of ruse soon falls apart.

Different groups of parents want different things. For example, in one elementary school, the parents of the children who come by bus may want to improve the lunch facilities and the transportation schedule; the Spanish-speaking parents may want to increase the number of bilingual teachers; the parents of the children in the top class may want French taught in the third grade. All of these demands are legitimate. All of the various groups should be encouraged to meet by themselves and prepare their own list of grievances and demands.

Parents must then come together and decide *priorities*. Which issues are the most important for all parents? Be careful that you don't concentrate only on those issues which the most powerful members of the parent association want. Be sure that you *hear* what all the various parents are saying. Be sure you include a wide cross-section of grievances and demands on your final list. (The UFT* goes into bargaining sessions with more than six hundred different demands from all the various teacher chapters.)

Your parent group must be representative, but, even more important, it must include, in large numbers, those parents who have the most serious grievances.

Many parent groups fail because they are not truly representative. Usually parent associations are heavily weighted to include mainly those parents who are satisfied with the school and trust

---

* United Federation of Teachers, the New York City chapter of the national American Federation of Teachers.—ED.

the administration. Those parents will have an extremely narrow list of grievances. In a sense they are the "company union." It is crucial that parents do not argue with each other over the validity of a particular grievance. For example, if some parents believe that some teachers are bigoted, this is a very real issue to them. Just because other parents do not share this grievance is no reason to eliminate it. All parents want qualified, unprejudiced teachers. This is a good and legitimate demand.

Many parent groups fail because some of their members feel obliged to defend the school system from all criticism. Parents should defend and protect their children and other parents; it is up to the school employees to defend the system. If the parent association has become a "company union" you may want to set up your own parent group, or you may want to challenge the parent association to run a new election. However, a split of this sort is potentially dangerous and might weaken your group. If you can pull all the parents into a common group first, try to do so. But, priority should go to those parents whose children are suffering the most in the school. Parents whose children are doing all right simply will not fight as hard, nor will they risk very much. If keeping the parents united means losing the support of your angriest parents, forget it. It would be better to split.

Do your own research. Gather facts carefully to support your demands.

Fact-finding is a good organizing tool. As parents try to gather more information about their problems, they can get angrier and angrier with the system.

However, they can also get worn-out. The most important fact for you is the way the parents and students feel about your school. Document your stories and grievances, and be sure to *protect* the *anonymity* of everyone concerned.

When fact-finding, go directly to the source if you can. For example, if you want to find out about Title I regulations, go to Washington to find out how things *can* be done; don't go to board headquarters in Brooklyn,* because all you will learn there is why things cannot be done your way.

Use various resources to help you gather data. Church groups, community agencies, and colleges that wish to support you can

---

* Headquarters of the Board of Education of New York City.—ED.

be really helpful in securing the information you need. Just be sure that they only want to help you and don't intend to take you over.

Don't believe things you read or things you are told, if your eyes tell you differently. Often the Board of Education will show parents some facts on paper which will testify that all the children are reading or that the school is not overcrowded. Our own eyes tell us that they are lying. We see that the kids can't read and we see how crowded the school is. Believe what you see, not what they tell you. And make them come and see what you see.

Publicize your grievances and demands and broaden your support.

Many parent groups take their grievances to the officials too soon. Once you develop your list of demands, you must first be sure that most of the parents agree with you. Hold meetings, distribute flyers, encourage other parents to add to the list and provide additional documentation for those grievances they support. Get some community groups to support your demands—early in the game before you run into any trouble. And remember, "support" means just that. You are not inviting them to veto your demands or modify them. You are asking their support and sponsorship. Invite community leaders to come into your school and see for themselves why you need what you are asking for. But don't let them try to supervise you, censor you, or manipulate you. You can appreciate their advice, but remember, a parent campaign must be run by parents. If your demands are good ones, undoubtedly there will be some teachers in your school who will be willing to support you. . . .

Once you get a meeting to present your grievances, be sure to:

- take a good-sized group representing a cross-section of parents. Do not limit your group to only two or three members; this will antagonize too many parents. The UFT negotiating team consists of twelve or more members.
- find out how long your meeting will last. If you prepare a half-hour presentation, but the meeting is scheduled to last only a half hour, you will have let them off the hook because there won't be enough time to force them to answer you.
- find out in advance whom the board plans to have attend the meeting. If they are inviting many "experts," bring along your

own experts. If they are inviting other parent groups, find out in advance and decide if you still want to go under those conditions. Or perhaps you will want to caucus with those other parent groups in advance.

- doublecheck on the morning of your meeting to make sure the person you think you are seeing will really be there. Decide in advance whether or not you will keep the appointment if he keeps you waiting or if he delegates an assistant to you.
- have one member of your group take minutes. But insist that the school official put all promises into *writing.* You might want to stay there while he dictates the "agreement" to his secretary, or else you may be surprised that the letter you receive later in no way resembles the agreement you thought you had.
- if the school official tells you he must "study" the matter further, give him a time limit within which he must render a decision or meet with you again. Schedule a follow-up appointment then and there. . . .

Never, never, never attack other parents or parent groups.

- Don't let the Board of Education divide and conquer you.
- If you walk into a meeting where other parents have been invited to argue with you, ask to meet with them without any professionals present, or else leave. Take on those parents in private; don't fall into the system's trap by fighting among each other, and letting the school officials off the hook.
- Even when you agree to disagree with the other parents, you can fight the system for what you want without fighting the parents.
- Never take away something from another parent group. Always demand that you get as much as they got, but don't be trapped into fighting another group to give up something for your sake. There is enough to go around for everyone, but the school system likes to make us fight . . . each other for crumbs while it controls the real pie.

Keep your neighbors informed and keep broadening your local base of support.

- Don't get so wrapped up in meetings "downtown" that you lose contact with your fellow parents and neighbors.

- During any negotiation, keep local demonstrations, rallies, and picket lines going. Distribute flyers telling everyone what is happening.
- Don't depend on citywide media to tell your story. If you take lots of parents to all the meetings, they will see what is going on and they will spread the word.
- Never stop inviting other local organizations to join with you. Go to churches, political clubs, antipoverty agencies, and everyone else to tell them about your campaign and invite their sponsorship. This will prevent the Board of Education from calling you extremists or other unfavorable names. Get the most legitimate groups in your community to lend their support. If you are campaigning for things parents really want, this should not be too difficult. . . .

Keep your sense of humor and find ways to deflate and ridicule the officials.

The struggle is hard and long. If you get too intense or uptight, you will be worn out long before you can win. There is humor in the most critical situations. Learn to seek it out, for it will keep you going.

Stokely's Speech Class
recorded by Jane Stembridge*

The most important class was "Stokely's speech class." He put eight sentences on the blackboard, with a line between, like this:

I digs wine.	I enjoy drinking cocktails.
The peoples wants freedom.	The people want freedom.
Whereinsoever the policemens goes they cause troubles.	Anywhere the officers of the law go, they cause trouble.
I wants to reddish to vote.	I want to register to vote.

* This class was conducted by Stokely Carmichael, a field worker for the Student Nonviolent Coordinating Committee (SNCC), for high school–age SNCC field workers at an extended SNCC workshop in Waveland, Mississippi, in 1965.—Ed.

From Miriam Wasserman, "Two Classes," *This Magazine Is About Schools,* Vol. IV, No. 2 (Spring, 1970). Copyright 1970 by Outerbridge & Dienstfrey. Reprinted by permission.

Stokely   What do you think about these sentences? Such as. "The peoples wants freedom"?

Zelma   It doesn't sound right.

Stokely   What do you mean?

Zelma   "Peoples" isn't right.

Stokely   Does it mean anything?

Milton   "People" means everybody. "Peoples" means everybody in the world.

Alma   Both sentences are right as long as you understand them.

Henry   They're both okay, but in a speech class you have to use correct English.
           (Stokely writes "correct English" in corner of blackboard.)

Zelma   I was taught at least to use the sentences on the right side.

Stokely   Does anybody you know use the sentences on the left?

Class   Yes.

Stokely   Are they wrong?

Zelma   In terms of English, they are wrong.

Stokely   Who decides what is correct English and what is incorrect English?

Milton   People made rules. People in England, I guess.

Stokely   You all say some people speak like on the left side of the board. Could they go anywhere and speak that way? Could they go to Harvard?

Class   Yes. No. (Disagreement.)

Stokely   Does Mr. Turnbow[1] speak like on the left side?

Class   Yes.

Stokely   Could Mr. Turnbow go to Harvard and speak like that? "I wants to reddish to vote."

Class   Yes.

Stokely   Would he be embarrassed?

Class   Yes! No!

Zelma   He wouldn't be, but I would. It doesn't sound right.

Stokely   Suppose someone from Harvard came to Holmes County and said, "I want to register to vote." Would they be embarrassed?

---

[1] Hartman Turnbow, a black farmer from Mileston, Mississippi, the first black man to attempt to register to vote in the Holmes County registration campaign of that decade. A popular indigenous leader of extraordinary poise, charm, and courage, he used the common "reddish" for "register."

Zelma	No.
Stokely	Is it embarrassing at Harvard but not in Holmes County? The way you speak?
Milton	It's inherited. It's depending on where you come from. The people at Harvard would understand.
Stokely	Do you think the people at Harvard should forgive you?
Milton	The people at Harvard should help teach us correct English.
Alma	Why should we change if we understand what we mean?
Shirley	It is embarrassing.
Stokely	Which way do most people talk?
Class	Like on the left.
	(He asks each student. All but two say "left." One says that Southerners speak like on the left, Northerners on the right. Another says that Southerners speak like on the left, but the majority of people speak like on the right.)
Stokely	Which way do television and radio people speak?
Class	Left.
	(There was a distinction made by the class between Northern commentators and local programs. Most programs were local and spoke like on the left, they said.)
Stokely	Which way do teachers speak?
Class	On the left, except in class.
Stokely	If most people speak on the left, why are they trying to change these people?
Gladys	If you don't talk right, society rejects you. It embarrasses other people if you don't talk right.
Hank	But Mississippi society, ours, isn't embarrassed by it.
Shirley	But the middle class wouldn't class us with them.
Hank	They won't accept "reddish." What is "reddish"? It's Negro dialect and it's something you eat.
Stokely	Will society reject you if you don't speak like on the right side of the board? Gladys said society would reject you.
Gladys	You might as well face it, man! What we gotta do is go out and become middle class. If you can't speak good English, you don't have a car, a job, or anything.
Stokely	If society rejects you because you don't speak good

	English, should you learn to speak good English?
Class	No!
Alma	I'm tired of doing what society say. Let society say "reddish" for a while. People ought to just accept each other.
Zelma	I think we should be speaking just like we always have.
Alma	If I change for society, I wouldn't be free anyway.
Ernestine	I'd like to learn correct English for my own sake.
Shirley	I would too.
Alma	If the majority speaks on the left, then a minority must rule society. Why do we have to change to be accepted by the minority group? (Lunchtime.)
Stokely	Let's think about two questions for next time: What is society? Who makes the rules for society?

"Girls Don't Play with Cars, Linda"

by Phyllis Taube MacEwan

For the past two years a group of Boston area teachers in child care centers and nursery schools have been trying to figure out ways to confront the sex-role stereotyping that young children express in their play. In . . . this paper, I will describe several incidents that took place in our centers—what the children did and how we responded. . . .

Most of the experiences described demonstrate that adults' actions with children regarding the issue of sex roles can bring about positive and visible change. However, it must be recognized that, given the social pressures of the media, family, etc., efforts to help children grow up in a new way can meet with frustration, and change is often slow and not as visible as in the experiences

From Phyllis Taube MacEwan *Liberating Young Children from Sex Roles: Experiences in Day Care Centers, Play Groups, and Free Schools.* Copyright 1972 by Phyllis Taube MacEwan. By permission of the author, published by New England Free Press, 60 Union Square, Somerville, Mass. 02143.

discussed here. In fact, working with children between the ages of two and four years gives one a rare opportunity to promote new attitudes and self-concepts, which is not the case when working with older kids. . . .

The [following] situation took place in an experimental elementary school. The children involved were in a "family group" that ranged in age from five to ten.

Seven-year-olds Eddy and John were engrossed in playing with Hot Wheels on an elaborate home-made ramp structure. After watching them race for a while, Linda, a sturdy five-year-old, walked up, picked up a car, and silently joined the boys in their racing.

"You can't play here, Linda," asserted one boy.

Without responding she continued playing with her car. Both boys repeated their demand for her to leave, getting progressively louder and more annoyed. Over and over they repeated, "Girls don't play with cars!" While she didn't appear to be intimidated, she finally stood up and stared at them, holding on to one car. For a few moments she simply stood there and looked at them, unsure of what to do next.

At this point the teacher intervened, saying, "Girls can play with cars as well as boys can." The boys looked bothered by the teacher's statement.

"We'll talk more about this later, but right now I think you will have to let her play." Play resumed, although the boys played separately from Linda, excluding her from the racing and measuring.

At their regular group discussion time that day, the teacher brought up the incident and asked the kids why it was that boys and girls did not play together.

"Sometimes we want to play alone," one boy said.

"Why do girls ever need to play with cars? They don't drive cars," another boy commented.

A nine-year-old girl responded. "Look, that's silly to say because ladies drive cars. Like Marian [the teacher], so we can play with cars too."

Another girl pointed out that one of the bus drivers was a woman. The teacher asked them about their own parents. It came out that mothers drove as often as fathers. The result of that discussion was to show that the boys' line of argument was simply not true: both men and women drive.

The teacher continued the discussion by asking, "Why do you

think that boys usually play with cars and trucks and girls with dolls? I want you to go home and think about this for the next few days. Look at your toys and at your sisters' and brothers' and try to think why boys and girls play in different ways."

At the suggestion of a child, the teacher reintroduced the issue a few days later. She began the discussion by asking if the children had noticed if their fathers ever helped out with the babies or with housework. Most of their fathers helped only on Mother's Day or when their mothers were sick. This happened whether both parents worked or not.

"How do fathers get that way? How come that happens?" the teacher asked.

"That's why young boys should take care of babies, 'cause they are going to be fathers and fathers should help too," one older girl replied.

"Yeah, that's why boys should play house with girls; they need to learn how to do that kind of thing," added another girl.

It was quite clear that the kids understood that role-playing in childhood taught people their adult roles.

"Look, remember our problem was the business of boys and girls playing with cars together?"

"But that's how it should be," insisted one boy.

"How did you learn that?"

"Tonka."

"Where do you see Tonka?"

"On TV, only the boys play with the trucks."

Then proceeded a very involved 45-minute discussion about other things that kids see on TV regarding roles: mothers cooking with their daughters, using Pillsbury; fathers fishing or hiking with their sons, smoking Kents, etc.

"Do you girls like to play with trucks?"

"I do." "Sure." "Yeah." "Not me." "Sometimes."

"And do you boys like to play with dolls?"

"Yeah." "Sure." "Sometimes." "Me too."

"Where do you do it?"

"I play with my sisters' dolls," a few boys commented. The same was true of girls using their brothers' trucks. When the teacher suggested that the boys ask their parents for dolls and the girls ask for trucks for their next birthdays, the response was a united "No" from all the kids. The teacher's final comment was to point out how early in their lives they had learned from their parents and TV what they could and could not do.

Throughout the year this topic cropped up in various ways. The kids, even though they didn't dramatically change their own behavior, certainly became aware of how they got that way.

Toward a Movement

by Patricia Michaels and BARTOC

Folsom High School, its students will tell you, is the tightest school in the Bay area. It still has a rigid dress code which is strictly enforced and a principal who has publicly stated that if he has to be the Hayakawa of the school district, he'll do it; he does it every day.

Folsom certainly has an order to it, as any teacher or visitor will tell you, but underneath, and not too far underneath, the surface is an anger that goes beyond anything I've ever seen in students after three years of teaching in fairly rough schools.

Even as a substitute teacher, I felt a knot in my stomach every time I worked there because I knew that from the moment I entered the classroom I would have to choose between the repressiveness of the school and the students' response to that repressiveness. I remember the first day: We were having a pretty heated discussion in one class when the principal walked in and told us that our behavior (he treated me as he did the kids) was appalling and that there was too much noise in the halls. When we didn't quiet down, he kept the whole class after school for an hour.

But the biggest confrontation came over passes to the bathroom. There was a constant cat-and-mouse game between the administration and the students over smoking regulations, and, because the kids knew that I wasn't about to ask them every time they left the room whether they really wanted to go or whether they wanted a smoke, they converged on me for passes, which I freely gave.

Usually I had one-day stands at Folsom and that was quite enough. But one day this year I was called in to do a three-day stint with a "low achiever" science class. The teacher I was subbing for was a very big, authoritarian male and the students literally breathed a sigh of relief when they saw me. Some laughed because they knew this would be an easy three days. The regular teacher left detailed lesson plans ("Have them read pp. 109–117 and answer the questions at the end of the chapter") and strict orders that none of his equipment was to be handled by the students. I timidly and embarrassedly read the assignment, and when the students groaned, I felt a sense of relief and anguish, relief because I felt uncomfortable administering such a nonsensical assignment, and anguish because I knew that if I didn't administer it, I would have to deal with all of the pent up hostility that had been lying there for an entire year. So I just said, "He'll be expecting this work, do it at your own pace, do it together if you want, feel free to talk, but let's keep it cool."

Five minutes later two boys came up to the desk and asked to go to the john. I let them go, only one at a time. About ten kids left during the period, some of them freely borrowing cigarettes and matches from their friends. We talked about the absurdity of the regulations, which made them sneak their way out of classes and through the halls to the johns.

Things went pretty well until the fourth-period class of thirty-five boys. (The teacher had described them in his plans as animals, and so they understandably acted out his expectations.) My pleas for quiet went unheeded; they told me not to bother writing the assignment on the board, and went about the room throwing the equipment that they had been told not to handle. After about fifteen horror-filled minutes, during which time I franticly tried to take roll, I yelled, "Please tell me why you're so angry. I know that having a sub means letting loose but I really sense that something else is happening here." One boy said, "This is a goddamn prison and we're just breaking out." Another boy said something else. In about three minutes, we had reached in this discussion of what was wrong at Folsom the order which the teacher had wanted to have around his assignment. But the noise of the previous few minutes had somehow carried. While one student was enthusiastically laying out his ideas for organizing some kind of strike at the school, the science teacher from next door was standing, arms folded, at the door. The student looked up at me and then at him and said, "Mrs. H., do you think if we had a strike here they'd call the cops?" And I, feeling like the floor was giving under me, not having the good sense to walk over to the door and ask the science teacher what he wanted, not wanting to break the discussion, sympathizing with the boy's desire to let the spy from next door know that he was not going to be intimidated, said, "Well, the police have been called into other places when that's happened, but it hasn't stopped people from fighting for what they believe." At that point, the science teacher noticed a kid playing with some lab equipment in the back of the room and, not knowing how to react to the whole scene, he screamed out, "Get your hands off that; it's private property." The kid looked back at him and yelled, "No, it's not! It's public property and this is a public school and I can touch this equipment," at which point the bell rang and the science teacher said, "Don't think I won't report what's been happening here back to your teacher when he returns."

The kids filed out and I walked up to the intruding teacher and just poured out what I had been feeling. I told him I didn't know how teachers were able to teach anything in a school like this, where students were so angry about the way they were treated and where teachers had to live in continual fear of the administration. He softened a little (he didn't like the principal too well either). At the end of the conversation, I felt like we had at least a temporary reprieve.

After lunch, classes continued in the same way. I told the kids some of what had happened earlier and that we ought to be cool about passes to the bathroom and noise. I suppose I could have expressed my own anxiety about losing my subbing job—but on the basis of one day they had no reason to trust me or to give a damn about whether I lost my job or not. The thought of sending someone out never crossed my mind, because I knew that I could never use the hated authority of that school.

The last period of the day came and I thought I was already at home and free, when, midway through the class, the principal came in. He pulled out of his pocket about five passes he had collected during the day, slapped them on my desk, and asked, "Is this your handwriting?" I answered "yes." He said, "Well, we don't give out passes except in extreme emergencies." I told him that I had no way of knowing if a student really had to leave the room and that I wasn't about to humiliate myself or the student by asking. He said, "Well, I'll solve your dilemma for you. Starting tomorrow, no one in any of your classes leaves your room for anything." He walked up and down the rows checking out what students were doing and left.

The next day I told the students what had happened and that no one could leave. They listened, muttered something about the principal, and I went on to show a movie that the regular teacher had scheduled for that day. About fifteen minutes into the movie, I smelled smoke and realized that the students were lighting up cigarettes all over the room. I went over to each group and told them, "Hey, listen, I just told you what went down yesterday. We're all going to get into serious trouble." (Me mostly, I thought, since a five-day suspension for smoking is welcomed by a lot of kids!) As each group I spoke with put the cigarettes out, another group lit up, and round and round it went until, in desperation and anger, I flicked on the lights and what I saw were looks of terror, kids frantically putting out their cigarettes, waving the smoke away from them, and some heads bowed with guilt. What struck me in that moment was that, while they sneakily defied the rules every day, in some part of them they believed that what they were doing was wrong; that in fact, their marching off to the bathroom was not . . . a way of confronting the system but, in some strange sense, was a reaffirmation of the principal's legitimacy and of his definition of them as troublemakers. And so I said to them, "You know, you're right in everything you want, but the sad thing is that you don't know you are. Whatever you're sneaking around to get, whatever you're hiding, you have the right to ask for in the light of day, and when are you going to start doing just that? When are you going to stop telling me and each other that there are only five kids in the school who'll stand up and demand anything, when there are twenty kids right here who took a chance and smoked." And I added, "Let's go, all of us right now, and light up in front of the principal. Or if you don't want to do that, why don't you start with something else, like wearing your hair the way you want to," and then I muttered something about its being their school and their having a right to say something about how it runs. No one said anything for a minute. Then a boy asked if he could open a window to clear the room of the smoke. We talked a little bit, until the end of the period. I told a few of the kids about student unions being formed in the city, about what black and white kids were doing at Balboa, and that it wasn't impossible to get some of the things they wanted. The bell rang and the rest of the day was quiet. Kids had heard about what had happened in the first-period class, and they somehow ordered their classes themselves that day. A few of the kids started asking for passes, and other kids said, "No, not today—she'll get in trouble and so will we." A few said they had heard about the student unions and asked if I could get them something to read on them. My assignment ended, but I continued to go back to Folsom periodically for the rest of the year and talked with as many students as I could. A few things did happen. At a rally in early May, the principal ordered the students back to class after somebody set off a cherry bomb. Most of the students refused to leave the auditorium and began chanting in protest. A few organizations got started, and I attended one meeting where kids were making plans to write a letter to the community telling it about some of the things that were happening at Folsom and inviting it to a meeting to discuss possible actions. The meeting never came off as far as I know, but something had begun and I think will pick up again this year.

There were several things that I learned from my experience at Folsom. As a sub—or even as a regular teacher—you don't often know what are your own failings and what is the function of an impossible job or situation. But what I did see is that you can't teach independence or creativity in science or in anything else in a prison-like atmosphere. At some point, you have to start confronting the general repressiveness of the school. You can't delude yourself into thinking that *your* classroom will be different, because the anger carries over and you have to deal with it whether you have created it or the principal has.

The question of how to deal with that anger is a more difficult one. The movement talks about the kids who rebel today, it revels in stories about fires being set, riots in schools, and the like. What I learned at Folsom, where rules are continually broken, where vandalism abounds, is that this doesn't necessarily result in kids getting a better conception of themselves or in getting them to work together to change things. As radicals and as radical teachers we have to stop saying "Right on!" to every individual act of defiance. We have to begin helping students to understand that their anger is legitimate and what their acts of defiance mean. Only with this kind of self-consciousness will students and teachers move from what are now individual and desperate acts of rebellion toward building a movement that will change the prison-like atmosphere of our schools once and for all.

Bibliography

Caution!

This bibliography is not complete, objective, unprejudiced, or well balanced. It consists of the recommendations of one opinionated reader to other readers whose opinions she would like to influence.

However, my readers deserve an explanation of my criteria, how ever rough, for selecting the items. They have been chosen from among the following classes:

1. Books and periodicals that I happen to have chosen to buy and keep on my shelves, library research being so arduous in these days of tragic library neglect
2. Writings that captured my imagination or deepened my thinking or gave me pleasure by their quality or rang so true for me that I wished I had written them (A few have done all, or almost all of these.)
3. Writings that I believe have influenced other people strongly and whose influence I wish to comment on or in some way modify
4. Writings that I deem useful in unraveling and then reweaving the many strands of the school crisis
5. Writings and other resources that may be of practical use to radical teachers, students, and parents

In respect to coverage of the various topics in this book, some very important topics and phenomena are relatively less well represented by bibliographic entries than others. Topics about which there has been a great deal of well-publicized material (such as school oppression of black children) are less well covered here than topics about which material may be harder to find (such as oppression of girls, Mexican Americans, native Americans).

There are a couple of exceptions to this rule. There are too few entries on the very important topics of oppression of working-class or poor white children, on curriculum as mystification, on oppression of teachers. This is because I could not find much material on these topics. (Maybe I didn't try hard enough.) Anyway, the world is our best resource for those. I hope that people will be writing or discovering writings on these topics to be included in another edition of this bibliography.

Again, I hope that readers will accept this bibliography for what it is. It is not a final word on all the writings about school that a radical has to read. It is an offering of books and other writings by one who cherishes the written word when it is used to clarify rather than to mystify our world.

Books, Articles, Pamphlets

ACKERMAN, FRANK, and ARTHUR MACEWAN. "Inflation, Recession and Crisis, or, Would You Buy a New Car from This Man?" *Review of Radical Political Economics,* 2503 Student Activities Bldg., U. of Michigan, Ann Arbor, Mich., 48104. August, 1972. Helpful for an understanding of the fiscal crisis of schools as part of the fiscal crisis of the public sector.

ARIES, PHILIPPE. *Centuries of Childhood: A Social History of Family Life.* Trans. by ROBERT BALDICK. New York: Random House, Vintage, 1962. How modern ideas about childhood, the nature of children, obligations to children developed. Gives pleasure by frequently jolting some of one's lifelong certainties.

ASHTON-WARNER, SYLVIA. *Spinster: The Story of a Teacher of Maori Children.* New York: Simon & Schuster, 1968. A novel by the author of *Teacher.* Describes her renowned "organic" method of teaching reading and portrays with great sensitivity the oppression of the teacher as a woman.

BARATZ, JOAN C., and ROGER W. SHUY. *Teaching Black Children to Read.* Center for Applied Linguistics, 1717 Massachusetts Ave., N.W., Washington, D.C., 1969. Articles, theoretical and practical, from the linguist's point of view, recognizing the significance of dialect differences.

BARATZ, STEPHEN S., and JOAN C. BARATZ. "Early Childhood Intervention: The Social Science Base of Institutional Racism," *Harvard Educational Review,* February, 1970. A most important contribution to the literature of scholarly protest against the myth of cultural deprivation. Authors' cultural-differences model is presented as a viable alternative to the existing genetic-inferiority and social-pathology models, both of which are based on a view of the black man as a "sick white man."

BARLOW, WILLIAM, and PETER SHAPIRO. *An End to Silence.* Indianapolis, Ind.: Pegasus, 1971. A good analytic account of the intentional class bias of California's master plan for higher education is contained in this report on the longest student uprising ever to occur on an American campus: that at San Francisco State College in 1968–69.

BARRY, KATHLEEN. "A View from the Doll Corner," *Women: A Journal of Liberation*, Fall, 1969. One of the few pieces of published writing that deal with the crucial topic of the role of interpersonal classroom relations in early sex socialization.

BERG, IVAR. *Education and Jobs: The Great Training Robbery.* New York: Praeger, 1970. Boston: Beacon, 1971. Demonstrates how schooling functions more to credential than to train people for careers and thus helps deflate one of the sustaining myths of American schools.

BERNARD, ANN, and JOHN HURST. "The Chemistry of Classroom Control," *Edcentric* (double issue, "Education and Drugs"), March, 1972. An excellent review of the institutional use of drugs in child-pacification programs.

BERUBE, MAURICE R., and MARILYN GITTELL, eds. *Confrontation at Ocean Hill–Brownsville.* New York: Praeger, 1969. A compilation of documents and articles about the notorious community-control–union struggles in New York City in 1968–69.

BHAERMAN, ROBERT D. *New Currents in Education: A Preliminary Review.* Washington, D.C.: American Federation of Teachers, n.d. Good short definitions of several institutional reform strategies: merit pay, accountability, behavioral objectives, PPBS, performance contracting. Bibliography.

BILLINGSLEY, ANDREW. *Black Families in White America.* Englewood Cliffs, N.J.: Prentice-Hall, 1968. By analyzing the history and strengths of the black family, gives the lie to the Moynihan thesis of the "pathology" of the black family, on which so much of the myth of cultural deprivation is based.

BIRMINGHAM, JOHN, ed. *Our Time Is Now: Notes from the High School Underground.* New York: Praeger, 1970. A collection of articles about the student underground and youth revolt.

BODENHEIMER, THOMAS. "The Poverty of the State," *Monthly Review,* November, 1972. A very much condensed and easy-to-read version of O'Connor's fiscal-crisis theory. (*Cf.* JAMES O'CONNOR, *The Fiscal Crisis of the State,* below.)

BONE, ROBERT. "Teaching Negro History: An Interdisciplinary Approach," *Integrated Education,* February–March, 1967; also in MEYER WEINBERG, ed., *Integrated Education: A Reader* (Glencoe, Ill.: Free Press, 1968). Argues that serious study of black history touches deepest feelings in the students—"For the white children, guilt and fear. For the Negroes, shame and rage."

BULL, JENNY. "High School Women: Oppression and Liberation," *Women, A Journal of Liberation,* Winter, 1970. The dilemma of the high school woman with respect to academic achievement versus sexual achievement.

CAHN, EDGAR S. *Our Brother's Keeper: The Indian in White America.* New York and Cleveland: World Publishing, 1960. The chapter "Education as War" is a frightening but good summary of the special destructiveness of schooling for native American children.

CALLAHAN, RAYMOND E. *Education and the Cult of Efficiency.* Chicago: University of Chicago Press, 1962. An account of the attempt to apply assembly-line principles of scientific management to the running of public schools. Older readers may recall the great proponent of scientific management Frederick W. Taylor. A tragicomedy which makes good reading if depressing history.

CARNOY, MARTIN, ed. *Schooling in a Corporate Society: The Political Economy of Education in America.* New York: McKay, 1972. A compilation of articles dealing mainly with the classism of schooling in the United States.

CHANNON, GLORIA. *Homework: Required Reading for Teachers and Parents.* New York: Outerbridge & Dienstfrey, 1970. An account of a middle-aged teacher's struggles to overcome her own and her students' fears of freedom in the classroom. Realistic, if sometimes painful, support for struggling teachers, men as well as women.

Chinese-Americans: School and Community Problems. Chicago, Ill., Integrated Education Associates, 1972. School problems of and discrimination against Asian children tend to be ignored or minimized because these children are likely to be far more docile ("well behaved") than many other low-status children. The articles in this booklet explore the problem and also show that their good behavior and good grades do not earn for Asian students full and respected citizenship in U. S. society.

COLEMAN, JAMES S. *Equality of Educational Opportunity.* Washington, D.C.: U.S. Department of Health, Education, and Welfare, 1966. An elaborate statistical documentation of the fact that black children and poor children perform worse in school than white children and well-to-do children. Perhaps the ultimate in violation of Ockham's razor, almost always more honored in the breach than in the observance by social scientists. (See WILLIAM RYAN, *Blaming the Victim,* below.)

COLES, ROBERT. *The Migrant Farmer: A Psychiatric Study.* Southern Regional Council, 52 Fairlie Street, Atlanta, Ga. 30303, 1965. A compassionate study that stresses the strengths as well as the sufferings of the families of migrant children, by the author of the renowned *Children of Crisis* series.

Dick and Jane as Victims: Sex Stereotyping in Children's Readers. Women on Words and Images, P.O. Box 2163, Princeton, N. J., n.d. Analysis, examples, illustrations, statistical tables demonstrating sex stereotyping in children's readers. Consistent ridiculing and devaluing of girls and women are shocking when gathered in such concentration.

Dissent and Disruption in the Schools: A Handbook for School Administrators, Institute for Development of Educational Activities (IDEA), an affiliate of Charles F. Kettering Foundation, P.O. Box 628, Dayton, Ohio, 45419. Strategy and tactics for the "prevention and control of activism" on high school campuses. How to substitute cool manipulativeness for brute oppression.

DYER, HENRY S. *Controversial Aspects of Educational Accountability,* New York: United Federation of Teachers, 1970. A critical review of accountability, vouchers, and performance contracting with reference to the notorious Texarkana project.

ENGELHARDT, TOM. "Ambush at Kamikaze Pass" *Bulletin of Concerned Asian Scholars,* Bay Area Institute, 604 Mission St., Room 1001, San Francisco, Calif. 94104, Winter–Spring 1971. The contribution of westerns to the destruction of the American soul: "They have successfully tied extermination of non-white people to laughable relief, and white racial superiority to the natural order of things. They have destroyed any possibility for explaining the various ways in which non-white . . . people could resist invasion, colonization, exploitation and even mass slaughter." An analysis of westerns could provide good experiences in a history classroom.

Equal Educational Opportunities: Hearings Before the Select Committee on Equal Educational Opportunity of the U.S. Senate, 1971–72. The twenty-one volumes cover many manifestations of unequal education. Especially useful for providing economic and fiscal data. The volume *Selected Court Decisions Relating to Equal Educational Opportunity,* March, 1972, contains the texts of important decisions relating to desegregation and school finance.

FARBER, JERRY. *The Student as Nigger.* New York: Pocket Books, 1970. Sharp essays by the absurdly irreverent author of the famous title essay.

FIRESTONE, SHULAMITH. *The Dialectics of Sex: The Case for Feminist Revolution.* New York: Morrow, 1970; Bantam, 1971. The chapter "Down with Childhood" is an excellent analysis from a radical feminist point of view.

FORBES, JACK D. *The Education of the Culturally Different: A Multicultural Approach.* Berkeley, Calif.: Far West Laboratory for Research and Development; Washington, D.C.: Government Printing Office. The author is an anthropologist-educator of Powhatan descent. The booklet has useful material for the teacher.

———. *Mexican-Americans: A Handbook for Educators.* Berkeley, Calif.: Far West Laboratory for Educational Research and Development; or Washington, D.C.: Government Printing Office. History, culture, assets of Mexican-American schoolchildren; suggestions for teachers and administrators; bibliography and list of audiovisual materials. Useful for educators who wish to overcome their own cultural deprivation.

FREIRE, PAULO. *Pedagogy of the Oppressed.* New York: Herder and Herder, 1968. A Brazilian teacher and revolutionary describes a method whereby peasants learn to read as a part of the process of perceiving and seeking to overcome their oppression. In the tradition of important revolutionary writings, this book is hard to read, though deeply poetic. It is also a useful corrective for elitism among revolutionary as well as liberal educators but is subject to being misunderstood and used for quite other political-educational purposes than the writer probably intended. However, it is a basic work for the radical educator.

FREUD, ANNA. *Psychoanalysis for Teachers and Parents.* Trans. by BARBARA LOW. Boston: Beacon, 1935. Despite its want of political perspective and its many distorters, psychoanalysis has much to contribute to our understanding of children's "nature." This book is a simple and compassionate exposition, with many practical implications.

FRIEDENBERG, EDGAR Z. *The Dignity of Youth and Other Atavisms.* Boston: Beacon, 1966. Essays about schools, youth, and other matters by one of the all-time wittiest and most perceptive writers about education. Good descriptions and examples of schools' alienating function in respect to middle-class youth.

GINTIS, HERBERT. "Education, Technology and the Characteristics of Worker Productivity," *American Economic Review*, May, 1971. A refutation of the common notion that "the main effect of schooling is to raise the level of cognitive development of students and that it is this increase which explains the relationship between schooling and earnings." Gintis is difficult to read but solid.

——. "I.Q. in the U.S. Class Structure," *Social Policy*, January, 1973. Argues that the statistical association between adult I.Q. and economic success derives largely from the common association of both with social-class background.

——. "Towards a Political Economy of Education: A Radical Critique of Ivan Illich's *Deschooling Society*," *Harvard Education Review*, February, 1972. Argues that "despite his forthright vision of the liberating potential of educational technology, Illich fails to understand fully how the existing educational system serves the capitalist economy."

GRAUBARD, ALLEN. *Free the Children: Radical Reform and the Free School Movement.* New York: Pantheon, 1972. An account of the so-called free-school movement combining good firsthand observation, serious politicoeconomic analysis, and a tendency to intellectual overelaborateness, which sometimes obscures important points.

GREER, COLIN. *The Great School Legend*. New York: Basic Books, 1972. The legend is that American public schools were the vehicle in which the poor of previous generations, mainly immigrant, rode to successful middle-class status. Greer demonstrates that the legend is a lie and that, in fact, the schools have always taught the children of the poor to fail, not to succeed, and still do.

HENRY, JULES. *Culture Against Man*. New York, Vintage, 1963. A cool anthropologist describes U.S. society as a total cultural system and parents, children, and schools as integral components of the system. Two chapters on school provide the best real-life data published on how the schoolroom forges the American character. This book, like those by Waller and Hollingshead cited below, is a classic in the genre.

————. "Education for Stupidity," *New York Review of Books*, May 9, 1968. An invaluable critique of social studies textbooks that shows clearly how they distort history in order to convey the mythology of imperialism.

————. *On Education*. New York: Vintage, 1972. Selected short essays.

HERNDON, JAMES. *The Way It Spozed to Be: A Report on the Classroom War Behind the Crisis in Our Schools*. New York: Simon & Schuster, 1968. An amusingly self-deprecating account of how one teacher and his students coped with their cultural differences. Herndon is less romantic and cooler than other writers in this genre and therefore for some readers somewhat less inspiring, while for others more believable and delightful. But a student reader is said to have told him about his classroom stance, "Looks like you were just there watching, not really involved."

HERZOG, ELIZABETH. *About the Poor: Some Facts and Some Fictions*. Washington, D.C.: Children's Bureau, U.S. Department of Health, Education, and Welfare, 1967. The former head of the Children's Bureau writes refreshingly about some realities, by contrast with some myths, about the life of the poor. Good reading for teachers who might tend to see all their poor children's school difficulties in terms of their own stereotypes of the children's home lives.

HOLLINGSHEAD, AUGUST B. *Elmtown's Youth: The Impact of Social Class on Adolescents*. New York: John Wiley, 1949. How the social class of their parents was meticulously reproduced in the youth of a typical (all-white) Midwestern town in the early 1940's. Striking incidents of school reinforcement of class differences and prejudices. Fascinating reading.

HOLT, JOHN. *How Children Fail*. New York: Delta, 1964. The American father of the "free school movement" writes with warmth and insight about children's learning. But admirers of the early Holt should be cautious in respect to the later Holt: His empathy with children exceeds both his empathy with adults and his political perspicacity.

HURST, JOHN. "Education: Tool of an Emerging Fascist State?" *New School of Education Journal,* University of California at Berkeley, Spring, 1971. Argues that many changes being introduced into schools support conditions tending toward an American form of fascism.

ILLICH, IVAN. *Deschooling Society.* New York: Harper & Row, 1971. Analysis of the socio-economic functions of schools in Western society, along with a seductive proposal to abolish schools, which has given rise to a small cult among educational radicals. The sharp analysis appears to lead to, but actually conceals fatal flaws in, the conclusion.

Indian Education: Hearings Before the Special Subcommittee on Indian Education of the Committee on Labor and Public Welfare, U.S. Senate, 1967–68. A gold mine of firsthand information on the degradation of American Indians by and in schools and schoolbooks. Overwhelming evidence of the way schools can contribute to destroying individuals' and whole peoples' human identity and self-respect.

JOHNSON, HENRY SIOUX, and WILLIAM J. HERNANDEZ, eds. *Educating the Mexican American.* Valley Forge, Pa.: Judson Press, 1970. A collection of materials covering a great range of topics, including bilingual education, historical and cultural background, adult literacy, problems of migrant children, and special programs. Useful for focusing attention on the schools' rather than the children's failure.

KATZ, MICHAEL B. *Class, Bureaucracy, and Schools: The Illusion of Educational Change in America.* New York: Praeger, 1971. An important piece of revisionist history that enables us to see that (1) bureaucracy is not a dispensable epiphenomenon of classist-racist schools but a basic component; (2) U.S. public schools have long been an instrument for socializing the children of the poor for a poor place in the work world; and (3) some of our dominant social institutions have grown out of conscious decision-making by men of power, not only out of the vague "forces of history."

KEIL, CHARLES. *Urban Blues.* Chicago: University of Chicago Press, 1966. Description and analysis of a profound American literary tradition that is almost never given legitimacy in school curriculums. Takes you to the backstage settings of some of the blues masters. Fine discussion of the black family.

KING, A. RICHARD. *The School at Mopass: A Problem of Identity.* New York: Holt, Rinehart & Winston, 1967. A case study of an extreme case of school alienation, this anthropologist's account of a residential Indian school in the Yukon is written with great compassion for both the oppressed and alienated Indian children and the oppressed and alienated white personnel. Sad, but helpful for understanding all the other, mostly less extreme, cases.

KOHL, HERBERT. *Thirty-six Children.* New York: Norton, 1968. Teacher's notes and students' writings from a New York City school for black children. This book, along with Kozol's cited below, began to arouse adult Americans to what the children had known for a long time. There is a slightly dangerous innocence in respect to what schools, schoolteaching, and schoolteachers are all about.

KOZOL, JONATHAN. *Death at an Early Age: The Destruction of the Hearts and Minds of Negro Children in the Boston Public Schools.* Boston: Houghton-Mifflin, 1967; New York: Bantam, 1968. A call to conscience from a young teacher in a Boston public school. The degree of Kozol's horror at what poor schools have generally been about. Along with Kohl and Holt, Kozol has helped to bring the miseries of poor children to the attention of well-meaning, well-to-do adults.

LAUTER, PAUL, and FLORENCE HOWE. *The Conspiracy of the Young.* New York and Cleveland: Meridian, 1971. A politicoeconomic analysis of the youth movement of the 1960's, with a good chapter on schools.

LEACOCK, ELEANOR BURKE. *The Culture of Poverty: A Critique.* New York: Simon & Schuster, 1971. Interesting collection of pieces on "cultural deprivation," language, non-U.S. classrooms. "The Integrity of the Cherokee Student," by Mildred Dickeman, demonstrates the cultural deprivation of the Anglo teacher in a Cherokee classroom.

Let Them Aspire: A Plea and Proposal for Equality of Opportunity for Males and Females in the Ann Arbor Public Schools, Marcia Federbush, 1000 Cedar Bend Drive, Ann Arbor, Mich. 48105. A good example of what a small group of women can do to survey and begin to counteract school sexism.

LEVIN, BETSY, *et al. Paying for Public Schools: Issues of School Finance in California,* The Urban Institute, 2100 M Street, N.W., Washington, D.C. This booklet, addressed primarily to the issues posed by the *Serrano* case, is helpful in untangling many of the fiscal contradictions of public schooling.

LURIE, ELLEN. *How to Change the Schools: A Parents' Action Handbook on How to Fight the System.* New York: Vintage, 1970. Practical organizing advice from the training director of a New York City activist parents' group. Tends to be rather harshly antiteacher.

McDERMOTT, JOHN. "The Laying on of Culture," *The Nation,* March 10, 1969. Shows how teachers who are liberal, intellectual graduates of Ivy League colleges and big universities scorn and fail to identify with their working-class students in community and other small colleges. Offers some suggestions for connecting with their historical past in the labor movement.

MARX, KARL. *Early Writings.* Trans. and ed. by T. B. BOTTOMORE. New York: McGraw-Hill, 1963. The few pages entitled "Alienated Labor" and "Money" are profoundly intricate and beautiful explications of some of this great thinker's greatest insights about people in a capitalist society. They should help to give weight to the thesis of alienation training. For most benefit, read them several times over an extended period.

MÉSZÁROS, I. *Marx's Theory of Alienation.* London: Merlin Press, 1970. An analysis and interpretation of Marx's theory of alienated labor as developed mainly in his early writings.

Natural History Magazine Special Supplement: "Play," December, 1971. Articles on play among children, adults, and monkeys illustrate its significance as a developmental function. Useful for understanding alienation in work and play.

The Negro Family: The Case for National Action. Washington, D.C.: U..S. Department of Labor, March, 1965. Known as the "Moynihan Report" after its principal designer, Daniel Patrick Moynihan, this report exemplifies the ethnocentric thinking that often lies behind notions that their own "pathological" family structure, rather than the whole society in which they are cast as victims, is responsible for black children's performance in school. Should be read in conjunction with the cited works by Billingsley and Ryan.

NEILL, A. S. *Summerhill: A Radical Approach to Child Rearing.* New York: Hart, 1969. The British inspirer of a good deal of the free-school movement in the United States writes of his beliefs and his experiences in the famous school he founded. The warm humanity is stained by sentimentality regarding children and softheadedness regarding capitalist society—both of which stains continue to spread.

New York Civil Liberties Union. *Student Rights Handbook,* Students Rights Project, 84 Fifth Avenue, New York, N.Y. 10011. The local and state branches of the American Civil Liberties Union and of the National Lawyers' Guild in many localities publish similar handbooks.

NORDSTROM, CARL, EDGAR Z. FRIEDENBERG, and HILARY A. GOLD. *Society's Children: A Study of Ressentiment in the Secondary Schools.* New York: Random House, 1967. Makes an interesting connection between teacher distress *(ressentiment)* and student turning off, but fails to explore the former.

NYERERE, JULIUS K. "Education for Self-Reliance," in *Ujamaa: Essays on Socialism.* London and New York: Oxford University Press, 1968. The President of socialist Tanzania, a former teacher, provides an interesting possible alternative model to the prevailing model of education by competition. Conceptualizes an education system in which it is not necessary for many to fail in order that a few may succeed.

O'CONNOR, JAMES. *The Fiscal Crisis of the State.* New York: St. Martin's Press, 1973. A Marxist analysis of the fiscal crisis. Heavy, but worth the weight. (Readers not up to it should read Bodenheimer's article cited above.)

OLLMAN, BERTELL. *Alienation: Marx's Conception of Man in Capitalist Society.* London and New York: Cambridge University Press, 1971. To understand the process to which children in school are being subjected, we have to understand the process to which adults in society are subjected. This book helps explicate some heavy Marxist theory worth working on.

OPIE, IONA, and PETER OPIE. *Children's Games in Street and Playground.* London and New York: Oxford University Press, 1969. Through these precise anthropological descriptions of urban children's unsupervised play, we see boy-girl differences outside of school and home, how children manage competitiveness among themselves, and children's ritualizations of fears, humiliation, and other "negative" emotions. Provides fascinating glimpses into children as they are where we are not.

PARKER, STANLEY. *The Future of Work and Leisure.* New York: Praeger, 1971. Extensions of theories of alienated labor and alienation into contemporary work-leisure problems and definitions.

PARSONS, TALCOTT. "The School Class as a Social System: Some of its Functions in American Society," *Harvard Education Review,* Fall, 1959. An important conservative sociologist analyzes the "structure of the public school system . . . and the ways in which it contributes both to the socialization of individuals and to their allocation to roles in society."

PRATT, CAROLINE. *I Learn from Children.* New York: Cornerstone Library, Simon & Schuster, 1948. The progressive educators of the early decades of the century have much to teach contemporary free-school educators about the correct proportions of allowing and creating learning. A founder of the City and Country School of New York City (still in existence) gives her recipes. Unfortunately, somewhat hostile to parents.

Proceedings of the Conference on Educational Accountability, June, 1971. Princeton, N.J.: Educational Testing Service. The contributions of Erick Lindman and Henry Dyer are good critiques of accountability and evaluation from the point of view of supporters of the system.

Report on Sex Bias in the Public Schools, National Organization for Women, New York City Chapter, Anne Grant West, 453 Seventh Street, Brooklyn, N.Y. 11215. One of the first compilations of materials documenting sexism in public schools.

ROSENTHAL, ROBERT, and LENORE JACOBSON. *Pygmalion in the Classroom: Teacher Expectation and Pupils' Intellectual Development.* New York: Holt, Rinehart & Winston, 1968. Some interesting speculations, based on experimentation, that children's success or failure in learning may depend on their teachers' expectations.

ROSSMAN, MICHAEL. *On Learning and Social Change.* New York: Vintage, 1972. Some good essays on overcoming the totalitarian classroom.

RYAN, WILLIAM. *Blaming the Victim.* New York: Vintage, 1971. A beautiful, coolly passionate statement of how the oppressed get blamed for their oppression. The chapter "Savage Discovery in the Schools: The Folklore of Cultural Deprivation" contains a refreshingly comprehensive and sensible critique of the famous Coleman Report. (See JAMES S. COLEMAN, *Equality of Educational Opportunity,* above.)

SCOGGINS, WILL. *Labor in Learning: Public School Treatment of the World of Work,* Institute of Industrial Relations, University of California, Los Angeles. An analysis of antilabor bias, lack of practical, realistic material for future workers, and distortions of history and economics in social studies texts.

Selective Service, "Memo on Channeling," reprinted in *Ramparts,* December, 1967. How subtle manipulative pressures are used to direct young men to "socially" desired pursuits and careers. An interesting analogy to subtle school tracking.

Sexism in Education. Minneapolis, Minn.: Emma Willard Task Force on Education. Descriptive material, bibliography, lesson ideas, consciousness-raisers. Very useful.

SEXTON, PATRICIA CAYO. *Education and Income.* New York, 1966. Using the schools of one Midwestern metropolis as an example, the book shows the striking discrepancies in inputs of all kinds between schools for the poor and schools for the middle class.

————. *The Feminized Male: Classrooms, White Collars and the Decline of Manliness.* New York: Random House, 1969. Harshly criticized by several writers for its emphasis on the damage done to boys by the "feminine" atmosphere of classrooms, this book, nevertheless, contains much good material on boy-girl differences and discrimination in schools.

SILBERMAN, CHARLES E. *Crisis in the Classroom: The Remaking of American Education.* New York: Random House, 1970. Astonishingly light for its bulk and price, this book is nevertheless useful in that it makes official some truths about schools that we all have long known to lie behind the myths. It is hard to believe, however, that either the author or his financial backer, the Carnegie Corporation, is really so innocent as to believe in Silberman's explanation of the school crisis.

SPINDLER, GEORGE D., ed. *Education and Culture: Anthropological*

Approaches, New York: Holt, Rinehart & Winston, 1963. Contains some very valuable essays by Jules Henry, Spindler himself, and others. Also some good material on schools and education in other cultures.

Students of Barbiana. *Letter to a Teacher.* Baltimore: Penguin, 1970. One of the two or three classics on education produced every second or third generation. Combines hard critical documentation, considerable analytic insight, great but controlled passion and compassion, and high literary skill.

TOLSTOY, LEO. *On Education.* Trans. by LEO WIENER. Chicago: University of Chicago Press, 1967. A great writer reflects on his experiences as a schoolmaster in a school for children of peasants, not only revealing a lesser-known facet of his greatness but demonstrating that many of the great truths of teacher-pupil relations are part of the wisdom of the ages.

TOOMER, JEAN. "Chapters from *Earth-Being*: An Unpublished Autobiography," *Black Scholar,* January, 1971. Early days of life and learning of one of the great writers of the Harlem renaissance of the 1920's. The description of how he learned "school things" at home and what he learned at school constitutes an interesting example of nonalienated versus alienated learning.

TRECKER, JANICE LAW. "Women in U.S. History High School Textbooks," *Social Education,* March, 1971. Answers in the affirmative the question "Are the stereotypes that limit girls' aspirations present in high school history texts?" pointing out that both the great women and women as women are either absent from history texts or presented as "supplementary material." The article does not offer suggestions for remedying the lack—a serious flaw.

U.S. Commission on Civil Rights. *Mexican-American Study.* Washington, D.C.: Government Printing Office, 1971. Mexican-American students, staff, administrators in the Southwest; segregation, discrimination, and isolation.

WALLER, WILLARD. *The Sociology of Teaching.* New York: Wiley, 1967 (originally published in 1932). Written as a textbook for prospective teachers to help them understand how the society of schools that they were about to enter really operates. As a textbook, it is—though a little outdated—rare for its honesty and depth. As an analysis of the school society, it is surprisingly in advance of its time.

WASSERMAN, MIRIAM. "Deschooling Society: The Respectable Revolution," *New Politics,* Autumn, 1971. Critical review of Ivan Illich's *Deschooling Society* and *Celebration of Awareness* as politically naïve.

———. *The School Fix: NYC, USA,* New York: Outerbridge & Dienstfrey, 1970; Clarion, 1971. Suffers from the author's over-ambitious attempt to provide an analysis of how a large urban school system operates; human-interest case studies; a gossipy account of the ins and outs of teacher-union and community-control politics at the time of the Great Strike in New York City; and a defense of community control and the student revolt of 1968. But thoughtful, well written, and useful in small doses.

————. "School Mythology and the Education of Oppression," *This Magazine Is About Schools,* Summer, 1971. A harsh criticism of *Crisis in the Classroom* by Charles Silberman in the light of the works of Paulo Freire.

WAX, MURRAY L., STANLEY DIAMOND, and FRED O. GEARING, eds. *Anthropological Perspectives on Education.* New York: Basic Books, 1971. A compilation of articles. The anthropological method helps to overcome some of the bias inherent in writing by participants in the educational process and some of the confusion caused by too strong adherence to the various school myths.

WEINBERG, MEYER, ed. *Integrated Education: A Reader.* Glencoe, Ill.: Free Press, 1968. A collection of articles that appeared during the early years of publication of the periodical *Integrated Education.* Helpful for understanding the mood, the problems, the resistance, and the hopes during the 1960's that school integration would solve the school crisis.

WIEBE, ROBERT H. "The Social Functions of Public Education," *American Quarterly* (University of Pennsylvania). Explores the social role of schooling since the 1830's.

YOUNG, MICHAEL. *The Rise of Meritocracy: 1870–2033.* Baltimore: Penguin, 1958. A nice satire depicting the author's vision of how it would be if the hypothetical meritocracy created by progressively competitive schooling were a reality.

Youth Liberation of Ann Arbor. *Youth Liberation.* Washington, N.J.: Times Change Press, n.d. A selection of pieces from FPS and student underground papers.

Periodicals, Bibliographies, Other Resources

American Library Association. *Alternatives in Print,* Office of Educational Services, The Ohio State University Libraries, Columbus, Ohio 43210, 1972. Lists publications, by categories, of hundreds of off-beat, noncommercial groups. Listings under "Education," "Schools," "Student Movement," "Teachers" contain materials about schools and for people in schools. Other listings (such as "American Indians," "Alternative Life-Styles," "Africa," "Labor History") are good for materials that can be used to create alternative curriculums and lessons.

Centerpeace. 57 Hayes St., Cambridge, Mass. 02139. $5 individuals, $8 libraries, $10 overseas. General articles about alternative education.

Changes. 2314 Elliott Ave. S., Minneapolis, Minn. About 6 issues annually. $3. Articles by and about alternative and radical education, specifically in the Twin Cities and North Country area.

Community Schools, Community School Workshop, 171 College St., Toronto 2B, Ontario, Canada. About monthly, students $2.50, other individuals $5, institutions $15. Promotes the community-school concept through a program of public education and community development. Refers specifically to Toronto.

Council on Anthropology and Education, *Newsletter,* 1703 New Hampshire Ave., N.W., Washington, D.C. 20009. Anthropology, of all the academic disciplines, probably has the most to contribute to students of schooling.

D & R Report, Council for Educational Development and Research, 775 Lincoln Tower, 1860 Lincoln Street, Denver, Colo. 80203. Useful for news about institutional strategies of reform and insights into the thinking of academia in education.

Edcentric, 2115 S Street, N.W., Room 30, Washington, D.C. 20008. $5 for 8 issues individuals, $8 institutions. College, alternative-school, public school news and analysis. Good resource directory.

Education Exploration Center *Newsletter,* 3104 16th Ave. S., Minneapolis, Minn. 55407. Monthly. $3 to $5. News of alternative and radical education projects and conferences in the Twin Cities and North Country areas.

Education Recaps, Educational Testing Service, Princeton, N.J. 08540. Ten issues annually. Capsule summaries of news about schools and the education world nationwide.

Expediteur: Contact Education, 10 Rue du Pelican, 75001 Paris, France. $8 airmail for 10 issues. Newsletter of the alternative-school movement in France.

Feminist Press, Box 334, Old Westbury, N.Y. 11568. Publishes feminist literature and children's books.

Feminist Resources for Elementary and Secondary Schools, by Carol Ahlum and Jackie Fralley, Valley Women's Center, 200 Main Street, Northampton, Mass. 01060. Resources about feminism and sexism for elementary and secondary classrooms.

Florida FL Reporter: A Language Education Journal, 801 N.E. 177th St., North Miami, Fla. 33162. Twice a year. $4 individuals, $6 institutions. Extremely useful for teachers of nonstandard-dialect speakers.

FPS/Youth Liberation, 2007 Washtenaw Ave., Ann Arbor, Mich. 48104. Triweekly. $5 movement and youth, $8 other individuals, $12 institutions. News service for the student movement and underground student newspapers below college level. Also publishes some special pamphlets for students and student organizers. Good for nonstudents who want to keep up with advanced student thinking.

High School Student Information Center, 1000 Wisconsin Ave., N.W., Washington, D.C. 20007. Publishes pamphlets on student rights, student organizing, student political involvement.

Inequality in Education, Center for Law and Education, Harvard University, 61 Kirland Street, Cambridge, Mass., 02138. Quarterly. Free to individuals, $6 libraries. Extremely useful for discussion and information on legal and paralegal questions about schools. Espouses a largely liberal, pro–civil rights point of view.

Integrated Education: Race and Schools, 343 S. Dearborn St., Chicago, Ill. 60604. Six issues annually. $8. Articles, speeches, reports mainly on race discrimination in schools.

Interracial Books for Children, Council on Interracial Books for Children, 29 West 15th Street, New York, N.Y. 10011. Quarterly. $3. Invaluable general articles and book reviews.

Libertarian Teacher, 180 Melbourne Road, Leicester, England. Journal of radical and liberation teachers in England, with news and analysis. Helps spread the idea that school problems in the United States are not idiosyncratic but systemic.

Little Miss Muffet Fights Back: Recommended Non-sexist Books About Girls for Young Readers, Feminists on Children's Media, P.O. Box 4315, Grand Central Station, New York, N.Y. 10017. Annotated bibliography of trade books only.

New England Free Press catalogue, 791 Tremont Street, Boston, Mass. 02118. Listing of pamphlet-size reprints of radical articles on schools as well as other topics. Indispensable for politically radical educators.

The New York Teacher, official publication of the New York State United Teachers, Inc., 260 Park Avenue South, New York, N.Y. 10010. Weekly, ten school months. $4. Tainted by what is sometimes very tricky politics, this paper, nevertheless, provides probably the best coverage there is on public aspects of teachers' lives, salaries, promotions, grievances, and so forth. The politics and significance of teacher unionism are topics far too often neglected by radicals in schools.

No More Teachers' Dirty Looks! Bay Area Radical Teachers' Organizing Collective (BARTOC), 388 Sanchez, San Francisco, Calif. 94114. $3 for 4 issues individuals, $6 institutions. Political analysis, classroom suggestions, news of the San Francisco Bay Area from a politically radical point of view.

Partial Bibliography of Materials on Sexism and Sex-Role Stereotyping in Children's Books, Lollipop Power, P.O. Box 1171, Chapel Hill, N.C. 27514.

People's Educational Resource Center, Albuquerque, N. Mex. Provides "non-racist, non-sexist, historically non-biased materials for educators, parents, and their children." Requests contributions of materials.

Quarterly Bibliography on Cultural Differences, compiled by California State Library, 801 Capitol Mall, Sacramento, Calif. An excellent annotated bibliography of new books and articles, both popular and scholarly, about minorities. Listings on American Indians, Mexican Americans, education, psychology, race problems, and other subjects.

The Red Pencil, c/o Wachs, 70 Manemet Road, Newton Center, Mass. 02159. Media and printed resources for radical teachers nationwide. Also special resources available in the Boston area. Back issues of a regular magazine by the same contain excellent analytical and classroom resource materials.

ROGERS, DAVID. *110 Livingston Street: Politics and Bureaucracy in the New York City School System.* New York: Random House, 1968. A very tedious but important book about a very tedious but important topic.

Science for the People, Scientists and Engineers for Social and Political Action, 9 Walden Street, Jamaica Plain, Mass. 02130. Bimonthly. $10. Lesson plans and ideas, analysis, news of interest to radical science teachers. Teacher Curriculum Work Center, 1400 East 53rd St., Chicago, Ill. 60615.

The Teacher Paper, 2221 N.E. 23d Street, Portland, Ore. 97212. Quarterly. $3. Practical classroom experiences and advice. Written by teachers. Some good, some funky, some doubtful.

This Magazine Is About Schools, 56 The Esplanade, Toronto, Canada. Quarterly. $4 Canada, $4.50 United States. The best liberal-radical education journal going. Formerly "Summerhillian" in tendency, now politically radical, with emphasis on Canadian matters but not exclusively.

Wisconsin Youth for Democratic Education, 216 N. Hamilton, Madison, Wis. 53703. Monthly newsletter. $2. Assistance for student groups.

Women and Psychology, Cambridge-Goddard School for Social Change, 5 Upland Road, Cambridge, Mass. 02140. 40¢. An excellent annotated bibliography, with a very useful chapter on "Sex Differences, Sex Role Development, and Socialization of Children."

Women's Studies Abstracts. P.O. Box 1, Rush, N.Y. 14543. Abstracts of scholarly writings relating to women, by categories. Good on education and socialization.

Women's Studies Newsletter, Feminist Press, Box 334, Old Westbury, New York, N.Y. 11568. Quarterly. $5 individuals, $10 institutions. Descriptions of women's studies courses, bibliographies, listing of conferences and job openings.

Women's Work and Women's Studies, 1971, by KIRSTEN DRAKE, DOROTHY MARKS, and MARY WEXFORD, Women's Center, Barnard College, New York, N.Y. 10027, or KNOW, Inc., P.O. Box 86031, Pittsburgh, Pa. 15221. Listing of over 1,400 books, articles, and other resources, by categories.

Work Force, Vocations for Social Change, 4911 Telegraph Ave., Oakland, Calif. 94609. Bimonthly. $5 individuals, $10 institutions. Jobs, news, institutions, people, resources, strategies outside the "establishment."